YANOÁMA

The new Shamatari chief

Valero, Helena

Yanoáma

THE NARRATIVE OF A WHITE GIRL KIDNAPPED BY AMAZONIAN INDIANS

As told to Ettore Biocca

Photographs by the missionary Luigi Cocco and by Ettore Biocca

Translated from the Italian by Dennis Rhodes

E. P. DUTTON & CO., NEW YORK 1970

First published in the U.S.A. 1970 by E. P. Dutton & Co., Inc. / Translated from the Italian, *Yanoáma,* Copyright © 1965 by Leonardo da Vinci Editore, Bari, Italy / English translation Copyright © 1969 by E. P. Dutton & Co., Inc., and George Allen and Unwin Ltd. / Published simultaneously in Canada by Clarke, Irwin & Company Limited, Toronto and Vancouver / Library of Congress Catalog Card Number: 69-10295

Second Printing June 1970
SBN-0-525-23888-3

CONTENTS

ILLUSTRATIONS

Photographs for plate nos. 1, 3, 6, 7, 8, 9, 10, 12, 15, 24, 30, 33, 36, 38 and 52 are by the author; the rest (with the exception of 21 by Baschíeri, and 22 by Niño) are by Father Luigi Cocco.

AUTHOR'S PREFACE

The biography of Helena Valero—a woman of Spanish blood abducted by the Yanoáma Indians, who lived for many years with them in the unexplored forest between Brazil and Venezuela—has been of great help to the recent scientific expedition which I directed in the tropical forest of America. The following pages represent a broad cross-section of the story and are published with the authorization of the National Research Council, which patronized and financed the expedition.

The opportunity of studying an unknown and wild group of Indians through the testimony of a woman prisoner who succeeded in returning to the world of the white men,[1] is a fortunate and exceptional event which, it seems, has no parallel in the history of American ethnology.

I tape-recorded the story while I was with my companions on the expedition—Bagalino, Baschieri, De Mello, Mangili and Ponzo—at the base of S. Gabriel, waiting for the crossing of the territory of the Yanoáma to begin.

It was not in any way my intention to put together a biography; I simply wished to have from Helena Valero all information useful for the expedition's work. But she replied to my questions on the usages and customs of the Indians, through the description of episodes in her own life: she narrated events as though they were taking place again at that moment before her own eyes, describing them in that vivid dialect of the Rio Negro, made up of Portuguese, Spanish and *lingua geral* Indian, which had been familiar to me ever since my first journey among the Indians. The images were like photographs in her mind and they came back, without a single contradiction, every time I asked her to repeat this or that episode. So then I decided to collect information on the Yanoáma by means of this woman's life-story, steering the narrative towards those aspects which I considered most important, without influencing, with appreciations or judgments, her recollections and her confessions.

[1] By 'the world of the white men' I mean to indicate culture and not racial origin.

This is how there was born, from my talks with Helena Valero, more than an ethnobiological documentation on the Yanoáma, indeed a new and unsuspected human documentation. It was life in the forest seen from within, seen by men who consider us whites as their eternal enemies, the creators of diseases and of death; it was the hatreds, the sudden acts of generosity, the betrayals, the agreements, the songs of the witch-doctors, the magic practices: it was a world, that is, completely new, which no white man certainly had ever seen, and which Helena Valero revealed to me.

All that has been written in this almost incredible story is no fruit of the imagination, but a report, sometimes dramatic, sometimes poetic, of a life that has been lived. The names of the Indian tribes are real, the names of persons and places are real, episodes are real. We, who have found again many of the people and of the Yanoáma groups with whom Helena Valero lived, have been able to confirm what she had described to us with such lucidity and clarity. The present account, which I have tried to translate into Italian preserving the hard form of the original, respects the narrative scrupulously, with the very object of maintaining all the value of a scientific documentation; whole sections which point out facts new to science, such as the preparation of curare and of hallucinatory drugs, the techniques of warfare, food, beliefs in the supernatural world and so on, have been set down in the volumes of the report on the voyage which are published by the National Research Council (E. Biocca (1966), *Viaggi tra gli Indi.* IV. volumes. Ed. Cons. Naz. Ric., Roma).

As the narrative tries to be a precise scientific document, so the photographic illustrations reproduce scenes from real life, partly taken by me, but above all by the missionary Luigi Cocco, among those very Indians with whom Helena Valero lived. The importance of some of missionary Cocco's photographs, especially those which refer to fights and to scenes of shamanism and of endocannibalism, may be understood in its full value, considering the danger of photographing at particular moments these Indians who are still so fierce and aggressive.

The ancient and recent history of the Yanoáma is still wrapped in mystery. Of all the regions of the earth still unexplored, that which extends for hundreds of miles between the Rio Negro and the Upper Rio Orinoco, just where the Yanoáma live, is perhaps the most vast and the most fascinating. Since the time of the conquest, all efforts to penetrate the interior of this forest have been useless. The old maps of the American continent showed, in the heart of this area, an immense salt lake which did not exist, Lake Parime, on whose banks was supposed to stand a city entirely built of gold, the home of El Dorado; women warriors, the Amazons, prevented anyone from entering these regions. Famous conquerors, from Gonzalo Pizarro to Walter Raleigh, had tried in vain to approach the land of El Dorado, which was reached only by the genial and satirical imagination of Voltaire, who sent his Candide, son of a decadent world of white men, to take lessons in civilization from the very inhabitants of this unknown territory.

When, with the expedition of Humboldt and Bonpland at the beginning of the nineteenth century, the mists of legends about El Dorado disappeared, contact began to be made and scientific studies carried out on the Aruak, Tukâno and Caraib Indians, who live around the territory of the Yanoáma, along the great rivers. But the virgin forest remained inviolate, with the great mountain chains enclosed within it, because of the hostility of nature and the fierce and obstinate resistance of a large Indian group indicated by different names—Waika, Shiriana, Shirishana, Guaharibo (which means screaming monkey)—a group which today we prefer to call Yanoáma, a word of their language which means 'those of the village'. Of these people there reached us, from time to time, only vague and frightening reports.

Towards the middle of the nineteenth century, Robert Schomburgk sailed up the Uraricoera, a tributary of the Rio Branco, to penetrate the basin of the Orinoco; during this marvellous voyage he received news of terrible Yanoáma Indian warriors, the Kirishanas, whose mere name struck terror into the guides. After him, the Brazilian naturalist Barbosa Rodrigues and the unfortunate Italian geographer and ethnologist, Count Stradelli, ventured up a northern tributary of the Rio Negro, the Rio Jauaperí, and had friendly contacts with a warlike tribe, almost certainly Yanoáma, who, after their departure, denied to all other white men entry to that river, which has remained unexplored to this day.

At the beginning of the present century, Koch-Grünberg repeated the voyage of Schomburgk and brought back the very first news of scientific interest concerning the Yanoáma of the basin of the Uraricoera. Less fortunate, later, was the American explorer Hamilton Rice, who, while trying to approach with his men the unknown sources of the River Orinoco, met in bloody battle with a strong group of Yanoáma, perhaps the Hasubueteri of whom Helena

Valero speaks, and was forced to give up the attempt. After this episode, the Yanoáma became always more aggressive and more threatening, from the Orinoco to the Rio Negro.

During my first expedition among the Indians of the Upper Rio Negro I did not succeed in approaching the Yanoáma; for hundreds of miles, I was unable to spend the night on the northern bank of this immense river, because my companions were so afraid of nocturnal raids. I was able, however, to study groups of Tukâno, Tariâna and Baniwa of the Upper Rio Negro. It was precisely during this first journey of mine that, on arriving at Taraquá on the Rio Uaupés, I learned that a pupil of that mission, Helena Valero, daughter of a Spaniard and a woman of the Rio Tiquié, had been abducted by the Yanoáma along the Rio Dimití. No one had had any further news of her.

On my return, I regretted not having been able to collect information on human life as it was lived beyond the limit marked by the banks of the great rivers, in the boundless forest, where there must surely exist a culture that was still unknown to us. I was convinced—and Helena Valero's life with the Yanoáma has confirmed this—that one makes a grave error if one supposes that the men of the forest are wild, primitive and wicked, simply because they are so remote from our own standard of culture; perhaps, for the same reason, the Yanoáma commit the same mistake when, with the one word '*nape*', they indicate the white man, the foreigner, the wicked man. Thus I considered the study of their organization and of their culture to be of the greatest scientific interest.

Meanwhile, in these last years, the first timid attempts to penetrate Yanoáma territory began to take place: the Protestant missionary Barker and then the Salesian missionary Cocco, with their brave companions, set out towards the Upper Orinoco and had contact with some groups of Yanoáma; from the Rio Negro the missionary Gois sailed up the Rio Cauaburí, guided first by the Tavares and then accompanied by Seitz. A great Franco-Venezuelan expedition, in which the biologist Anduze and the explorer Grelier also took part, with the support of the Venezuelan civil and military authorities, went up the Orinoco again and discovered the southern sources of this great river. The northern sources were discovered shortly afterwards by a group of the Venezuelan-Brazilian Frontier Commission, led by my friend the astronomer Pantchenko. Some young Frenchmen, in a risky expedition of which Gheerbrant has written, repeated in the opposite direction a journey similar to that carried out by Koch-Grünberg, and Vinci ventured into the northern distribution area of the Yanoáma, where he had those exceptional adventures magnificently related in the book *Samatari*. Finally the German scientific Frobenius mission, composed of Zerries and Schuster, established itself at El Platanal and collected material of great scientific interest, while in Brazil the ethnologist Becher, guided at first by the missionary doctor Bigiaretti, studied Yanoáma groupings of the Rio Demení.

Suddenly a sensational piece of news reached the Salesian missions of the Upper Orinoco and the Upper Rio Negro: Helena Valero, the girl who had been abducted twenty years before by the Yanoáma along the Rio Dimití, was alive and had come back to the white men, in a boat belonging to a Venezuelan who had sailed up the Upper Orinoco in search of precious wood. Journalists and scholars at once tried to approach and to interview her, but the difficulties, for some of understanding the Indian world, for others of following the dialect spoken by this woman, prevented a successful collaboration; only a nun, Sister Maria Sonaglia, drew inspiration from the adventures of Helena Valero for a short poetic story.

Father Bigiaretti, from his mission at Uaupés, informed me that the right moment had come to carry out a scientific expedition in the Yanoáma territory, making use of this exceptional woman's help. The National Research Council welcomed my plans. Thus our journey had been organized with Padre Bigiaretti and with Helena Valero, a journey which would take us from the basin of the Amazon to that of the Orinoco, by a route not yet followed by other expeditions—Rio Cauaburí, Ria Maturacá, Rio Baria, Rio Pacimoni, Casiquiare Canal and Upper Rio Orinoco—that is, crossing the Yanoáma country along ways of communication consisting of water.

But life in the immense forest, under which numerous groups of Yanoáma still operate and in which also Helena Valero's Namoeteri have again penetrated and spread out like shadows, remains an almost unknown world still to be explored, and one which this story has only begun to bring to light.

This documentation on the life of the Yanoáma has been made possible through the complete collaboration of Helena Valero, who held nothing back; through the assistance of two Salesian missionaries—Father Francesco Bigiaretti (a doctor) of the Missions of the Upper Rio Negro, and Father Luigi Cocco of the Missions of the Upper Orinoco—and through the constant co-operation of my wife

Maria Ippolito in translating and preparing the text. To them I dedicate this work.

ETTORE BIOCCA

YANOÁMA

The shaded area shows the portion of the unexplored lands of the Yanoáma Indians in which Helena Valero lived.

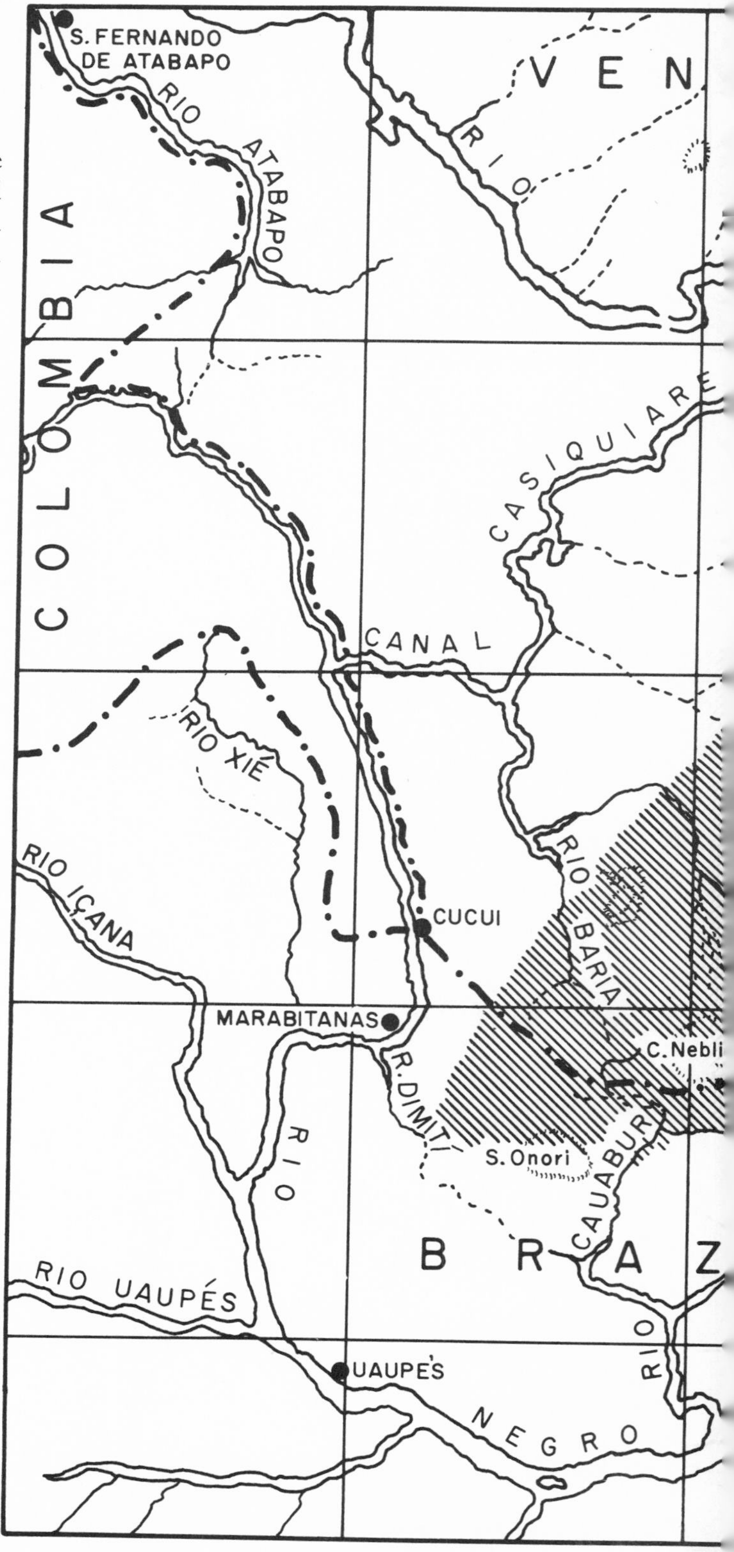

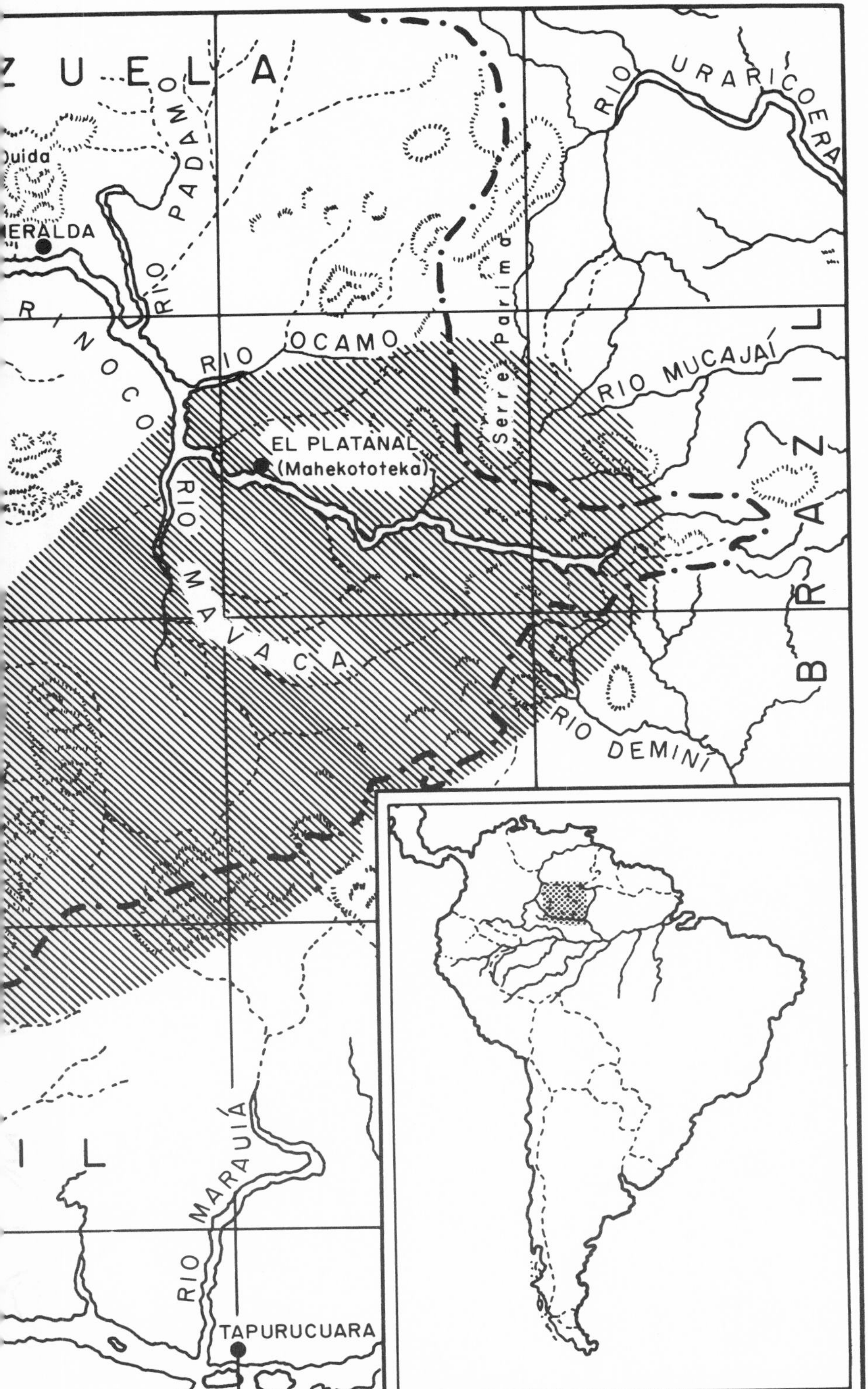

ZUELA
Ouida
ERALDA
RIO PADAMO
RIO URARICOERA
Serra Parima
RINOCO
RIO OCAMO
RIO MUCAJAÍ
EL PLATANAL
(Mahekototeka)
RIO MAVACA
BRAZIL
RIO DEMINI
IL
RIO MARAUIÁ
TAPURUCUARA

PART ONE

CHAPTER 1

On the Rio Dimití

I was a little girl; I was studying at the Mission of Taraquá on the Rio Uaupés. One day the director of the mission wrote to my father, asking him to come and fetch me, because the missions were made for the Indians, not for 'civilized' people. My father grew sad at this and took me back home to Marabitanas on the Rio Negro. Thus about a year went by; during that time we sailed down the Rio Negro as far as Santa Isabel to collect pará nuts in the woods. When we sailed back, my elder sister died in San Gabriel, where we are now.

It was 1937. My mother's brother came to Marabitanas with his family. For five years they had been living along the Rio Dimití; they had built two little houses and cultivated three *roças*, clearings, where they had burnt down the trees. Now they were leaving that place and offering us their houses and their *roças*. They were the only houses along the whole of the Dimití; they were beautiful, with doors and windows.

My mother in three days prepared the manioc seedlings to plant in the *roças*; my father prepared the big canoe. It was early in the morning; we set out, my father, my mother, my brother Luis, who was seven years old, my brother Anisio, who was still tiny and myself, about eleven or twelve. We had loaded the manioc seedlings and all our belongings; we didn't have to go very far. We went a little way down the Rio Negro and reached the mouth of the Dimití. It is a small river in the forest; here on the Rio Negro they call such a stream an *igarapé*. All day we sailed back up the Dimití; my father and my mother were rowing.

Every place had a name on the Dimití. I remember that a big dead tree, with very hard wood inside, was lying across the river. The huntsmen had told us that this trunk was an old *pagé*[1] and that everyone who passed by had to leave bananas and *bejú,* manioc cake, on the trunk, saying: 'Pagé, don't let it rain: keep the weather fine

[1] *Pagé* = shaman.

and sunny, so that I can go hunting. When I come back I will leave you the leg of an animal.' My mother left a piece of *bejú* on a branch of that great dead tree and we went on our way. I remember everything; but then, my father has told me about this journey so many times. In the evening we saw, near the river, a hut made by the huntsmen; we slept there.

Early in the morning we began once more to sail upstream in the canoe. The sun was already high, when my father said: 'I can smell smoke.' White smoke was drifting down the stream. My mother replied: 'Perhaps some huntsman is smoking his meat in my brother's empty house.' 'Perhaps,' added my father, 'they have come from Manadono to hunt for the Marabitanas feast.' Manadono is a small village near Marabitanas, along the great river. So we landed; the little houses were some distance away from the river. That low smoke was wafting down the river. My father said: 'I'm going to see who is there,' and he went away with his machete in his hand. He approached the little houses; no smoke was coming out of the houses: the smoke was coming from the edge of the camp.

My mother had got out onto dry land and I was sitting on the stern of the canoe. We saw my father running back towards us; he arrived very pale with his machete in his hand. Blood was trickling down his arm: a poisoned arrow had hit him, but he had pulled it out. My mother asked: 'Carlos, what's the matter with you?' My father did not answer; he couldn't speak. He pushed the canoe with his foot and jumped in. My mother helped him to push, began to row and asked him again: 'What's the matter with you?' He took the *cuia* in which we kept the salt; he rubbed salt on the wound and in a whisper stammered: 'Throw the bunches of manioc in the water, and let's get out of here; the Indians have shot at me with arrows.' My mother cried and threw all the seedlings in the river. We threw everything we had, so as to travel more quickly.

Around us all was silent as we rowed. We were already a good way off. 'Perhaps the Indians have stayed behind,' I thought; but the Indians were running along the banks. Suddenly arrows began to arrive from one side. 'Lie down in the canoe,' said my father. I ducked down, but an arrow pierced the skin of my belly and stuck in here, in my left thigh. I shouted out and tried to lift myself but couldn't. The arrow had fixed my thigh to my belly. I shouted and shouted; my dress didn't get torn because it was new. My mother seized the arrow, pulled it out and threw it in the water; the point broke; one piece remained in my belly and the other in my thigh.

My mother, with her fingers, pulled the piece of arrow out of my belly; the piece stuck in my thigh had gone deep and you couldn't see it any more. Then she tried to get hold of it with her teeth; she bit, she pushed, but the point did not show, it was so deep. In the end she succeeded in getting it out with her teeth; she spat it in the water.

Meanwhile my father was trying to row. My mother threw a glance along the river; in terror she said: 'Children, here come the Indians.' Down there, a long distance away, there were big rocks over the river; on the rocks lots of Indians with bows and arrows. Some were painted black, others were red: red on the chest, red on their shaved heads. The current was carrying us towards them. My mother was crying and shouted in the Tucana language: 'Don't shoot us!' My father said: 'We are not doing you any harm, don't shoot us!' My mother said: 'Don't shoot, we'll be friends, don't shoot!' But the arrows were falling on us. One struck my father on the back, another on his arm; eight arrows hit my father, but he managed to pull them all out. Then we all threw ourselves into the water; my head was spinning and I couldn't swim, but my mother held me up by the arm. We reached the bank; my father took me in his arms and began to run like a drunken man towards the woods, leaning onto the branches. I remember that all the trees were swimming around my head; my sight was growing misty. I could hear the shouts of the Indians nearby, for they had run towards the canoe. Then I remember only that I said to my father: 'Father, leave me, I'm dying.'

My father tells how, after leaving me on the ground, he saw me get up, then fall back and sit down. He broke two big branches in order to find the place again and ran stumbling into the woods, carrying with him my brother Luis. My mother had Anisio in her arms; she too ran into the middle of the forest and lost sight of my father: they found each other again after two days. So then they went back to Marabitanas. Then they came to look for me with soldiers, but they did not find me. The Indians stayed there many days: the soldiers did not come near, otherwise they would have found me.

CHAPTER 2

Prisoner of the Kohoroshiwetari

When I woke up it was night and I was near a fire; an old man was singing his witch-doctor's song; he had a little white beard. All around were lots and lots and lots of Indians, all naked, with heads shaven in the middle, and each man with his penis tied up. Men and women looked as if they had a swollen lower lip, because they kept a huge lump of tobacco between lip and teeth. I grew terrified. Near me was a woman; I thought she was my mother. I looked at her and I cried; the woman stood up, took a *cuia* of water and offered it to me. She thought I wanted water, but I took none and I continued to cry and cry. Then the men came up and spoke to me in their language; then they took their arrows and beat them to make me afraid. I cried even more. An old woman came up and pointed at the arrows; then I was afraid but I stopped crying.

The Indians stayed there, near my uncle's little houses, about a month. They had built all their own little huts, which we here call in *lingua geral, tapirí*; they were all close together, almost in a circle. I lived near the old woman, who was the headman's sister. She had come with her brother; her husband was dead. She also had a young daughter, who was with her man, and a son, who looked after the old woman's *tapirí*. The men talked to me, but I didn't understand. At night I did not sleep; my wounds hurt me too much. After two nights I felt a bit better, and, shuffling along the ground, I tried to run away. The old woman noticed me: I had hidden myself near her, behind a tree-trunk. The men made a big fire to light up the scene and they saw me. I tried to run: I couldn't for the pain. They caught me again, but they didn't do anything to me; they brought me back to my *tapirí*. The old woman gave me some *bejú,* honey and game to eat.

After a long time, when I was already with the Karawetari and understood their language, I listened to the story of what had happened. Three groups had come together to attack the whites: the Kohoroshiwetari, the Karawetari and the Inamonaweteri. They had reached the little houses as soon as my uncle had left: the ashes were still hot. They had found the *tipití,* that fibre tube for squeezing the manioc, and they had prepared manioc cakes. After capturing me, many men had gone to look for my father to kill him. They had sailed down the Rio Dimití as far as the Rio Negro, without finding anybody. Then they had come back about six days later, laden with honey, little wild boars, and other game.

One day, about a month later, we left to go to their big village. We travelled for eleven days in the wood; I counted all the days. I still couldn't walk and the women carried me on their shoulders, as they carry their babies. When one was tired, another took me. Sometimes they made signs to me to walk, but I showed them I couldn't, also because I hoped they would leave me behind. Instead they carried me all the time; but if I tried to walk, all my wounds would swell up.

During the journey the men went hunting, killing wild boar and birds. In the morning they set out in line with the women and children who went in the middle; when it rained, they stopped, covered themselves with branches and waited for it to stop raining. But if they were in a hurry, they went on walking. When it began to get dark, they broke down tree-trunks and prepared the *tapirí* for the night: they were little huts, with a roof only on one side. Those who arrived first began to build them for their families too. If they had no game to eat, the headman used to say about midday: 'Now put up the *tapirí,* then let everybody go hunting.' But if they still had some game, they would cook in the evening, when they stopped to make the *tapirí.*

The *bejú* came to an end; then they ate meat and nothing else. First they smoked the animals with their hair on, then they split them open and boiled them for a long time with all the hair in a big earthenware pot. Often the hair floated on the broth; they drank the broth, in which they sometimes put *bacabas,* after having taken the stone out. They ate the meat after they had pulled off the skin and the hair. If they killed monkeys, they burnt the hair, and then cooked them whole, after taking out the intestines. The old woman said to me: '*Yaro, yaro.*' But I could not eat those kinds of meat. Later I saw that, whenever possible, they ate the meat with roast banana or with maize cooked in the water or roasted.

I kept trying to break branches to leave signals, hoping to be able to run away and find the way again. But they did not follow a path, but went straight through the forest. They walked and walked:

then some young men climbed the tallest trees, from which they could see the mountains where their village was. Down below in the forest you could see nothing. Then one man up a tree would bite a branch with his teeth, break it off and throw it in the direction of the mountain; then he would come down and pass in front of the others to show the way.

Then the meat came to an end and there was nothing left to eat; there were no coconuts, there was nothing. Sometimes they found bees' honey. From my uncle's house they had brought a lot of pots; they squeezed into them the bees' nests, with all the young grubs. The old woman passed me that juice and said *'Koari, ķoari,'* and I drank it. When there was no more honey, they drank only the soft flesh of those young creatures; it was acid, it tasted like lemon and had a strong smell. I couldn't drink it and I spat it out. Then they found *inajá* palms; they cut them down and took the fruit. I had never eaten them before; they were rather bitter.

Their headman's name was Ohiriwe (*Ohi* means to be hungry: I learnt his name a long time after, because they don't allow themselves to be called by name); he made us walk up and down all the hills we came across. Perhaps he did this so that I should not be able to find the way back again. Eleven days later we reached the place where their wives were waiting: it was a group of *tapirí* still a long way from the big village.

Before we arrived, we stopped near an *igarapé* to have a bath. The old woman wanted to cut my hair in a crown; I didn't want her to, and I cried. She showed me her daughter's shaven head, but I wouldn't let them cut my hair, and cried. In the end she cut my hair all round with the bark of that little bamboo. Then she took red *urucú* and rubbed it on my body, making great red streaks on my back and on my chest, then on my legs and arms, only a little on my face. All the others painted themselves too. The men, who were already painted, began to go up to the huts shouting: *'Pei haw, aw, au, au.'* The women answered from a distance. Then they told me that the women had wept a great deal, because, not seeing them return, they had thought that the white men had killed all their men. When we reached their *tapirí,* a lot of people appeared. There were ever so many: old women, old men, women and children; all came around me and stared. I looked this way, I saw people; I looked that way, I saw people. Then I began to cry for fear. I thought they would kill and eat me, and I thought: 'Perhaps they haven't killed me before, so as to eat me here.' Many of the old men had *cotia*[1] teeth pushed through their ears. I cried and cried for fear. The old woman with whom I stayed spoke loudly to the others; the women and children went away from me. Only the old men, all painted red, stayed behind to look at me.

That same evening the Karawetari, who were also in great numbers, went with the Inamonaweteri, who numbered scarcely thirty, to Ohiriwe, shouting. I understood that they wanted to carry me away with them. Ohiriwe would not let them. They talked and talked; the old woman too, who was looking after me, had a lot to say. The Karawetari shouted and beat their arrows in anger. The same night they parted and the Karawetari went away very upset: they were by now enemies.

The next morning we too left: I began to walk, but my leg still hurt me. We slept one night in the forest and the following day we came near to the big empty village and there we camped. All around there was only forest and no mountains could be seen. The men went ahead to put the village in order; they call it a *shapuno*. On the Rio Negro we call an Indian village a *malocca*. They built a new roof of leaves, changel the rotting trunks which held it up; and cleaned the open space. The village was big, almost round, with a big roof all round and in the middle the large square; it had only two entrances.

One day Indians arrived in the *shapuno*: they brought four big dogs and gave one to Ohiriwe, one to his brother-in-law, one to Ohiriwe's son and one to his son-in-law. They also brought with them a white child whom they had made prisoner. He must have been about ten years old; his eyes were rather blue. I don't know where they had captured him; I asked the child, but he would not give me any answer. They had also stolen the white men's clothes. The little boy would not eat and they gave him to me to make him eat. The child came and sat down near me; I gave him some bacaba juice, but he cried, he cried all the time and would not speak. On the following days he kept coming to me; I gave him bananas, which I cooked for him, and those roots like potatoes which they call *uhina* and which the old woman prepared for us. At night those Indians who had brought him and who slept at the other end of the *shapuno* took him away with them. Then he began to talk to me: he spoke Portuguese and he told me that they gave him to eat the root of a liana which grows in the forest and is bitter. They dig, pull out the root, cut it and cook it; it is yellow. It was very

[1] *Cotia*—a kind of agouti (rodent mammal).

bitter to me too, but they said it was good. The boy didn't want to eat it and only ate game when they gave him any. He spent all his time with me. It seems that they said: 'This child is getting used to living all the time with that white woman. When he grows up, he'll run away with her towards the big river.' One day, while we were with the old woman in the *igarapé* fishing for shrimps, they took the little boy and led him away. I have never heard anything of him since; I have never seen him again.

CHAPTER 3

The Karawetari Attack

An old man arrived at the Kohoroshiwetari *shapuno* to warn us that the Karawetari would come and kill us all. Then the women began to cry and cry. One of them gave me a push and said: 'Must we all die because of this woman?' I was already beginning to understand their speech: I fell down and wept. The men began at once to plant in the ground tree-trunks which I think were about six feet high, all round the *shapuno,* tying them tightly one to another, so that arrows could not come through; the women put short tree-trunks in the low corner below the roof, to protect themselves better. Thus the arrows could reach us only if shot from the other side of the *shapuno.* The *tushaua,* or chief, had a watch kept all night. He sent five men along the path: two men a long way in front, two further back and one near the *shapuno.* They say that if they send more than five men, they begin to talk and laugh; the enemy approaches and hears them. Then he made some of them hide around the *shapuno,* one here and one there, and said: 'If you hear any people making a noise, run and call us, so that everybody can come out.' Several days went by and no enemy came near; then the men began to say: 'No, they're not coming; they're afraid of us, because we are so many and we have arrows.'

One morning two Kohoroshiwetari men had gone to get roots and bark to prepare the curare. From a distance they saw some Karawetari men who were crossing a large bridge suspended over an *igarapé.* The Karawetari saw them too, and shouted: 'You think we are only passing by. No, we shall return to our *shapuno* only when we have carried off all your women.'

That morning the daughter of the old woman who was looking after me wanted to go with some other women into the wood to get fruit from the *buriti* palm. Her mother told her: 'Take this girl along with you.' Then the woman gave me her little boy and I accompanied her. So we went under the *buriti* trees. I remember that I had sat down with the child while the mother gathered fruit.

Suddenly I heard shouts: '*Waiucape, waiucape* (the enemy, the enemy) . . .' and I saw the other women and the young girls who were running in front of us. The mother took the child from my knees, gave me a push and said: 'Let's run! Let's run!' So we all ran towards the *shapuno*; we found it almost empty. The men had gone running to meet the enemy; the other women, with their children, had run away. Only six men and the old woman had stayed behind to wait for us.

It must have been nine o'clock in the morning, and the sun was still low. It is easy to guess the time when the sun is shining. The old woman's daughter untied my hammock from the trunks; I took a basket of *buriti* fruit, hung it over my shoulders, holding with my forehead the long strip of bark with which it was tied, and we ran away. We ran and ran to catch up with the others, but we could not do so. At last we caught up with them. There were lots of women, youths, old women and children, but no men. We sat down to rest. Soon after a young man came running and said, 'What are you doing? Run away! The Karawetari have already reached that place where we were catching monkeys that day near the *shapuno*. Every one of them has a bundle of arrows in his hand. They have shouted that they won't go away without taking our women!' Then we fled again. We ran all day. We stopped to rest in the evening and the women said, 'We're a long way off now; they won't come this far.' Then they began to prepare the tents for the night.

It was well into the night when two men came running and said: 'Run away again; the Karawetari have shouted that they will capture you all.' Those Kohoroshiwetari men did not shoot any arrows at the Karawetari; they ran away without shooting and stayed between us women and the enemy. The Indians with whom I lived later did not do that. Whenever the enemy approached, they shot arrows straight at him. We picked up the firebrands which we had brought with us from the *shapuno* and we began to flee again. I, behind all the other women, fell down and wept; I was thin and weak. For some time I had eaten those bitter roots of theirs and I always had a stomach ache. I had spent the nights going to the *igarapé*.

At last we stopped: the night was dark. I lay down on the ground and fell asleep. I had perhaps just gone to sleep when I felt myself being shaken: 'Get up, get up,' said the old woman. Three youths were saying, 'The Karawetari have already arrived where you wanted to sleep and where you had begun to put up your tents.

They have already shot one of us in the shoulder and one in the leg.' The women were crying, because they thought the men were dead; they said: 'Where shall we go now? The big rocks are nearby.' The *tushaua* had sent those three men to guide us among the rocks; they must have known the way, because they had been hunting on that hill, but one of them said: 'Let's go that way,' while another said: 'No, that other way.' So we walked and walked all night. At last the old woman's daughter put the firebrand on the ground and said to me: 'Sit down'; she gave me the little boy and went to look for wood. I immediately went to sleep. It was just getting light again when they woke me up once more. Above us were some very high rocks; it was cold.

Two men came running; one had a child in his arms. 'Run away again,' they said, 'we can already hear the enemy shouting, "Miserable women, miserable women! Why do they run and fall among these boulders? Do they think we shall leave them alone?" ' Then the old woman said to me: 'I am going back down the hill to where my sons are; the enemy want to kill them. You go with my daughter. Climb up towards the top of the hill; you'll be safe, because they won't come up there; they must already be hungry. I'm going back to my children.' I never saw that old woman again.

We were now very high up. I looked down and saw the enemy, all painted black, running towards us: I pointed them out to the old woman's daughter. The three men, who had accompanied us during the night, met those who had arrived and they disappeared together. Thus we women were left alone with the children. We tried to climb up the rocks, but we could not flee any more; the Karawetari were by now quite close. They had split up into two groups. One group had climbed up the rocks and were already above us, while the other group was following us from below.

Then a woman began to shout loudly to the enemy, who were below: 'Karawetari! Have I by chance killed your fathers, so that you should persecute me like this? You have pursued us all night and still you pursue us!' While she was shouting, those who had climbed up the hill and were above us began to shoot arrows: tak, tak. Six or seven arrows fell, but did not hit us. A child, trembling with fear, climbed up a tree. Then the woman shouted louder: 'Karawetari, dirty bunch!' Behind us a voice replied: 'I'll carry you off to my *shapuno*; you have a big mouth for talking, but you can't frighten us. So much the worse for you, that you have no arrows and you have a husband who's afraid! He threw his arrows down on the path and ran away. I'll catch you and take you away with me.' Several times before the Karawetari had seized Kohoroshiwetari women, but many of them had succeeded in escaping. Meanwhile the enemy continued to shout: 'Kohoroshiwetari women, your husbands are miserable! They make you eat roots from the forest; we eat bananas and *pupugnas*. Your husbands make you eat only the roots of wild plants.' The women replied: 'Yes, we eat fruit out of the forest, and roots of plants, but we haven't come to ask you for fruit and bananas.'

In the meantime I had seen a little grotto among the rocks and I had gone inside; behind me other women had come to hide. Outside there were many women, a lot of them with children in their arms. The enemy were coming down from above and climbing up from below. The boy who had climbed a tree shouted at a man who was coming nearer: 'Father, don't shoot me!' 'I'm not your father,' shouted the man; 'if I had been your father, you would have been happy to run towards me'; and he shot him. The arrow hit the little boy from behind in the leg and came through in front. The child fell, picked himself up and ran with the arrow still in him.

The men began to seize the women; they caught them by the arms, they caught them by the wrists. '*Ahi!*' shouted the women. Some said: 'You won't take only us away; inside that grotto there are other women hiding.' The men came closer: 'Come out; if you don't come out, we'll shoot arrows inside.' One woman came out at once. Another wouldn't come out and hid in there, but the Karawetari pointed their arrows at her: 'Don't do that,' she said, 'I'll come out.' I was still hiding at the back, but I heard the voice of a woman who was saying: 'In there at the back is that woman whom they caught not long ago.' Then a man came and shouted: 'Come out!' He threatened with his bow as though it were a spear. I came out and stood in line with the other women.

One woman had a baby girl in her arms. The men seized the little child and asked: 'Is it a boy or a girl?' and they wanted to kill it. The mother wept: 'It's a little girl, you mustn't kill her.' Then one of them said: 'Leave her; it's a girl; we won't kill the females. Let's take the women away with us and make them give us sons. Let's kill the males instead.' Another woman had a baby boy only a few months old in her arms. They snatched him away from her. 'Don't kill him,' shouted another woman, 'he's your son. The mother was with you and she ran away when she was already pregnant with this child. He's one of your sons!' 'No,' the men replied, 'he's a Kohoroshiwetari child. It's too long since she ran away from us.' They took the baby by his feet and bashed him against the rock. His head split open and the little white brains spurted out on the stone. They picked up the tiny body, which had turned purple, and threw it away. I wept with fear.

So we began to go down the hill. The men held their women prisoners by the arms. When the forest had thinned out and they were afraid that the women might run away, they put them in the middle; one man stayed on one side and another on the other. While we were going downhill, we saw a woman hiding among the rocks; she couldn't run away any more. She had three children, one strapped to her back, one on her knees and the biggest by her side. They were near a precipice of rocks. One man came up to her, saying: 'What are you doing here?' He kicked the woman and the children and hurled them all down the abyss. They rolled right down among the rocks to the bottom. When we arrived, we found them all injured, but still alive: the blood was flowing from so many wounds and the children couldn't even cry. One woman prisoner recognized them: 'It's the wife: they are the children of the brother of that Kohoroshiwetari who lives with you.' A Kohoroshiwetari did in fact live with the Karawetari; his name was Matahewe (*Mata* is a big snake). He had married a Karawetari woman and had grown-up children.

Meanwhile from all sides the women continued to arrive with their children, whom the other Karawetari had captured. They all joined us. Then the men began to kill the children; little ones, bigger ones, they killed many of them. They tried to run away, but they caught them, and threw them on the ground, and stuck them with bows, which went through their bodies and rooted them to the ground. Taking the smallest by the feet, they beat them against the trees and the rocks. The children's eyes trembled. Then the men took the dead bodies and threw them among the rocks, saying: 'Stay there, so that your fathers can find you and eat you.' They killed so many. I was weeping for fear and for pity, but there was nothing I could do. They snatched the children from their mothers to kill them, while the others held the mothers tightly by the arms and wrists as they stood up in a line. All the women wept.

Meanwhile the Karawetari began to call and insult the Kohoroshiwetari, shouting in a loud voice: 'Kohoroshiwetari, Kohoroshiwetari, cowards, cowards; you ran away! Come and avenge yourselves and kill us! We have killed all your children, take vengeance on us!' No one answered. They went on: 'Kohoroshiwetari, from afar you are brave, at close quarters you are the biggest cowards! You run away and leave your women with their children! It's a good thing that we have killed your children!' So they continued to shout for a long time. Then a voice was heard from afar: 'You Karawetari, you are cowards too: you have the courage to take women and children among rocks where there's no way out. We'll see your courage when the Shamatari come and make war. Then you'll be the biggest cowards!' While he was shouting from a distance, the Karawetari were saying: 'We'll make him talk; we'll find out where he is and we'll go and shoot him.' They recognized him by his voice: once Kohoroshiwetari and Karawetari had been friends. The men shouted: 'Eh! Amiana, Amiana!' This was his name. 'Come here, come here.' The man did not answer. A group of Karawetari went among the rocks to kill him. They came back not long after saying they had shot arrows among the rocks where he was hiding, but they had not hit him: they brought back a bow.

All we women stood still together. It was perhaps eleven o'clock, and the sun was very high, when the Karawetari *tushaua,* whose name was Maniwe, arrived. He had been in the quarrel with the others; he said: 'Now let's go away; you have already done plenty of killing. I don't want any of these women for myself, because they are too clever at running away. The last time we caught them, they nearly all escaped.'

Shortly afterwards Matahewe, that Kohoroshiwetari who lived with the Karawetari, arrived, and saw his sister-in-law with her children all bleeding: 'Who has done this to my brother's wife and to my nephews? Children must not be killed.' He shouted and shouted: 'If I had been up there, when you hurled them down the precipice, I would have shot you!'

Then in a very loud voice he called his brother, the father of the three children who had been thrown down the abyss. We women were all in a line, waiting to leave. A voice was heard from a distance and soon the man appeared. The Karawetari looked at him; the brother, who was with the Karawetari, said to him: 'Why did you too run away from the *shapuno*? You should have waited for me with your wife and children. Have you seen what they have done to your family?' the other replied: 'You came with the Karawetari; you too came with the intention of killing my children.' 'No, it's not true; if I had been there, I would not have let them do what they did.' The other looked at that heap of dead children.

There were children of one year old, of two years, three years, and bigger ones. Matahewe said: 'Why have you killed these children? Children don't know what grown-ups are doing. We are here to make war on adults.' He shouted, and he wept also. The Karawetari looked at him and wanted to shoot him.

The Karawetari *tushaua* said to his own men: 'Let him speak! Let no one point his arrow at him; let everyone keep their arrows in their hands.' The man continued: 'Children don't know how to take an arrow or stretch a bow; why have you killed them? No; you shouldn't have killed them, you should have sought and killed the fathers. When I go to make war and give the command, I say to my men: 'Don't shoot your arrows at little children, at old men or at women." ' All listened to him without a word; even the Karawetari *tushaua* listened. At last the brother, who also had two grown-up sons with the Karawetari, said: 'Now we are leaving. If you want to come to us, to the Karawetari, you can; nothing will happen to you. The fault for all this is with the Kohoroshiwetari; their chief, Ohiriwe, speaks very badly of us. We wanted to kill him and his son-in-law, not your sons, nor yourself.' The brother replied: 'Now I will gather wood and I will burn the bodies of the dead.' The Karawetari left that man his wife and three injured children.

Before leaving, the men began to shout loudly, *'Au, au, au . . .'* in a ranting voice. This is the cry of the enemy when attacking and it is the cry which they make when they go away after the attack.

CHAPTER 4

The Women Prisoners and the Jealous Wives

They all stood in line, a man, a woman, a man, a woman. On the track, one behind another, they let go of our wrists, because it was difficult to escape. There were many Kohoroshiwetari women, perhaps about fifty. With the Karawetari there were only three women who came behind the fathers and brothers.

We heard a whimper among the leaves. One woman prisoner went up and saw that boy whom the Karawetari had shot at in the tree. With us was that Kohoroshiwetari who did not want them to kill the children. The woman called him and said: 'Shoriwe (brother-in-law), why don't you start a fire and warm this child?' The other Karawetari looked at him and wanted to kill him. The man said: 'Don't shoot him. He's got such a big wound that he will surely die; leave him alone to die by himself.' He took his hammock, hung it up on the branches, put the little boy in it and lit a fire nearby to warm him.

We walked and walked, and at last we reached a wood of *buriti* palms. The *tushaua* said: 'We are hungry and we have nothing to eat. Take these women to collect *buriti*.' Some women went with the men into the forest to collect the fruit, while others stayed behind; there were lots of them. In the *buriti* palm forest a young woman tried to run away: she began to run and run. As soon as the man who had captured her saw that she was now capable of escaping, he drew a hooked arrow, one of those pointed with monkey-bone, and hit her in the middle of the back. The woman fell face forward. She must have died; she could never have pulled out one of those hooked arrows. The men came back and said: 'A woman has run away, but we have shot her. She fell down; let's leave her there to die, let's go.'

We walked on and on. By the evening I was very tired and hungry. We stopped in a place where there were some old *tapiri*.

Some men came up to me and looked at me: 'Who took her?' they asked. 'With whom will she stay?' The young Karawetari girl, who had accompanied her brother and who I afterwards learned was called Xoxotami, said: 'It was my brother who caught her, she'll stay with us'; then she turned to her younger brother: 'Give this girl your hammock.' The youth gave me his hammock and lay down on the ground. So we settled down under that roof of leaves, I, the girl, the young lad who had given up his hammock and the other brother. Then the girl began to talk to me; I now understood everything. She said: 'We are going a long way, that way.' Meantime the men were cooking monkeys and had collected those roots out of the wood. They gave me a piece of monkey meat. Thereafter that girl stayed with me all the time.

Early in the morning we left and we walked all day. We reached that bridge where the two Kohoroshiwetari had seen the Karawetari crossing. It was dark now: the river was broad, but we all crossed and camped on the other side. Then the men cut the bridge right down, so that the women could not escape and the enemy could not come and make a surprise attack. The girl called me and made me hang my hammock near her. The younger brother lay on the ground. The older brother and the father put their hammocks up on the branches near us, and they made no *tapirí*.

No sooner had I begun to fall asleep than I heard: tuk, tuk, tuk . . . they were arrows falling nearby. The Kohoroshiwetari were shooting. The Karawetari then began to shout: 'Kohoroshiwetari cowards, you can shoot from a distance! In the daytime you didn't have the courage to show your faces, now you can shoot from afar, by night!' The Kohoroshiwetari on the other side of the river saw the fires and shot their arrows from a long distance: that is why they didn't hit us. The Karawetari covered up all the fires. The girl, who was with me, was afraid and said: 'Come and hide among the great roots of that tree.' So we ran and hid among those roots and there we stayed until dawn. During the night a woman came silently up to me. She was the one whose tiny baby they had killed. She said to me: 'I'm going to run away; you can go with them. Perhaps it's all right for you; you have neither father nor mother with us. You can go. They already seized me once before. You won't be badly off with them; they don't only eat fruit from the forest, but bananas and *uhina* roots.'

We continued our journey; the way was long. The Karawetari did not cross the forest and did not climb the trees to see a long way off, but returned by the same path which they had taken while coming. Some Karawetari had been wounded, but none had died. One had a wound in the shoulder, caused by that bamboo arrow-head like a spear: it was a big cut. Another had had an arrow hit him in the heel, another in the knee, and yet another in the chest. From the wound of this last man blood and bubbles were oozing out; he couldn't walk and his companions were carrying him. The other wounded, after two or three days, were already beginning to walk by themselves again.

Some men said: 'The Kohoroshiwetari are cowards, but they still follow us. They wait till they think we are a long way off and are unprotected and then attack us. We have taken so many of their women; they'll come to take vengeance on us.' A few other men replied: 'No, they are not following us: now they must burn their dead and so they are looking for them among the rocks.' The *tushaua* said: 'Don't say they won't come; they will come. Do you think perhaps that you have killed the sons of wild boar in the wood? No, you have killed the sons of Yanoáma; we Yanoáma love our sons very much. Certainly they will come; they are waiting for us to be off our guard to attack us.'

So after five days we arrived at a great *roça*. Three men went off to cut down an *inaja* palm tree and get its *palmito*:[1] suddenly an arrow came and stuck in the tree. They ran back to where the group was, shouting: 'The Kohoroshiwetari are attacking!' Then they all grasped their arrows in their hands. A fresh arrow fell near the running men. The *tushaua* said: 'I said that nobody was to go away by himself. If they had killed you, no one would have seen you.' Then he ordered seven men to stay behind on the path to keep watch. In front of all the rest went a group of men, then a man and a woman prisoner, a man and a woman prisoner. The line was very long; there were so many of us. I, with that girl and her younger brother who had given me the hammock, went ahead, near those who were leading the file.

Sometimes those who had taken the women did not want theirs and said: 'I took this woman, but I don't want her any longer; who wants her?' Some others replied: 'Give her to me.' Then the one who didn't want her any more gave her to the other and so he passed in front with those who were leading the way and had no women. The young man who had taken me, brother of that girl who was always

[1] *Palmito* in Spanish means the shoot of the palm: a delicacy eaten raw as a salad or *hors-d'œuvre* in South America. (Translator.)

with me, said to her: 'I want to give this woman to another man.' 'No,' answered his sister, 'she'll stay with us, I'll take care of her.'

We passed near a *roça* which belonged to the Kohoroshiwetari. The men went and found *cara* roots and tobacco leaves: they filled the baskets with them. Then they carried the *cara* to those who were leading the way. So we came close to a group of *tapirí*, where their women were waiting for them and which was still a long way from the big *shapuno*. When we got near we stopped; the men said to the women prisoners. 'Now you must all paint yourselves.' The women painted themselves red with *urucú* which the men had brought. The brothers of the girl who was with me had no *urucú* and painted themselves black with ashes and coal. I was still a child and so they did not paint me. The men who had killed did not paint themselves: they pushed two smooth little sticks through the holes in the lobes of their ears and tied two little sticks to their wrists.

While they were going into the middle of the *tapirí*, the Karawetari women came angrily to meet them, shouting: 'You, Kohoroshiwetari women, after they have killed your sons by beating them against the rocks, you, dirty bitches, come here all painted as if it were a feast!' They said all sorts of things, accusing them of everything. The Kohoroshiwetari women didn't reply; they went where the men took them. Then the *tushaua* said: 'We haven't brought Kohoroshiwetari women for you to quarrel with. They have been so hungry during the journey; just see you give them something to eat.' But the Karawetari women continued to shout and to insult them.

Xoxotami took me to her mother in her *tapirí*. 'Who's this?' asked the mother. 'Where does she come from?' Xoxotami replied: 'She is a *Napagnuma*.[1] She's that white woman whom our men captured together with the Kohoroshiwetari, the one whom the Kohoroshiwetari did not want to give up. This is why our men have become their enemies and have gone to fight them. Xoxotami continued: 'She's pretty thin; no one wanted her. I have helped her and brought her here; now she'll stay with us.' The mother looked at me and answered: 'There are lots of young men here who have no women. This white woman will stay with me; then nobody shall come to take her away.' Then she said in a load voice: 'Let everybody listen. There are so many men without women. Soon this one will become

[1] *Napagnuma*, in the Yanoáma language, means white woman, foreign woman.

a woman and then nobody must take her away from me.' She took me by the arm and led me to her hammock. 'Now have a rest; you'll be tired after such a long walk.'

Meanwhile the wives continued to insult the Kohoroshiwetari women who were now crying. They said: 'You come here all happy, painted all over. You are happy, you have found your husbands! If they had killed our sons, we should have come in tears. Not you, no, you come with painted faces. Does it give you pleasure that they have killed your sons?' None of them replied; all was quiet. During the journey some of the women had wept, but the men did not like it; when they saw them weep, they threatened them with arrows, saying: 'You weep because you want your husbands to hear you from a distance and to know where you are. If you cry loudly, we will shoot you.' Then the women had been afraid and had cried no more.

The next morning we resumed our journey towards the great *shapuno*. Nearly all the men went hunting and collecting *pupugnas*; the Karawetari stayed in the line to guard the women prisoners. The old woman said to Xoxotami and to another daughter who was big and tall: 'Let's go ahead; the women will shout all the time, I don't want to listen to them. The other time, when they took the women prisoners, our women shouted and shouted, and they beat them too; that's why many of them escaped later.' We reached an *igarapé*; Xoxotami's mother said: 'Let us catch crabs.' We stopped and we caught many large crabs. When the sun was already high, we began to march again. The other women, with the prisoners, came quite near to us.

While I was walking, I heard a noise behind me and I saw two young Kohoroshiwetari hidden amongst the trees; they were looking for their women among the prisoners. The wife of one of them, in fact, was a little way behind me. Suddenly one young man jumped out, gave a push to the basket which the woman was carrying on her back and caused it to roll to the ground. The old woman saw him and said: 'Let's go, come on, come with me; no one will come and take you away. If they come, I will hit them with this bow.' She was fairly old and old women, when they travel, lean on a long piece of a bow.

Meanwhile the two men, with the woman, ran off into the bush. The Karawetari women left their baskets on the ground and went after them. The husband allowed himself to be caught to give his wife a better chance to escape. They wanted to take his bow away;

the man said: 'Leave my bow, grandmother,' but the old women had surrounded him and wanted to kill him. One shouted: 'Let's catch him down below by his organs, so he won't have any strength left!' He tried to defend himself with the bow, but a woman seized him by one leg, shouting: 'Let's kill him!' The man fell down; his companion kept poking at the women with his bow as though it were a spear, to liberate his friend. The Karawetari women—they were only the old ones, because the young ones were afraid and had gone away—said: 'You can kill us with your bow if you like, but today will also be the end of this man who came to take his woman back. He came to get himself killed by us!' Meanwhile the man had freed himself, while his companion kept the old women off with his bow. So the two managed to escape, taking with them the woman who was running ahead. Then the Karawetari women shouted after the fugitives: 'Go on, go on! Go back to eating wild fruit and bad fruit. Stupid woman for running away! If you had stayed with us, you would have eaten *pupugnas* and bananas from our *roças*. Now you'll have to work hard enough to find wild fruit in the woods!'

So we continued our march, until we reached a group of old *tapirí*, where we awaited the men who soon began to arrive with baskets laden with *pupugna* fruit which they had found in a nearby *roça*. Then some Karawetari women began to say: 'You left us alone; the Kohoroshiwetari have come and got their women back!' The men, annoyed, said: 'It was all your fault. When they arrived, you maltreated them so much; now they have run away, you are so happy!' Then the women said: 'It's not true, they have taken only one.' The man who had captured her shouted: 'I'm going to get her back.' He wanted to kill the woman and her husband. He left with about ten men. We stayed in those *tapirí*; the old woman began to roast bananas and Xoxotami to cook *pupugnas*. Those men came back later: they said they had run, they had found the footprints; then the footprints became almost invisible. Afterwards, in the mud, they could see the footprints clearly again, then they disappeared altogether.

CHAPTER 5

Life with the Karawetari

Their big *shapuno* was nearby; the men went ahead to get it ready. Meanwhile the women loaded water and picked those long leaves which are used to cover the roof. The old woman gave me large bundles of them, which I carried on my head. The next day the men said: 'The whole *shapuno* is clean. We have pulled up the weeds in the inner square;[1] tomorrow we shall go and cut the big trees.'

Every woman of the *shapuno* said to her husband's female prisoner: 'Now you'll do as I say. You'll have to gather wood for me, and water in the *igarapé* for me. If you don't do it, I'll beat you.' One woman replied: 'I came because your husband brought me; I should have run away at once.' The husband said: 'Stop talking, else I'll give you both a beating.' The wife went on: 'No, I will kill her and then you will burn her by yourself; I will run off with other men.' I remember one man said to his wife: 'You stay with the children; this woman will come with me into the *roça* to help me carry bananas.' The wife, who was jealous and knew what her husband wanted to do with the other woman, waited for them to go out, cut down the woman's hammock and threw it on the fire; then she looked for the *urucú* with which the other woman painted herself and threw it away. When she met the other woman coming back with the man from the *roça*, laden with bananas, she beat her with a stick. She said: 'This stick is good for beating you with, *ihina*.[2] You've been with your dog, *ihina*!' The man looked on quietly. The wife hit the woman hard on the head; blood spurted out. Then the husband took a big stick and gave it to the other woman: 'Now you hit her on the head.' He seized his wife to hold her tight, saying, 'Hit her!' The woman prisoner was weeping with fear, but she didn't hit the wife. The husband said: 'Go on, hit her!' but the

[1] It is, in fact, not square in shape, but roughly circular. There is no appropriate English word to describe this central open space surrounded by the dwellings.

[2] *Ihina* means dog or bitch.

woman did not move. The wife too said: 'Hit me, hit me, and it'll be the end of you. I'll hit you next and I'll leave you to die.' The husband continued: 'Hit her; I want to see whether she's got the courage to kill you.' But the woman was bleeding, and trembling, and had not the courage to do it. The husband said: 'So you don't want to hit her? So now you can take my blows,' and with that he beat her himself.

The *shapuno* was very big; bigger even than that of the Shamatari, which I saw later. After three days, even the leaves of the roof had been renewed. The Karawetari were much more numerous than the Kohoroshiwetari. The men were more than a hundred and there were very many women and children. At night the men sniffed into their noses a kind of powder which they called *epená*; then one began to sing and to invoke the Hekurá spirits, so that thus the enemy should have nothing, so that the parrots and the other birds should ruin the *mirití* flowers and those of the other fruits, so that the fruit trees should not grow near the places where the enemy lived, but only near their own *shapuno*. They repeated the same things for the hunting animals. Sometimes there were two who sang like this all night, invoking fruit and animals for their own tribe and evil for the enemy. I had already seen the Kohoroshiwetari doing the same thing.

Some days later we went into the forest to get butterfly grubs: they call them *mana*. There are various kinds of these: those long, smooth ones, with no hair, those with long hairs, which when they are disturbed go tac, tac, tac and burn your skin. That day we went to catch the ones with the long hairs. They had climbed up the branches; there was a mass of them on every little branch. The men climbed the tree and slowly broke off the branches so as not to let the caterpillars fall. Meanwhile, along the track, we had picked large *pishaansi* leaves and had put them in the baskets. They eat them cooked or toasted; if eaten raw, they make you sick. They open them, put the soft flesh of those grubs inside *pishaansi* leaves and make a sort of packet. When we came back, everyone had prepared many of these packets. Then they put these packets of leaves on the embers; they turn them from one side to the other, until no more drops of liquid, sort of a broth, come out. At other times they fill the baskets with grubs, then they roast them in earthenware pots. They put them in flat baskets and rub them with stones to take off the hairs, which are hard, white, and can stick in the tongue and the throat. They eat them with bananas, if they have any.

When they go to look for them in the woods and find them, if they are not yet ready they open a few to see inside and then say: 'Let's not spoil them: they are still young, they are green.' Then they leave them on the ground; the grubs climb up again on to the trees where they were before. If a bit of the soft flesh squirts into your eye, it burns badly like pepper; the eye becomes red. A few days later they come back to get them; if they are late, the caterpillars all come down from the trees and go and bury themselves in the ground, where they turn into dark cocoons. Then a large, bluish butterfly emerges from these cocoons. When the Indians return and find that the caterpillars are no longer on the tree, they begin to dig in the earth where the cocoons are; these are long and smooth. If the butterfly inside is not yet dark, they eat it; but if it already has wings and big eyes, they do not eat it, because it irritates the mouth. They say: 'They are no longer good, let's give them to the old women.' These creatures do not eat the leaves of poisonous trees.

In the *ingá* nuts there are white worms. They break the nuts, take out the little worms, often mix them with salt water, prepared with the ashes of a tree or with little peppers, then put them in leaves and cook them. They don't eat them without that water, for otherwise, they say, they ruin the teeth. They do not know cooking salt. To cook worms, snakes and fish, they use salted ashes of a tree which they call *ķarorihekļ*. I saw what they did to prepare ashes. That salty juice which they obtain from that tree-trunk, and which they mix also with peppers, is called *ķaķorihuna*. They also use the ashes of a plant that grows in waterfalls and which they call *atahiķi*; they burn those leaves, but they prefer very much the ashes of that big tree.

I always used to go catching little fish with the women. One morning the old woman said: 'Let's go to the *igarapé* near here; there are lots of fish.' We passed near to a large *roça*; it was there that I saw how the Karawetari cultivate so many bananas. In the *roça* there was also tobacco and *urucú*. The Kohoroshiwetari, however, ate almost exclusively wild fruits of *balata*, *pirarana*, *puirana*, *sorba*, *patauá* and *bacaba*. We soon reached the *igarapé*, which was pretty wide. We could hear the birds singing and those little toads which go prin, prin, prin. There was myself, the old woman, Xoxotami, the eldest daughter with a little boy and a niece. They gave the boy to me and I sat down and stayed with him on the bank. The women broke branches and jumped into the water, beating it heavily with the branches, pah, pah, pah. They beat and beat the water, and the little fish all hid among the rotting leaves. Then the old woman said: 'Let's stop and see.' They allowed the water to settle; no fish could now be seen. Then they began to take large handfuls of rotten leaves; in the middle there were just two or three fish. Sometimes they dived in to get the leaves at the bottom. Then they bit the fish in the head and threw them out of the stream. When there were no more to find, they shouted: 'Let's go on; there are no more here.' In the end the old woman said: 'Let's go back; I am afraid the Shamatari will come and attack us.' They said they had seen tracks of the Shamatari around the *shapuno*. They were very frightened of the Shamatari. The old woman gutted the fish and put them inside leaves; so she made many packets. That day we ate a great deal of fish.

Not long after there was a heavy fall of rain and the water rose in the *igarapé*. When the *igarapé* began to dry up and the time came when fishing was good, we returned to fish at the spot where the *igarapé* made a sort of pool. The men came too: one of them saw an enormous anaconda on the bank. The snake was asleep, because it had eaten a deer. The man approached and hit it with an axe in the middle of the head, with all the strength he had. I was standing a good way off, but I was looking on; the serpent began to turn around. In the evening, in the *shapuno*, the man said: 'Let's go and get that snake which I hit on the head; it'll be dead by now.' The weather was bad and they did not go; three days later they decided to go. We walked for the whole of one day before we reached the place where that enormous anaconda was: in that pool there was a huge quantity of fish. We reached a *buriti* forest and the men prepared the little *tapirí* for the night. The next morning we went to see: the snake's body was emerging from the mud; it was dark and broad like that of a tapir. 'It's dead!' they said, and they began to fish in that pool. There were lots of those dangerous fish which give an electric shock; they don't eat them.

I approached that enormous serpent: the wound in its head was open and you could see flies all round it. I looked at it and the snake looked at me; it put its tongue out. I ran away. The women were beating the water to drive the fish into a narrow passage where the men were waiting with arrows. I ran to them and said: 'The snake is still alive; it looked at me and put out its tongue.' They replied: 'You're telling lies!' One man went near to the anaconda and beat it on the head with his bow; the snake didn't even move. He stuck the end of the bow into the snake's body and the creature then put its tongue out again. The man jumped and slipped: they all laughed, but they came out of the water quickly enough. They were very much afraid, because it was enormous, coiled up like that in the mud of the pool.

The men said: 'Let's kill it,' and they began to poke it with the points of their bows and to give it blows on the head. The snake began to twist itself round very slowly and to spit out of its mouth some rotten pieces of deer; it was one of those deer with horns. Then they took some big lianas and began to make nooses, which they threw around the creature's neck. All of them, men and women, pulled the brute towards the dry ground, but it attached itself to the tree-trunks with the point of its tail. At last they succeeded in pulling it out of the water; it was never-ending: many feet still remained in the water. They said: 'It's very big, it has a lot of meat; let us cut it up and smoke it.' They tied the lianas to a thick branch of a tall tree and began to pull, hoisting the beast up. When it was suspended well into the air, they began to cut it, starting from the tail. They rested the rear part of the creature over a trunk and cut it with their very sharp bamboos. They had already cut off seven very long pieces, when they came to where the intestine was: 'Here's the fat part,' said the women, and began to tear at it. Suddenly the anaconda began to lash out, coiled itself up, snapped the liana and again fell into the water. The water was all churned up again and turned red. We all fled at a run: they abandoned the fish which they had caught, they abandoned the pieces of the snake, and they never even went back to pick them up.

After five or six days, one man returned to see whether he could get the arrows which he had left behind in his flight. He climbed a tree and looked around: the water was clear; the serpent was still there, alive. He came back and said, 'It's alive, it's the nephew of *Rahara*!'[1]

All the Hekurá then advised them not to go back there ever again. They said that the pieces of tail had joined together again. I have seen plenty of snakes in that *igarapé* and in those pools, but that one was enormous.

In the *shapuno* there was a sick woman. The old *Shapori*[2] had tried to cure her by sucking her and chanting their songs. They had said that the woman's *Nohotipe*[3] had fled and that this was why she

[1] *Rahara*: an enormous mythological serpent.
[2] *Shapori* or Hekurá: shaman, witch-doctor.
[3] *Nohotipe*: the spirit, soul or shade.

was so ill. That illness was *noreshi*. The woman was always complaining. Then they built on the compound of the *shapuno* a kind of enormous cage about three feet high, fixing in the ground some thick sticks and tying others over the top: it was the harpy's nest. Some men painted themselves black around the eyes, around the mouth, on the chest, on the legs; they entwined long *assai* leaves in their hair and hung them behind their head like a tuft: they said that thus they were imitating the harpies, those big birds. Others painted themselves black around the mouth and the eyes, and on the legs: they were the monkeys.

In the afternoon, after three o'clock, they nearly all went outside to look for the *nohotipe*. The harpies with their cry, *fio, fio* . . . with leafy branches under their arms, beat their arms as if they were wings. The sick woman had stayed with a few men. At the big entrance to the *shapuno* a woman was answering the cries made from far away by those who had gone into the wood to search for the soul: 'Look here, here is our home.' Those who were pretending to be monkeys were shouting, jumping, waving the branches which they had in their hands. Those who were painted like otters were repeating the otter's cry. Even the children were following the others, painted like little falcons. The *tushaua* had said: 'You will be falcons which look down from above and are the cleverest at finding; you monkeys, look among the branches.' The women swept the branches along the ground like brooms. They think that they can find the *nohotipe* and thus drive it towards the *shapuno*. Many women carried their babies before them slung from their necks, because they were afraid that if they left them in the *shapuno* they too might have lost the *nohotipe*. After they had gone round an area where they thought the soul might have stayed, they went back into the *shapuno*. They passed round all the braziers and, with the branches, swept under the hammocks, in the corners, and they scattered the fire; then they again went outside the *shapuno*. They once more went right round it; when they came inside again, the most important Shapori said: 'The soul is weeping in that place where we went that time.' They all ran in that direction.

The sick woman did not improve: then they lifted her on their shoulders and carried her outside to look for the soul together and to put it back in her. At length they returned inside the *shapuno* and one man squatted on that enormous cage which they had prepared: then another one jumped up on it, then another: they were the harpies and the monkeys. They also put the sick woman in their midst and, with the branches, began to strike her on the face. They thought that thus the *nohotipe* would more easily re-enter the body.

The monkeys stayed on the edges of the cage, jumping and shouting *eih, eih . . .*, while the harpies shouted *fio, fio . . .* and beat their wings. The women, the boys and all, as they came back, threw over the big cage the branches which they had in their hands. They say that that big cage, with the branches over it, is the harpy's nest. They all squatted over it. They turned the sick woman round and lifted her up; the harpies went *tak, tak . . .* beating upon the sick woman's body as if they were killing ants. According to them ants had entered into the *nohotipe* when it was lost in the wood.

At last a woman brought water in a *cuia* and some leaves which sent out a very strong odour. They are leaves which grow over the nests of certain ants called *kuna kuna*. Then they rubbed these leaves hard in the water and drew them over the sick woman's body and head. Slowly the woman began to improve: no more saliva came out of her mouth, nor did she groan any more.

They also believe that a man's soul is that great bird the harpy. When a man is ill, they say: 'Perhaps he has fallen out of the nest, and cannot fly; that is why he is ill.'

One morning the old woman said to us: 'Go and get water.' I and Xoxotami went; we did not know that the enemy were hidden along the bank of the *igarapé*. I filled my *cuia*: the water went pin, pin, pin . . . as it entered. I stopped up the *cuia* with a cork made of leaves, placed it against the root of a tree and went back to the *igarapé* to take a bath. Xoxotami too entered the water to bathe; she rubbed her body with leaves.

I looked up above and saw many men, all painted black. One made a sign to me with his hand not to shout. I dived into the water and came out at a run. Xoxotami saw them too and shouted: 'Don't shoot us, we are only women!' and then she ran away shouting, 'Enemy, enemy, look out, look out!' Another woman, near us, began to shout, 'Enemy, enemy,' and we all fled to the *shapuno*. The men took their bows and arrows and yelled: 'Enemy, enemy! This is the shout that our ears want to hear!' The old woman asked me: 'Have you seen them? Are they Kohoroshiwetari?' The men ran out, but did not find them. They came back in the evening, saying that they had only found the spot where the enemy had sat down, then their tracks disappeared in the woods. I said, 'Yes, I saw some men.' The old woman added, 'The other girl also saw some men.'

An old man arrived one evening at the *shapuno*; his name was

Shoamao. He had both his eyes, but from one eye he could not see us. He was carrying a large earthenware pot. The old man said: 'I have come to invite you to the Hekurawetari. They have many ripe *pupugnas*; they invite you.' He spoke much; he sang as he spoke, as they do when they come to invite people. The *tushaua* replied: 'I cannot come now; I have only just cleaned up the *shapuno*; the bananas that I have hung up are not yet ripe; the *pupugnas* are ripening. If I come, they will all go bad. If I come, the Kohoroshiwetari will come here and destroy all my trees. I want to await the Kohoroshiwetari here: our men have killed so many of their sons and captured so many of their women. They will come for sure; if they don't find me, they'll say I have fled. I want the Kohoroshiwetari to come here to kill my sons in the *shapuno*, I don't want them to find me travelling. On a journey one is unprepared and the women are following behind. In the *shapuno* we leave the women and children; we go out into the forest nearby only with great care.'

Then Shoamao came to the father of Xoxotami and said, 'You come, if the *tushaua* does not wish to come; at least you can come to the Hekurawetari, who have sent me to invite you.' Xoxotami's father replied, 'Yes, I'll come. I don't mind leaving the fruit. Other people can eat my bananas and my *pupugnas* too if they want to!' But the others did not want to go, partly because Shoamao had said that the Shamatari were about to come and fight the Hekurawetari. The headman of the Hekurawetari was called Hekurawe, from *Hekurá*, which means a spirit, also called *pagé*.

CHAPTER 6

Wild Shamatari

The old Hekurawetari, who had come to invite us, left early the next morning. Xoxotami's mother and father, two big sons, a daughter who was also grown up, a younger one and I all left a little later. The first night we slept in the forest and the second night we reached a place where there were lots of little wild coconut palms. The nuts were in groups of two or three to each tree, and they were low down: we could reach them with our hands. The Karawetari used to go from their *shapuno* to gather them. Those nuts were good and had the same taste as real coconuts. There were some big rocks nearby. In the morning we broke open those nuts on the stones. I was still weak; Xoxotami broke them for me.

The third night we reached an *igarapé* near the *shapuno*. 'This is the water of the *igarapé* which the Hekurawetari drink,' my companions said. 'They live near the springs.' The next day, along the *igarapé*, we found their footprints and some little arrows. 'Here is where the boys came yesterday to fish.' So we went back up the *igarapé*, which kept getting smaller, until we came in front of an old *roça*. There we stopped: 'We must paint ourselves to go into the *shapuno*,' the Karawetari said. The old man painted himself brown on the chest, legs and face. When they are in a hurry, they paint their whole body, then with their nails they make different lines. If they have time, they paint themselves with thin lines; they do it with a little piece of slender liana chewed at the end, which they dip in *urucú* and use like a brush. While we were painting ourselves, another Karawetari came up to us with his wife and a son: they too had decided to come. 'You are painting yourselves,' the wife said. 'Aren't you painting this girl here?'

'Yes,' replied the old woman, 'when I have finished painting my daughter.' I had already been painted once before, before entering the *shapuno* of the Kohoroshiwetari; then they had also cut my hair all round. In the Karawetari's *shapuno* Xoxotami's mother had shaved my hair in the middle. She began to paint my back; she made designs on my chest, legs and face. We all painted ourselves. We had not yet finished when two young Hekurawetari arrived, saying: 'Our father has said: "Who knows; perhaps they are painting themselves. Tell them to come into the *shapuno* right away." We are expecting the enemy, the Shamatari. They say it is three days since they left their *shapuno* to attack us. Still they haven't shot at us.' Then we all entered the *shapuno*. Those who had joined us painted themselves with large stripes only.

These Hekurawetari had once lived with the other Karawetari; then they had quarrelled amongst themselves and split up. There were not many of them; forty or fifty persons. Many men had gone hunting. There was the headman Hekurawe with two sons. There was an Aramamiseteri: he was a great Hekurá. They told me that he had been the one to warn them that the Shamatari had set out three days ago to come and attack. When the headman saw us, he shouted: 'The Karawetari have brought a strange woman!' Meanwhile we stood still on the compound of the *shapuno*; four men came up and called Xoxotami's brothers and the others who had joined us, to follow them near to their braziers. So they all separated and went to their friends. The old woman, the old man, Xoxotami, I and the other unmarried daughter, all stayed together. Meanwhile they began to talk; they told them who I was and how they had taken me from the Kohoroshiwetari.

The daughter-in-law of the *tushaua* there came and called me: 'Here is *pupugna* for you. Eat with us, not with those with whom you came.' This woman's mother continued: 'Don't go back with them to the Karawetari. The old woman wants you with her; but I have my own children. You stay with me and with my son.' I didn't know what to say: I was like one stupefied. The wife of the elder son came up too; she called me to one side and said: 'Don't go back with those people. There are many there; soon they won't let you live with that old woman any longer. The men will take you and share you between them; there are so many men. Here, no; here you can live quietly. There aren't many of us. No one will take you, you will live with me.'

The next morning the chieftain Hekurawe said: 'Let's go right away to gather *pupugnas* to give to these people who have come. Soon the men who have gone hunting will come back.' Xoxotami's mother said to her daughter: 'Go and call Napagnuma. Let's go and get *pupugna* fruit and let's go back soon; these people talk too much.' She had understood what they had said to me and she wanted to go back home. We all went to pick *pupugnas*: there were so many of them. The men climbed up the thorny palms. With lianas they tied together four stout sticks, crossed over two by two, making the trunk go through the first hole. Thus they climb up to where the bunches of fruit are, without pricking themselves on the thorns. They carried long lianas with which they tied the bunches of *pupugnas* and pulled them down.

Suddenly those big birds that cry when they see people began to sing their song: *can, can*. Hekurawe cried out, 'The enemy are coming to kill me, now that I am alone! My sons have climbed the *pupugnas* and the others are hunting. There is no one who can defend me!' Actually it was nothing. The men quickly came down from the trees and said: 'Take the *pupugnas* away at once; perhaps the Shamatari are arriving!' The old Hekurawe said to me: 'Choose the bunch which you want of these *pupugnas* of mine.' There were yellow and red *pupugnas*: I chose a bunch. My old woman tied them up for me and took three more bunches; one she put in the basket and two she prepared to have them brought to Xoxotami, then she said, 'Let's go away at once.' 'Yes,' added Hekurawe, 'you women hurry up and go ahead to the *shapuno*. I'm staying with the men to put the *pupugnas* in the baskets. Maybe tomorrow those who have gone hunting will arrive. It's already so many days since they went away,' and he showed eight fingers. They filled those baskets so full that they could not even hang them from their foreheads and hold them on their backs.

When we returned to the *shapuno*, the wife of the *tushaua* Hekurawe called me and made me rest in her hammock. In the evening, Xoxotami's mother scolded me for not having eaten with her. 'She called me and gave me something to eat; I didn't know,' I replied. 'She doesn't want you to eat with me; she gives you *mingau*[1] and other things. They want you to stay with them, but you won't stay, you will come back with us.' 'I don't know whether we'll return,' I replied, 'because everybody's saying that the Shamatari are near. I don't think any of us will return.' 'There are no Shamatari,' said the old woman.

The next day, when the sun was already high, the wife of an Aramamiseteri, who was on the opposite side of the *shapuno*, came up. She said to Xoxotami's mother: 'My husband wants to see Napagnuma, I am cooking *pupugnas* for her. Let her come, I will paint her. How can a strange woman stay in the *shapuno* without being

[1] *Mingau*: banana pulp.

painted? I will smear red *urucú* over her, so that when the hunters return, there will only be the black colour to put on her.' 'Go on, then,' said the old woman to me. Xoxotami came with me also. The Aramamiseteri man looked at me: 'Is this Napagnuma? I thought she was a grown and beautiful woman. Napagnuma's reputation comes from afar. There, among the Aramamiseteri, they told me she was with the Karawetari. They were anxious to see her and they said they wanted to come and take her. Everyone knows about Napagnuma; perhaps only the Shamatari know nothing.' Then, turning to his wife, he said: 'Give her some *pupugnas*; it's better that she should go with the Shamatari on a full stomach than an empty one.' He was joking. The Aramamiseteri's wife came up and said to me: 'Let us go and bathe and paint ourselves with these *urucú* seeds. We will make delicate designs, because I think the men will arrive today.' Xoxotami also came with us.

The woman began to take the *urucú* seeds from the basket and to run *urucú* on my back. Suddenly I heard a noise: a dry branch breaking—*trak*! 'Xoxotami,' I said, 'did you hear anyone snap the dry trunk?' The girl exclaimed: 'It must be the enemy.' I was seized with terror; all those *urucú* seeds fell to the ground. Four children came running up; they were small. The smallest could hardly talk yet; he said: 'Run—all black—enemy!' They ran in front of us into the *shapuno* to warn them. The children said that in the *igarapé* they had seen men all painted black, who had said: 'Quiet! Don't shout, or we will shoot you. Go quietly to the *shapuno*.' At that moment we too arrived and the woman said: 'How can the enemy be there, if these girls can come without being worried?'

An arrow fell behind us. The enemy had followed us and had waited until we entered. Other arrows began to fall: tah, tai, tai . . . Near me I saw an arrow that was sticking in a bunch of bananas: it kept on waving about for a long time. A little girl started to run into the compound. An arrow—tah!—hit her on the back of the neck, and the child fell. Her mother ran to pick her up and, while she was lifting her, an arrow hit her on the knee. The mother shouted; another woman ran to pick up the little girl. She was already dead; the woman laid her on the hammock. Inside the *shapuno* there were eleven men; they did not reply to the arrows, which were falling on all sides. Finally Xoxotami's brother, whose name was Pausiwe, shouted, 'Let's shoot!' Then from inside the *shapuno* they began to shoot arrows from this side and that, through the straw roof, without seeing where they were falling. The enemy's arrows, too, were penetrating the leaves of the roof and falling on the floor. The woman said to the old Aramamiseteri: 'You go and hide; you are a great Hekurá, so hide.' I went up to the roof of the *shapuno* and parted the leaves a little. All around the enemy were crouching. When they attack and are afraid of being hit by those inside, the warriors squat down so as not to be seen. They keep an arrow ready in the bow and, at the moment when they wish to shoot, they stand up and shoot the arrow. They wait for the enemy arrows to fall before they stand up and shoot.

In the *shapuno*, when the arrows stopped falling, the women ran out onto the cleared space to pick them up. In the middle of the area there was a large tree: the men hid behind it in order to shoot their arrows better. The men said: 'Now let us flee!' They formed up in a long line; man, woman, man, woman, man and so on. We tried to flee, but the arrows were falling on all sides; we went back inside.

Pausiwe, Xoxotami's brother, shouted again: 'Who are you? I want to know who you are who are shooting at us.' A silence followed; the arrows ceased to fall. He repeated: 'Who are you? Karawetari, Kebrobuetari, Aramamiseteri? I want to know.' A loud voice very near the *shapuno* answered: '*Kamigna Shamatari* . . . I, Shamatari. I am the son of Pocecomemateri;[1] I am a Shamatari . . . I am that Shamatari whose name you always hear.' When that voice was heard, silence fell in the *shapuno*. They again formed a line to flee in—a long line. We ran out, but they immediately hit a son of Hekurawe in the chest. They all went back inside; I, however, stayed outside and hid behind a large tree-trunk. Three young warriors saw me; I heard them saying among themselves: 'There's somebody behind there.' I saw they were looking at me; one, perhaps thinking I was a man, stood up pointing his arrow. Then I shouted: 'Don't shoot me; I belong to another race. I am not a Kohoroshiwetari or a Karawetari, I am a different kind of person!' They came running towards me: one of them took me by one arm and the other by the other arm. They dragged me running inside the *shapuno*.

Meanwhile the *tushaua* of the Shamatari had already entered; also his brother, his cousin, his brothers-in-law and other Shamatari. Not even one man of those in the *shapuno* was standing up. The old Hekurawe was there, dead, with arrows in his body; the Aramamiseteri, too, was lying dead not far away. There was a girl who had fallen on her face. They said: 'She's pretending.' A man turned her

[1] *Pocecomemateri*: I don't like to say it, it is a nasty word, it means that the hole in his behind is closed up. (Reply by H. Valero.)

over; the arrow was not to be seen. The point had entered below the breast and had broken off. Only a trickle of yellowish liquid was coming out. It was a poisoned arrow and the young woman was dead. Then they said: 'She really is dead.' Further on was another woman; down there another dead man, near that big tree in the middle of the square. One of Hekurawe's sons was also dead. Only one son of the Aramamiseteri, one son of Hekurawe and that Karawetari who had arrived after us succeeded in getting away. The only man not wounded was the old Karawetari, Xoxotami's father. The two sons were wounded, but alive. One was wounded in the chest: red blood and froth were coming out of the wound. The other was injured in the leg; he was trembling all the time.

Then Xoxotami's father said to the Shamatari *tushaua*: 'Cousin, why have you shot my sons? See how they are wounded!' Rohariwe (this was the *tushaua's* name) looked at him and said to his own men: 'Don't shoot any more.' Then he continued: 'What have you come to do here, Karawetari? My men have shot your sons, my relations, without wishing to. Why have you come to disturb me? I was coming to make war on my enemies. You knew very well that this is my time for coming to make war. I am not responsible for the wounds of your men.' He took the sharp point of the arrow, one of those made of bamboo, and opened the flesh of that wounded man in the chest to get out the point of the poisoned arrow. He called one of his men and said: 'Pull this arrowhead out.' Then he continued to reprove the old man: 'When the arrows fall, how can we know if they hit our own relatives? Go away from here and don't ever come back among these men.' The old man replied: 'They had called me for a *reaho*.'[1] Meanwhile they had pulled out the arrowhead from the son's flesh. Then the Shamatari *tushaua* said to him: 'Now you lie down quietly in the hammock. When you are better, all of you go away and don't come back.'

Two men continued to hold me by the arms. Others also took Xoxotami. The Shamatari warriors were looking for the women, who were hiding in the corners of the *shapuno*. There were two enclosures of palm leaves: inside were two young girls 'of consequence'; that is, in puberty. An old Hekurawetari woman said: 'Don't touch my grand-daughter! It's only three days that she's been of consequence. If you take her, *Gnaru* (Thunder) will kill you.' The girl began to cry, but the old woman continued: 'Don't cry; it's bad to cry when you are like this. If you cry, you die.' They opened

[1] *Reaho*: large collective feast, usually held for the celebration of the dead.

the shelters and dragged the girls out. They also took one of Hekurawe's daughters. She was beautiful, pleasant and nice; the nephew of the Shamatari *tushaua* took her. Then the *tushaua* saw her and asked: 'Who has taken this woman?'

'It was your nephew.'

'This woman is for me.'

Meanwhile the men began to bring the women prisoners together. They held them firmly by the arms. There were many and they were young. Other men continued to go around the *shapuno*, taking baskets, earthenware pots, bananas, *pupugnas*. They put everything in the baskets and passed them to the women to carry. No bodies of little children were to be seen. The only live men were the father and two brothers of Xoxotami. The mother was weeping and saying: 'I came with my sons and you wanted to kill them for me!' The *tushaua* replied: 'They will not die. I have already had the poisoned arrowhead pulled out of this son of yours. The other one has been wounded by a bamboo point, which is not so bad.' That second son still had the wound of an arrow-shot received in the fight with the Kohoroshiwetari. The old women began to say: 'Go away; the men who went hunting will be here very soon.' They said this because they wanted them to go away, so as to be able to look for the children who had hidden around the *shapuno* and to see whether they were still alive.

The women were weeping; an old woman shouted: 'Yes, you are *tushaua*, brave at killing women when the men aren't there. I look forward to the day when I shall hear that you have been killed.' 'I? I shall not die, old woman; I shall come back to visit you again. Perhaps some day, when I'm old, they will kill me, but not now. Meanwhile weep for your dead sons, for your dead husband.' The Shamatari left in the *shapuno* the ageing and elderly women; they took only the young ones who had no children.

It must have been ten o'clock. We all went out of the *shapuno* of the Hekurawetari in a line and went not far off to where there was another old *shapuno*. The Shamatari were asking the women prisoners how many men there had been in the *shapuno*; the woman replied that there were only those men whom they had killed or wounded. None of the Shamatari were dead.

The men took Xoxotami away as well; she was near me and she wept. Her mother had told us always to keep together. They asked: 'Those two, whose daughters are they?' The women prisoners replied: 'One is a daughter of that Karawetari, the father of those you wounded.' 'And the other?' 'The other, they say she's Napagnuma, a white woman.' 'We won't take this one,' they said, 'she's too thin, she won't be able to follow us. We shall have to walk day and night, without rest, and we shall not be able to wait; we have killed men.' 'She's too thin,' said the *tushaua* Rohariwe also. 'I am sending her back to the old women. It's true, she's too weak, she's not strong like the others.' While they talked like that I felt happier, because I thought they would not take me away with them.

In the meantime they made us line up again. The *tushaua* said: 'Make her get up; I want to see her; I want to see if she is big enough.' I had sat down near Xoxotami and I stood up. That Hekurawetari woman, strong and beautiful, whom the *tushaua* had chosen for himself, said to me: 'Stand up, stand up.' I stoop up, and the woman said: 'She's not thin, her body is just like this.' The *tushaua* asked: 'Who has taken her?' 'It was we two; I and this man,' they replied. 'Right then, you will take her.' One answered: 'I don't want to have a child with me; I want a big woman, with a woman's body. Then this one will not walk fast and I shall want to kill her. It's better that she should stay here.'

Then the *tushaua* saw his brother's father-in-law and said to him: 'Take her. Your woman is very good. She will look after this child, who will be useful to her, since she has many little children.'

'I am afraid of women who are daughters of white men,' he replied. 'If she had been a daughter of these people here, I'd have taken her.'

Then the *tushaua's* brother pointed out the father-in-law to me and said: 'Go with him.'

'Take her,' repeated the *tushaua*, turning to the man, 'when she's a grown woman, you will have daughters by her and she will be my mother-in-law. I want to have a woman of another race, who is not a Shamatari, not one of these here.' I was weeping and all the other women were weeping.

The warriors had also taken two young girls. The mother, a big fat woman, came up to the *tushaua* and said: 'I want to come too; I want to follow my two daughters who are still too young. I will come with you and stay with you always to accompany my daughters.' It was a lie; she was coming because she wanted to escape with her daughters. The men did not want her to come and said: 'Go back to your *shapuno*, or else we will shoot you.'

'I'm not going, I'm coming with you.' And she came.

CHAPTER 7

The Unucai Warriors

Then they raised their shout: '*Au, au, au*,' with a cavernous voice, and we began the journey. We marched and marched. It was already late, more or less five o'clock (in the forest everything is already getting dark by five o'clock), when an arrow fell between us women and the warriors who were coming behind. The men shouted: '*Pei haw, pei haw*!' because they wanted those who were in front to hear and to stand on guard. They picked up the arrow; the women prisoners looked at it and said: 'It's Hiriwe's arrow.' They recognized it because it had the three stripes, like the snake that Hiriwe was in the habit of drawing on his arrowheads. So the Hekurawetari hunters had come back. Only Hiriwe had run back, because they had taken his woman: perhaps the others had stopped to burn their dead. The women said: 'He has shot an arrow so that his woman may know which way to flee. If he had wanted to kill he would have shot the men from the rear.' They all stopped to see if other arrows fell, but no more did.

During that night, while the others were asleep, a woman escaped. The next day we walked all the time and no woman could run away. The third day, that big woman who had wanted to accompany her daughters fled with the two daughters and took with her one of the girls 'of consequence'.

In that part of the forest there were many *haiu* trees, which have those good red fruits. They nearly all went to eat them. The men, who had killed in battle, were *unucai*, as they called them. They could eat only bananas and a few other things. They say that if they eat, a sickness attacks them, and so they fast. The *tushaua's* brother said to these men: 'While we eat these fruits, you go ahead towards that *roça* where there are bananas, which we saw when we came.' A woman said to the man who was guarding her: 'I am going to eat fruit with the others: there are many men.' He let her go, but the woman pretended to follow the others and fled. Later they noticed that she was not there any more. Then the *tushaua* said: 'He who guards a woman prisoner must follow her always. If she goes into the thick bush, he must follow her; if she goes along the path, he must follow her. You have left her alone and she has run away. Well done! Now she has gone back to her *shapuno* and I don't want her to be followed. The enemy, who are coming behind us, might be there, and if they find you alone, they will kill you.'

Xoxotami was all the time near me and she was crying. I said to her: 'Let us run away, let's go back to where we were.' She replied: 'It's already too far,' and she wept. 'Then you'll cry even more later on,' I said, 'if you don't want to run away with me now: I have the courage to flee.' 'I'm not afraid,' replied Xoxotami, 'but the jaguar will eat us.' 'No,' I said, 'the jaguar will not eat us.'

In the evening we reached the bank of a wide but shallow river which came down from rocky hills. It could be crossed without a bridge. They called it Sukhumumo, which means river of the little parrots. We stopped on the bank of this river. The *pupugnas* which they had taken from the Hekurawetari *shapuno* were nearly finished and we were beginning to feel hungry. A youth came up to me—he was the son of the Shamatari *tushaua's* uncle—and he said: 'I am going to gather *bacabe* nearby; do you want to come?' I went with him and we started to collect *bacabe* in large leaves. Then we brought them back and put them in the earthenware pots which they had carried off from the Hekurawetari. We heated them and ate the softest. When they are hot and soft, you squeeze them and drink the juice by itself or with bananas. We also took some to the *unucai* warriors, who could eat *bacabe*. That evening the youth lay down to sleep near me. He was an intelligent young man. Xoxotami also wanted to sleep near me and not with that man who had taken her; the man let her come with me.

Near our camp the mountainside fell away. During the night we heard not far off the sound of someone slipping on the rocks and a voice saying: 'Go quietly, don't make a noise.' It was the Hekurawetari, coming back from hunting, who were following us. The Shamatari heard and said amongst themselves in a whisper: 'The enemy, the enemy. Let us shoot that way so as not to allow them to cross the river.' So they began to send arrows in that direction—*ta, ta, ta, crai, crai, ta*. No one shouted. At last the Shamatari shouted: 'Hekurawetari, don't run away. Wait for daylight and wait for us.' No one answered. The Shamatari then shot fresh arrows: they had taken many of them in the Hekurawetari *shapuno*. You could hear when the arrows stuck in the distant tree-trunks. But all was silent; the others did not shoot, perhaps for fear of hitting their own women. The Shamatari covered all the fires. Then the Shamatari *tushaua* shouted: 'You poor wretches, coming after us; I will leave you all dead along this *igarapé*. Fools! To follow us you have left your dead. Miserable lot, you will not get back one of your women. Go back, smoke your dead and eat them!' A Hekurawetari in the night replied: 'Wild Shamatari, do you think your day will not come? It will come and you will be slain with an arrow.'

But the Shamatari *tushaua* was not wicked. During the journey he said: 'Why have you killed all these people? You shouldn't kill like this!' The men replied: 'You told us to kill them all.' 'I said it only in a manner of speaking. You should not have killed like this; they were only few.' The others added: 'They are not few, those who had gone hunting were many: they still have women and soon they will have other children and they will again be very many.'

But that night no man slept. They all sat with their arrows in their hands. I fell asleep leaning on Xoxotami. The boy, near us, was resting against a *haiu* tree. In the morning, some Shamatari passed by the river again to see whether they could find the enemy. They saw where they had been sitting, where they had slipped. They also brought back two arrows, which the others perhaps had not found in the night when they had set out. They were arrows with poisoned heads, but the dew in the night—said the men—had melted the poison. The night moisture melts the poison and leaves the point clean. But the sun dries it and the poison remains attached to it. The fire also dries the poison and therefore they apply it to the arrowheads and dry it over the embers.

All day we walked. We slept again, then set out once more and so we came to a large empty *shapuno*. It was already quite full of weeds. Nearby there was a *roça*. The men left the young women in the *shapuno* and went with all the women prisoners to the *roça* to load bananas. I stayed with Xoxotami and said to her: 'Let us say that we are going to get water and let us run away.' 'How can we run away,' she replied, 'if we are so far away? I am afraid.' 'You are afraid to run away with me? Don't cry then, when they scold you and beat you as the Karawetari did the Kohoroshiwetari women.'

'But we are too far away: we can no longer escape.'

'You didn't even want to run away when we were near,' I said. Meanwhile the men returned from the *roça* with the women laden with *pupugnas* and bananas.

The next morning the *tushaua* came up. Near me was that young boy; the *tushaua* said to him: 'Listen; give this girl the bananas.' He did not yet speak directly to me, because he had decided that I would be his mother-in-law. The Yanoáma are unwilling to speak or approach those who are, or who they think will be, their mothers-in-law. Then the boy said to me: 'Bring these bananas.' I took two little bunches and put them in the basket with the *pupugnas*. Xoxotami also took bananas and came with me in the line. That day the Shamatari said to the women prisoners: 'Walk fast, because we are near.' For them it was near, because they walk so much, but really we were not at all near. Evening came and we slept in some old huts. The next morning that youth said to me: 'This time we really are near. I have been here to hunt with my father; we shall arrive tomorrow.'

When they have killed, they become *unucai*. Then they put those little sticks in their ears and tie them also on the inside of their wrists, quite long. From this you can tell that they have killed. The *tushaua* Rohariwe, on the journey back to their *shapuno,* walked like a stunned man, because he had killed many enemy. He was strong, and white-skinned; he was happy when he was talking with people. The first day he had said: 'I feel stunned. I have shot eight arrows and all of them have hit human flesh. My sight is growing dim; it is growing dim. I believe all those I have shot are dead.' Every so often he would sit down. They say that when enemies die, the whole body of the man who has shot the arrows grows soft. The next day he said: 'Yesterday I felt all soft; I have slept and my strength has returned. Perhaps one of those whom I hit is not dead, but is better.' If they feel better, it is because the wounded man is better. Then Rohariwe asked: 'Who has felt soft in his body?' One replied: 'I felt soft in my body.' 'Then the man you shot is dead. Don't eat anything and go and prepare those smooth little sticks for your ears and your wrists.' All those who felt their bodies growing soft knew that they had killed and so they put on the little sticks. Those who have killed do not eat; I think this is why they feel weak and soft in the body.

One of those who had felt his body to be really soft, said two days later: 'Today I woke up feeling strong. I think the man I shot is not dead; I want to throw away the little sticks.' He took them off his wrists and out of his ears and threw them away. They eat only roasted bananas; three in the morning and three in the evening. The bananas must not be burnt, because this would signify death, as for girls who are of consequence. The girls do not eat, because they say that they would fill themselves with wind, they would vomit and suffer stomach aches. With those pains they might die and therefore they remain for a long time 'of consequence'. After some days, the men's companions seek the honey of small bees and give it to them in a *cuia*. No one else may take any out of that *cuia*. After they have drunk, another man washes the *cuia*.

One who had killed, after some days, sat down, went *scah!* . . . and threw forth a worm from his nose. Then the others said: 'The man whom you killed has not yet been burnt. They have certainly put the body up on high, tied to those tree-trunks twined together, and already the worms will be coming out. They are worms that later change into flies.' In the evening he again went *scah!* Two more white worms came out, and how they wriggled! It was the first time I had seen them coming out of the nose. Then the *tushaua* said: 'Those whom we have killed are still all fresh; they have not burnt them. One of my arrows, I think, has killed a woman; I can smell that my breath is very bad. We shall go for many days without eating game.' When they kill women, they say that their breath becomes fetid.

We came near to the *shapuno*; the *unucai* men went ahead. Those who were guarding the women said: 'Do not say that we have captured all these women.' In the *igarapé* they all washed, rubbed their bodies with leaves, and painted themselves red, with stripes and designs on their legs, on their body, on their faces. They put the feathers of birds in their ears.

We went inside the *shapuno*: there were many people, more than a hundred. There were the Patamanibueteri, who had come to live with the Shamatari before the latter left to attack the Hekurawetari. They were awaiting their companions, who had come with the Shamatari to make war on the Hekurawetari. They told me that the headman of the Patamanibueteri was a brother of Rohariwe, *tushaua* of the Shamatari; a short time before, they had quarrelled because of a woman. Then the Patamanibueteri had separated from the others and gone off to live by themselves. The *Patamanihena* is a tree with a long, broad leaf that is whitish underneath; when it shakes, the white looks like tapioca falling. They had gone to build their *shapuno* in the middle of the forest, where there were many of those trees, and this is why they are called Patamanibueteri, but they were Shamatari like the rest. Some of them had come to make war together with the Shamatari; they had taken three women, but during the journey two had succeeded in escaping. Only one young girl had remained with the Patamanibueteri.

Those who had killed remained isolated; they ate only those long bananas. They were forbidden to talk to the others. Only some old men could talk to them; they were absolutely forbidden to talk with the women. They had not washed before coming nor had they painted themselves: they were dirty. The black which they had on their bodies when they had come to make war had melted with the rain during the journey back. They say that when the body of the man whom they killed is burned, their breath smells like that fetid smoke. One day a *unucai* said: 'Last night while I was asleep, the fetid smoke came out of my nostrils.' 'Then the man you have killed,' replied the father, 'has now been burned. In two days' time you will go and bathe.' They say that when they have felt the fetid smoke come out of the nose, they feel lighter. The *tushaua* also said: 'I too feel light—I feel as though I haven't even got a body when I walk. Tomorrow we will go and bathe in the *igarapé*.'

The *unucai* slept on fibre hammocks, not on those comfortable cotton ones. When they had finished their expiation, they went to bathe; not in the usual place, but in another *igarapé* which is somewhat hidden. Many men, with bows and arrows, accompanied them to protect their journey and in order that they might bathe in midstream. They said that they took many leaves, of the kind which scratch, and rubbed themselves down well. Their hair had not been shaved any more and was growing ugly. After a long time they came back washed. They were still wearing those little sticks on their wrists and in their ears. I remember that their companions then shaved their hair and scraped their heads. Then they painted large designs and snake-like lines on their bodies and on their arms; on their faces they made red and black lines.

Then when I was with the Namoeteri, I saw instead that those who had killed never painted themselves, but went bathing every day, rubbing themselves with rough leaves which scratch, to cleanse themselves more quickly of their crime. No one was allowed to bathe in that place, because he would have received a wound which would never have healed. After the last bath, they painted them.

Meanwhile, their companions prepared tree-trunks, the white, hard kind; the *unucai*, before taking their last bathe, fixed their hammocks to the trunks with lianas. In the evening, in a line, they took those posts with the hammocks tied on, and, all painted, went into the thick forest, looking for one of the tallest trees to tie on the top the trunk with the hammock. They bound it tight, because, if it had fallen, it would have been a signal of death for the *unucai*. Together with the hammock, they hung up there at the top those little sticks which they had in their ears and on their wrists, and the *cuia,* from which they had taken bananas and honey.

He who has killed is held in great esteem. If he returns to the fight and kills again, he is considered even more highly. He who has killed one who has killed, is called by the others *waiteri,* valiant. When he dies, the women sing, weeping: 'He was *waiteri*; *waiteri* in the battle; he was *waiteri,* and he never stayed behind.'

CHAPTER 8

Curare

In the *shapuno* the *tushaua* said to his brother's mother-in-law: 'My uncle seems to be afraid of the daughter of a white man. Take this woman with you.' The woman replied: 'Yes; I need some company for the little children. When I go into the wood, I don't know with whom to leave them.' Then, turning to her son, she asked: 'Which one is it?' 'It's this one standing behind me.' She said to me: 'Come, come,' and I went. Xoxotami followed me: she was beginning to be a woman, although her breasts were still small. The man who had taken her in the *shapuno* of the Hekurawetari, said to her: 'No, you come with me; I left you with Napagnuma for the journey, not for always. Now you must come with me. You two must split up.' He took her by one arm. Xoxotami shouted and wept, but he took her with him to his fireplace. That man already had two wives. One of the wives said: 'You should have taken a bigger woman who could carry fruit for me. Instead you have brought this one, who is still almost a child and has no strength.' Then turning to Xoxotami: 'Don't cry; why are you crying? You'll be all right with me.' So we parted company.

A few days later Rohariwe decided to prepare curare and began to speak aloud in the *shapuno,* just as the priest does in his sermon: 'I shall prepare *mamocori*; anyone who has none may now learn how to make it; if anyone has some, let him go on to the track to watch out against the enemy. Let everybody listen to me; no one must go and misbehave with a woman tonight. I shall then try *mamocori* on a monkey; if the monkey does not die, it will mean that you have been with women during the night; in that case, the next time I shall chase you all out and make my poison by myself.'

Many other times I have seen how they prepare the curare. They look in the hills for some large lianas, which do not grow in the lower regions and which they call *mamocori,* like the poison: these have short branches which end like hooks. When they go hunting and find these lianas, they mark them so as to find them again later;

then they come back and cut them down. They at once build *tapirí* to protect themselves from the rain because, they say, the weather grows dark; it is the master of the poison who is protesting. Then they scrape the trunks on large leaves and make sure it does not rain on the part they have scraped, for otherwise the poison will be weak. Then they enclose the scraped part in big packets of leaves, put them in their baskets and go back to the *shapuno,* where they have already prepared a kind of tall cage over the fire, made of *bacaba* sticks, on which they place the package to dry. They say that if the children touch or sit on that scraped liana, they become sick and ill.

The next morning, all the men who had to prepare the curare had painted themselves black with coal on the face, on the body, on the legs, because they said curare is useful for war. They didn't eat that day: they said that the women who stayed to watch must not bathe, because the poison would no longer kill animals or men. Pregnant women must not be present because, they said, the babies whom they carried in their stomachs make water on the poison and the poison becomes weak. They do not begin to prepare the poison too soon, because at that time the deer is still walking about in the wood and urinating: the deer urinates a long way off, but for them he urinates on the poison and makes it weak. Towards six o'clock in the morning, Rohariwe and the others went into the forest to gather other plants, especially the plant *ashukamakei*, which is used to make the poison become more sticky; it is a plant with long leaves.

When they came back, they set about preparing the curare, one here, one there. Rohariwe sent two children to get water from the *igarapé* and said they must not put their feet in the water, but on trunks and roots; if they had got wet, he would send others. He put some broad leaves on the ground and poured over them about two or four pounds of that dried, scraped *mamocori*; then, resting over the top of it two burning brands, began to blow in order to set fire to the pieces of bark. He mixed it all well with a little stick and, when he saw that it was all nicely dark, he put the fire out. Meanwhile he had mixed the scraped bark of the *ashukamakei,* which he had heated over the fire in leaves and which was fresh and soft, with the dry scraped bark of *mamocori*. With the heat, a liquid came out of the *ashukamakei* bark and was mixed with the rest. Then he rubbed very hard, with his hands tightly clasped between his legs, the roasted *mamocori* barks with those of the *ashukamakei,* until he reduced the whole to a blackish powder. While he was rubbing, he invoked the old Mamocori, mother of the poison. At last he said: 'Now it is becoming strong: I can feel that my hands are going to sleep.' When he had finished rubbing, he put the powder together in the big leaves, he folded the leaves over and pressed them. An assistant tied three big leaves tightly together and made a funnel which he pushed into a round holder made from a thin liana wound round and held secure on pieces of a bow fixed into the ground, and dug a hole beneath the funnel where he put some ashes and set half a *cuia* in position. He filled the funnel with the burnt powder and very slowly poured boiling water over it, which he took with a little *cuia* from a cauldron on the fire. All the powder became wet, but still nothing dripped out. After some time, tac, tac, the drops began to fall into the *cuia* which was below; they had the colour of very strong coffee.

He had already prepared the arrowheads of *pupugna* wood; (sometimes I have seen them also made of *pashuba* wood). These heads have three deep incisions, in order that, when they break, the pieces may remain in the flesh. He pushed about twenty arrowheads, one next to the other, all the same, on to a kind of hard handle, prepared with big leaves folded over and tied well together. He took a kind of long brush, dipped it in the dark liquid in the *cuia* and painted the arrowheads many times with it, holding them over the embers, three times on one side and three times on the other side. When the poison began to grow like a resin and made dark bubbles, he passed the brush only once over one side and then over the other: he was very careful not to let it burn, but to make it evaporate slowly. Finally he touched the arrowheads with his fingers to feel whether the poison had become dry. Two hours later he tried again, but the curare had begun to melt and had become soft. Then he said: 'It's soft!' He took some *urucú* paste in his mouth and spat on the arrows to fix the poison better, painting with the brush again over the heads which had been heated by the fire. When they prepare the poison, they don't touch water and then they don't wash their hands in water, but they clean them with leaves; they say that their hands are still very bitter after two days.

'Tomorrow we shall try the poison,' said Rohariwe at last. 'Be careful not to shoot the *uisha* monkey; otherwise all the arrowheads that we have prepared will grow mouldy.' The *uisha* is a bearded, ashen-coloured monkey, the males long-tailed and the females short-tailed. They say that they can be killed only with old poison. It was already evening and some men had not yet finished painting their arrowheads with poison. Then the *tushaua* said: 'Pick up the rest of your poison, put it in one *cuia* only; dig a hole in the ground and cover it up. Tomorrow morning you will go on putting it on your arrowheads.' The next day I saw him shoot a monkey on a tree. The animal did not fall right away, but kept on jumping among the branches, then sat down, looked down, urinated and remained there like a drunken man; then it hung itself up by [illegible] Roharíwe shouted: 'The poison is bad! I told you [illegible] women; now the poison is spoiled. If the enemy [illegible] be able to kill them; you'll only be able to give [illegible] your arrows!' They went back into the *shapuno,* s[illegible] and made new poison.

A few days later they went hunting; they kil[illegible] wild boar. The meat, around the spots where th[illegible] had entered, was dark, but they ate it, although [illegible] They also said to the children: 'Eat this meat which [illegible] has made bitter, so that when you are shot with *mamocori,* [illegible] resist better.' They did not wash the meat of the animals they killed with the fresh poison, because otherwise, they said, the poison would not have the power to kill any longer. Instead they washed the meat of animals killed with old poison.

In the *roça,* near the tobacco plants, the men cultivate in secret certain magic plants for hunting and for war: they are especially those kinds of onions which grow underground. They tear off the branches and the leaves and cover the roots with the bark of trees, so that other men cannot find and steal them. The women do not know them or pretend not to know them. For hunting the tapir, they use the onion of a *piripirioca,* which is shaped something like a tapir's eye. They let it dry by the fire, then they mash it up and rub it, mixed with *urucú,* on their own bodies, on the arrows and on the noses and paws of the dogs. The juice has a stupefying action: it should also stupefy the tapir, allowing the hunters to come close to him. For every animal there is a magic plant. The wild pig is hunted after men, arrows and dogs have been rubbed with a root shaped like the pig's snout. The *mutum* bird, the toucan, parrots, monkeys, armadillos, and so on, all have their plants.

CHAPTER 9

The Apprentice Witch-Doctor

When the Shamatari heard a strong wind, they often shouted: 'Take the children, the Hekurá are arriving!' or: 'The Hekurá of the white men are coming from the great river!' Then they would look into the distance: 'There they go, there they go, far away. . . .' When they said this, I thought: 'Can the great river be near?' But I said nothing to anyone.

In the middle of the compound of that great *shapuno,* there was an isolated hut or *tapirí.* Inside that *tapirí* a young man went to live, with his hammock and nothing else. They told me that he was going to learn to be a Hekurá. No woman could approach the *tapirí* where that young man was, not even his mother, because, they said, the Hekurá detest women and flee from them. Only one boy, who was not yet fifteen years of age, went to sleep with his hammock in that *tapirí* to blow the fire and put wood on it. He who was learning must not bathe and must try not to touch the ground with his feet, otherwise the Hekurá would return to the mountains from which they descended to come to him. The young man could eat almost nothing. He was absolutely forbidden to eat meat. After he had been isolated a couple of days, the men went to get bees' honey, put it in one of those conical earthenware pots and gave him a little of it in a small, white, well scraped *cuia*; they had scraped it with those leaves which are rough as files. In the night they gave him a little more, again in the morning, again towards midday, and so on. When the honey came to an end, they had to go and look for some more. At last the men said: 'We can find no more honey.' Then the *tushaua* replied: 'Go away early in the morning and seek it a long way off, until you find it.'

He could never go out of the hut. When he was tired of lying down in the hammock, he could sit on two pieces of tree-trunk, well smoothed with those tough herbs of theirs. One day, while the old Shapori master was instructing the youth, some neighbours started to burn the hair of a monkey, to cook the animal. The old man began to shout and run, saying that the Hekurá spirits were abandoning the *shapuno* and returning to the mountain from which they had been called. During the night the old man's song could be heard as he repeated: 'We Hekurá will not come again to you; we live very far off and we will not return.' Then the young man wept and despaired.

The youth took much *epená,* a vegetable powder that causes visions; it was not the master who blew *epená* into his nose, but a boy who had not yet known a woman. He blew three times into one nostril, three times into the other, then retreated. He also continued to take *epená* into his nose by night; his face grew dark with the *epená.* The master, who went to him early in the morning, checked to see that the boy remembered to blow into the pupil's nose, and said: 'Remember always to blow *epená* into his nose.' The old Shapori who was teaching also took *epená;* it was the other men who blew into the master's nose.

So the apprentice began to know the Hekurá; first he learnt to invoke the Hekurá of the toucan, then the Hekurá of that smaller toucan, of the little parrot, and of the wood peacock with the white wings. Then came the more difficult Hekurá: the great armadillo, the little armadillo and so always new Hekurá, which only the oldest know how to invoke. The master taught so many things: one does not know really what, because he taught only at night. He made them put out the fires, because, he said, the Hekurá cannot approach if there is light. We, who lived around, could not make a fire: the old men said: 'Put out all the fires.' Once I was reviving the fire and the old Shapori master shouted: 'Whose daughter is making a fire? I will beat her with this stick.' The old woman said to me: 'Put the fire out at once!' and I threw banana skins on it. As soon as the old master finished speaking quietly, he began to chant: then one could light the fire again.

When the apprentice was so drunk with *epená* that he could not even stand on his feet, a man stood behind him and held him up, while the teacher went back and forth chanting, so that the youth should do the same. He had to repeat the chants that the master was teaching. He repeated the first and the second chant; then the old man walked away, saying: 'Sing more loudly; I cannot hear anything; more loudly.' The youth sang more loudly; the old man went further away still and repeated: 'Sing . . . I can hear nothing,' and sent someone to blow more *epená* into his nostrils. If the youth made mistakes over the words, or forgot them, the old

Shapori repeated and repeated them, until the pupil had learned them. The master made the youth, who was stupefied by the *epená,* get up, made him go back and forth, shouting and chanting with his arms open. He had to go slowly, because, he said, if he had gone quickly the route of the Hekurá, which was not yet well formed, would be broken and the Hekurá would not come again at his call.

The other men, who were already Shapori, were sitting and saying: 'Good! That's good!' After some time the old man who was teaching said to another old Shapori: 'Now you teach for a few days.' The master could change. One evening I heard the young man chanting by himself: 'Father, the Hekurá are already arriving; they are many. They are coming dancing towards me, father. Yes, now I shall be a Hekurá too! From today on, let no woman come near my *tapirí* again!' A woman, painted with fragrant *urucú,* passed near the hut; then the youth despaired and wept. 'Father, this evil woman has passed near me; now my Hekurá are leaving me. Already they are taking away their hammocks.' He was truly in despair: 'Father, the Hekurá have left me alone; those whom you had put into my breast have already departed.' Then the old men shouted and shouted against us women. For one woman alone who had passed by thus painted and scented, we were all given the blame.

The youth had, after a few weeks of taking *epená* and eating so little food, become so weak that he could scarcely any longer stand on his feet. Then his mother began to weep, because her son had not even voice enough left to answer his master. The mother, the aunts, began to say from a distance: 'Our son has no more strength; do you really want to make him die of hunger? It's time to leave him alone.' But the old Shapori were not worried. At length the master called the boy who had always blown the *epená,* ordered him to heat water in the earthenware pot and to wash the youth, rubbing him well down; then made him dry him with bark. Another youth, who knew how to paint, painted beautiful wavy lines on his legs, body and face with *urucú* mixed with coal.

When he finished, after so many days, perhaps a month, he really was weak. They said that he could easily have lost his Hekurá. He had a young girl, who had been promised to him; but he left her with his mother without going near her.

They say that if the young men, who have just learned to be Hekurá, commit any misdeeds with women, the Hekurá speak to them thus: 'I was coming to live with you, but you have soiled me. I am going away with your other Hekurá; do not call us again, for we will not come.' I have often heard, in the dead of night, a youth chanting and weeping: 'Father, the Hekurá are leaving me; come and keep them here for me.' Then came the old man who had instructed him and said: 'Do not weep, invoke.' The youth continued: 'Hekurá's daughter has turned her back on me and gone away; all the Hekurá now despise me, call me *shami* (dirty). Hekurá's daughter now speaks to me; she says: "I thought you were our father, but you have soiled me, you are worth nothing, so now you will be alone."' Sometimes the master said: 'Very well; you have gone with women, you have not respected what I had told you; now your Hekurá have fled.' Then the youth wept and wept. At other times two or three old Hekurá came, took *epená,* blew it into the youth's nostrils, and then said: 'Call; we too are calling the Hekurá for you,' and they chanted: *'Hapo he, Hapo he, Hapo he . . .'* Through their mouths the Hekurá replied: 'We are never coming back; he is *shami,* he is dirty, he is worth nothing.' Then the old men said: 'It is no use calling them; their hammocks are already mouldy; they have left you.' They say that those who are old Hekurá can, for the sake of mischief, frighten off with their Hekurá those of the young men.

CHAPTER 10

The Jaguar

Meanwhile the Patamanibueteri, who had gone along with the Shamatari to make war on the Hekurawetari and to seize their women, decided to return to their *shapuno*. They went away rather discontented, because they had only been able to take one woman. After they left, Rohariwe said: 'It's better that we go away too; that part of the *shapuno* that is in front of me has been emptied. When it's like that, sickness appears, Poré comes, the Hekurá enemy come and take the children.'

The following day Pocecomemateri, father of the *tushaua*, who had three wives and was in command in the *shapuno* when the son went away, asked: 'I have heard that you want to leave the *shapuno*; where do you want to go?' 'I want to go where my little *roça* (cleared field) is; I want to enlarge it and plant crops.' 'I shall not come,' said the old man; 'I shall go and eat *mumu* fruit. They have told me they have seen much *mumu*, which is beginning to ripen. I think it is good now. When the *mumu* begins to fall, I will send you word. Meantime you stay near your *roça*.' They call *mumu* that fruit which in *lingua geral* is called *conorí*. It is like the fruit of the rubber tree, but of a reddish colour.

I went with the father-in-law of Rohariwe's brother, with Rohariwe, his brother Sibarariwe (*sibara* means knife) and his brother-in-law. There were only five or six men and many women. The *tushaua* had four wives: one Shamatari, one Aramamiseteri, one Karawetari (whom they had stolen on another occasion), and that beautiful Karawetari, whom they had taken at the same time as me. Xoxotami also came with her man, who had his *roça* along with that of the *tushaua*. I was with the father-in-law of the *tushaua's* brother, who had his wife, a daughter with her husband, two other big daughters and three little children.

We walked all day, up hill and down. Their *roça* was on the other side of the *igarapé*. There were many bananas; they had four different kinds. The wife said: 'There are no long bananas, which people roast; let us take these which are not yet ripe.' She took a bunch, split it and had half brought to me and half to one daughter. There were also many *uhina* plants with the broad leaves, rather fleshy. The old woman said to me: 'Once *uhina* was the food of the Jurupuri (worms), which, at that time, were people. It was they who showed the Yanoáma how to plant *uhina*, how to cut its roots so as always to have more. Today, when the worms gnaw those roots, the Yanoáma say that they are the former masters who are coming to eat their fruit.'

We stayed there some days. The great river must have been very far off. We could see only rocks; we could hear birds singing with strange songs. At night from all sides the little *Tesiroruma* were whistling: no, they were not birds, they were spirits of the forest. Those Indians are not afraid of birds, but they were afraid when they heard the whistles of the Tesiroruma.

Some days later Rohariwe's old father sent a man to tell us that the *mumu* fruit was falling and the water of the *igarapé* was all red with fruit. One of the *tushaua's* wives said: 'I am going right away; I love to eat that fruit with armadillo meat.' Rohariwe came back, but he said: 'I haven't been back long; I have not planted all the banana seedlings and I still have to burn a piece of forest.' We stayed: I looked after the children while the others went to work in the *roça*. There were six children.

After three days we too went to those who were picking *mumu* fruit. I saw that when they want to preserve the fruits, they first dry them over the fire and then hide them in caves, on shelves of wood where it is dry, and where they also put the other things. When they want to eat them, they put them in water. To take away the poison, before putting the *mumu* fruits in water, they boil them to make them soft. They eat them with the meat of armadillos, crocodiles, or birds, after having cut them up in thin slices with a kind of knife, made out of the lower part of a tortoise shell. Those who have no cooking pots use those big barks which are used also for preparing the *mingau* of bananas at their big feasts. Then they peel off the bark of the *akorimanosi* tree, and with the hooked arrowheads they pierce the ends of the bark; through the holes they push lianas and tie them. They put big sticks, which they tie at the ends, so that the bark shall stay stretched out, and a stick across the middle, so that the two sides of the bark shall not join together. Then they tie the two ends of the bark more than three feet above the ground and throw into it *mumu* fruits and water which completely covers them. First they take off the hard peel of those fruits. Then they make a fire below: it is the men who cook, because, they say, women get distracted and then the fire grows too big and burns the bark. But the men are squatting down and watching it carefully. Soon it begins to boil, *po, po, po, po*; it boils very well. It begins here; they move the fire over a bit that way, and then it all boils up. It boils and boils; the man stirs it with a stick so that the fruits on top shall not remain hard. When they prepare the bark of that tree, they don't like to see pregnant women, because, they say, the bark would break. They boil those fruits to make them soft, then they put them in the water of the *igarapé* so as to take away all the poison. I have only seen *mumu* fruits cooked in these bark vessels. At their feasts they throw into these vessels the *mingau* of banana, prepared in the earthenware pots. The widows, who have no earthenware pots, sometimes use for cooking small pieces of bark that the little children bring them.

One day the *tushaua's* brother's father-in-law said: 'Along the *igarapé* there are many shrimps. Tomorrow we will go.' The following day we went with the wife, the daughter, the son and another smaller boy. We walked a long way and reached the bank of the *igarapé*. The man found an armadillo's hole. When they find the tracks of these animals, they follow them until they reach the hole, which is almost always close to the water. They stand and listen, and if they find that the armadillo is in the hole, they put branches in the entrance and go and look for old wood to make smoke. They light the fire outside, burn pieces of *cupim* (*cupim* is a termite's nest) which makes much smoke, put them inside and stop it up with earth and mud, so that the smoke cannot get out. They leave only a little hole to blow the smoke. When the armadillo is about to die, it scratches, then goes *uaiii* . . . and dies near the entrance to its hole; they then get it out with their hands. Sometimes they find two or three armadilloes in the same hole. I have seen those small wild boars which take refuge in the hollow trunks of trees caught in the same way.

The man made smoke, then said: 'The armadillo is dead inside.' He tried to widen the hole, digging with a pointed stick. He crawled in but could see nothing. He took a longer stick and went in again. He said that he could feel the armadillo's body on the end of the stick. He dug again and his daughter crept into the hole, seized the armadillo by the tail, but could not pull it out. The man dug again: at last the girl managed to pull it out.

The man went down into the river, cut open the armadillo and threw away its intestines. The woman said: 'I want to cook the liver.' She pierced the liver with little sticks; she threw away all the bitter part. She took the heart and pierced it; she took the spleen and the kidneys and pierced them. She wrapped it all up in *pishaansi* leaves and closed the packet. The fire was ready.

Meanwhile the man was smoking the armadillo over a high gridiron without taking the skin off. He cut off the tail and put it over the fire to roast. Then he said to the woman: 'You turn the armadillo, while I go back to my hunting.'

From a distance the man shouted to us: 'Come and eat *inajá*.' The woman took the bundle of leaves away from the fire. The man had cut down an *inajá* tree: everyone took a piece of the central shoot and we returned to where the fire was, while the husband continued to hunt. We put the liver back to cook; a yellowish liquid was still dripping from the leaves. The woman said: 'It isn't cooked.' So she continued to turn it around, until it started to come out like clear water. Then the woman said: 'Now it's done.' We also cooked the *inajá*.

Soon afterwards the man returned from hunting. He was carrying a little live monkey, of the kind they call *uishá*. He had shot the mother, who had fled and had let the baby fall. The wife said: 'Let's take it back; I want to bring it up.' The man took the armadillo, which was now smoked and he placed it away from the fire to cool it down. The woman opened the bundle with the liver inside and shared it between us, saying: 'Now it's cooked, you can eat it; like this it won't do you any harm.' They tied the armadillo with lianas. 'You will carry it,' said the woman to me and she tied it with lianas behind my back, putting a piece of *inajá* on top.

We walked as we ate that *inajá*, uphill and downhill on that horrid mountain. The weather grew dark, and a thunderstorm came. I remained a short distance behind, then started to run after the others. I entered a path, thinking it was the one which led to the *tapirí*. It was raining hard and I ran; so I came to the bank of an *igarapé*. I looked for their footprints in the mud, but I did not find them. 'Perhaps the rain has made it impossible to see footprints,' I thought. I continued along that path, calling all the time, but no one answered.

The rain stopped. Near me I saw some big rocks and recognized them. I had already been there, when I was coming with the women prisoners whom the Shamatari had taken from the Hekurawetari. I remembered that the men had said that there were jaguar lairs. I shouted: 'Where are you?' Only the birds replied. The sky was darkening again; I saw in front of me the middle of a huge rock. 'This is the very rock of the jaguar, which they showed me when they were coming!' We had run fast below it. The men had said to us: 'Run!' It was morning that day and we had seen among the rocks, as if in a window, a jaguar's head. It was a kind of jaguar which I did not know: it wasn't one of those spotted ones or those red ones that they call *kintanari*. It was a brown jaguar and it had long hair on its head: it was the rock jaguar.

This time I was alone; I passed near its cave. The beast roared: *eu, euuu . . .* it roared horribly. I was so afraid, I ran away. 'Now the jaguars have answered me. I have come back onto the path of the Hekurawetari.' Night fell, while I continued to run and to call. I went down in the direction of an *igarapé*, then climbed up the rocks again on to an ugly hill: the night was black. I was tired; I left the piece of *inajá* on the ground and kept on walking.

In the darkness I found myself in front of a big rock and I climbed up it. It was covered with plants. I reached the top: there were lianas in front of me. I slipped, grasped a plant, which began to come down with me; then all the roots broke off and I fell headlong. I could not see anything; all was dark. I rolled down between two great rocks, hitting my forehead. A great deal of blood ran down; a big blister formed on my back. The armadillo, with that hard skin of his, finished up under me.

I don't remember how long I stayed like that. I suddenly heard the water going *tac*, *tac*, *tac*, on the stones and I opened my eyes: everywhere was dark. I was thirsty, my throat felt dry. I tried to get up, but I could not. Then, very slowly, I stood up; the liana, with which the armadillo was tied, was pulling at my neck: I bit it and it broke. I left the armadillo there. I could hear the noise of a waterfall. 'That water is near, I want a drink.' That dryness in my throat, that pain in my back! On one side it all felt as if it had gone to sleep. I tried to get nearer to the waterfall, but it was so dark in the forest; I could only see the stars in the sky. 'What shall I do now if the jaguars come?' I looked for a slender tree to climb. 'Jaguars do not climb up slender trees,' I said to myself.

I started to climb up a tree-trunk. A poisonous ant, a *tocandira*, stung me in one leg, another on the foot. I tried to pull them off, but one stung me on the hand. I came down and fell on their nest. They stung me all over. Then I really did cry! 'Where shall I go now? Oh, God! Where can I run like this? I should have died in that cave!' I thought, and I wept. I walked a bit farther, but I couldn't go on; I had too many pains all over. 'I will sleep here.' I recognized a small plant with which they prepare the *epená* which the *Hekurá* inhale. It had branches, open like an umbrella around the stem which grew in the middle. I could hardly breathe for the pain, but I climbed up and reached the first branches. 'It's too low here; there are jaguars.' I got to the second branches. 'It's still too low here.' At last I arrived higher up. There were two branches, one here and one there. I sat down between them and with my legs grasped the trunk in the middle. Mosquitoes came too that night. They were those big mosquitoes. There are many kinds of mosquito: red ones with a white behind, which they call *jacamin* (bird) mosquitoes; all red ones, called stag mosquitoes; whitish ones, called armadillo mosquitoes. I hurt all over; I prayed and I wept.

I don't know what time of night it was. I heard a jaguar walking under the tree: he was puffing like an ox. Terror struck me and I held my breath, I stopped crying and clung more tightly to the trunk. The jaguar scratched the trunk with his claws, *crei*, *crei*, *crei*; the tree moved. 'If he climbs up, what shall I do? I shall break a branch; *epená* wood breaks easily, so I'll hit him while he is climbing.' I looked down. It was very dark and I could not see anything. Not even the stars were shining now and the weather was black again. 'Where shall I escape, if he climbs up? He will claw me, he will drag me to the ground and eat me.' I started to cry again. But the beast did not climb. After a short while he went away, then came back on the other side. He was puffing and breathing like a big cat. Now he puffed loudly, now softly, now he stood still below me, silently. Thus he persecuted me all that night. I was up there trembling. When the pain and tiredness were making me begin to fall, I thought: 'It's morning.' I looked up, but it was not morning; I saw the stars. 'When will day come?'

As soon as it began to get light, the jaguar went away. I looked down, but I was too scared to come down. Then I heard a voice calling me. I didn't answer: it was that woman, the wife of the *tushaua's* brother's father-in-law, who was looking for me and had seen my footprints. She shouted: 'Napagnuma, daughter of white men, what are you doing all alone here? Come to me.' Then I answered: '*Oo-oo-oo*.' The woman ran towards me. When she was near to me, I climbed down and sat on the ground. She looked at me and wept. 'Which way did you go?' I replied: 'You abandoned me; I called you, but you ran ahead. I fell among those rocks. The armadillo is still there.' The woman said: 'Perhaps you have broken something?' She made me turn around and she pinched me hard in the swelling on my back. She wept with sorrow for me; I too wept. 'Poor little thing! How could you climb with this great swelling?' She squeezed it again.

'The armadillo, where is it? Show me where you fell down.' We went to the rock. 'Didn't you understand that it was a rock?' 'No,' I answered, 'it was night, it was all dark; I climbed up, thinking I was on firm ground. When I began to slip, I could no longer hold myself. It was all coming away with me.' Then she picked up the armadillo, tied the liana which I had broken with my teeth, put it on her shoulders and said to me: 'Now let's go; let's go slowly; you can't walk fast.'

We reached the *shapuno*. She prepared for me some *bacabe* juice and gave it to me with *mumu* fruit. When I had eaten it, she said: 'Now lie down in the hammock.' She heated some water and began to bathe the part where I was swollen; I felt the pain. 'Now lie down and go to sleep, because you didn't sleep last night.'

CHAPTER 11

Puberty. The Great Toad

We all went back into the great *shapuno* where there were two girls of consequence. When girls are twelve to fifteen years old and are just about grown up, at the time when they begin, they are shut up in a cage made with *assai* palm branches and other branches of *mumbu-hena*, which I have seen only in those mountains. They tie all the branches with lianas, very tight, so that the girls cannot be seen. They leave only one little entrance. The men and boys must not even look that way. Inside the cage there is the fire and the girl's hammock. The hammock must be stretched out well, otherwise, they say, the girl will become a hunchback. Her mother may enter to make the fire; her girl-friends may also make the fire for her. The fire must burn all the time. If the fire is going out, the weather too, they say, becomes dark. Then the old men ask: 'Are you making a fire in that cage? Don't you see that the weather is growing dark and the Thunder will send lightning?'

The girl must stay in her hammock without speaking. She cannot even weep. Because of this, when the Shamatari took the two Hekurawetari girls of consequence, the old woman said: 'Don't weep, don't weep, otherwise you will die young.' For their needs of life, the mother leaves one of those large leaves with which they then make a packet. The father and brothers, if there are any, are in hammocks nearby, outside the enclosure.

Throughout this period the young girl scarcely eats. The first day she takes nothing; the second she drinks only water, from a *cuia* from which she must suck it with a little bamboo. She cannot drink it straight from the *cuia* because, they say, she would ruin her teeth. After three days the mother prepares those short bananas, which they here call São Tomé, by putting them under the embers. They must not get burnt at all, because, if they get burnt, this signifies death. When they are soft, the mother throws the skin away and gives the girl three bananas. On the following days the mother continues to give her only these very few bananas.

After about three weeks, early in the morning, when it is still dark, the mother takes away the cage of palm branches and ties them together with lianas. The girl cannot yet look towards the middle of the *shapuno*, nor can she look at the men, for otherwise, they say, their legs will tremble when they climb trees. She may begin to speak, but very softly, *sottovoce*. Meanwhile the mother heats some water and bathes the girl with lukewarm water; then she takes *urucú* and rubs it all over the girl's body, but without making designs.

Finally, after some days more, the mother burns dry banana leaves near the girl; she takes her by one arm and makes her walk round the fire. From that moment she will be allowed to talk. Then the mother, with other women, accompanies her daughter into the woods to adorn her. They take the young leaves of *assai* palm and open them, making lots of thin strips. Some women tie these leaves with cotton thread and make pretty bunches, which they fix onto her arms, like flowers. To adorn her, they always look for a rock, because if they adorn her on the ground, the girl will soon die. Her hair is long, then the mother says to one of the women: 'Come and cut my daughter's hair,' and the woman begins to cut it. In fact, to soften the hair, they spit on her head, tuh, tuh, and they scrape and scrape; sometimes they spend hours over it.

The mother has also brought a packet of red *urucú*, one of black *urucú*, large and small threads of cotton. One woman begins to rub a little red *urucú* over all her body, which becomes pink. They then design wavy black lines, brown on her face and body; they make lovely designs. When she is completely painted, they push through the large hole in her ear those strips of young *assai* leaves, one near the other; they pull them from behind until they all look nice and equal, of the same length, and they cut them as necessary, forming two pretty, large, yellow bunches in her ears.

Then they take coloured feathers and push them through the holes which they have at the corners of their mouths and in the middle of the lower lip. One woman also prepares a long, thin, white stick, very smooth, which she puts in the hole that they have between their nostrils. Around the wrist, and the ankle, and below the knee, they put twisted cotton, broad and white, which they wind to a width of about two fingers. They put a strip of cotton around the chest, crossing it behind and below the breasts. This cotton must be white; that which has become red with the *urucú* of the body is no good for these girls.

The young girl is really lovely, painted and decorated like this! The women say: 'Now let's go.' The girl walks ahead, and after her come the other women and the little girls; many of them are painted. They all enter the *shapuno* in this way by the entrance which is farthest away from the mother's hearth, in order to be able to cross the whole of the compound; thus everyone can see how beautifully decorated the girl is. She walks across the compound slowly, goes towards her parents' hearth and sits down in the hammock. It's the mother who looks after everything. The men take no part in this.

So I spent some months in the *shapuno* of the Shamatari. I was always with the *tushaua's* brother's father-in-law: now there was a little tiny boy sleeping with me in the hammock. Another, who was still at the breast, slept with his mother. I took the little boy with me everywhere; for this reason his mother, too, loved me. The Shamatari treated me well. The *tushaua* had said: 'Napagnuma is not used to eating the roots which we eat; when you have some fruit, give her some too.' Then the women, when they came back with fruit, always gave me some.

There were some Karawetari women who were jealous of me. One always used to say: 'These people give everything they eat to Napagnuma, nothing to me, never anything to us; we have to carry water, carry wood.' She said that they were badly treated while I was well treated; that I should not go with the men into the forest to work. The Shamatari women, in fact, when they returned to the *shapuno,* said to me: 'Napagnuma, take this,' and gave me a fruit: 'Napagnuma, it's for you.' That woman, and other Karawetari women too, were very angry.

Unfortunately, after some months, Rohariwe's brother's father-in-law, with whom I was staying, left with his family. They went to an old *roça,* where there was a lot of *urucú*; the woman wanted to take me with them. 'How can you?' said the husband. 'Don't you know that the Karawetari and the Hekurawetari are always around us, trying to steal our women? Let's leave her with my brother's wife,' and they went away. The brother's wife had a little girl and I looked after her. They said to me: 'Don't ever leave her alone. Wherever you go, take her with you.' So I stayed with that other woman. She too was kind; she never scolded me.

Only a few days after they had left I went with that woman, her daughter, her niece and many others into the forest to look for honey. Only a few men stayed in the *shapuno*. In the forest we found one of those fruit trees they call *mucugnas*; they look like banana trees, but have their bunches high up. They cut the tree down and we picked the fruit. Then the man shouted: 'Here's some bees' honey.' 'What kind is it?' asked his wife. 'Those bees with little spots on them.' So we took much honey. We were going back home; the hillside was rocky. Before me, among those stones, I saw a huge toad, somewhat brown in colour. I looked at it; it looked at me, opening and shutting its eyes. 'Napagnuma has found a toad,' said the little girl who was with me, and she took it by one foot. Meanwhile, in the *igarapé*, the man had squeezed the honey into a big leaf and we all ate it. They killed the toad, skinned it, cleaned it: that kind of toad they call *uanacoco*. They threw its head away (although they eat the heads of other toads); with their teeth they pulled out the creature's claws, *tac, tac, tac*. A woman said: 'Open up the veins well and let the blood come out, because there's poison in the blood.' 'Can there be poison?' I asked. They opened the feet, broke the veins and squeezed them; thus they drew off the blood from the whole of the flesh. That toad had many eggs. The women said: 'Now let's go.' A Karawetari woman, the one who always said that she was maltreated while I was well treated, took the eggs, made a little packet of them and gave it to me: 'Take this packet,' she said; 'it's to eat.'

We reached the *shapuno*. The woman with whom I now was, lit the fire and we lay down in the hammocks. She gave me her child and said: 'Now I want to cook my fruit, then you cook yours.' When she had finished, I put on the fire that packet of leaves with the toad's eggs inside; while they were cooking, I could hear *tac, tac*; it was the eggs. 'What is it?' the woman asked me. 'I'm not sure,' I replied, 'Karawetarignuma[1] gave it to me.' After it was cooked, I opened the packet. The little girl asked me: 'What is this? I want some.' I answered 'I don't know; I have never eaten it, because my mother never gave me any. Who knows? Perhaps they eat these toad's eggs.' The child put a few eggs in her mouth and said: 'It smells, it has a nasty smell.' There was also with it a bit of flesh of the toad's belly. I tried it: it was very bitter and I spat it into the fire.

Another little girl came and ate those eggs. A little later she said to her mother: 'I want to be sick.' The mother replied: 'Go and be sick outside, behind the house. You have eaten too much honey.' The little girl went out and soon came back: she had been sick. She lay down in the hammock, then got up like a drunken person. The

[1] *Gnuma* means woman in the Yanoáma language.

mother asked her: 'What's the matter with you? What are you doing?' She hugged her. The father wasn't there; a man came running: 'What's the matter with you? Is it the enemy's Hekurá who want to kill her? They held her in their arms and stood around her; soon after that the little girl died. The mother began to cry and shout. Everybody wept and wept; they didn't understand why she had died.

The other child, who had tasted the eggs, also began to be sick; she had froth in her mouth. They asked her: 'What have you eaten?' 'I have eaten the eggs of that toad,' she replied. A big strong woman, whom they had stolen from the Namoeteri, said: 'So you don't know that the eggs of that toad are poisonous? When I was with the Namoeteri five children died after eating the eggs of that toad. Are you joking? We had gone to pick *mumu*, and the children, who stayed behind with only the old women, had cooked the toad's eggs. They had died, one here, one there, all five of them. That toad's eggs are poisonous.' The woman asked: 'Who gave them to her?' 'Napagnuma gave them to me.'

The dead girl's mother looked at me. Then she began to shout: 'Kill Napagnuma! Kill Napagnuma! I want her to die as my daughter did! I don't want to see her alive in this world any longer! If she goes on living in this world, my grief will only grow.' I said: 'Why do you want to kill me? I knew nothing; I did not know it was poisonous. They gave them to me: I knew nothing.' But the woman continued to shout amid her weeping: 'Kill her, kill her, kill the white man's daughter; I want to see her dead like my daughter! Kill her; she must die this very night!' It was a weeping chant: 'I shall only be happy if you kill her. Kill her! If you don't kill her, I shall say that you are not *waiteri*; I shall say that for you it is better to carry women's baskets!'

In the middle of the night, the woman with whom I lived shook me in the hammock: 'Get up,' she said, 'run away! Do you see that fire? They are putting poison on their arrows to come and kill you. They will kill you with poison, as you have killed with poison. Run away, run away!' The old woman repeated: 'Run away, run away! They'll kill you! They are putting poison on their arrows.' 'Let them kill me; I am tired; I don't want to run away; I have done no harm to anyone.' 'Run away, for no one will defend you!' She pushed me among the straw of the low roof, and gave me two firebrands for the fire, repeating: 'Run away, run away at once! Stay at a distance for some time; then come back, for after that they won't kill you.'

I ran into the forest towards the *roça*. I was already some way off, when I heard the men shout, who had come to look for me in the hammock. The woman replied: 'Napagnuma is not here, Napagnuma is not here.' Then they came to look for me outside: I had started to walk slowly. It was night and it was full of thorns, so that I had to go slowly. Near the *roça* a deer was resting; as soon as it saw me, it jumped up making a noise and ran off into the forest. The men thought it was I and they shouted: *'Pei haw, Pei haw, Napagnuma ka*!' and they began to run after the deer. I, from the *roça*, among the banana trees, heard them as they ran. At last they saw the footprints and knew that it was a deer. I heard some of them say: 'Napagnuma has turned into a deer! Napagnuma has turned into a deer!'

After a short time all was silent again. I sat down on a tree-trunk; I had covered the brands, so that they should not see them. The Indians in the forest began to call each other by making bird sounds: one whistled on one side, one on another, one on another. I heard their voices again. One was asking: 'Haven't you seen her?' 'No, it was a deer.' 'She hasn't come this way, perhaps she is still there, behind the roof of the *shapuno*.' Meanwhile they were whistling with bird-calls, to call back those who were further away. After they had gone away, I leaned up against a trunk: I was afraid. From afar I heard the women weeping and the men shouting; I thought: 'Why do they want to kill me? I should have stayed.' I began to weep and weep.

I went farther away; the moon began to light up the forest. Near me, on a tree, a bird was singing: *tu, tu, tu*. I looked and I climbed a little way up: the bird was on its nest. I took a stick, climbed up again and hit the bird hard on the head; it fell from the branches to the ground. It was a pretty big bird and had long claws. 'Shall I be able to eat this bird?' I had never seen it before. I picked a big leaf, climbed up again, put the eggs in the leaf and came down. I stayed under the tree: the moon was going in and I thought of going to get bananas in the *roça*. I left the bird and the eggs near the firebrands; I went to the *roça*, took a few bananas from a bunch and a few from another and went back. When one runs away in the night, it's a long time before morning comes.

Daylight was returning to the forest: all the time I heard from afar the weeping of those people. Then some voices came near; they were talking amongst themselves and saying: 'Can she have run far?' 'No,' replied another, 'where can she escape? She has no father, no mother, she does not belong to other Yanoáma.' They passed near, but they did not see me. When it was quite light, I made a packet of leaves with the eggs, one with the bananas, one with the bird; I put them all together, tying them tight with lianas. Then I covered over carefully the place where I had been and began to move off. I didn't know where, but I had the fire with me.

At a distance I saw some big rocks. I approached them and went inside a grotto; I could see light from the other end. I passed into another cleft between the rocks. There was water; I remember that the little toads were going *prin*, *prin*, *prin*, *prin*. The sky was clear. I was now a good way from the *shapuno* and I could no longer hear the weeping. I rested, sitting on those rocks, then I looked for a *cupim* and dry wood. With those brands I made a nice fire. I looked with fright at the smoke. The smoke rose high. When the smoke does not rise, but stays low in the forest, they smell it from afar, follow it and soon find the fire. I cleaned the bird in a nearby stream, put it into leaves and roasted it on the embers; I also cooked the eggs and some bananas. While I was eating, I heard distant shouts: '*Au*, *au*, *au*.' I think they were going to hang up the dead little girl, high in the branches in the forest, and afterwards to burn her. I heard weeping women go by. One was calling me 'Napagnuma, come!' I did not reply, but hid myself still better.

Soon afterwards I came out from the rocks: those birds which go *can*, *can*, *can*, saw me. They sang very loudly and I went back to hide. When all was silent, I again took the brands, loaded onto my back the packages with the bird, the eggs and the bananas, and began to move off once more. I thought I would find a path that would lead me to another tribe. I found in the wood a big, clean path; they had told me it was the one that led to the Patamanibueteri. They lived in the middle of the mountains, but they too were Shamatari. I wanted to go, then I thought: 'Those to whom the little girl belonged, they will know, they will come and catch me and kill me.'

In the evening it began to rain and I was afraid for the fire; I covered it well with leaves. I saw two bunches of wild bananas, the kind of forest bananas they call *ḳoaboḳa*. With a stone I had found I started to beat on one side of the soft trunk until it was all squashed, then I hit it on the other side and I succeeded in felling the tree: I was strong then. The fruit was ripe, I picked the bananas, lit the fire and cooked them. That day I ate only the fruit and I kept the bird. I piled up branches of *assai* palm around the fire and lay down on a stone; I had no hammock, I had nothing. That night I prayed constantly.

When day broke, I began to go along an *igarapé* with my packages and the fire. I climbed up a hill to see into the distance. I thought: 'Who knows, perhaps there will be some *balata* worker?' I shouted as loudly as I could, but no one answered. Then I felt that great feeling of sadness. 'Now I am lost,' I said, and wept and wept. From up above I saw only forest and another hill. It was like a hill I had once seen when I was with my father, and I thought: 'It might be the Serra where that friend of my father's used to live, whose name was Alosio. It was a Serra near the great river.' I climbed higher; I shouted and called. Nobody replied; I heard only the monkeys in the distance, imitating my call. If you had been people, I thought, you would have come to see my tears! and I cried again.

From the height of the hill I could see no rivers, I saw only the great mountains and the forest, beautiful, blue and green here, blue and green there. I thought: 'Where can the Cucui mountain be? It is very high, I ought to be able to see it. Where can it be?' I looked into the distance, but I recognized nothing. I went back, ate a little of the bird, and fell asleep. The next day I found that same enclosure of branches I had piled around the fire and I finished eating what I had. In the morning I remembered that the Indians said that on the mountain there were potatoes of wild *cara*. I found them, and that day I ate forest *cara*.

At night I dreamed: a voice was saying to me: 'What are you doing here? Do you not see that beautiful water which rises in the forest? Every night a jaguar comes to drink of it. If you stay here, the jaguar will eat you.' I woke up, sat down, made the sign of the cross, and looked all around: there was no one. I thought: 'It must have been a spirit. Perhaps it was the ghost of my sister who died at San Gabriel, who came to warn me?' I sat and thought: 'What shall I do? If I go back to the *shapuno*, they will kill me. Why must I suffer like this? Why did God bring me here? What have I ever done wrong? Why does God wish to chastise me thus? I have done no harm to anyone. So why has God thrown me into this place to suffer so?' I wept so much! 'Let them kill me then! Let them kill me today, I'm going back; I can't stand this any longer.' I was more afraid of that wild beast in my dreams than of the arrows. I took the fire, prayed, and started to run. Two big tapirs were eating: 'Oh, tapirs, why are you not human? If you had been men, you would not have appeared before me!' I continued to run. In the afternoon, about three o'clock, I heard human voices. I whistled to call them, then I was afraid, made the sign of the cross, prayed, and ran off again. Thus I came back close to the Shamatari *shapuno*. I climbed a tree to hear better; a man had taken *epená* and was chanting. I remember that song: 'The Hekurá have come, have sat on my breast and have sung this song. But I have frightened them away; when they came, I was never with a woman!' I thought: 'Perhaps the *tushaua*'s brother's father-in-law has come back? Is it he who is singing? But it was not he. I recognized the man who was singing: his name was Kuirasi.

I thought: 'I have done no wrong to anyone; I am going to that woman with whom I last lived. Perhaps within an hour I shall be dead. They will want to take vengeance for the child, because they think I killed her!' I made the sign of the cross, thinking that perhaps this would be my last prayer.

I went behind the *shapuno* as far as the woman's hearth; I drew aside the leaves of the roof and entered. The girl recognized me and exclaimed: '*Napagnuma ka*!' The woman was getting some thorns out of one foot; she looked at me in surprise: 'I have come back,' I said. The woman replied: 'I'll give you something to eat; I am going to get water,' and she went out.

I was afraid to stay alone with the husband, because, that day, he too had wanted to kill me with the rest. The man got up and took *urucú*. He began to paint himself red on the chest; then he made black lines on his chest and around his mouth and big red lines on his legs. I thought: 'He is painting himself ready to kill me!' Still no one had realized that I had arrived. The man finished painting himself, then took his arrows, which he kept high up above the fire. He took an arrowhead, sharpened well the monkey bone and tied it crosswise on the head. Then he pulled out of his bamboo quiver a poisoned arrowhead and placed it in another arrow. 'Now, he will kill me,' I thought, and my heart beat violently for fear. Then he took his bow, pulled and let go the string, *tak*, *tak*, to see if it was well stretched. It was not well stretched; he undid it at one end, twisted it again many times and threaded it in again. This is what they do to tighten it better, when they are going to shoot. He picked up the arrows and went off.

The woman was returning with the water and I was beginning to feel less frightened. The woman said: 'Perhaps he will get an animal or two and we shall need the water, don't waste it.' She gave me some bananas. I was hungry, but I had not the courage to eat: I was afraid the man would walk around once and then come back inside and shoot me. The man did not come back. 'Lie down in the hammock,' said the woman. I lay down, ate a little fruit and went to sleep. The next morning the woman said to me: 'Get up; prepare this fruit and cook it.' It was fruit from the forest; one breaks the shell, washes and eats the good white seeds which are inside. The woman repeated to me: 'Cook this fruit; then go behind the *shapuno*. There you will find a dead tree-trunk. Take a bit of wood so that we shan't be without fire tonight!'

They all knew now that I had come back, but nobody had said anything to me. I think they had decided to kill me at the moment when they were burning the little girl's body. I began to see that each man was taking a burning firebrand from his own brazier. They were taking that fire to prepare the pyre and to burn the child's body. The body had already been in the forest many days, tied high up. They came out to get the body, each with his own fire. There were only a few men, since many had left. I remained alone in the *shapuno*, but I was afraid and suspicious.

Later an old woman arrived, whose name was Ucuema: 'I heard them talking about you,' she said. 'Why have you come back? I didn't think you would.' I replied: 'I came because I didn't know where else to go.' Meanwhile I was roasting and eating that fruit.

CHAPTER 12

The Poisoned Arrow

Evening was already coming on and the sun was low [illegible] that wood as the woman had said. I had not seen anyo[illegible] While I was beating on that dry wood to break it . [illegible] poisoned arrow entered and passed through the othe[illegible] leg. 'Ah!' I shouted. I trembled and looked, but I coul[illegible]ne. I pulled the arrow, but its poisoned head stuck in my flesh.

I began to run along the path; but it hurt too much, I couldn't run. I sat down and tried to pull the arrowhead out. It was impossible; a big bubble of blood had formed inside. I thought: 'I must pull it out!' I squeezed, I broke the blood bubble, seized the head and pulled it out of the flesh. The wound was a big one and bleeding freely. 'If I run and leave a trail of blood, they will find me and kill me.' I put rotten leaves over the wound, but it continued to bleed. Then I took some mud; I cleaned off the blood and put mud on top. When the mud was all red, I threw it away and put some more on, because I did not want them to see the drops of my blood.

I went down a slope and sat on a rock. The blood wouldn't stop flowing; I kept cleaning it with leaves, but it continued to come out. Meanwhile I felt that the poison was beginning to kill me; I was like a drunken woman. I saw the yellow trunks, in the midst of a kind of smoke; I looked on the ground and saw all the leaves, as if they were yellow. I could now no longer stand up; my legs felt terribly heavy. My arms too were heavy and I could scarcely move any more. I heard them arriving: their footsteps among the leaves went . . . *sharara, sharara* . . . I wanted to run away, but I could no longer move. With one hand I still managed to pick a few big *embauba* leaves and put them on my head.

The forest was beginning to be dark: they came near me. One said: 'Let's go away; she is already dead.' Another: 'No, you have only wounded and frightened her with your arrow, coward! *Shirishiwe*. If you had waited for me, I would have shot her in the stomach, in the chest, in the neck, so that she would have died instantly.' I was afraid they had seen me; but they had not seen me. Then I prayed; I prayed that they would not see me, because I would not have been able to flee. I could no longer move; my whole body now seemed to be asleep. One repeated: 'Let's go; she's dead; it's the same poison which we tried yesterday on that monkey, which died at once. She's near here and she's dead. The flies are already putting worms in her mouth, in her nostrils.' I heard them laughing: 'Have you seen her blood? There were ants and bees eating it!' Then I heard no more, I saw no more. I spent the whole night like that: I didn't move, I heard nothing, I remember nothing.

In the morning I began to feel the water beating here in my ears, *tac, tac*. Then I felt cold. It had rained in the night and the water was running down my neck. Lots of rotten leaves had settled round me. I wanted to open my eyes, but I could not; my neck was stiff. I only felt that cold. Then a bird began to sing: I heard it well. 'It must be already evening,' I thought, 'these birds sing in the evening.' I managed to open my eyes: the sun was high. I saw the reflection of the sun between the branches, red and yellow; everything was beautiful. I felt no pain, only cold. The sun was now high and I began to feel softer. Near me there was a branch; I grasped it and dragged myself up: I succeeded in sitting. My leg was purple around the wound; it looked as if it were painted blue. Then the sun got hotter and I began to remember. I saw around me only rotten leaves; then I really did cry! From the arrow wound a kind of bloody water was oozing out; the leg was swollen and purple; it looked like the leg of a toad.

When my body began to feel warmer, the pain increased; at first I only felt cold and hard. I remember it all well and I wept. My leg kept hurting more. . . . My mouth was bitter, very bitter, as if I had been chewing quinine. Already the sun was no longer lighting up the place where I was sitting; by dragging myself along on all fours with hands and knees, I brought myself into the sun again, then again behind the sun. At last I succeeded in standing up; it was already nearly evening. I dragged myself to an enormous trunk with huge roots. My leg kept hurting more and more.

Later a group of women passed by, looking for fruit in the forest and collecting firewood; they were talking among themselves. One was saying: 'Napagnuma really is dead.' Another: 'Have you seen how it rained last night? It's she who is making it rain.' Yet another one said: 'They told me she died among the rocks; the flies have left lots of worms in her mouth.' While they were talking like this, I was saying to myself: 'What a lot of things they are making up!' With these women went a sister of the *tushaua,* whose name was Uipanama and who had always been well disposed towards me; she called me 'niece'. I heard Uipanama saying to the others: 'You always follow after me, when I go collecting wood.' 'We came because we have no axe and we are waiting for you to give us yours.' 'Here you are; take it, and leave me alone to collect my wood in peace.' The women took the axe and went away.

I crawled on all fours towards Uipanama; I gathered up a bit of mud and threw it out beside her. The woman looked around and did not see me. I took another handful, squeezed it and threw it again. She saw me, ran towards me, hugged me and wept: 'Napagnuma, what have you come to do here?' 'I have come to ask for fire! When night falls, bring me the fire; I will wait for you near the *shapuno.*' 'They told me you had died near the grotto; one man said that he had beaten you with his stick on the head and had flattened it like a rotten leaf.' The old woman looked at me and wept: 'You will not stay alone in the forest; no, you will come with me and stay with me in the *shapuno.* My brother Rohariwe only yesterday was shouting at these people, saying: "You have shot her, because I wasn't there. I had given her to my brother's father-in-law, because, as soon as she was grown up, I wanted a daughter by her. You very people, who didn't even come to fight, but stayed behind in the *shapuno,* were able instead to kill this girl! If I had been present, I would have broken your arrows and killed one of you to avenge her." So said my brother.' Then the woman continued: 'When it's dark, men will come by these parts, because they'll be going hunting. As soon as all is quiet, come to the *shapuno* by the path.'

The old woman went away. I stayed by myself behind a trunk. When it was well into the night, the hunters passed by. Then I went up behind the hearth where the old woman was, made a noise among the straw on the roof, and the old woman said: 'Wait, wait.' She first dampened down the fire with banana skins, so that the others should not see me, and let me in. The husband was stretched out in the hammock and he already knew; the woman had told him. Uipanama made me lie down on her net and gave me some bananas and a piece of armadillo; I ate a little.

Soon the young daughter came running: 'Mother, they say you are hiding that woman they shot yesterday! They are putting poison on their arrows.' I stopped eating. The woman shouted: 'Yes; I am hiding her; what do they want?' and she ran to her brother. I heard her saying to the *tushaua* Rohariwe: 'I was in the forest collecting wood; there in the forest I found her almost dead with her leg wounded on both sides. It was I who brought her here; now they again want to kill her!'

Then Rohariwe stood up, went right into the middle of the *shapuno* compound and shouted aloud: 'Why do you want to kill her? You who have not travelled afar over high and difficult mountains, as I have, now want to kill her? You, sister, give her a hammock; light a big fire near her, so that everybody can see her and kill her! If you kill her, I will kill you this very night. She has no father, no mother, no relations to defend her, and so you want to kill her. I have not gone to war to bring back women just so that you may kill them. If you shoot her, even if you then run away to another *shapuno*, I will come there with my men.' Rohariwe continued: 'Leave her to die by herself; she is already badly injured, she is mortally wounded.'

The woman too was shouting against those men who wanted to shoot me and she insulted them; she said they had the courage to kill only those who had no relations to avenge them, but were afraid to kill anyone who had relations. Then she came to me and said: 'Don't be afraid, my brother won't allow you to be killed. Sleep.' But I was so afraid, I thought: 'They'll kill me while I am asleep.' I wanted to escape again into the forest, but the woman would not let me go and so I stayed. The night went by; I prayed all the time.

Early in the morning the *tushaua* again shouted: 'You who are *waiteri,* go and shoot tapirs and wild boar, not women, whom no one eats. Let all go hunting tapirs, monkeys, armadillos: I want to hear what taste the meat you get will have. You would like to kill only people; I cannot drink broth made of people; broth of game, yes, I drink that broth and fill my stomach with it. Let no man come back tonight without game; thus I shall believe that you are indeed *waiteri*!' Then those who wanted to shoot me got up and all went into the forest to hunt. One of the *tushaua*'s wives came near to me, saw me wounded as I was and wept; other women came up too. They all looked at me and wept for sorrow. Thus I stayed with them for some days.

Meanwhile they burnt the body of the little girl; they collected the bones and hung them above the hearth. Now they had to prepare the banana flesh to mix with the ashes of the dead child and eat them. The bananas were all hung up and were ripening. The hunters had gone hunting to give the game to those who had made the pyre; they came back after two days.

The old woman said to a young woman, who was nearby: 'Now they will pound the dead girl's bones. Cut Napagnuma's hair all round and shave it off in the middle of her head. Then smear *urucú* on her body and take her a long way off, into the cave on the mountain. When all is dark, you will go back and fetch her.' My leg was less swollen, but the wounds, where the arrow had passed through, were open and a yellow watery liquid was coming out.

The old men had begun to cook the banana flesh; the bones were not yet crushed. The woman cut my hair and shaved me on top of the head with a blade of small bamboo bark; then she took a piece of wood with fire and said to me: 'Let's go.' We entered upon a path. The woman added: 'Now walk, walk straight ahead all the time, and you'll come to the mountain. Up there, a long way off, you will find a grotto. Don't stop near here, because when they pound the bones to make the powder, they will come and look for you to kill you. Other relatives will also arrive: they have had news and they also want to kill you. When we are weeping for the dead, the men will come to seek you to take vengeance. You come back only when it's the dead of night.' The woman then left me and did not come as far as the grotto.

CHAPTER 13

Boundless Forest

I continued walking alone; the leg was now giving me less pain; I covered the brand well with leaves which I tied below so that it should not go out. In the *shapuno* they were preparing the bones. When they prepare them, no one leaves the *shapuno,* but all stay together. I walked along the path, thinking: 'How can I go back? In two, perhaps three, days they may kill me; it's better that I run away.'

I reached the spot where they had suspended the little girl's body before burning it: it struck terror into me. I went into the nearby *roça,* took a bunch of bananas, tied them with lianas and loaded them onto my back. From a low *pupugna* palm I broke off a bunch of *pupugnas.* I walked a bit further, but the groin was swollen and gave me much pain; from the wounds that watery matter kept coming out. I saw some old abandoned *tapirí*; I was on the path that leads to the Hekurawetari. I lit the fire with dry wood, because I thought: 'No one will come to search for me today; they are pounding the bones.' I also found some big dry bamboos; I broke off four pieces, leaving the knot on one side, to carry water. In the stream I got water and closed up the bamboos with leaves. Near me I saw a big tree whose bark was almost detached; I pulled it and a piece fell off, like a little canoe. Then I collected wild banana leaves, put them in it and lay down.

Night was falling and I thought: 'Perhaps it's better to roast all the bananas, because they weigh less. No, bananas last longer like this, ripening gradually.' With an ants' nest (those they call *cupim* here) I made a nice fire and cooked the *pupugnas.* I ate some, drank the water which I had got, prayed, stretched myself out again in the bark and slept all night. In the morning I picked up my things and tied them securely; I found a piece of bow with a point. 'I'll carry this with me always!' I thought. 'It'll be useful for killing animals.' They had told me that if you meet a jaguar and strike him hard with the point of the bow, the jaguar gets a kind of shock and you have time to escape. I took the brands and my other few things and started to walk.

That day I kept on walking farther away, because I was afraid that they would pursue me: towards midday I heard men hunting monkeys and shouting loudly: '*Uh, uh, uh . . . Ih, ih, ih.*' They go like that to frighten them: then the monkeys can no longer run away and the men can shoot them. In the evening I found a tree with big roots. With *assai* palm and *bacaba* branches I surrounded it all and lit the fire; I cooked some bananas and lay down. My leg had swollen again and was hurting me a great deal: during the night I had to get up for the pain. I was afraid the fire would go out. *Cupim* burns very slowly. The next morning I left four big pieces of *cupim* alight, one here, one there, and went away with all my possessions. I passed over a thick and rough hill, full of *piassaba* palms. In the evening I came right to the *tapirí* where the *tushaua's* brother's father-in-law and his wife had gone; the father of the dead girl had gone with them too. The Shamatari had warned them and they had already left to return to the big *shapuno*, because the father had to eat the banana flesh with the dead girl's ashes. They took a different path from mine, and luckily I did not meet them. After a long time I found with another tribe the woman who had always been good to me. She told me that on the journey the dead child's father kept saying: 'I must look for Napagnuma and well and truly fix my arrow in her stomach.'

Under those *tapirí* were *pupugnas,* some mouldy, others good, and an abandoned dog. I was glad because I thought he would be company for me. Soon after I heard a man coming back whistling and calling; I hid in the thick of the forest. The man found the dog and beat him: *cui, cui, cui* . . . shouted the dog. Then he went away with the dog. When I could hear no more noise I came back; I found a basket, put the *pupugnas* in it and continued to walk.

I no longer recognized the path: eventually I found a deserted *shapuno,* where I had passed by when they had seized me from the Hekurawetari. The enemy had come and had burned it. I decided then to make a *tapirí* for myself: I had seen many times how they built them and I tried to do the same. I took four big poles not completely burned and went into the forest to prepare other smaller ones. I bit them with my teeth on one side and pulled; the pole went trac and broke. When they are gnawed with the teeth on one side, it suffices to gnaw a little on the other and pull, so that they snap: my teeth cut like knives. Then I looked for that tree which has the bark which is used in strips like rope: I tied three big posts in a triangle, to make a sloping roof. With hooked branches I caught some big palm leaves and broke them off. Thus I covered the roof to keep the water off me. I also put on top those big wild banana leaves. Then I thought: 'It's too open around; the jaguar will come in.' I found a *pataua* palm, broke off many leaves and put them all round. I slept inside that little hut; my leg was still very swollen.

During the night I thought: 'I must look for that path which leads to the Karawetari; they are friends of the Aramamiseteri.' I remembered that when I was with them, some Aramamiseteri had come with big knives; I had asked what those knives were called and they had replied: '*Terçado*.' So they must have had them from white Brazilians, because I remembered my father calling them *machete*; perhaps they had got them from white men lower down, towards S. Isabel. They had also brought a tin of manioc flour and they called it 'farinha', as on the Brazilian side. Then the Karawetari had said to me: 'To go to the Aramamiseteri you cross a river where the whites sometimes come,' and they had shown me a big hammock belonging to whites, with green and yellow stripes, the colours of Brazil.

All day I looked for the path leading towards the Karawetari; but I found nothing. I remembered that when they had seized me from the Hekurawetari, who live in the direction of the Karawetari, we had climbed down from a high mountain; on the left there was a higher mountain, on the right a lower one and in the distance one with two peaks. Then, further on, a mountain consisting completely of rocks which they called *Amiana*, and straight ahead other rocks which they called *Amini*: I remembered them well. All day I searched; I climbed up and down. Night came; I had nothing left to eat. I returned to my hut and went to sleep hungry.

Next day I found a wild sorb-tree, which in *nheengatu* they call *kuma*: it was laden with fruit, those big ones. The monkeys had been eating them on the tree, and, by shaking the branches, they had made a lot of fruit fall off. The tree was still full of fruit. I tried to climb it, but the trunk was too big, and a great deal of that yellow stuff was still coming out of my wound. When you suffer great hunger, you no longer feel very hungry. I ate only a little of that fruit, put the rest in leaves, tied them up tightly and went back to my hut. I hid the sorb-fruits, which were not yet ripe, in a hole which I dug in the ground to soften them.

Next day I continued to search for the path to the Karawetari. I heard from afar a noise . . . *luk*. It was *ukoqui* fruit falling; they grow also along the Rio Negro. They are scented; they have a big kernel and around it a pulp which you eat. There were many of them on the ground, and many had been nibbled by the tapirs. So I saw a nice path and followed it. It was not a human-made path, but the path of the tapirs. I made a little hut near that big *ukoqui* tree. In the night I heard a loud noise near me; I was terrified because I thought it was a jaguar. I had not the courage to blow on the embers, because I had heard the Indians say that, when the jaguars see a fire, they leap on it. I would have climbed the tree, but I did not have the courage to move. It was not a jaguar; it was a tapir, which had come to eat *ukoqui* fruit. In the middle of the night another tapir also came. But I had been very frightened and the next day I returned to my old hut near the burnt-out *shapuno*.

I had made a hammock of strips of tree-bark, such as they make. I spent a lot of time there; in the daytime I covered the embers over well and took the fire with me; thus, if it had gone out, I would still have found some fire where I had slept. Actually in the evening the embers were still alight. I finished the *ukoqui* fruit; the sorb-fruit was already finished, and I had nothing else to eat. There were those big *cupim*: while the *pupugnas* are ripening, you find many *cupim*. You make a hole on one side with a little stick with a sharp point; thus all those little white animals fall out, and you gather them up in leaves. The black ones run faster and escape. The Indians press them well between the leaves, put them on the fire and add that salt water which is prepared from the ashes of a tree. They are good like the *sauba* ants. They eat them just when they are about to have wings. There are two kinds: those which live in big, tall houses, and those which instead have a low house. If you eat them raw, they make you sick. While I had the fire, I ate them, and also ate crabs, shrimps, ants' eggs and ants.

One day it rained heavily; I went back to my hut and went to sleep. When I woke up, I looked for the fire. The water had almost put it out, and there were only hot ashes. I began to blow and blow; I put dry wood on it and blew again, but the fire went out completely. I wept and wept, because I had no more fire. I thought: 'I'll go back and steal fire from the Shamatari.' I walked for two days towards their *shapuno* and came near, then thought: 'Now, if they find me, they'll kill me; better to run away.' So I went back to my hut without any fire.

Meantime my leg had healed and I climbed up the lianas. There were many *mamocori* lianas, which the Indians use to make their poison. I climbed the lianas and got fruit from the trees; I had nothing else to eat. With long branches I made hooks to shake the fruit down; if it was not ripe I kept it and waited for it to ripen. In the forest I always went looking under the trees for fruit which the monkeys had nibbled. If I found any, even if I did not know what sort it was, I ate it just the same, because monkeys only choose non-poisonous fruit. On the other hand, if I found nice fruit which the monkeys had not touched, I did not eat it. When I found fruit which the monkeys had begun to eat, I collected it, put it in leaves and went away at once, because jaguars often come around those trees.

When there was no fruit, I ate only those ants which I had seen the Indians eat. I filled some leaves with them and then ate them. I took only the front part, not the stomach, because it's dirty. There is a wood-ant which makes its home small; if you push a stick through it, lots of big ants drop out. I ate very many of these. There is a season in which those ants have wings, but fly only by night: but I only ate ants without wings. After I had caught many of them, I let a few days go by and then came back to get more.

If I saw the muddy road of those ants which have their homes on the trees, I took a little. First I made all the ants come out, then I blew and blew, and when there were no more inside, I put it in my mouth. This way I ate several mouthfuls: it had no taste, just as if it were manioc flour with no taste.

There were many crabs and shrimps in those parts. The crabs were big and lived under the stones; I tried to catch them with my hands, but they bit me. Then I put a fat leaf in front and succeeded in getting them. I tried eating them raw: I opened them, tasted the flesh, but it was sweet and I couldn't swallow it, so I spat it out. I also tried shrimps, but they had a bad taste.

One day I reached an *igarapé*; there was that white, fine mud. I had seen them eat it. I squeezed it with a leaf and ate it; I thought: 'Perhaps I shall walk with more strength,' but it was not so. The next day I ate it again. I did not know how to eat it and it stuck in my throat. Ahi! I couldn't breathe. From that time I have always been afraid to eat sand. Near the *igarapé* I found a big path; it was the path of the Shamatari, which led to an old *roça*. I came to the *roça*. There was some *urucú* and I painted myself. There were also those potatoes which they eat. I thought: 'I'll eat these potatoes raw, and so at last I'll die.' I still had that basket in which earlier on I had put the *pupugnas*. I went down into the *igarapé*; I washed the potatoes, peeled them with my teeth and ate them. I took many back to my hut.

That night too the jaguar came, but he did me no harm. It must have been about eight o'clock in the evening and I heard, *sha, sha,* along the *igarapé*. Then a heavy breathing coming nearer; it passed around my little hut, around the palm branches. I had a big stick in my hands: I thought it was a deer. It walked past many times during the night and went away only towards morning. It came back also the following night; it went past and then it went away. In the daytime I saw the jaguar's great tracks, but I still stayed there to sleep, because I was nicely hidden and I thought the Shamatari would not find me. One night two jaguars passed by: a mother with her son. The mother called: *hua, hua* . . . and the son answered. In the morning I went to see where they had been; the mother had vomited some wild boar flesh which was still fresh.

I found an old *roça* full of *pupugna* trees. I tried to eat them raw, but it was impossible. I thought: 'What a pity I haven't the fire; I must try again to make one!' I knew that the Indians make it with two small sticks: they put on the ground a flat piece of dry wood of wild cocoa, which they hold firm between their feet, and they rotate quickly over it a small stick of the same wood. After they have rubbed it three times, smoke begins to come out and a small ember forms in the pith of the stick, which they drop on a piece of *cupim,* or on dry fibres. Then they blow and blow, and so the fire is born. All the evening I spent rubbing wood: the sticks heated up well, smoke came out, and more smoke, but no flames. I put all my strength into it: my hands were full of blisters, but I didn't succeed. I found cotton and *urucú* branches in that *roça*: they also use branches of those plants to make fire. I tried for so many days, but I never succeeded.

I kept looking for a new path; I climbed up tall trees. I always hoped to meet some worker who had come to seek for rubber or *balata*; I shouted: 'Hey, heyyy . . . Is there nobody over there?' Only the birds and the monkeys answered me. Then I wept and wept. All throughout those days my job was to look for a path which I did not find.

One day, while I was sucking wild cocoa fruit near an *igarapé,* I heard a noise, as though people were approaching: it was a jaguar which saw me and puffed loudly. I ran away; I remember that, when I stopped, there was in front of me a small snake which put its tongue out and looked at me. The jaguar did not pursue me. Two days later I returned to pick up the cocoa fruit and saw in the mud of the *igarapé* the huge footprints of that jaguar.

One evening I was on the bank of an *igarapé* now dry, and full of rocks. The place was beautiful and a gentle breeze was blowing. I heard a whistle, as of a person calling me. I thought: 'It must be the Shamatari who have found my footprints or the Karawetari who have come to steal women!' I stood up straight on to a rock to look. Two enormous snakes were coming, one next to the other, gliding slowly between the rocks. Their bodies were whitish, with three black spots within round rings. When they were near and I saw their great heads, I ran away. The two serpents did not follow me, but from time to time did their whistling noise and continued to glide along one next to the other. I thought: 'Who knows if they have been trained by some man, as I have seen done on the Rio Negro, and are going back to their master? Who knows whether there isn't some man in this forest?' Then I began to follow them. They went ahead of me and I saw them clearly; every so often they stopped, raised their heads a little, put out their tongues, then started to move off again. I followed them for a long time: they came near a great rock that covered a dark, deep cave. The sun was now going down and they slowly entered the cave. I saw their enormous tails, which became constantly shorter: the tail of the first one disappeared, while that of the second snake was still outside. I stayed to watch from a distance, until the other tail also disappeared: then I went away. Later the Indians told me that those great snakes make the whistling sound of agoutis, in order to attract and catch them. The Indians call them *okhoto* and eat them.

Every day I looked for a new way: this was my salvation, for at last I found an old *roça*. There were many bananas of different kinds: I took the ripest, squashed them, made a paste and ate it. I ate too much of it and felt ill. I took two bunches, tied them up and carried them to my hut: they were not yet ripe, and I hung them up to eat them as soon as they should become ripe. The next day I made other excursions and my hut was filled with hanging bunches of bananas. If I had not gone on seeking them all the time, I would certainly not have found those bananas. Then I knew that it was an old Shamatari *roça*. It seems that once they lived in a clearing nearby, where the Waika attacked them, killing many: after that attack, the Shamatari had gone down towards the Cauaburi.

I made my new hut not too near that *roça*, because I was afraid they would find me. To reach the *roça* I had to pass through a clearing and, not far off was another one full of canes for making arrows. When the wind blew, the canes beat against each other and went *shaaa*. . . . They find the plants for their arrows near the rivers, take pieces of roots and plant them in the *roças*. They call these arrow canes *hama*; in the *roça* were *hama* arrow canes and wild arrow canes. After that second clearing one walked uphill to a flat area near the source of an *igarapé,* where was the *roça* full of bananas. In the background you could see high chains of mountains, on the side other mountains. I spent much time in that hut. I renewed the dry leaves of the roof three times. From the big trunk that I had planted in the ground, two shoots were sprouting. I thought: 'How time flies!'

This is how time is measured in the forest. When a moon grows small and then vanishes, it is already a month. Then when it disappears a second time, it is another month. When you ask the Indians: 'How long will you be away?' they reply, 'This moon comes and goes, another moon comes and goes, another moon comes and goes, and at the end of yet another moon, before it disappears, we will come back.' That makes four months. I did as they do, I counted the moons: in this way seven moons went by. My hair, which they had cut the day they had crushed the bones of the little girl, had grown long. When I threw it in front, it reached down to my chest. I took slender lianas and tied my hair very tight behind. When I took a swim, my hair covered me down to the chest.

One night the jaguar came round my hut; the next day I ran again far away and built another hut. Then I returned, because I was afraid of that new place; near it passed a path made by man. When I walked in the forest and found a path, I went slowly on tiptoe. I picked leaves and carefully put them over my footprints, only old leaves. I had seen how they did it to hide their traces with dead leaves. If there were trunks, I walked on the trunks and not on the ground. Far away from the paths I did not hide my footsteps.

CHAPTER 14

The Namoeteri

One day, near that *roça,* I saw human footprints. I thought: 'Perhaps they have found my tracks and are seeking me: it must be the Shamatari.' I couldn't go on living like that, without fire, without clothes. At night I was cold, I shivered and shivered, I rolled myself up like a ball. I began to follow those tracks; I reached a low wood, and at last I found their empty *tapirí.* Bunches of ripe bananas and four bundles of arrow canes were hanging on the trunks of the *tapirí.* They hang those canes up so that they do not get spoiled. I sat down and thought: 'Can they perhaps be Waika?' They had told me that the Waika kill even women. 'Better for me if they kill me.' I went up to a hanging bunch of bananas and tried to pull a few off; many ripe bananas fell to the ground. I picked them up, pressed them inside *pishaansi* leaves and ate them. 'Let them see them, let them look for me, and so they will find me.'

I saw some *urucú* on the ground, picked it up and painted my whole body red; I scraped the red colour with my nails and made colourless stripes across my body. Then I mixed a little *urucú* with burnt wood which I found where they had made their fire and I drew dark lines on my face and my body. I wanted to paint myself like them, so that they should see that I was human like them. I thought: 'They will certainly come tomorrow to get the bananas; they won't let them go bad.' I took a few bananas, tied them up in a packet of leaves which I hung round my back and went away. I thought of the fire which I didn't have and of the jaguars, which knew where I was and which one day, when they were really hungry, would eat me.

I had come close to the *igarapé,* when I heard in the distance the loud laughter of men. One was saying: 'Keep quiet, there are human footprints.' They had seen my tracks. 'It must be the Waika,' answered another. They spoke more or less like the Shamatari; I hid behind a big tree which they call *sokokuma*; every so often I raised my head, looked and listened: 'This is no man's footprint, it's a woman's. Perhaps they are women who have run away from the Shamatari and have come into our *tapirí.*' 'Yes, yes, it's a woman's footprint.' 'Careful,' replied the other, 'it might be a man with a woman's footprint, there are small men'; and they laughed.

I saw them pass near me all painted red; there were four men, and, behind, three women with children: one was carrying the baby in a basket. 'Can they be Shamatari?' I thought. I looked at them closely and saw that the shaved part of their heads was bigger than that of the Shamatari. Soon after another man walked past whose head was shaved the same way as the Shamatari.

In the *igarapé,* between the rocks, a kind of enclosed pool had formed. I had found little water tortoises and I kept them in there; when I passed, I would throw fruit or peel to make them grow bigger. I hoped always to find fire and thus I would have been able to cook them. I was afraid those people would find them; so then I caught them, broke the shells with stones, pulled off the little feet, the flesh and the liver, which I put into leaves, and decided to follow those people. While I was walking, I thought of stealing fire from their *tapirí* and then running away again, to look once more for the road back to the Karawetari.

The men were beating hard on the trunks of *pupugna* trees to find *mushiba,* those fat larvae which live under the bark of *pupugnas* and *bacabas,* and which are good to eat. I heard a woman saying in a loud voice: 'Go at once and get *pishaansi* leaves to put *mushiba* in, because it's raining.' One man ran in my direction, because I was following them, hiding among those very same big leaves. The man came near to me and began to get the leaves, breaking the stems with his teeth. I was all painted red and the man saw me; he let the leaves drop and exclaimed in fright: 'Who are you? Are you maybe Poré?' He thought I was Poré, that spirit of which they are afraid, and he looked at my long hair. 'No, I am not Poré,' I replied. The man started to shout: 'Bring me arrows to shoot Poré.' 'I am not Poré, I am Napagnuma.' The man looked hard at me: 'No, Napagnuma is dead; she died some time ago. Already a big *cupim,* a nest of ants, has formed over her bones. How can you be Napagnuma? You are Poré.' 'Don't shout,' I said, 'don't call the others, I am not Poré. Tonight I will come into your *tapirí.*' 'Will you really come?' 'Yes, I will come. And who are you?' 'We are Namoeteri.'

The man continued to stare and stare at me; he picked up his leaves and walked off saying: 'Porekewe, Porekewe.' He thought

I was Poreкewe, the restless spirit of the dead woman, of Napagnuma. I was afraid the others would come; I ran away, I hid at a distance. Then I began to think: 'I can't go on living like this, I have no fire, the jaguars know where I live, the Shamatari too will find me and will finish me off.' Then I remembered that into the Shamatari *shapuno* one day some Namoeteri men had come to bring two dogs; these men were of the same tribe.

They call the spirit of people who die Poré; they are afraid of it. They often say that in the *roça* they have heard whistling and beating on the tree-trunks. They go to see and they see no one; it was Poré who made those noises. Sometimes in the forest there are sounds like coughing or cutting wood or the falling of trees, crash! . . . you go and see and there is nothing. It is the souls of the dead, and that is why there is nothing to see. Until the ashes have all been eaten by the relatives in banana pap, Poré or Poreana, with eyes of fire, goes roaming about at night. It is the spirit that has remained in this world to protect the ashes, it will depart only when the ashes of the bones have been finished. They say to the children: 'Don't go far away, don't go alone into the *roça*, otherwise Poreana will strike you.' The Poré of those who get lost and die without being burnt and without their ashes having a chance to be eaten, continues to wander. The women often asked: 'Where can the Poré of that man be, who wasn't burnt?' They are unwilling to die without having finished the ashes of their dear ones, in order that the soul may go freely towards the House of Thunder. This is why I had often heard them say in the evening in a loud voice: 'I may die: a snake, an arrow. . . . Death gives no warning, it comes without warning; I would not like these ashes to be left over, I want to make a feast'—the feast that they call *reaho*. When the ashes have been finished, the Poreana becomes *Peikaneporebe*.

When all was dark, I approached the *tapirí* very slowly. The men had brought back much game: there were monkeys and *mutum* birds. I saw the fires and I saw that they were cooking the meat; I heard them talking about me. The man was telling them how he had seen me; the Shamatari said it wasn't true, but that I had been dead some time. Then I went into the *tapirí* and said: 'Is there any fire? I am very cold.' They muttered under their breath: 'Poré, Poré.' They made the fire bigger to see better; I was lit up on one side and I squatted down among them. One man said to his wife: 'Go away, it's Poré, it's not a human!' 'Don't shoot me,' I exclaimed. 'I am not Poré! It is true that the Shamatari have shot me;

I spent one night as though dead, then I returned to their *shapuno* and then I ran away. Since that time I have been fleeing in the forest without fire. This is why I have come to you, because I want to come with you; do not shoot me,' and I started to cry.

Then a woman came up and touched me: 'Are you really Napagnuma?' I did not answer and continued to cry. 'Why are you crying? Come here, near the fire, and sit down here; lie down in my hammock. I will cook the bananas for you.' Meanwhile the others began to talk among themselves: 'But is it really Napagnuma? They had said that the worms had eaten her all up; how can she be alive?'

While I was listening to them I began to be afraid that I really was dead. Then I thought: 'No, I am not dead; how could I have come back here among the living? It is true, I was dead for one night; then I recovered. Here is the mark of the arrow.' The woman came close and I showed her the scars; the other woman came too, looked at me and said: 'Yes, it is true, it is Napagnuma.'

Meanwhile the woman said to me: 'Stay in my hammock; I will sleep in the hammock with my man. We have been to the Shamatari to give them these big hammocks, but since they had nothing to exchange, we have brought them back again. Sleep in my hammock together with my little boy,' and she passed me the child, who must have been three years old. When day dawned, I heard the men saying: 'Let us see if it is Poré. If it is Poré it won't be there any longer; if it is Napagnuma, she'll still be there.' Then the woman said: 'Yes, it is Napagnuma; can't you hear how badly she speaks our language? If she had been Poré, she would have spoken differently!'

The Shamatari had begun to paint himself all black. He came up to me and asked: 'Where is the mark of the arrow?' The woman answered: 'Look here,' and pointed to my leg. He sat down and kept on painting himself black. Then the Namoeteri men said to him: 'We are four and you are one; we are four Namoeteri and you are one Shamatari. What can you do by yourself against us?' The Shamatari answered: 'I will take her with me to the *shapuno*. I'll take her away.' He said he would take me and give me to the *tushaua*. The Namoeteri replied: 'It's better for you if you keep quiet and go away, if you want to return alive. We are four. You wanted to kill her and you have already shot her.' At that time I had begun to grow up a bit, and to have a certain shape; perhaps because I had eaten much fruit. The Shamatari tried to take me, but the others put themselves in between us. 'So you want to die? You mean nothing to us.' The man moved off and went on painting himself black. In the meantime I was saying to the woman, who had given me her hammock: 'I don't want to go with him, I want to come with you. They have already shot me, and they wanted to kill me.' The woman said: 'You will not go with him; now let's go away.'

We formed up in line; one woman, I, another woman, then another woman and the children. The men, the four Namoeteri and the Shamatari, stayed in the *tapirí*. We were already a good distance away when the four Namoeteri arrived. They told us how they had said to the Shamatari: 'Come with us.' He had not replied and had kept on sharpening the arrowheads in silence. Then they had said to him: 'Don't try to shoot while we are on the march, because we will follow you right to the gate of your *shapuno* and we will kill you.' The man had not answered; the others had come away leaving him on his own.

That day we walked until about four o'clock; then they made the *tapirí* and we slept. The *shapuno*, where the Namoeteri lived, was nearby; we walked all the next day and slept. We went on the following day too and slept near an *igarapé*. That evening they said: 'We shall get there early tomorrow morning.' On the journey the men went hunting and those who had wives smoked the game to take it to their mothers-in-law. The next morning we reached an *igarapé*. They all bathed and painted themselves. The woman cut my hair and shaved my head in the middle, and drew long, broad red lines on my back and narrow lines on my face: they were red lines of *urucú* and a few black lines.

Near the *igarapé* there was an empty *shapuno*; the roof no longer had even its leaves. It was large and round, with a big compound in the centre; one opening led out towards the path which went to the Shamatari territory and the other towards the *igarapé* and the path of another tribe, the Hasubueteri. It was a *shapuno* of the father of my first son. I recall that, as soon as we entered, my head began to swim and I fell. The woman picked me up and held me in her arms, saying: 'Our country is strange to her! Perhaps she comes from afar off.' Then she took some small branches and slapped me on the back with them. I was lying on the ground; I opened my eyes and began to sweat and sweat. I heard shouts from a distance: '*Haw, haw, haw. . . .*' It was the old men who were saying: 'Hurrah! Our sons are arriving!'

We were all painted by now. I stood up again; I could walk once more. So we went to the great *shapuno* of the Namoeteri. They all came near to look at me. There were so many of them, men and women. I followed the woman who had given me the hammock, and went with the child to her hearth. A woman came up to me and said: 'Come with me.' 'No,' replied the other, 'I have brought her from afar, she must stay with me; no one must take her away from me.' The headman's brother came and asked: 'Is she already a young lady or is she still a girl?' 'I don't know,' replied the woman. 'With whom will she stay, then?' continued the man. 'She will stay with me, she is my companion, she is my fortune; I have not brought her for anyone, you all have women.' 'All right, keep her, we shall see,' said the man somewhat angrily and went away.

From a distance came the headman, whose name was Fusiwe; a number of women followed him. At that time he was the headman of them all. His father was still alive, but very old and infirm, and had given the command over to his son. The headman said: 'Is it Napagnuma? How did you find her?' Then they began to tell the story of how they had found me. 'And did you have the courage to speak to her that night when she came to you?' 'Yes,' said the woman, 'they wanted to shoot her, but I defended her. If I had been another woman, I would have let them kill her.' 'And now what do you want to do with her?' asked the headman. 'She will stay with me; I brought her,' answered the woman. 'Let her stay then,' said the headman, 'your husband is more important than I am here, isn't that so?' He turned and went.

Then I realized that that was not his true feeling. They told me that he went to his father and said: 'Father, she is already a woman; I will not leave her with them, I'll take her.' The father, they told me, replied: 'Leave her; you already have four wives, think of them and of the children you have to bring up. Leave her with the others. The woman who brought her has a brother-in-law who has as yet no woman.'

A few days later that woman with whom I was living went with her family to the banana *roça*, which was called Wakaweteka, because it was of red earth. I went with them. We travelled for one day. The next day we came to where they had their *tapirí*, near the *roça*. Three of that woman's husband's brothers came with their wives, the husband's father, a man who had no woman, and one who had a wife, the son-in-law of the old man; there were about ten men, many women, four young girls and many children. In the *roça* they did not pick up fallen bananas; they said: 'No, don't pick them up off the ground; it's dirty, there are worms wriggling about inside; pick a bunch off the tree. There are toads, spiders and snakes on the ground; it's better not to look among the dry leaves.' They are afraid of a small toad, which squirts poison into men's eyes. But when they are hungry and can find no more bunches on the trees, then they also pick up fallen bananas.

Some days later some Namoeteri arrived and told how, when we had left, the chieftain Fusiwe had said: 'That woman is taking the young girl away, because she is afraid I want to have her. If I had wanted to, I would have taken her the moment they arrived and would have led her to my hearth. I went close especially to have a good look at her. She is still not a grown woman, she's not yet round enough. If she had been a full-grown woman, I would have taken her and no one would have said anything, neither the woman, nor the husband who is *shirishiwe* (a coward) and cannot order me around.'

Meanwhile the woman began to say: 'Now you are almost a woman. How can you adorn yourself, if you have no holes? Come, we will make holes in the middle of your lip and at the corners of your mouth.' I already had holes in my ears. I answered: 'You make your holes, for you are of this race; I am not.' But the woman continued: 'Come, it doesn't hurt at all.'

It was a young Hasubueteri woman who pierced the corners of my mouth. She pushed through two *pashuba* palm thorns, broke them off at the two ends, and left a small piece in my flesh. It hardly became at all inflamed; sometimes, however, there is a big wound. When it healed, they pierced my lower lip in the middle; this time, however, it became very inflamed. The lip is much harder; with *pashuba* palm thorns it is impossible to make the holes. It was a man, the husband of the woman with whom I was living, who prepared a fine point with very hard *bacaba* wood and pierced my lip. With *inajá* wood it becomes inflamed, and so they don't use it. Before pushing it through, he burnt the end a little, so that it should not become inflamed. The lip was hard; he pushed and hurt me. It remained all very painful and half paralysed until it healed. With these same sharp points of *bacaba* wood they make the holes through the nose and the lobes of the ears. In the case of males they always make a hole in their lower lip and their ears. Many young Namoeteri and Karawetari also had their mouths pierced at the corners. But only a few men had a hole through the central part of their nose; only five or six among the Namoeteri, who were very numerous. The women, on the other hand, nearly all had holes in their noses; and sometimes they were big holes. Those small holes can easily be seen when they dance, because they put feathers or little sticks, made very smooth, and with feathers on the end, through them. On the small stick which goes through the nose they sometimes put those white vulture feathers that look like white cotton balls.

While I was with those people, the time came when I became a woman. The old woman made me an enclosure in the *tapirí* with *assai* palm branches and with leaves of another tree which doesn't grow here, but which is used for this very purpose, and she made me stay there by myself, leaving me little space. She tied lianas carefully across the entrance; I could never go out, I could do nothnig, not even blow the fire. 'When you are tired of lying in the hammock,' the woman said, 'sit down.' After three days she gave me only three roasted bananas, a *cuia* of water and a little bamboo with which I had to suck the water. Sometimes I tried to drink the water straight from the *cuia*, but if she saw me, she scolded me: 'Don't do that, because it ruins the teeth.' After I had been eating nothing but those bananas for about two weeks, they went and got some ants in the forest; the woman roasted them and made me eat them. I had become terribly thin; I was nothing but bones.

Some time later a few Namoeteri came to invite us. When it was dark and the Namoeteri had gone away, the old man with whom I was staying said: 'The *tushaua* (who afterwards became the father of my sons) has sent us to invite you because they are having a *reaho*. He has also invited the Mahekototeri[1] to bring pots and dogs. I have answered that I will go to him.'

The woman spoke with her daughter and her daughter-in-law. So once more they cut my hair, which during the time I had been 'of consequence' had grown again; they cut it all around and shaved it in the middle. They painted my whole body red, even my head and face; then three young women chewed lianas and made wavy black lines on my legs, chest, back and face, around my mouth, and on my cheeks; then they put the cotton bands under my knee, on my foot, around my wrists and breasts, crossed over at the back. I really looked beautiful.

So we came near to the *shapuno* which stood high up. I was ashamed, very ashamed. I had heard tell that the men would take

[1] The Mahekototeri were afterwards visited and photographed by Father Luigi Cocco and by me.

me. The woman who wanted to give me to her son said to me: 'Do not ever leave me these days, but stick always to my side. My son is still young; his father says that it is still too soon for him to become a Hekurá. But you stay with me. If the men try to take you away, run back to where we are.' The other women also said to me: 'Run away and come to us, if they try to seize you.' 'How can I flee inside the *shapuno*?' I replied. We reached the *shapuno*. They told us: 'The *tushaua* Fusiwe has gone away, he has gone to get some dogs to go hunting for the feast. He has said that you are to make your *tapirí* here.' It was a part of the circle of the *shapuno* which was still empty.

The men looked at me, but no one said anything. The next day I went to the *roça* with the woman to get wood. 'Paint her again,' she said to her companion; 'the young girl in this condition must not stay as she is without being painted in colours. If she is not painted all the time, she'll soon grow old.'

CHAPTER 15

Violence

I was lying in the hammock; I saw lots of men, all painted. They went out from an opening in the *shapuno*, turned around, and came back in one after the other. Towards me came one all painted black; behind him, one painted black above and red below. They came near; I was afraid, started to cry and said to the woman: 'I am going to run away; see how they are coming to get me!' 'No,' she replied, 'don't run away, there are my sons, my nieces; they will hold you and they won't let them take you.' 'You are few,' I said, 'you won't succeed.' I would have run away into the thick bush, but the daughter-in-law also said to me: 'Don't be afraid, don't run away.'

They came; there were many, so many of them: there must have been fifty. The first one came up with his arrows in his hand and stood still looking; next to him another, then another. I turned my face towards the *shapuno* roof; I wanted to escape through the leaves of the roof. The man who stood in front of all the others squatted down. Then the one standing behind him gave him a little kick on the back with his foot and said: 'Go on now, have you lost your courage? Go on, you invited me, now you must put your hands on her.' The other did not reply. Behind him there was a long line of men, all standing. The man who was squatting down then stood up, dropped his arrows and took me by the arm. I was still turning my head towards the roof. The man said: 'I have come to take her.' Then the woman began to weep and shout: 'Yes, I have done all the work, I have looked after her; now you come to take her away! You should have taken her when I brought her, when she was so thin. Then nobody would look at her, now you are all looking at her!'

While the woman continued to shout, the man pulled me roughly by the arm. I curled up in the hammock, holding myself tight by my arms and my legs; the man pulled me, but could not get me out. Then, turning to the others, he said: 'Come and help me; you pull, too. You sent me, now don't you want to help me?' One grasped me by the other arm and managed to open the hand which I held on to the hammock. I gave him a sharp bite on the arm and he let me go. Then I clung to the trunk on which one end of the hammock was tied. The women in that small group ran to my assistance, but not one of those men moved to defend me. The woman said to them, 'They will say that you are great cowards; that you let her be taken away under your very eyes.' She shouted and wept, but they, lying in their hammocks, didn't even look; they turned their backs.

Meanwhile the women succeeded in snatching me from the men and told me, 'Lie down in the hammock.' They all stood around keeping me flat. Then the men began to untie the hammock from the poles; the hammock fell to the ground. Once again I grasped the pole; I was very strong—much stronger than I am now. I pressed myself tight against that tree-trunk with my arms and my legs. They tried to pull me, to drag me away, but they could not. In the end they said: 'Will there really be no way of carrying her away? Let us take her with the whole tree-trunk.' Then they started to tug at the pole to which I was clinging. 'Do you want to pull my *tapirí* down?' shouted the old woman. 'Leave her alone; you have women already; this one is ours.' Her son said: 'Don't destroy our *tapirí*! If you pull it down, I will first shoot her, then you.' 'Who's afraid of you?' they answered. 'Just you try to shoot if you dare! Shoot her if you like!' The women kept me on one side, and the men pulled on the other. They pulled at those bands of cotton that I had on my wrists, under my knees, over my foot and around my chest. Those strands of cotton cut into my flesh. I shouted with the pain, I shouted in despair.

Night was falling. The old woman stoked the fire, saying: 'I want to see whether you kill her.' The men gave a few pushes to the women who were holding me, throwing them down, but the women got up again and grabbed me once more. The trunk to which I was clinging was uprooted and I fell to the ground. Then the men dragged me towards the middle of the compound, while the women continued to pull me in the opposite direction: they wanted to carry me outside the *shapuno*. Those bands of cotton I had around my breasts came up to my neck; the men continued to pull. I could not breathe and I no longer felt anything.

The women afterwards told me that when I suddenly went limp the men shouted: '*Pei haw, pei haw,* now we have really killed Napagnuma! Now she will no longer be either ours or yours; her back has been broken. We'll throw her head on one side and her legs on the other. Smoke her and eat her! Since you loved her so much, take her, pick up her bones and eat them!' I now felt nothing. When they all realized that I was senseless, they left me alone.

Then the *tushaua*'s sister—so they told me—ran to her mother: 'Mother, they have killed Napagnuma!' The mother replied: 'Who knows, perhaps the cotton band has tightened round her neck. Let's run and see if she is still breathing.' They took a firebrand and came up to me. The old woman felt that I was still warm. 'I think she's still alive; let's try,' said the old woman. Then the son-in-law took me to their hearth; they began to pull my fingers, and my ears, to throw water in my face, on my head, beating and slapping me, until I began to breathe again. The old woman said: 'Now she's coming back to life, so leave her with me.'

I woke up while the *tushaua's* sister (the son's aunt) was holding my head up and the old mother (the son's grandmother) was pouring water on my head. It was the middle of the night. The old woman started to cut those cotton bands, saying: 'They have cut all your chest, all your chest!' My back too was covered with cuts made by those bands; on my body I had lots of scratches full of earth. The *shapuno* compound, where they had dragged me, was of stone and red earth.

The old woman and her daughter washed me; I ached all over, and my body was burning. By my side, the *tushaua's* father looked at me; he was old and had many ancient wounds which had never healed. They had been made by the enemy. I sat down, I was burning all over. Blood was flowing from the cuts on my chest and my wrists. Then the old woman said to me: 'Yesterday I finished a new hammock for the baby; lie down in the old hammock, it's bigger.'

During the night, those with whom I had come, filled with rage, took their belongings and went. The woman wanted to give me to her son as soon as he had learned how to be a *Hekurá*. I do not know why they had brought me into the Namoeteri *shapuno*. They all imagined why; I too imagined why, and trembled for fear and shame. The *tushaua,* his son-in-law and his brother were not in the *shapuno* when the men seized me: they did not know what their men were doing. The *tushaua* had gone to get two dogs to hunt tapirs for the feast to which they had invited the Mahekototeri.

CHAPTER 16

Fusiwe, Headman of the Namoeteri

After some days, the *tushaua's* mother sent me one evening with the children to the *igarapé* to get water. Along the path at that moment came the *tushaua* Fusiwe, returning with other men; behind them came a huge dog. The children said: 'Here comes that bad dog!' Then I exclaimed: '*Shami watiwe* (dirty, bad!).' I threw myself into the water, I was so scared, and stayed in the middle of the *igarapé*. A woman, cousin of those with whom I had lived, heard me and told the *tushaua's* mother that I had called him 'dirty, bad', and that I had said: 'I will not go and live with that scoundrel who has so many women!' It was not true. I had said nothing, I had said those words only to the dog. That woman probably wanted to see me killed. The mother called the *tushaua* and—they told me afterwards—spoke to him as follows: 'You are a grown man, the strongest among all these men here; do you allow yourself to be called dirty and wicked by a woman? You are not *shami*, *watiwe*, you are the handsomest man here. Kill her at once!'

I went back; I knew nothing of it. I started to prepare *pupugnas*. I saw the *tushaua* approaching me with bow and arrows in his hands. But I was innocent and suspected nothing. He looked at me intently and I turned my head. 'Here's the woman who says I am ugly and dirty!' I turned round and saw that he was pointing his arrow in my direction: I made a leap over the woman who was squatting down near me. The other women threw themselves on this side and that, and the small son ran with his bare feet into the fire. I parted the palm branches of the roof and jumped over the palisade. I don't even know how I did it, I was so frightened. They told me when I came back: 'But how high you jumped!' While I was running, there came an arrow. It did not enter my flesh, it just hit me, tac, on the arm, like the blow of a stick. The arrow fixed itself into a *pashuba* trunk: it was a poisoned arrow. They told me he shot two arrows.

I ran and ran, came to the *igarapé* and threw myself into the water: I walked in the water so that they should not see my footprints. I came to a trunk in the middle of the *igarapé* and thought: 'I will get out of the water by this trunk so as not to leave a trace of my footsteps.' I jumped up on it, dried the soles of my feet and leapt from one rock to another towards the thick bush.

Thus I came to the edge of the *roça* and sat down. I thought: 'Why must I suffer so much in this life? Everybody is my enemy. The Shamatari want to kill me; now the Namoeteri too want to kill me. Only the Karawetari did not want to kill me, but I cannot find the way back to them; I don't know any others.' I had nothing to eat and no fire. While I was running, a great thorn had entered my leg above the knee. I could not pull it out and it swelled up badly. Later it came out with a lot of pus. I stayed on the edge of the *roça* until nightfall and there I slept. The next day I went wandering about and found nothing to eat. 'Let me die!' I thought. And so I came to a new *roça*. They had only recently cut down and burned the trees. One trunk, burned inside, had become like a kind of canoe. It was now evening; I covered the trunk with leaves, lay down and went to sleep.

I began to dream. I was entering a church; it was all lit up with candles. I looked inside and the church was empty. I prayed and said to Our Lady: 'As you have opened up the way for me to come here, so open up to me the way that I may find the great river again; please do this miracle.' While I was dreaming this way, an animal bit me in the leg and I awoke. In a trunk near where I was sleeping, I could see the embers. I looked towards the sky; it was full of stars. I prayed and wept. But I had found fire. When a big tree-trunk burns, the fire goes on for days and days until the whole trunk is burned.

The next day was very miserable. I thought: 'I will not make a hut again; I will live as the animals live, I will sleep on fallen trees; if I find no trunks, I will sleep in the living trees, among the rocks, like the animals.' That day I climbed up the tallest tree on the mountain, but I could see nothing but forest on all sides: forest and mountains, distant mountains, mountains closer by, but no river.

I returned to the *roça* to get bananas and I heard a noise. I hid in the bush and saw a man with a short axe and arrows in his hand. Then I knew that he had said in the *shapuno* that with that axe he would like to cut off my head. I lay down flat on my chest: the man looked all around. He had two big scars on his head. He looked up towards me but did not see me. He had with him two dogs, which luckily did not bark; other men passed by too, but no one saw me.

When they had gone away, I ran after them, walking in their footsteps on the tips of my toes so as not to let myself be found; thus I came to a path. I thought: 'It must be the path which leads to the Mahekototeri. Along this part will come the Mahekototeri whom they have gone to invite to the *reaho*. I will wait for the Mahekototeri to come back and then I will follow them.' I had heard that the Mahekototeri (*mahekॢo* means knee) live near a great river, where the river forms a knee. They said that white men had passed along that river. I imagined the Mahekototeri would come soon, because there were already many ripe bananas and *pupugnas* in the *shapuno*. I remained four or five days on that path. I also went close to the *shapuno*, thinking that they would not look for me because they were preparing the feast. Many men had gone hunting, while the rest were gathering *pupugnas* and bananas for the *reaho*. I went so close that I could hear their voices.

One evening I went down near the *igarapé*: some women came to get shrimps. There were mosquitoes everywhere. The women were talking among themselves and I listened to them. Meanwhile a mosquito was biting me and I went tap with my hand to squash it. 'Listen,' one said, 'somebody has killed a mosquito. Can it be Napagnuma?' Then I ran away, hiding in the bushes. They returned to their *tapirí* and warned their men that they had heard someone kill a mosquito with his hands.

It was now late at night when three or four men came into the wood with burning brands; they called and whistled. I stood quiet and they did not see me. They said to one another: 'I don't think there is anyone. Perhaps it was a fruit which fell on a leaf, that made that noise—pah!'

Next morning I heard the loud voice of the *tushaua* in the *shapuno*, shouting: 'Get wood and make a fire. Hurry up and prepare banana pap. I don't want those who are coming to dance today to arrive late. If they are late our enemies can hide nearby and attack them; I don't want us to be blamed for this. Let two men go out to meet those we are expecting and tell them to come while the sun is high, because I want to dance while the sun is high. Let them hurry up and paint themselves, and come into the *shapuno* without waiting a long time outside.' I continued to walk around outside the *shapuno*, keeping myself hidden and listening.

In the afternoon I heard the Mahekototeri arriving. They spoke almost the same language and I understood easily. I heard them saying: 'The children are hungry, they have hardly eaten anything, only *pataua* juice.' They stopped outside the *shapuno* and I tried to look at them to see what they were like. Soon after I heard shouts from the direction of the *shapuno*. '*Pei haw, pei haw* . . . Give these two Mahekototeri and these two Kashorawetari something to eat!' I knew that when a group goes to a feast, they stop near the *shapuno*; two, and if there are many even four, go ahead with the baskets. The *tushaua* gives them game, *pupugnas*, and bananas to take to their companions who are hungry and are outside the *shapuno*. Those who had been in the *shapuno* came back and shouted: 'In the *shapuno* there is lots to eat. The bark-vessels are full of banana pap, covered with banana leaves. You can see these pieces of bark, full, everywhere!'

Then I saw that they were painting themselves; there were more than a hundred of them. I heard the mothers saying to their children: 'Now go and do what you have to do in the woods; when we are inside the *shapuno*, you mustn't make it dirty. Once we are inside, we don't want to go out just to look after you, no. We don't want to get their enemies' arrows outside, because you little ones want to go out. Don't make a mess inside, for we don't want them to speak badly of us after we have gone.' They painted themselves and set out for the *shapuno*. First the men, then the old men with the earthenware pots and hammocks tied to their backs, then the women. When they reached the *shapuno*, I heard the loud voice of the *tushaua* shouting joyfully: '*Ai, ai, ai, ai* . . . our brothers-in-law and our friends are arriving . . .' Then late in the evening I again heard him: ' *Pei haw* . . . Kashoraweteri woman, Mahekototeri woman, sing. Our women will sing later. We will learn your songs and you will learn ours!' First the women sang; then, late at night, the men sang. I spent all night listening to their songs.

Very early in the morning some who were going away passed along the path near me. When the sun was high, the others began to pass by with the women. I would have liked to follow them, but I thought that perhaps some Namoeteri would be going with them, would see me and kill me. So I went back to where I slept, took some *pupugnas* and entered an *igarapé*, where there were some little fish. I crossed it, went a long way, made a fire and cooked the *pupugnas*.

What did those Namoeteri do? They told me later that when all the Mahekototeri and the Kashoraweteri who had come together had left, they began to say: 'Those young Mahekototeri left too early this morning. Perhaps they have caught Napagnuma on the road.' In the afternoon, they told me, the *tushaua* shouted loudly: 'I think those men, who left early, found Napagnuma in the forest yesterday and have left her near to where they stopped to paint themselves. That's why they left so early today, and why they ran.' The others, it seems, replied: 'Let's go back. That's what they must have done. We will not take Napagnuma, but their women!'

They took bows and arrows and ran after those who had come to dance with them and had been their friends. It seems that towards evening they caught up with the Kashoraweteri and entered their *tapirí*. The Kashoraweteri grew afraid and their *tushaua* asked what they wanted. The Namoeteri, who were very numerous, did not answer and began to look among the *tapirí*. The Kashoraweteri *tushaua* shouted: 'Why do you come to search like this? You have entered without speaking to me. First the *tushaua* should have come in and spoken with me. I would have replied to whatever he asked.' The brother of the Namoeteri *tushaua* said: 'You must know. Those who left early this morning have found Napagnuma, who was a fugitive in the forest.' It seems that the chieftain replied: 'I saw no women with them. Four of our men, who had left at the same time as they did this morning, are here. They had left early, because, when we were coming to you, they had found an armadillo's hole and had closed it. Now today they have gone to catch the animal and smoke it.' Then, it seems, he called the four men and asked whether they had seen women or women's footprints. 'No,' they replied; 'neither women nor tracks of women along the mud of the *igarapé*, only our own footprints.' Then the Kashoraweteri shouted angrily: 'You, proud Namoeteri, should not have behaved like this with us, threatening to kill us.'

The Namoeteri went out without shooting and assembled along the *igarapé* nearby. There they decided to pursue the Mahekototeri. The *tushaua* Fusiwe ordered his men not to ask whether they had seen Napagnuma but to take the women, those young ones without children, and carry them out of the *tapirí*. They told me later that, when it was dark in the wood, they came to where the Mahekototeri had made their *tapirí*. They began to enter threateningly among the huts; the old men and women took fright and shouted: 'The enemy, the enemy, the Namoeteri, many of them!' So they took seven young women; one was even pregnant. They did not kill a single man, because, they said, the men had left their bows and arrows and fled into the woods.

At night I heard when the Namoeteri returned. The women were weeping; the men were saying: 'Don't cry; why do you weep for your men who are old and ugly? You, so young, live with old men whose hair is already white! Be happy! You will enjoy life with us, we are many, and we are strong; no one will be able to recapture you. You were never at peace with them, fleeing all the time for fear of the enemy.' I followed them and listened to them without letting myself be seen. Later I came close to the *shapuno*. The *tushaua* was saying in a loud voice: 'I have been on the attack; one of these women is for my brother. I have come from the Kashoraweteri; the old man said to me: "There's no woman here; Napagnuma is not here!" He was angry as he spoke to me. Does he think perhaps that I am afraid of him? If I had wanted my men to take all their women, I would have done it. I took pity on him, as he has other enemies, and I did not want to go on being his enemy.'

The next day I went away from the *shapuno* and came near to a *buriti* wood. When the ripe *buriti* fruit fall in the water, they go bad and attract fish. Among the holes, in the mud, near those trees there are the fish; two, even three, to every hole. It is easy to catch them; I caught them with my hands. That was the last day that I lived out in the forest.

CHAPTER 17

Fusiwe and Rashawe

They said that that day, while I was catching fish beneath the *buriti* tree, some men passed by, saw my tracks and found where I had made the fire and where I had been sitting. They followed my footprints and saw that they went round the *shapuno*; they told it to the *tushaua*. Then they told me that he was angry. 'It's her fault,' he said, 'if I am now the enemy of the Kashoraweteri, because I have had a search made inside their *tapirí*. It is her fault if I have made my young men capture women from the Mahekototeri. Now I want to see her footprints.'

I had cooked my fish near the *igarapé*; I had then jumped into the water and had walked quite a long way in the water. The *kupari* birds, those evil birds which sing when they see people, had seen me and had sung their song: *cau, cau, cau*! The *tushaua* had seen my footprints and the fresh fishbones, had heard the birds singing and had said: 'It is indeed she who is in these parts. These footprints go all around here; she cannot be far away.'

The *tushaua*, they said, returned to the *shapuno* and spoke to his mother: 'Mother, I have found the footprints of Napagnuma.' The mother—so they said—replied: 'If you catch her, don't kill her, because she is fleeing for fear, not through guilt. She is fleeing for fear of your arrows.' The father also said: 'Don't kill her, she is not to blame. It's not good to kill this kind of people: you are used to killing Yanoáma.' The *tushaua* replied to his mother: 'Tonight I will hide near the *igarapé*. If she is in these parts, she will come to drink in the same spot where we drink. The other water is a long way off.'

I had lain down; then when it was quite dark, perhaps eight o'clock, I got up and started to cook the fish which was ready in the leaves. The packages are made with five *pishaansi* leaves. Banana leaves are no good, because they burn too quickly and the fish remains uncooked; the *pishaansi* leaves, however, burn very slowly and the fish cooks. If the fishes are small, you put several together.

On the embers you can hear it boiling inside the leaves; the package rises and juice comes out. At the beginning it is actually blood, but then, when the first leaves are burnt, no more juice comes out and the fish is cooked.

I thought: 'Now I'll go and get water.' With two firebrands I set out quietly, passing through the two old *roças* and went down to the *igarapé*. I heard all those toads calling: *cro*, *cro*, *cro*. I did not know that at that dark hour, on the other side, the *tushaua* was waiting for me in hiding with a brother and another youth.

I left my brands in the bush and lowered myself into the water. I heard a noise and already the *tushaua* had caught me by one arm. 'Now you deserve to die!' he said. 'It's your fault that I went to capture the women of those who had come to my *reaho*. It's your fault that they are now angry with me.' He pushed me: 'Let's go to the *shapuno*!' The younger brother, who was still a boy, said to me: 'It is true; they have taken those women. One has escaped; the others are weeping in the *shapuno*.' I was afraid; I walked ahead. Behind me came the *tushaua*, who pushed me, then the brother and the other youth. I was ashamed and afraid to get there: 'Now they really will kill me, and nothing will save me!' I prayed as I walked.

We reached the *shapuno*: those who lived near the entrance had gone away. They were those who today are called Patanaweteri. The others said that before leaving they had said: 'You have taken the Mahekototeri women; they are friends of the white men. They will come with the whites to kill you.' About a hundred persons had stayed behind. As soon as we entered, the *tushaua* said to me: 'See, that part of the *shapuno* has been emptied; it is without braziers. They have left out of fear. You are responsible; if they come back with the white men, they will attack us and kill us.' He took me to the hearth where his oldest wife lived and said: 'Here is the woman about whom you always used to think. Be glad that she is now here, you who wanted to defend her!' The woman came near to me and said: 'Come.' I was weeping; near me one of those women whom they had stolen was weeping too. It was the pregnant one.

The *tushaua* went away. I heard him say to his mother: 'Mother, I have taken Napagnuma when she came to drink. She is over there, weeping, near my oldest wife.' The mother replied: 'Don't kill her. You already have four women; if you don't want her, bring her to me. She will stay with me until this last son of mine becomes a man.' The father said: 'Why do you want to kill her? She has no father, no brother, no one in these parts. It is not her fault if you have captured the Mahekototeri women. You captured them because you wanted to. No one had said that she was with the Mahekototeri. Your mother asked the women of the Mahekototeri, when they came to the feast: "Have you seen that white man's daughter who has run away from here?" They answered that they knew nothing. You have stolen other men's women because you wanted to steal them.'

Meanwhile a strong young man came up to the *tushaua*; he came from the other side of the *shapuno*. It was Rashawe (*rasha* means *pupugna*). He spoke as follows, while I listened: 'Brother-in-law, whom do you want to kill?' 'I have taken Napagnuma while she was drinking; now she is there, with my woman.' 'Why do you want to kill her?' 'I want to kill her, because she will escape again. She is responsible for the Mahekototeri now being our enemies. This is why I wish to kill her.' Rashawe continued: 'You are the greatest man in this *shapuno*, our chief, but listen to my advice. Do not kill her! She was going about alone in the forest, all alone for a very long time; when she arrived the first time, you remember, she was as thin as could be. Now she has grown into a woman: now you must let her live. Leave her with your oldest woman or with your mother, so that she may be a companion to your mother or to yourself. You will not kill a woman who is here without any relations. If you kill her, who will weep for her? Who will burn her? Who will take her ashes? It would be a great wrong to kill her.' Then the *tushaua* replied: 'You ask this of me; you ask me not to kill her. I will do as you ask.' Rashawe added: 'One day you will say to me: "It was true what you wanted. Take this banana *mingau* that she has prepared." That's what you will say to me one day.'

The two men approached me. The *tushaua* said to his oldest wife: 'Give a hammock to this companion of yours; she will stay with us. I wanted to kill her just now, but, while I was talking to my father, he came'—and he pointed to Rashawe who was standing nearby—'and he did not want me to do so.' Rashawe looked at me and asked me: 'Where were you going?' 'I was just walking around here,' I replied. 'Now don't run away again, stay with *Shoriwe* (brother-in-law). I have defended you, so that he should not kill you, but you must not run away.'

The *tushaua* went towards the corner of the roof lit up by the brazier and took an enormous bundle of well-worked *pupugna* wood. 'With this bundle,' he said, 'I wanted to kill you. This young man has defended you and has allowed you to live; from today consider him as your brother. I wanted to kill you, because owing to you I have taken these women and I have those enemies.' I listened and wept.

Rashawe said to me: 'Live always with him and with his family; do not run away again.' I did not reply, I only wept. Then, turning to the *tushaua,* he continued: 'I feel so sorry for her; my old father also feels so sorry for her. You are a great *tushaua*, but you have listened to my advice. My father loves this woman because she has no one. My father said: "She could live with us." You have found her in the woods, so treat her well, do no harm to her. She has been a lone fugitive in the forest for so long.' 'Do not run away any more,' he repeated to me. 'You have no relatives to escape to. The Mahekototeri are afraid. We ran after the Mahekototeri with our *tushaua* and we caught up with them. They nearly died of fright. The old women shouted, the old men shouted, and all the men ran away.' Rashawe was the *tushaua* of the Pishaanseteri: he had gone with Fusiwe and some of his men and he had come back with two Mahekototeri women. After a few days Rashawe and his Pishaanseteri returned to their *shapuno,* near their *roça,* in the centre of a mountain.

I stayed with the Namoeteri. From that day on I never escaped again. Fusiwe was tall and strong.

PART TWO

CHAPTER 18

Wife of Fusiwe

So I began to live together with Fusiwe's other four wives; we lived separately, but with our hearths near each other. The first and oldest wife, a Namoeteri of the Patanaweteri group, had a grown-up married daughter and a small daughter; her relations had moved away and gone to live alone; they were called Teteheiteri: she was the one who gave the orders to everyone else. Then came Sherekuma, the Aramamiseteri wife. Fusiwe had seized her as a child while she was bathing in an *igarapé*; his mother had brought her up. Another was a Hasubueteri: he had taken her after a feast while her people were returning to their *shapuno*. The fourth was a Namoeteri, the youngest and the prettiest: her name was Tokoma. Lastly there was myself.

They do not like to hear themselves called by name and I only got to know their names after a long time. Once the *tushaua* said: 'How come that they don't find nice names to give to their children? One wife answered: 'Your name too is ugly,' but I did not ask it I recall that one day, after I had been living with him for a long time and already had a son, a man said: 'Fusiwe has killed a tapir.' I asked: 'Whose name is that?' They answered me: 'Your child's father!' *Fusi* means lip. Fusiwe had a small son by the Hasubueteri wife, by name Komohiwe. I called him 'Father of Komohiwe,' the other woman called him 'My son's father'; the aunt called him 'My nephew's father.' I learnt the name of my sons' grandfather, Fusiwe's father, only after his death; his name was Hayamamukuwe (Deer's Eye). They may say the names of the small children, but when they grow up they no longer call them by name. Not even the women are called by name; they say 'Child's mother', if she has a son. When the person is absent, the others sometimes call him by name, but never if he is present. In battle they shout out the name because then they are enemies.

The Namoeteri were formed of the Namoeteri of Fusiwe, the Patanaweteri, the Gnaminaweteri and the Pishaanseteri. When they were together, Fusiwe was in command of them all; there were very many of them: much more than a hundred men with their wives and children. Fusiwe's old father had been chieftain, before his son, of that group which, even when it split up, continued to be called Namoeteri (*Namoe* is the name of a great mountain).

An uncle of Fusiwe, younger brother of the old man, who already had two Hekurá sons, was chief of the Patanaweteri, who were the most numerous. Then there were the Gnaminaweteri: their old chief always said: 'I want to go and live alone, *gnami*,' and this is why they were called 'the solitary people'. Rashawe, the one who had saved me, was of another family. He commanded the Pishaanseteri (*pishaansi* is a great leaf). His father too had been a headman; he was not the eldest son, but the strongest; the one who, they said, was the greatest Hekurá.

Near our *shapuno* were two big *roças*: one full of bananas, the other full of cotton, which I did not yet know, because the Shamatari do not cultivate it. One day Fusiwe said: 'The humming-birds are beginning to ruin the cotton on the plants and the rats to nibble that which has fallen to the ground; let's go and pick it.' We worked for three days, because we had to get it without even one dead leaf. It was not yet ripe and we put it on banana leaves in the *shapuno* compound in the sun and not near the fire, so that it would not go yellow. It is the men who plant cotton: they pull up the weeds in the *roças,* burn them and plant the seeds. They make a hole in the ground with a broken bow or with a pointed stick and put in two seeds. If too many germinate, they leave only two seedlings. They say that some people have a bad hand at planting; then the cotton grows too tall and gives little fruit.

The *tushaua* told me the story of the cotton: 'Once humming-birds were men and had cotton hammocks; to this day humming-birds steal cotton to make their nests. The Yanoáma saw those hammocks and asked *Tensho* (humming-bird) how they had prepared them. He then took them to his *roça* and showed them young plants; farther on he showed plants with fruit, and farther on still plants which had no more fruit left. Then he spoke thus: "Make a small *roça*; do not mix other plants, because they take away strength from the earth. Sow your seeds so that you get young plants, then plants with fruit, then old plants; in that way you will always have cotton." He returned to his home, gave the seeds to the Yanoáma and said: "When the plants are fairly tall, pinch the top out; thus the branches will grow stronger.' Then he took a long stick, a piece of *cuia* round and smooth at the bottom, and made a spindle and taught them to spin. When the men were changed into animals, then the Tensho too became humming-birds.'

The oldest wife loved me. Sometimes the others were against me; they wanted me to make their big knives and clothes because I was white and ought to know. They went to Fusiwe shouting, 'Hit her; she's a white and she doesn't make cooking pots or machetes for us.' The old headman of the Gnaminaweteri always defended me and said: 'I don't think that white women know how to make those big knives, no! Napagnuma is alone and does not know how they are made. Why do you want to hit her? Don't be angry with her, don't go on like that!' He was good. The women continued, 'She is a white woman, she must know; yet she doesn't want to make clothes, machetes, or cooking pots for us; hit her! If she doesn't know how to make them, it means that her father is not a white!' I answered: 'My father did not know how to make machetes; he didn't make them himself. He didn't know how to make clothes; he took them as payment for his work.' The *tushaua* did not tell me to make machetes or clothes, but he did not defend me when the others shouted. The old mother said: 'Why do you want him to beat her?'

At the time of the maize *reaho*, and when it was time to divide the ears of grain between the women of those who had come, the oldest wife had to share them out: she separated the short from the long ears, then said to me: 'You go on that other side and, when they have finished collecting them, divide them.' I did not want to, and said: 'I don't want to, because I should perhaps give more to one and less to another;' then I counted the ears of maize and gave the same number, fifty, to each. The old wife often said to me: 'You take charge.' When there was a shortage of wood, she said: 'There's no more wood, make the other women go and get some.' I said: 'Go and get wood and bring it here.' At first I did not want to be in command and I wept. If they answered me, 'Why don't you go?' I would say: 'They have ordered me to tell you, and that's why I tell you. I am not going, because they send you to do it.' 'What? You, who don't belong here, have to be in charge, and we who belong here must obey you?' I referred the matter to the oldest wife who said to me: 'If they talk to you like that again, warn the *tushaua*; he will put it all straight.' After I had been there some time, if the oldest wife was not present, I used to say to the other women: 'You go and get water, you prepare banana *mingau*.' The others obeyed. When there were women from other tribes, the old wife wanted me to accompany Fusiwe's other wives: 'Go with them,' she said, 'because, if they go by themselves, they start talking, they bathe together and they waste a lot of time. If you are there, the others won't come, because they are afraid that you will come and warn him. Don't you carry the big basket, but only a *cuia*.'

The *tushaua* had said to me: 'If you see any man put his hands on you or on your companions, do you know where death is?' 'No,' I replied. 'Get hold of him between the legs and squeeze him with all your might; you will see that he falls down dead.' In the *shapuno,* in general, men respect women. Then I said to the men: 'Be careful with me; don't think that I will catch you by the arms or by the neck; I'll catch hold of you right there and you will shout and shout but I will not let go of you.' They said that once a woman had killed a man in this way and had then run away to another *shapuno*. But there was a young girl, daughter of a Namoeteri father and a Shamatari mother, who was persecuted by men. She was afraid and always wanted me to accompany her every time to the *igarapé*. When I went with that young woman, the men would say to her: 'Why do you go with Napagnuma? What is she? Your mother or your husband?' One day we were in the forest with that girl, I, the *tushaua*'s daughter and that girl's aunt. Some men jumped upon her: the young girl clung to a tree-trunk and crossed her legs. The women pulled her from one side and the men from the other. The girl held herself tight to the tree but they pulled her off; she clung to another tree but they pulled her off that. The *tushaua*'s daughter defended her, but the men pushed her and sent her away. The poor girl shouted: 'Napagnuma, save me; I came out with you, I will always come with you, save me!' I left my basket and said to the men: 'I will kill you! You have poisoned arrows, but I am not afraid.' One said: 'Anyone who puts his hand here is in for trouble.' I went into their midst, took hold of the girl and said: 'Let go of that trunk; come away.' The men lacked the courage to do anything, while I shouted loudly: 'Pack of dogs, do you think perhaps that I am like those women who sit down and wait for you to finish? No, I'm not one of those. I am a woman, but I feel sorry for my woman companion.'

I entered the *shapuno* shouting in this way. They then began to ask each other: 'Who was it?' I pointed: 'There are their wives,' and they all asked anxiously: 'Have they done any harm to the girl?' 'No,' I replied, 'truly no! They tried to.' I was terribly angry and I thought my heart was bursting. I said to the young woman: 'You talk to everybody; a woman who already has a husband must not talk to everybody.' I was weeping with rage. The *tushaua* saw me, came up and asked me: 'Why are you crying? Who has made you cry? Now I'll try my *nabrushi*[1] on them. Who was it?' Meanwhile those men had arrived and answered: 'We have not laid a hand on Napagnuma nor on your daughter.' 'No, but you must not risk doing these things to women in their presence. You are a dirty lot.' He got a big *nabrushi,* scraped it and would have hit them on the head with it. Then he shouted and shouted: 'If you think you can do this in our *shapuno,* it is better for you to make a change. Go to the Hasubueteri, who are used to behaving like that with their women. If you do it once more, I will kill you. I will follow the women who go into the forest to gather fruit or to get crabs, and, if I hear shouts, I will run and kill you.'

Many women were always faithful, others not. It often happened that the mother, the father, or the brother-in-law said to the son of the betrayed man: 'Warn your father that your mother has gone with another man while he was out.' Sometimes the father replied: 'I don't mind; let her go with whom she pleases,' but often the man was jealous. I remember that one woman, who had her fire near us, offered banana *mingau* to her husband on his return. The man threw away the *mingau* and hit her on the head with his *nabrushi.* The old mother ran up shouting, but he said: 'She's like a bitch! While I am out, she does as she likes with other men.' Then he looked for the man who had betrayed him and did battle with him with blows from his *nabrushi.* The wife stayed with her husband; but every so often the husband remembered and hit his wife again on the head, saying: 'Go away, go away with that man of yours.'

There was another married woman who loved a man younger than her husband. She waited for her husband to go hunting a long way off and sent to tell the youth to meet her in the *roça.* When the husband came back he got to know of this and gave her so many beatings, and burnt her with live firebrands on the chest; her skin remained attached to the brands. But the woman who had this weakness said, 'He has beaten me; now I'll behave even worse.'

Fusiwe's mother talked with me a great deal: mothers-in-law don't like to talk to their sons' wives, but she told me so many things. She said that she was not afraid of me and that I must not be afraid of her, because she was very old. The men, on the other hand, were very much afraid of their mothers-in-law and said that, if they

[1] *Nabrushi*: stick or club for fighting.

looked at them, it was as if they saw a flash of lightning. She told me of an evil thing which sometimes happens amongst them. When the first son is born and dies, and the second is born and dies, and the third is born and dies, if the woman changes her man, the son who is then born does not die. Sometimes the babies are born very yellow; then they say that the father has eaten the ashes of a dead man only recently prepared. For this reason, when the wife is pregnant, they do not eat the ashes of their dead.

One woman always had children who were born very yellow and then died. An old Hekurá inhaled *epená* and said to the husband that, if he wished to have children, he must send his woman with another man. The husband disapproved of this and refused, but I heard the old man say: 'I am not saying anything wicked; I am giving you advice for having children. You should not go with your wife any more, because it is your fault if the baby dies.' But that man refused to follow this advice and the children continued to be born yellow and afterwards to die. I remember three other occasions when the husbands arranged with other men to have children. One woman did not want to go with the man chosen by her husband and came to weep with us, because her husband wanted her to go and beat her.

There were some women who were friendly with each other, but the others found this very repulsive. One day some girls were saying to one: 'That is your woman.' The girl's mother listened and said nothing; it was a girl who did not want men and fled from them. Some time later the same girl was asking her girl friend to go with her to collect wild *caju* in the forest; the other girls wanted to go, but this one said: 'No, we are going on our own, because you never collect anything.' The others answered: 'Go on your own, then, for you are husband and wife!' Then the mother took a stick, ran after her daughter, knocked her down and gave her such a rain of blows.

They have a great feeling of modesty when a man goes with a woman. The *tushaua*'s mother gave him much advice. When we were all together, I often heard her say to her son: 'Son, there are many women here; this one has no child, that one has a child already, that one has grown children. When you go into the forest, take with you that one who has no child; when her belly is very large and she is about to have a baby, leave her in the *shapuno* and take with you only the one who has no child, for the children must not see.' Fusiwe replied: 'Mother, you are making me feel so ashamed.' 'No, my son, this is no shame. I tell you this, so that the other women shall not be angry when you invite one of them. I repeat this to you in the presence of all: do it in secret and don't let anyone see you.' He listened and did not reply; then he too said that the children must not see.

We lived happily in those days; in our *roças* there was much tobacco. They let the tobacco dry over the fire and take away the hard part which is like a stem in the centre of the leaf. They leave a part of the stalk which is used to hang it high up over the fire. When the leaves are dry, they throw away the piece of stalk as well and keep the leaves one on top of another. Some tie the bundle of leaves with thin lianas, so that the wind does not blow them away. Then they line a basket carefully and fill it with leaves and begin to use those which are a bit spoilt. Before using them, they put them in a *cuia* with a little water; then, near the fire, they mix the leaves with ashes until they are dry again. Generally they take three leaves, beat them to remove the ashes and then roll them one over another. If the leaves are very long, they double them over several times, until they make a big long sausage which they put under their lower lip.

The women also put it in their mouth; but I always refused to do this. I made a kind of cigarette and smoked it: Fusiwe said to me: 'If you wish you may smoke in the evening when it is dark; but don't let the others see you.' Even he was annoyed by the smell of smoke. Sometimes the women prepare the ball of tobacco and first put it in their own mouth and so have it ready to pass to their husbands. There are some men who don't like this, who find it sickening and, if the woman has already put it in her mouth and passes it to them, throw it away saying: 'Prepare me another one.' I used to prepare it for Fusiwe.

Fusiwe told me the story of tobacco: 'When animals were people, one day *Washo*[1] met a Yanoáma man and invited him to try tobacco; the man found it good. Then Washo took the tobacco seeds, which he kept in a little bamboo tube, just as it is kept today. He put some in a *micuemi* leaf and said: "Make a fire in the *roça* with *cupim* which burns easily. After three days, blow these seeds on the burnt earth and just cover them slightly; when the young plants show, transplant them and protect them from the sun with big leaves, but not completely. When the days of one hand have gone by (five days), if the seedlings are healthy, take off the leaves you have put on top and leave the young plants in the sun. With the

[1] *Washo*: a bat.

sun you will be able to have strong tobacco; with rain the tobacco will be weak." To this day the Yanoáma plant their tobacco in this way; the men invoke Hekurá of Washo and say: 'It is not I, it is Washoriwe who is planting.'

One day Fusiwe said to me: 'The Hekurá have told me that white men put their dead under the ground. Is this true?' 'Yes,' I replied, 'I have never seen white men burn their dead.' 'Then it really is true.' He added, 'Once we attacked a white man's hut, but the whites had fled. One of us said, "The whites, when one of them dies, make a hole in the ground and put into the hole, together with the dead man, all the things he had before he died, machetes, knives. . . ." We dug; we found a corpse all swollen, inside a hollow trunk, but nothing around it. Then we covered it up again.' I replied: 'No, they don't put anything near the dead man.'

Then I asked him: 'Why do you not also put your dead in the ground? That is what they did where I lived as a child with my father.' Fusiwe answered: 'If the body remains there, with the earth weighing on its chest, Poré cannot get out. You put your relatives under the ground and the worms eat them; you do not love your dear ones.' 'Yes,' I replied, 'you burn your relations, children, grown-ups, old people; it's not enough for you that they are dead, you also roast them in the fire.' Then he took a stick and ran after me; I fled laughing. Then he called me back, saying: 'Come here, come and talk quietly; you are talking very loudly.' I stopped and looked at him; I thought: 'If I run away, he will think that I am running away because I am afraid; I must finish what I have to say.' I went back and said: 'When you die, I will make a big hole in the ground and put you in it.' The *tushaua* laughed and I went to get wood in the forest. When I returned, I sat down near him in my hammock: 'Why did you run after me with a stick?' I asked. 'What did I tell you? I told you to do as the whites do, as my people do; this should not have made you run after me with a stick.' 'But you too make me angry,' he said; 'You speak and answer with a voice that is louder than a man's.' 'Yes, it is true,' I then said. 'You burn the body, then you collect up the bones and crush them. Even after he's dead, you make him go on suffering. Then you put the ashes in banana pap and eat them. Then after you have taken them, you finish up by going into the forest to do your dirty business; those bones still have to go that way.' The *tushaua* looked at me seriously and said: 'I hope no one has heard what you have said.'

They believe that people go on living after death. Fusiwe's mother used to say to me: 'I want to die, so as to go to the Thunder's *shapuno* and live in peace; I am tired of suffering in this world.' I asked: 'Is it really true that Thunder has a home?' 'Yes, it's true, it's true,' she would reply. 'My grandmother, my great-grandmother used to tell, and I used to listen. Those who lose their senses and appear to die and then come to life again, tell us these things. After death, the son of the Thunder calls the shade: "Come over here." The son of the Thunder stands on a mountain, near the Thunder's *shapuno*. The path that leads to him is not beautiful; a beautiful path, all surrounded with flowering trees, goes downhill a long way off and you cannot see the end of it. At the far end of this road, the earth is covered with fresh and beautiful leaves, which hide a precipice where there is boiling resin: they call it Shopariwake. Near the Thunder live all our dead: they are painted and they are more beautiful than when they were in this world, because now they have become Peikeneporebe. The Thunder is great, and handsome as the *tushaua*,' said the *tushaua*'s mother, 'he has a *shapuno* like that of the Yanoáma. The souls who live there do not work the *roça,* nor do they think about doing anything; they all eat avocado and *mukama,* which is that little black fruit of the forest, because the trees are full of fruit: there are lovely girls and you smell only the most scented flowers. They all find their own dead, if in life they were good. They are all young, and never suffer pain or sickness. If they were not good, when they come near to the Thunder and ask: "Where is my mother, or my father?" they reply: "They are there; they have gone to Shopariwake." Those who have been wicked in life do not listen to the call of the Thunder's son; they enter upon the beautiful road. When they come to the precipice covered with beautiful leaves, they fall into Shopariwake, without realizing it. They will stay there for ever, shouting, without being able to get out; and they will never see their dear ones again.' This was also the story that Fusiwe told me.

Sometimes, when it was not raining, but you could hear far off that noise of a thunderstorm, they used to say: 'It's the dead who are boiling inside Shopariwake, weeping and shouting. Listen to them; they are wicked people like you! Poor things! How hot it must be in there!' I used to say to those who killed: 'You, evil men, will go into the fire of Shopari.' 'No,' they replied, 'it will not be us who will go.' My son's father used to say to me: 'You will go, because when anyone takes your *cuia* or your other things, you protest and shout. If anyone wants your bananas you are jealous of them; you are jealous of all your things and you will not give them away. Those who have and who reply to those who ask: "I have nothing; if I had it I would give it," those who have and do not give to him who asks and is hungry, they are the ones who will go to Shopariwake. This is the worst sin of all.' The old woman used to say: 'I am very frightened of Shopariwake, and so I give away everything that they ask of me.'

CHAPTER 19

The Surrendered Wife

We, the women of Fusiwe, went fishing one day in a distant *igarapé*; in the evening, when we came back, each one of us lit her own fire. We had caught a lot of fish and we cooked our parcels of leaves with the fish inside. The Hasubueteri wife had a little son and a daughter who was slightly bigger; while I was cooking my fish, the little boy began to cry. Fusiwe asked: 'Why is he crying?' 'I don't know,' I replied, 'he was eating fish eggs.' Then the *tushaua* went up to the fire and blew on it strongly to make light: 'Don't blow like that,' I said; 'there are packets with fish eggs on the fire and by doing that you burn the leaves of the packets.'

He went to look for the child's mother, and called her: 'Shabottami.' The woman was not there. Fusiwe asked me: 'Where has she gone? Have you seen where she has gone?' 'I don't know, she is not my daughter and I am nobody's guardian,' I answered. Then Fusiwe took the little boy and said to the other Aramamiseteri wife: 'You, take her hammock, go to all the hearths without letting anyone see you; as soon as you hear her voice, give her the hammock. Whoever she is with, my brother or anybody else, give her the hammock and tell the man with whom she is staying: "My husband gives you the hammock and the woman, so that she may stay with you always, seeing that you are pleased to talk together; let her never come back."'

The woman untied the hammock, went and found the other wife who was in fact talking to the *tushaua*'s younger brother, around his fireplace; she did not have the courage to say anything. Soon after she came back saying: 'I haven't found her; I don't know where she is.' 'Haven't you found her?' shouted Fusiwe; he then took a big *nabrushi* and gave her a very savage beating. The woman shouted and fell. 'Where is she?' continued Fusiwe. 'She's there, with your brother.' 'Why haven't you handed over the hammock?'; he gave the woman three more terrible blows and then, with the same *nabrushi,* went towards the other younger wife and hit her hard on the head; that woman, too, fell down. I thought he would not strike me, but instead he gave me a hard blow with the *nabrushi* which made me fall down; I got up again and ran away to where his mother was and squatted down behind the old woman.

The mother shouted: 'Why are you quarrelling among yourselves like this? You have come back from the forest with your fish and you should now be eating happily together, but instead one runs away and another weeps. And you? Why do you go on like this with the women? Go and lie down; your father says: "Man is the son of woman, and so he must not beat her." Do you no longer remember what your father says? You have struck even Napagnuma and I don't want you to maltreat her, Napagnuma is the one who obeys me most of all.' I was weeping. When his mother told him off, Fusiwe remained silent all the time and obeyed; but his brother never listened to his mother. Then Fusiwe said to his mother: 'You protect these women.' 'Yes, I protect them, because I know that when I have some little wound, I feel pain. They too are humans like me, like you.' Then the *tushaua* went away.

A little later the old woman said to me: 'Go now and cook your fish; he won't strike you again.' I had a big swelling where he had hit me and I went back to my hammock weeping. Then Fusiwe said to me: 'It's her fault; of course I did not think of hitting you. I hit you because I was so angry, for the child was crying. Now you, Napagnuma, go and take her the hammock, so that she lives over there from now on. Perhaps my brother will not find another wife and so he will be glad to live with her.'

I took her hammock and said: 'Yes, I'll take it to her; I don't want to be beaten again through her fault; I've had enough already, and if she comes back I'll be the one to hit her.' I walked slowly, limping, because my leg hurt me. The *tushaua*'s brother was eating bananas, lying in his hammock. 'Here is her hammock,' I said to him, and, looking at the woman, I went on: 'Her son's father has sent the hammock so that she may live here always with you and never go back to him. She has left her packet of fish over there and now she has come here. Let her stay here.' The woman answered: 'I had come to bring him the wood for which he had asked me.' 'Has he by chance no mother,' I replied, 'who can give him wood? Then, when one brings wood to someone who has asked for it, one leaves it and comes away at once; that's what I do and I do not behave like you. Because of you I have been beaten, and if you come back tomorrow, I will bring your hammock back here.'

The woman remained silent. The man became serious and shouted: 'I don't want her.' Then he threw the hammock on the ground and said: 'Take it back to him and tell him that I don't want the woman!' I picked up the hammock and replied: 'No, you like the woman; if you didn't like her, you would not have kept whispering, but you would have said: 'Go back at once, for your son is crying'; I then threw the hammock on the woman.

Meanwhile the *tushaua*'s mother, who had come up to us, began to shout: 'I don't want an old woman for my son; I don't want an old woman for my son; I don't want a lazy woman for my son. Son, take the hammock to where she lives. I don't want this lazy woman for you; she waits for the others to go and get water so that she may then drink!' The *tushaua*'s sister also said: 'I don't want this woman for my brother! I have asked for a young woman for him; I have already spoken with the mother and that one must be his wife.' 'Let him stay with them both,' said I. Meanwhile the man continued to say, 'I don't want her, I don't want her, I don't want her.'

I went back to the *tushaua*; behind me came also his mother who said to him: 'Why have you sent the hammock? I don't want that woman for my other son.' Fusiwe replied: 'Mother, let her stay with him; let her live with him as he has no other woman. In the meantime let him take this one; when she is older still, he will look for another, younger one.' The mother answered: 'But I think you are jealous of her and that's why you have sent to give her the hammock.' 'If I had been jealous, I would not have sent the hammock, but I would have struck your son and the woman with my *nabrushi*. I am certainly not jealous of my brother; I think, poor brother, he has no wife and I have so many, I'd better give him one of mine. For days I have been thinking about it and now today I have my opportunity.' Then his mother went up to him and said quietly: 'Then, if that's how it is, you should give him another one, the youngest; otherwise everybody will say that you have given him the oldest.' Then that woman came back with us.

CHAPTER 20

Hallucinatory Drugs

One day four men and two women arrived in the *shapuno*: they were Konakunateri and they spoke with an accent somewhat different from that of the Namoeteri. Some time later other Konakunateri came back: there was also a young woman, the wife of one of them. The Namoeteri took her and said to the husband: 'Don't you do anything, or we'll kill you immediately.' The husband and the other men went away. The Konakunateri lived a long way off, in the heart of the *Kunakuna* mountain (mountain of the ant). To reach them it was necessary to pass near the *shapuno* of the Aramamiseteri and the Mamupatukaiubeteri. Before I knew him the *tushaua* had made war on the Konakunateri to steal women.

Once some Namoeteri went hunting and killed three wild boars: on the way back, when they separated, they gave only one boar's foot to one huntsman, who was a Pishaanseteri. This man said: 'What? You give me only one foot? There were three wild boars! I am not a dog.' He threw the meat away, took a *nabrushi* and hit his companion over the head. The man fell, got up again and hit the first man on the head; thus began the fight. Then the others took their *nabrushi,* which they always have ready, hidden under the roof, and started to fight. Eventually all the Pishaanseteri went away from the *shapuno.*

After a long time they decided to become friends again and invited themselves. When they arrived, the men said: 'Now take banana *mingau* calmly, for if you begin to inhale *epená,* someone will go almost mad, and will run about and knock over the big bark vessels with *mingau* in them.' When they had finished eating, they took away the pots and the remaining things. The following morning, about eight o'clock, after having sung all night, the *tushaua* and the other men began to paint themselves black. The *tushaua* said: 'Bring some *epená.*' Then one man came and poured *epená* powder into that kind of earthenware plate, and another came and poured *epená*; all those who were Hekurá poured their own *epená*. Then the *tushaua* shouted: 'Now let's take *epená,* and when we are drunk, then we will talk just amongst ourselves.'

Those who had come, left the *shapuno* to go out and paint themselves black with coal, without *urucú*. The women began to be afraid. It was the first time I saw it and I asked: 'Why are they so afraid?' When those who had come to the feast had painted themselves black and decorated themselves with feathers, the *tushaua* shouted from inside: 'Come.' Then they began to go inside in line.

The smallest boys came first, and they too were painted black, each one with a *nabrushi*; they shouted: '*Hai, hai, hai. . . .*' They did not come near the *epená*. Behind them came the bigger boys with bigger *nabrushi*; they too shouted: '*Hai, hai, hai, ho, ho, ho . . .*' and they struck the ground hard with their *nabrushi*; then came the men. Then, with those thin canes which have a little hole on one side treated with resin, they began to blow *epená* into their noses. The hosts first blew *epená* into the noses of their guests. Sometimes they even blow into the nostrils of young boys. After all those from outside had come in, the young men who had to fight on home ground arrived; each with his *nabrushi* and his bow. One shouted: '*Hai, hai, hai . . .*'; another: '*Hochea, hochea . . .*', and another: '*Hi, hi, hi . . .*'; yet another: '*Fu, fu, fu . . .*'; all in a row. The others, who had already taken *epená* and were beginning to feel stunned, started to blow the powder into the noses of those who were standing in line; one received *epená* and went away, the next received *epená* and went away, and so on.

After half an hour the youngest began to shout; their older comrades said: 'Don't shout boys, stay seated, bow your heads and resist . . .' But they did not resist and shouted. One stood up, ran forward and said: 'Mother! My mother is dead!' while the mother was right there, following him to hold him. Another shouted, 'Father! Father! Where are you running?' but the father was not running. The women tried to hold them, but generally they did not succeed. Another shouted: 'Mother! Mother! The *shapuno* is spinning round me'; or, 'My father is standing on his head.' The bigger ones said, 'Resist, don't do that!' Yet another one said, 'You have huge faces, enormous teeth!' It was frightening: some youths and old men had become almost mad; they ran out, took those thorny branches and struck anyone who stood near; others came shouting and wanted to shoot arrows. The women ran in all directions to hide. I hid behind the posts.

When they were half drunk with *epená*, those of the *shapuno* said: 'You are upset, we are upset, we must calm ourselves', and then they began the fight. Two men stood opposite each other; the first raised his bent arm and the man on home ground gave him the first blow with his closed fist, a very powerful blow on the chest. Sometimes they gave even two or three blows one after the other, then said: 'Now you,' and the other returned the blows. Some fell after three or four blows. Some raised their leg and rested the foot behind the knee and then gave the blows, and others crouched down opposite each other and gave their blows.

They had prepared *nabrushi* which were thicker at the end which strikes and thinner at the end they hold in their hands. They wanted to fight in order to become friends again. They choose *nabrushi* of heavy wood and they prefer them not very long, because, often, with long *nabrushi* they cannot hit each other well on the head, but hit on the arms instead. There is a plant, they say, that makes men grow afraid; it has long leaves and small roots. The old women scrape that plant and the men mix the scraped part with *urucú* to spread on their *nabrushi*. They say that, if they hit a man on the head with a *nabrushi* soiled with those roots, he falls down at once; if he stands up again, his legs tremble on account of that plant.

They began in twos, but if one fell, his brother came to take his place, or his brother-in-law, or his father-in-law. If four, five, or six gathered around one man, the *tushaua* said, 'No, no, the contest is for two only; stand aside. He who has fallen must avenge himself.' They picked up the fallen man, threw water on his head, pulled his ears, wiped the blood, picked him up again and gave him the *nabrushi* once more. Then the other leaned on his *nabrushi* and awaited the blow, lowering his head. They must strike in that part where the head is shaven. They strike their blows by holding the *nabrushi* in two hands. While they struck they said to each other: 'I sent to call you to see whether you are a real man. If you are a man, let us now see if we become friends again and if our anger passes . . .' The other replied: 'Say so, say so, hit me, and we'll be friends again.' When one fell down and did not stand up again, the others carried him away. The women took fright, the old mothers shouted: 'Eat him, then, eat him! You want to kill him to eat him!' Each man had only one opponent at a time. Even the small boys had other small boys as opponents and they beat those of the same age.

After the *nabrushi* they took axes; they had seized them a long time before from a group of rubber workers. The *tushaua* gave two blows with the blunt end to the man who stood opposite him, on one side of his chest, and the other fell. He was replaced by his brother, who gave in return four blows on the *tushaua's* chest, but Fusiwe did not fall. Then Fusiwe said: 'Now you fight your best,' and gave him two blows. The youth grew very pale and fell down. The women ran and picked him up. Another brother came and gave the *tushaua* many blows on the chest with his axe; but the *tushaua* was strong and resisted. He gave the blows in return and the other fell. Finally there came Rashawe's brother, whose name was Maharashiwe, and he said: 'You fight well with those who are younger and who have not your strength. Now try with me!' The *tushaua* raised him arm and the other gave him blows, tuk, tuk, tuk. 'Go on,' said Fusiwe, 'carry on with the axe until you knock me down.' Maharashiwe delivered blow after blow, but the *tushaua* did not fall. 'Enough, now, that's enough,' said the bystanders. Then Fusiwe picked up his axe and with a few blows on the chest knocked Maharashiwe down.

Then came Rashawe, the most *waiteri*, the most courageous, the man who had defended me. 'Now it is my turn,' he said, 'just try on me.' Already five young men had fallen under Fusiwe's blows. The *tushaua* struck him with his axe on one side and then the other, but Rashawe did not fall; Rashawe was indeed strong. Then he returned the blow. They strike each other and the blows increase in strength until one falls. I was standing to one side looking on with that other wife. In the end Fusiwe sat down and vomited warm blood from his mouth.

When they had all finished beating each other, they remained friends and said: 'We have beaten you hard and you have beaten us hard. Our blood has flowed, we have caused your blood to flow. I am no longer troubled, for our anger has passed.' If anyone dies, it is a different matter.

As soon as the fight was over, the *tushaua* said: 'Now go your way, here is the meat, here is the rest,' and he had baskets of meat, of *pupugnas* and of maize given to them. 'If you are tired and cannot walk, sleep near the *shapuno* or sleep tonight with us; you will then leave tomorrow. We have fought by hand, with the axe, with *nabrushi*, not to be enemies, but to calm down our wrath. I sent to fetch you in order to calm you down with a fight. I had learned that you were against me and I don't want to be your enemy, because we are the same race.' Fusiwe's brother, too, said: 'Do not continue to be angry. We have called you to be friends. We sent for you because your boys have called my name, have shouted my name. We made you come so that we could test you. If you are not men fit to fight by hand, it will be a battle with arrows. It is better that from today on there shall be no more anger between us, that no wicked words are spoken between us, because we are not the men to fight with arrows.'

The *tushaua* Fusiwe beat himself often; he became all swollen and purple. Where he pushed his finger in, there remained a hole in his flesh. Then he spent the nights groaning and not sleeping. They fought, they beat each other, I don't know why; they said it was in order to be more peaceful and to be friends.

One day the men had all gone hunting; the *tushaua's* daughter said to me, 'I want to prepare my father's *epená*.' The women and children are not allowed to touch bamboo tubes or those *cuias* with a small mouth, in which the men keep their *epená*. A woman may touch them only when her husband says to her: 'Go, get me the *cuia*.' She heated the pot, rubbed it, filtered it and said: 'Let us inhale to see what its smell is like.' We drew up into our noses that powder which goes straight to the head. For those who are not used to it it burns like a pepper. I think I inhaled it four times; then I sat down. I felt unwell, stunned; when I stood up, my feet would not move properly. I said to her: 'If I take any more, I shall not stand up again.' She took more than I did. She did not inhale directly like me, but she got another woman to blow that powder into her nose through one of those canes that the men use. 'This *shapuno* is moving all round me,' she said afterwards.

We went down to the *igarapé* to bathe. I did not go into the water, I was too stunned. I understood what they said, but I felt that if I had taken any more I would no longer have understood anything. I kept going about in a dazed state, with my feet weighing heavily; this all lasted perhaps an hour, but my head kept on aching for a long time. 'Are you still stunned?' the *tushaua's* daughter asked me. 'Less now, but my head aches,' I replied. I only tried it that once; it was *epená* of tree-bark, not the strong kind made of seeds.[1]

Epená when ready is a greenish-grey powder, very light, which

[1] These Yanoáma hallucinatory powders, studied by the author in collaboration with Marini-Bettolo (see Biocca, *Viaggi tra gli Indi*) are prepared with plants of the genus *Piptadenia*, *Virola*, etc. and are very rich in alkaloids active on the central nervous system.

they keep often in bamboo quivers. The Shamatari, the Namoeteri and the others who live near them prepare *epená* from forest plants, not from cultivated plants. They seek the *epená* tree, which has big leaves and branches that grow out in a circle around the trunk, and they scrape, from the inside of the smooth, yellowish bark, long, very thin, resistant strips which they dry first in the sun and then by the fire. They use the inside part of the bark of that tree with big leaves also to cure the skin disease which they here call *curuba*: it burns terribly on the wounds.

There is another tree, with small leaves, which they call *hama-azita*. They take the bark of this tree, dry it in the sun, break it into little pieces and then, with firebrands, burn it on the outside and take it away from the heat so that it does not turn completely black. Then, with their hands held tightly between their legs, they rub hard the fibres of the *epená*, dried in the sun and the heat, with the singed fragments of the *hama-azita*. In this way they obtain a very fine powder, to which they add a strongly smelling herb called *mashi-hiri*, which is also dried first in the sun and then by the heat of the fire.

Even stronger is the *epená* which some tribes prepare with the dark seeds of a plant which does not grow very high. On a big leaf called *miuma-hena*, they drop the fine ashes of the bark of the tree known as *hama-hahi*, then take those seeds, like beans, of a plant that is not very tall and rather red, drying them slowly over the fire; they rub them between their hands over some big leaves together with those ashes. Those seeds are always somewhat damp, so they keep adding new ashes to dry the mixture, but they never put too many, for otherwise, they say, they cause injuries in the nose. They drop this mixture onto a piece of hot earthenware, and it disintegrates with the heat. The little pieces go pa, pa, pa as they jump. If they jump very much it means that the *epená* is strong. Then, with a piece of smooth stone, they rub on that piece of terracotta until it all becomes a very fine powder. While they are rubbing, the powder grows cold. They filter the powder and collect it on another leaf; then they put back on the heated fragment of terracotta the pieces which are not filtered, until they become almost red. When they begin to cool down, they rub them again and then mix this powder with the other.

The Namoeteri did not have those plants with the fruit and had the seeds given them by the others. Once the *tushaua* Fusiwe planted them on one part of the mountain, after having cut down the trees.

I remember that one day, perhaps four years later, he came carrying a little basket with the beans in it. He said to me: 'Look at this *epená* which I have planted; the plants are still small, but laden with fruit; the mountain is very good!' I went with him and saw the plants full of fruit.

They say that it was Omawe who taught the Yanoáma how to prepare *epená*. Omawe was carrying his bamboo, with *epená* in it, hanging on his back. The *tushaua* said to me: 'I am doing as Omawe did: I hang my little bamboo full of *epená* on my back.' Sometimes, when they travel or go hunting, they say: 'I must carry my *epená* against those spirits, so that they do not persecute us.' Then, instead of carrying it in the bamboo tube or in the *cuia,* they put the *epená* in a packet of leaves tied tight, which they tie round their neck. They take *epená* in the night if they hear the noises of those spirits of the forest. They inhale it to drive them away, as the priests here do when they give benediction.

I wanted to know who was Omawe. Near the *roça* of the Namoeteri, in the wood, on the high mountain, there were many *pupugna* trees. While we were standing under those trees, Fusiwe's old mother told me this story: 'No one knows when Omawe and Yoawe were born. It was Omawe who taught men to shoot and to avoid arrows, by throwing oneself to the ground, or jumping on one side. Omawe was good, Yoawe no: he did evil to others. Omawe knew how to do everything. When he wished to make fish appear, many fish appeared. When a Yanoáma died, Omawe took that dead body, shook it, pulled one of its arms or an ear, and the dead body returned to this world. Time passed; the Yanoáma set themselves against Yoawe and Omawe. Then Yoawe said to his brother: "I will prepare *mamocori* to kill all these people. I want to kill them all, without letting them see who it was who has killed them." Omawe replied: "They must not be killed with *mamocori*. I will make the water rise to kill them." Then Omawe prepared a kind of raft to save himself. With a bow he made a hole and water gushed out which flooded everywhere; even these *pupugna* trees, which are so tall, went under the water. The seeds floated to the surface and when the river began to dry up, the seeds began to sprout; this is why they have the *pupugna* trees in the forest. When all was under water and not even the forest could be seen, Omawe and Yoawe began to go down river with that kind of canoe that still stands across there, where the river ends. While they were going downstream the great raft spun round and the sons of Yoawe wept. Even today the Shapori sing: "The sons of Yoawe are going weeping towards the bottom. Their weeping is disappearing; already they are far away." Yoawe answers: "My sons, my sons, do not weep. The sons of Yoawe are Parimi, are eternal, are like the Hekurá." Omawe and Yoawe grow old; their sons too grow old, but they never die. They are always down there, singing with the Hekurá, where the great river ends. *Mukakao* is that great river which flooded everything. When it rains hard and begins to flood, they say: "Can it be that Mukakao is coming and the water will increase as it did once and will it submerge everything?" '

When the old woman finished telling me this story, I said to her: 'If I had been born a man, I would have gone to where this river ends, to see whether it is true.' 'The river is very big,' she answered. 'Here there are only *igarapé*, but the river is always bigger. It was Omawe who made the river large, where there are animals of enormous size that swallow people; there are *Rahara*, *Waikugna*,[1] and huge fishes. At the mouth of the river, there is the raft on which they cross. Omawe and Yoawe live down there, because they are not dead; they never die.' I thought: 'Can it be true what this old woman is telling me?' I asked the other women and they replied: 'It is so.' I have now told these stories to my father, who has said to me: 'Who knows? They believe these things which their grandparents have told them; perhaps it is true.'

[1] *Rahara* is a mythological serpent and *Waikugna* is the anaconda.

CHAPTER 21

The Amahini, Spirits of the Wood

One day a child went out of one of the big entrances of the *shapuno*. As soon as the mother noticed that her son had wandered away, she asked: 'Where is my son? Has he gone to the *igarapé* with the other children?' They searched and searched for him, but he was not there and the other children had not seen him. The father, who was the son of the *tushaua's* uncle, asked: 'Have you by chance seen my son? Has he by chance come here?' The man was so terrified, he was going about like a madman. It was his first son. During the night he went with his mother, his wife, and his brother to look for the boy with lighted torches in the forest, calling out in desperation: 'Shamatari, Shamatari.' The little boy's mother was a Shamatari and they called the child Shamatari. In the morning they came back to the *shapuno*. They had gone a long way, as far as the bank of a big river, because they thought the 'enchanted ones', who live in their beautiful *shapunos* under the water, had seized him and taken him with them. These 'enchanted ones', whom they see when they inhale *epená*, would abduct men, girls and children; they would take them under water and never let them go.

For three days they sought the child. After three days they decided to go afar, towards the source of the *igarapé*, where the water rises from a muddy hole. We always used to go to those parts to get wild cocoa fruit, because the *igarapé*, small and pretty, had a steep bank full of cocoa trees. They said afterwards that, near those springs, they at last saw the child sitting on a tree-trunk. He was all painted with white mud, with lines like serpents on his body, his cheeks and his chin. The father said in a whisper: 'Look! Shamatari is sitting down there.' The mother called him; the child looked and fell into the water of the *igarapé*. They ran and reached that spot; but there was nothing there. But the child's footprints were there, on that little muddy beach. The woman called; the others called. Those who were searching nearby came, and they too saw the child's footprints.

One who passed by that way later said that he heard the child crying and calling: 'My mother, my mother. . . .' He ran, but saw nothing. On the fourth day the old Shapori said that the *Amahini*, those of the water, had stolen the child and taken him with them. The Amahini are tiny little men who live underground. The following morning they went back to look for the child, while it was still dark, saying: 'Who knows? Perhaps they are accustomed to appear early in those springs of the *igarapé*.' They told how, when daylight came they again saw the child sitting in the same place, all painted. During the night the Shapori had taken *epená* and blown it on the *Amahini* to keep them away. The tree trunk on which the boy was sitting above the *igarapé* was swaying and the child was holding on to a branch with his hands. The men approached silently, went behind without letting the boy see them, and when they were close, the father took a leap and caught him by one arm. Fusiwe, who was searching in another direction, heard the shouts and ran there: the little boy was there, all painted.

Then they told how the *Amahini* beat him all the time with lianas. He was all purple on the bottom, on the back, on the legs. They asked him: 'What were you eating?' The child was intelligent, but could not yet talk; he simply said: '*Nape, hape* (mamma, father)'; but he already knew how to walk well and shoot arrows with his little bow. The last day, the 'enchanted ones' had not painted him with white mud, but with streaks of red *urucú* on his body.

The boy grew bigger, but remembered nothing. His father took him hunting, but made him climb trees every time he had to chase the animals, since he was afraid that the *Amahini* would come back and capture him. His mother often burned peppers and threw their smoke over him to protect him.

The *tushaua* Fusiwe was a great Shapori: he knew so many songs, he knew all the Hekurá. The Hekurá spirits live in the mountains. In the great mountains live also the daughters of the Hekurá; they are the Hekuragnuma, lovely young girls, splendid with designs on their faces and bodies. He would say to us women: 'Do you think that the Hekuragnuma are like you? No, they are very beautiful. They have the scent of that sweet white flower of the forest. When one smells that scent, all hunger and thirst disappear.' They did not invoke the Hekuragnuma to help them in war, but they invoked them to cure the sick, that they might pass their hands over bodies hot with fever and over parts that gave pain, and so drive away the sickness.

Against the enemy, on the other hand, they used to invoke the Hekurá of the great anteater; with their hands they carried behind them a palm leaf, like a tail. When they invoked the Hekurá of the wild pig, they went to make themselves dirty wherever they saw ashes, filth, banana skins; they mixed the whole lot up around the *shapuno,* as though they were really wild pigs. When Fusiwe was departing, he said that he was not taking all his Hekurá with him, but only two or three; Wakariwe, Okoriwe, or Pashoriwe (Hekurá of the great armadillo, of the small armadillo and of a monkey). He left the others to protect the *shapuno.*

The Hekurá of the anaconda, Waicugnariwe, is invoked during storms; they say: 'Come, Waicugnariwe, you who have strength enough to hold up the trees; twist yourself around their trunks and do not let the wind break them.' They also call upon the Hekurá of spiders, Hamoriwe, Waikosheweiriwe, that they may spin their webs around the plants and protect them: 'You are small, but you have so much strength.' When they invoke the Hekurá of Hamoriwe, they rub white ashes over their chests and bodies to represent that spider. They themselves chant: 'It is I, Hamoriwe; I was an old man, I had climbed to the top of the *jatuba* tree, from where I fell down, broke myself to pieces, and became a spider; no longer am I a man. Why have you called me? Why have you disturbed me in my den and in my peaceful sleep? What do you want from me?' The man himself replied: 'Hamoriwe, I am calling you to make you blow upon those Hekurá who pass and break down the trees and branches.' Then the man rises and with that same thin cane which he uses to take *epená,* he blows all around the *shapuno*; he says he is aiming the sting of Hamoriwe against the enemy Hekurá. The *tushaua* Fusiwe would hurl abuse against other tribes; then he would say: 'I felt such a stinging, they have blown upon me with the sting of Hamoriwe.' Then he sent for water and poured it on his head. If the thunderstorm passed, they said that it had been their Hekurá who made it pass. I saw nothing, but they pretended that they had seen the Hekurá.

Once I said to the *tushaua*: 'The wind is no longer blowing, because the storm has passed, not because you have launched the sting of Hamoriwe against the enemy Hekurá.' Fusiwe answered me: 'You usually have doubt about the Hekurá; one day they will make you deaf; they will blow upon your ears and you will hear nothing any more. Perhaps they will blow on your eyes and you will become blind.' I replied: 'They do not exist, they can blow nothing on to me. They are not listening to me; you are the only one who is listening to me!' 'Yes, they are listening to you; they do not wish to harm you, because they are Hekurá friends of mine. If the enemy Hekurá were to listen to you, they would blow into your eyes and you would no longer see anything.' Then I began to laugh: 'Blow then, let them come; I want to see whether I lose my sight!' 'No, no, for no one will then come and carry you on the journey. You have no sons to help you, you will have to go blind, all by yourself, finding your way on all fours.' The women asked me: 'Don't you believe it?' 'No,' I answered, 'I can't see anything, I have never seen a Hekurá.'

When they sing their Hekurá chants, they do not wish the women to repeat them. One day I was repeating one of Fusiwe's chants, which said: 'The Hekurá found me: I was alone on a day of silence. The daughter of Hekurá came dancing in beautiful circles; when she came near me she pushed me and I fell. She opened my breast and my throat, cleaned out all my blood: she tore out my tongue and put in its place Hekurá feathers. I was lying dead, but I heard all that the daughter of Hekurá sang. She was beautiful; there is no woman as beautiful as she. Since the visit of the daughter of Hekurá, I now sing well. They have put a new tongue into my mouth; this is why I know and sing the songs of the Hekurá. . . .'

Fusiwe listened to me and said: 'If you repeat the songs of the Hekurá they will blow on your ears and you will become deaf. Even if you sing their songs here, they will hear you from afar.' This is why I never repeated them. He told me that they can blow a little thorn into the eyes and only the Shapori can suck it out.

Another time I was repeating a lovely Hekurá song which an old man was singing. Fusiwe told me: 'No, don't do that; it is not allowed!' Then he went to the old man, who was a great Hekurá, and said to him: 'If you listen to this woman of mine repeating your songs, do not blow on her ears.' 'No,' answered the old man, 'I only blow on the ears and in the eyes of those with whom I am angry; I am not angry with her.'

There are no women who are Hekurá. They said that there was only one among the Aramamĩseteri, whose name is *Shinarimi* (cotton). She is tall, strong, white and beautiful; she adorns herself as though she were a man. She knows how to suck, to draw away pain, to sing the songs of Hekurá and dance with open arms. She knows how to steal the shades of the enemy's children. They said that, once, she had come to the *shapuno* and the *shapuno* roof was overthrown by the wind.

CHAPTER 22

The Old Man, the Young Girls and the Hasubueteri

A long time later two young Hasubueteri arrived in our *shapuno*; before entering they had decorated themselves well. The men shouted: *'Pei haw, pei haw . . . Hamacape haw.'*

The Hasubueteri *tushaua* said that he was Fusiwe's brother-in-law; Fusiwe's wife Hasubueterignuma was his cousin. Fusiwe had captured her in a *reaho* to which the Namoeteri had invited the Hasubueteri. When the guests were returning to their *shapuno,* Fusiwe had seized the girl by one arm and had kept her; the girl, they told me, shouted and shouted, but the *tushaua* would not let her go. Some time later the Hasubueteri came back to take her and they had a fight with *nabrushi,* but they did not succeed in taking her away: so for a long time they remained enemies. The Hasubueteri did not come to the feasts of the Namoeteri: only the father and mother of that woman came to visit her. By degrees they calmed down. Now they had come for the first time to invite them to their *reaho*.

The two stood still for a long time waiting on the compound before being called near to a fireplace. Towards dusk they approached the *tushaua,* and remained crouching before him, as he was also squatting down. One of them began to speak, declaring: 'The head of my *shapuno* sends us to say that he wishes to hold a *reaho*; the bananas are almost ripe. He said that he would hang them up three days after our departure. The headman says that he has no one to invite and that he invites you.' When he had finished speaking to the *tushaua,* he went and squatted down in front of another man and repeated the invitation; thus they continued all night in that sing-song manner of speaking of theirs.[1]

At last Fusiwe said: 'Day is about to break: I do not wish to go

[1] Ceremonial speeches spoken with rhythm follow precise rules, both in the manner of speaking and in the positions or the actions of the interlocutors.

on talking in daylight, because the enemy could be around. If we are talking and off our guard, they might shoot.' The Hasubueteri concluded: 'The Hasubueteri *tushaua* invites all the Namoeteri.' The Patanaweteri and the Pishaanseteri at that time were divided; they had gone to their *tapirí,* near to some of their *roças*.

Then all the Namoeteri assembled together and we left. There were very many of us; we walked slowly. Towards three o'clock we stopped and the men made the *tapirí*; they covered them with palm branches. About seven o'clock in the morning we started out again. With the women and so many children who cry in the forest, it is impossible to make speedy progress. One evening we reached an *igarapé* full of fish; the men prepared little arrows with slender *inajá* branches, which easily pierce the fish. They shot these and sometimes even caught two on one arrow. The girls enjoyed themselves too! They said: 'Let us shoot arrows!' The men were not much pleased, because when there are a lot of people, if the arrows do not hit the fish they might hit the legs of those who are standing in front.

In the forest they saw an enormous bird's nest at the top of a very tall tree; underneath it only animals' bones were to be seen. The men climbed up and took a big baby bird, all white; it appeared to be made of cotton and did not have its wing feathers. This bird cried loudly. A little later its mother flew in; her wings were extremely wide. The men shot and killed her: she was a harpy. The baby of that great bird was still alive, but a man shot and killed it, saying: 'How can we keep it alive, if its eats only game?' Fusiwe's old mother wept, another woman wept, a man wept. The old woman said: 'You kill this great bird; perhaps it is the spirit of our relatives! Why have you killed it? It is like killing a child!' They pulled out of its body all those white feathers, like cotton, left them in the sun to lose their lice and preserved them for use in their dances. At the feasts, when they have no white harpy feathers, they use the white chest feathers of those vultures which have white wings.

We were now near the *shapuno* of the Hasubueteri, when a young man arrived saying: 'They send to tell you to go at once: those who have gone hunting, are about to return.' When he had left, Fusiwe said to his men: 'Why are they in a hurry? It is better that we halt a long way from their *shapuno*. Who knows whether they have hidden our enemies near their *shapuno* to attack us when we arrive? Let everybody today make their *tapirí* near to each other!'

To get near to the Hasubueteri we had passed beautiful mountains, high ground, and woods of *pataua* palms. They live on a mountain higher than the others; it was necessary to climb and climb to reach them. The next morning, early, they came back to invite us, saying, 'In the *shapuno* they have already begun to prepare the bananas, come soon.' Some girls and some women were afraid and did not want to go. They said that the Hasubueteri invite people, and when the guests go away, they take the young girls, then they maltreat them, beat them and burn them with fire.

The old women, however, who had sons, went, and so did many women who were still young. Only one old man, named Hikokotewe, stayed with us; he was bent with age as he walked and he had one eye that opened and shut. The men had left him three arrows, saying, 'Grandfather, stay here with these arrows and kill those who come to steal the women.' The old man had a dog with him. Night fell; we women were all nearby in the *tapirí*. In mine there were six of us: the *tushaua*'s daughter, two others above, and two on the side. The two *tapirí* nearby were also full. None of us could sleep. The dog began to bark. 'Can it be the jaguar?' I thought, but the others said: 'The young Hasubueteri have certainly thought that many women have stayed in the *tapirí* and are coming to seize us!' Then we took the fire and fled with our hammocks into the forest. One woman had a little child; she called: 'Wait for me, I cannot run with the small baby,' and the others waited for her.

We fled without saying anything to the old man, who, a short time later, began to look for us. He shouted: 'Come, come,' but the girls said: 'Let us not answer; maybe the Hasubueteri have taken the old man and are making him call to make us go back and then to take us too.' At length one woman shouted: 'Are the Hasubueteri there?' The old man answered: 'The Hasubueteri are not here. The dog is barking because he can smell the jaguar. Come back, otherwise the jaguar will get the little baby.' Thus we went back close to the *tapirí*. The old man said to us: 'Why did you run away without saying anything, leaving me all alone?' Then the girls began to make fun of the old man. One said: 'Let's make him cry!' The old man continued: 'You should not have left me alone; if the enemy had come and killed me, you would never have been able to tell the *tushaua* how they had killed me. Now you may rest in peace; before daylight I will put myself on guard over the path, a long way from here, near the *igarapé*. Tomorrow morning, if you do not see me, do not be afraid, I will be on guard over the path.' The girls laughed: 'Perhaps you wept with fear because you were left alone!' 'You called us because you were afraid!' 'I have my arrows,' replied the old man, and he showed us those three arrows, but the girls laughed and laughed.

That night nothing happened. The next morning came the *tushaua*'s old wife, who was thinking of her daughter who had not eaten. Fusiwe had said to her: 'Go back to the women, take them to gather *pataua* palm fruit, which is nearby.' This is what we did; we found trees with lovely, dark bunches of fruit. I climbed up a tree and, with an old axe, I cut off a big bunch. 'I cannot hold it, because it is too heavy!' The others said: 'Throw it down.' I dropped it, puf, and the fruit scattered. I said: 'I am going to look for another bunch; you pick up the fruit and pile it together for me too.' I and the *tushaua*'s daughter always climbed together; the others were afraid. That day I climbed up seven *pataua* palms, of the kind which have fruit with a big nut; the trees are tall and smooth. In the evening my body was covered with scratches. Fairly late they arrived from the *shapuno* with maize, bananas and those big roots; then came also some men who had been hunting and had brought smoked meat.

The *tushaua*'s old wife told us that when the Namoeteri entered the *shapuno*, those who were still angry with them began to utter hostile shouts: '*Pei haw*! Here comes the game that we were waiting for. Let's kill them right away.' The women too egged them on: 'Those about whom everybody talks have come, those who think themselves the most *waiteri*; take advantage of it, men, to give them enough blows to make their bones all soft. We shall see then whether they really are men.' Then the other Hasubueteri shouted: 'Women, keep quiet! Women always talk when they shouldn't: with an evil mouth against our friends!' The Namoeteri stood still in the middle, suspicious; then the others called them to their various hearths. At last, after they had talked in loud voices for a long time, almost singing one after the other, the Hasubueteri *tushaua* got up and said: 'Who is coming to eat my food does not die of hunger; do not think this of me! These arrows that I carry in my hand are for shooting birds. Do not be afraid, they are hunting arrows. Your women will sing, our women will sing, all will be joy, we shall be admired.'

But in the night the Hasubueteri had begun to shout loudly: 'Namoeteri, let us dance with your women.' But the Namoeteri were suspicious, because they said that the Hasubueteri ask to dance with women, then seize them, run off and never come back. Their custom is to dance holding one woman in between two men, singing and going to and fro across the compound of the *shapuno*. The young Namoeteri, who had brought young wives with them, answered: 'If anyone of you dares to come and ask my woman to dance, and takes her by the arm, I will transfix him with my bow.' They took bow and arrows and kept them ready under the hammock.

The *tushaua* Fusiwe said: 'You may dance, but no one must go out, neither from this entrance nor from that. You may dance only on the compound; if you go out with the women to escape, we will do the same. We are in this world to avenge ourselves; if you do it to me, I will do it to you.' The Hasubueteri laughed and only the men danced; they said: 'They are troubled, they are jealous.' Then the Namoeteri continued: 'Do you not wish to dance with our women? The women are here. Why do you not dance? Are you afraid? When you come to us, we will make all your women dance; we will take even the old ones in our arms and dance together!' But the Hasubueteri did not ask for them again and sang and danced up and down all night, men only.

In the morning the Hasubueteri were troubled. When the Namoeteri went to ask for gifts of arrows, they replied: 'We don't give these away; we need them to shoot those who want to kill us.' The Hasubueteri have so many arrows, because in their mountains the canes from which arrows are made grow well, while in the plains of the Namoeteri they do not grow well. The *tushaua* Fusiwe said: 'Let's go away, because many of these men have an evil look on their faces.' The Namoeteri came back to where we women were waiting for them, and so we all returned to the big *shapuno*.

CHAPTER 23

Maramawe

Meanwhile I was expecting a baby and my time had almost come. During those days many Namoeteri decided to go to the Wakawakateri (*waka* is the great armadillo) to ask them for gifts. They had learnt that the Wakawakateri had many machetes. The journey was long.

In the morning we women of the *tushaua*, with the *tushaua*, his daughter and many others, went to look for *buriti*: my stomach was already very big. On the way back we crossed an *igarapé*; the women killed little fish and shrimps. I brought a big packet of them back. Later they found *bacaba* palm trees on a piece of high ground. The men climbed up the trees, took those bunches and said: 'Collect all these *bacabas*, quickly; it's late, the enemy might be near.'

I began to feel a big pain in my stomach and sat down; a woman friend asked me: 'What is the matter with you?' 'Nothing,' I answered and remained seated in silence. The *tushaua*'s daughter was also expecting a baby and her belly was big. 'Let's go on,' she said; 'they walk fast and we cannot.' The others had also found a wild cocoa tree with fruit and the *tushaua*'s daughter went back to eat some. I said to her: 'Tell them I have gone ahead, and not to wait for me.'

When I felt the sharp pains, I sat down; thus, slowly, I came to the bank of the *igarapé* and bathed in the stream. Near the *shapuno* I met Fusiwe's old mother. 'Does your stomach hurt?' she asked. 'No,' I answered. 'Yes, it does hurt you,' she repeated. Thus I came to the *shapuno*. I sat down in the hammock; I put the big packet of fish to cook. At that moment the *tushaua* arrived and I said to him: 'The fish is ready.' I got down from the hammock and divided the fish; I gave some to the *tushaua*, some to his father, his mother, and his daughter, and sent some to his two brothers, together with bananas which I was roasting. I divided up the bananas I had prepared, among the *tushaua*'s other women, too. They had taught me how to share with everybody and that is how I did it. But the pains increased; I spent the night with those pains and said nothing.

The following day some men returned to the *igarapé* to fish; I remember that the small children did not want to stay in the *shapuno* with the old grandmothers, and they wept. The *tushaua* said to us women: 'You go and get *pupugnas*; let them be ready when those who have gone fishing come back; when one goes fishing one eats nothing and comes back hungry.' I took a small basket and went after them. I came to a clearing. I sat down near a trunk, and I had such pains. I thought: 'If I shout, these people will see me,' and I went deeper into the bush. I heard them looking for me and calling me, but I did not answer.

I had lain down near a big tree-trunk, when I heard at a distance shouting in the *shapuno*: there was a great confusion taking place. I then found out that one of those who had gone to the Wakawakateri to ask for machetes, had come running back and had said that they had killed all the Namoeteri and that only he had escaped.

About nine o'clock the baby was born: he was all purple, and did not move. I looked at him and thought: 'He is dead! What must I do? I'll go and get *pishaansi* leaves; I will wrap him up in those leaves and bury him in an armadillo hole.' I had seen a den nearby. I went away sadly, slowly, to look for those leaves; already I felt no more pains. There were none of those big leaves nearby, but I saw them on a rock. I climbed up a liana growing like a ladder, which we call a *jabuti* ladder, and I picked many. I could already walk well. Slowly I returned towards the baby. When I was near that big tree, I heard a cry: '*Ah, ah, ah.*' I ran. It was the baby all covered with ants, which were biting him all over; he was completely covered with ants.

I had done nothing to my baby; I had not cut the umbilical cord. When I was a child, my brothers had been born, but my aunt had not allowed me to enter and so I did not know. I had not asked the women there for anything. I thought of cutting the umbilical cord: there were little bamboos nearby. I broke one off and tried it on my hair; it cut. Then I cut the baby's cord and did not tie it up; it began to bleed. I saw later that they do not even bind up the cord. I took the child in my arms; he could not breathe, but went *cr, cr, cr. . . .* I remembered this, for they had told me as a child: 'If a baby is born and cannot breathe, suck the water from its nostril which is always there.' I sucked. Nasty water came out; the baby breathed better. Then I put into the leaves all that had been born with the baby, made a parcel, and thought: 'I'll go and put it in the armadillo's hole.' I felt no more pain.

While I was walking, I met an old man with a little beard. He said to me: 'Do you hear those shouts in the *shapuno*? They have killed all the Namoeteri who have gone to the Wakawakateri. The men want to go today to take vengeance; this is why they are shouting.' Then he looked at the baby and exclaimed: 'But you have a baby. I had heard groaning and I came to see. I thought it was the baby of a deer. Then I saw a baby crying, kicking and no woman near. I thought it was the son of Poré. I was afraid and I ran away.' He had gone up to the child while I had gone to look for leaves.

I went up to the armadillo's hole with the packet, put it inside and trod the earth well down over it. I saw the *igarapé* and thought of taking a bath to wash myself. My father now tells me: 'It was a miracle of God that you didn't die!' but it is not easy to die. I put the baby down on a rock, on a big leaf; I sat down nearby in the water and washed him well on the head with that cold water. Blood continued to come out of his navel. When he cried and drew himself in, the blood came out. I felt very cold and returned to the *roça*, where I sat in the sun with the baby, who first cried and cried, then kept quiet. When he had grown warm, I thought of returning; I was now hungry. In the *roça* I picked some ripe bananas and, with the baby in my arms, set out for the *shapuno*.

Many babies had been born before mine among the Namoeteri: the father does not stay in the hammock, as the Tukano do, but he does not eat tapir meat, large wild boar, or monkey, for a long time. The small wild boar, on the other hand, could be eaten by the father and the mother. 'This little wild boar is one of Omawe's animals,' Fusiwe's mother said, 'and does no harm.' Birds too could be eaten.

I looked through the palm branches of the roof and saw the man who had come running. He was talking to the *tushaua*, who was looking at him with his bow and arrows in his hand. The women were weeping, because they thought their relations were dead. I did not have the courage to enter, but I entered slowly and got into the hammock. The *tushaua*'s mother came up and said to me: 'They have killed your husband's son-in-law, and that is why they are weeping. Can it be true?' 'When anything happens,' I thought, 'my heart grows tender and I weep; this time no tears are falling.' I was frightened and answered: 'I do not believe it is true. This man is lying.'

The *tushaua* looked at me, saw the baby and asked: 'What is it?' 'It's a boy,' answered his mother. He came close to me: 'Then treat him well; you must bring him up well. Remember that the Shamatari are not my friends; the Wakawakateri have killed my son-in-law and my nephews. We have enemies on all sides. This baby, some day, will look after you.' Then he went away. Later, not even an hour afterwards, he came back and sat down near me; he remained silent. Then he stood up and shouted: '*Pei haw, pei haw*. . . . Let's go today.' The uncle's son replied: 'Yes, today, otherwise the Wakawakateri will say: 'They are *waiteri* in killing enemy; let us see whether they come to kill us.' This is what they will say for sure.' I said to the *tushaua*: 'I don't believe it, it cannot be! The Namoeteri, who have gone there, were many; it cannot be that not a single other man has escaped. Wait a bit longer! My tears are not falling; it means that these people are alive. You wish to run, to shoot, to kill; first wait, to learn whether it is true!' The *tushaua* replied: 'These men will say: "We want to see whether he faces up to the Wakawakateri." I want to face them to see whether they will kill me and whether these men will then avenge me.'

Then came a man who had come to visit us; he came from the *shapuno* of the Mahekototeri. He was Akawe, he who afterwards became the father of my other children. *Aḳa* means tongue. He had listened to the *tushaua*'s words and said: 'You are the *tushaua* of the Namoeteri and it must not be you who goes to meet them. I must face them: I know where the Wakawakateri live, and on which side is the entrance to their *shapuno* towards the river and from which exit they leave to go out hunting. I am from there; I know what has to be done and I understand everything.'

Meanwhile the women were standing around looking at my baby; he was beautiful and white, but he had hardly any hair. Then the women began to say: 'This is not a human being, this child has no hair. When our babies are born they have plenty of hair; kill him, kill him! Kill him at once!' I replied: 'No, I do not know how to kill children. My mother has never killed children; how can I kill him?' 'Put him on the ground, put a tree-trunk over his neck and tread on the trunk.' They say that when they kill newly born babies, they put a trunk on the neck and press down on the neck until they die.

The *tushaua* listened and came to us: 'What are you saying?' 'They want me to kill him, because he hasn't got a human face and because he has no hair.' 'Why do you say this? Who has ever told you to kill your sons? As you love your own, so she loves hers. Let her bring him up, even if he has no hair!' The women answered: 'But he has no hair!' 'If he has no hair, his mother can worry about that, not you. Let the child grow up; some day he will work for her and defend her. Go away, go and cook *pupugnas* for your husbands who soon have to leave.' They then began to go away, one one way and one another. When he was left alone, he said to me: 'If you had been another woman who was afraid, you would have gone and killed him.' 'No, I will not kill him,' I replied. Fusiwe rested his hand on my shoulder while I wept.

The men were ready to go against the Wakawakateri. They all painted themselves black and gave a shout, which made the *shapuno* tremble: '*Haw, haw, haw*! . . .' They beat their feet on the ground of the compound, shouting very loudly and waving their arrows; it was enough to strike terror into you.

The day after my son was born, I was already out in the forest gathering wood; when they have babies, they do not care about themselves, and so I was working. I heard a strange noise and thought it was a jaguar. I looked towards the sky and saw a white airplane, which passed low over the *shapuno*: I had never seen one before. When I was a child, my grandfather had told me about the airplanes. I thought: 'Can there really be people up there?' I put the baby on the ground on a large leaf and covered him with another large leaf. I ran to the *shapuno*; I found it empty; they had all run away. The men and women had hidden themselves in the thick of the forest; some had squeezed themselves in between clefts in the rocks. All the fires were extinguished: they had thrown water on all the fires.

Then I shouted, called and made signs with *embauba* leaves. The airplane, which had seen the *shapuno*, had come down low and was circling round. The Indians thought it was the spirits of the dead come to eat them. 'Poré capé, Poré capé!' I explained: 'It is not Poré, it is the white men. My grandfather used to tell me that the white men can fly through the air.' They did not believe me and answered: 'No, it is Poré.' They were troubled because they had seen that I had tried to call the airplane.

During the night they all said they felt ill; they were trembling and they had headaches. Perhaps they had been too frightened and this is why they felt ill. The next morning they went to the *igarapé* and rubbed that white mud all over their bodies to cool them down. I had no fever and did not tremble. Then the women said, 'You are not a human being. Your son isn't human; you are animals, and so you have no fever.' I replied: 'No, the sickness understands that we are human beings, and so it leaves us alone. It recognizes, however, that you are animals and so it attacks you.' Then the old men blew towards me, so that the sickness might attack me, but I said: 'Blow, blow as you will, for the sickness will not come my way,' and I laughed.

Those who had gone to fight the Wakawakateri came to a big river which I believe was the Orinoco. They told us later that Akawe, the man who had offered to guide them, crossed the river by holding onto lianas and tied the lianas on the other side; thus they all crossed holding onto those vines. They had scarcely finished crossing, when the Namoeteri who had been to the Wakawakateri began to arrive from the other side of the path. They were carrying gifts: one had machetes, another a cooking pot, another bananas. Their companions asked, 'What happened?' 'Nothing; they have given us presents.'

They all returned together. When the men entered the *shapuno*, they let out shouts: the man who had told a lie obviously thought they would kill him, and ran into the forest. He spent the night at the top of a tree and came back a day later; the others did nothing to him.

The *tushaua* said to me: 'The name of this son of ours will be Maramawe, because it was not true that the Wakawakateri have killed the Namoeteri.' *Maramao* means deception.

Near the great *shapuno* there was a *roça* of maize. To cultivate it the woman carries the seeds to the river in a basket: she leaves them in the water. After three days, her body painted with red *urucú*, she goes back to take the seeds out of the water and puts the basket in the shade; three days later still, the seeds have germinated. Then they all go to the *roça* together to plant the maize. While some make holes in the ground, others drop in the seeds. When maize is planted, no one in the *shapuno* can eat crocodiles, because the shoots would be born without teeth, nor can they eat *jabuti*, otherwise the wind would ruin the plants.

It was the *sauva* ant which taught the Yanoáma how to cultivate maize. Fusiwe told me: 'One day a Kuie man (*sauva* ant) planted maize; he was married to a Pupumari woman (a bird which sings *pu*, *pu*, *pu*). His mother-in-law wanted to gather maize; the man made his wife tell the mother-in-law not to go among the plants, but to gather the grains on the edge of the *roça*, because among the plants she would get lost. The mother-in-law went to the *roça* with her little grand-daughter. She said: "On the edge the grains are small," and she went in between the plants. Then a strong wind began to blow and the old woman got lost. She shouted three times; her daughter heard and ran to her. She called "Mother!" The old woman answered: "*Pu, pu, pu,*" and turned into a Pupumari bird, her voice coming from farther and farther away. The woman ran to the *shapuno* and called her husband. They went back together; they heard the distant cry: *pu, pu, pu.* The husband said: "Now we can do nothing more." ' Fusiwe knew how to invoke Kuieriwe, because he was a great Hekurá. The Yanoáma, when they plant maize, invoke Kuieriwe (Hekurá of the *sauva* ant), because he taught men the use of maize and because he is very industrious and is not lazy.

Once Fusiwe and the men had gone hunting: we women had stayed behind with the children. I was eating *murame* fruit, when from a distance we heard the cry of Kumareme. The old grandmother said: 'Let no one answer, for it is Kumareme.' The weather had meanwhile grown dark and a strong wind had sprung up and was blowing hard. We heard trees falling in the forest and Kumareme shouting: '*Eheee . . .*' The old woman seized a post and began to beat on the trunk which was holding up the roof in front of us. She wanted the Hekurá of Fusiwe to wake up and run to our defence; she shouted: 'Get up, get up; your master is not here. Wake up, come and defend our sons, since your master is not here.' She spoke like this because the men had gone hunting. We all, women and children, huddled together and were very frightened.

They say that when the weather becomes dark, sometimes a woman's voice is heard shouting: '*Ehee . . .*' I did not believe it, but later I heard her shouting in the woods and I had to believe it; but I have never seen her. She is a very beautiful woman with long hair that falls all about her. One may not even speak of her; the men who see her are enchanted. Her body is beautiful, not painted, but all surrounded by her hair.

The *tushaua* told me that when he heard a woman's voice shouting in the forest, he took his bow and arrows and ran. Once he had hidden with his brother behind a tree and seen her run past. She was very lovely, all wrapped up in her hair. If she looks at a man she drives him mad; the man runs after her shouts and gets lost in the forest. When he told us about Kumareme, the old mother said, 'You have been fools to try to see her. She has looked at you, but she has not seen you; if she had looked you squarely in the eyes, you would have run after her and you would have got lost. How can you, who have many sons, not be afraid to go and see Kumareme? She entices you and carries you off; then your sons remain alone in the hands of others.' From that time they never again tried to see Kumareme. When Fusiwe took *epená* he said 'Hekurá of the Kumareme comes from afar, drawing behind herself the Hekurá from other mountains, because she is so beautiful!'

CHAPTER 24

Brutality and Repentance

One day we were at the *roça*; the *tushaua*'s son-in-law had killed a crocodile. They dig above the hole and when they see the crocodile's head below they stick the point of the bow between its eyes. Sometimes there are even two crocodiles in the same big hole. At other times they push into the hole a pole to which is tied a long cord of lianas; the crocodile bites the cord and they begin to turn the pole with the cord around the animal. When they can feel that the pole cannot turn round any more they begin to pull out the crocodile, tied to it. One above and the others to either side stick the bow in his body and so kill the animal. The man was lighting the fire to cook it. I and the *tushaua*'s daughter arrived from the wood, where we had been to collect *buriti*. Fusiwe said to me: 'Do you know how fire was born? Once the Yanoáma did not know fire; Omawe had not shown them how to make it. Then the crocodile began to go "*Ah, ah, ah* . . ." and spat an ember from its open mouth; with this they made fire. This is why the crocodile has so short a tongue; the fire has burnt the end off.' Then Fusiwe started to inhale *epená*; he looked at me and said: 'Prepare a lot of *buriti* juice; I want to drink it, so let it be nice and tasty.' I began to prepare it in the big earthenware pot, while the other wife was cooking the crocodile. The *tushaua* divided the crocodile up into pieces, while his brother distributed it.

I was preparing the *buriti*; it seems that, at that moment, my child went up to his uncle who gave him a piece of meat from the crocodile's foot. Near the child was a black and white dog, very beautiful, of which the *tushaua* was very fond. The dog snatched the meat from the child's hands, and the boy began to shout. The dog quickly swallowed the meat and choked itself: in two minutes it was dead. While the child came crying towards me, I heard them saying: 'Napagnuma, the dog is dead!'

I saw nothing; I only felt a very heavy blow on my arm; I fell and lost my senses. It was Fusiwe who had struck me, because, he said afterwards, I had not kept the child near me and that was why the dog was dead. The arm broke completely. Slowly I opened my eyes; I felt that cold feeling in my body. I sighed and saw Fusiwe's old mother weeping near me, while the *tushaua*'s daughter held my arm which was completely folded over and very swollen; I felt almost no pain, but it all seemed to have gone to sleep. The daughter said to me: 'He has broken your arm, because your son has caused the dog to choke to death with the meat.' The old woman said: 'But why has he broken your arm?' Then she went up to Fusiwe and repeated: 'She has no father, and no mother here; why have you broken her arm rather than anyone else's?' The *tushaua* came to me and said: 'How can it be broken? I only gave you one blow.' The old woman replied: 'You took the stick with both hands, and the stick isn't even dry, but still alive and fresh.' He asked: 'Where is it broken?' The arm was divided in two, and where he had struck me there was a big dark blister. He took the arm, pulled hard and said: 'Yes; it is broken. It is not my fault; it is her fault, for leaving the little boy to go by himself to eat.' I wept.

The arm was all twisted; the old wife began to straighten it; the bone went crac, crac. On one side the bone was under the skin, on the other the arm hung down. The woman pulled the arm hard and straightened it with her hand; when she did not pull, the bone stuck upwards and hurt all the more. The *tushaua*'s daughter was weeping near me: 'Yes, it's broken! Yes, it's broken!' I said: 'Now I don't ever want to go with him again!' Meantime the *tushaua*'s daughter ran to get arrow canes to prepare a splint, as they do when someone breaks a bone. She broke those arrows into pieces the length of my arm, tied them tightly together, one next to the other. They were the arrows of her husband, the *tushaua*'s son-in-law; he had many, because he kept those short ones which he had already used on wild boar.

Thus they made a bandage of arrows, one tied well to the next. They took balls of cotton and, after the old woman had carefully set the bone with her hands, they bound up my arm from the shoulder to the wrist, inside that bandage of arrows, while they pulled my hand so that the arm should stay well stretched out. Then they put long fresh strips of a thin, resistant bark around it to keep it all in place.

It must have been about three o'clock when he broke my arm, and I stayed there until it was nearly dark: I felt more pain all the time. The old wife accompanied me as far as the *shapuno* and made me lie down in the hammock, while the *tushaua*'s daughter tied a high rope to the roof of the *shapuno* with two knots; she tied one very near my shoulder and the other to my wrist, so that the bone should remain horizontal. I could neither bend nor move the arm. At night I felt the pain gnawing at me inside and I groaned. After a few days, they undid the bandages to see whether the bone was beginning to knit together: it was dark, purple, and painful. They tried gently to move it; but it still made a faint noise, cric, cric. Then the woman said: 'Your arm is still soft; don't move it, otherwise the bone will stay broken and it will be ugly.' When she untied the bandages, the others held my arm tightly stretched; they heated water and massaged it while they pulled. It was the *tushaua*'s daughter who rubbed me with hot water; she wept so much for me. The women stood around me and wanted to give me something to eat; but I replied: 'Leave me to die; I don't want anything; he treats me like this.' I lived by weeping.

One day Fusiwe was taking *epená*; he came and sat down beside me. He said to me: 'Now the Hekurá are making your arm heal well.' I replied: 'I don't want the Hekurá to make my arm heal. I have not the strength to stand up; otherwise I would run away from you. Those who strike others ought to have their arms broken to learn what pain is,' and I began to cry. Then he wanted to touch me with his hand; but I didn't want it; I pushed him away. I really wanted to die; I would not eat, but I did not die. A woman came; she left me some *mingau*: I did not eat it. Another woman came; she left me some more *mingau*: I would not take it.

There were three people who looked after me; they often changed those bark strips around the arrow canes; because, when they are dry, they do harm. The baby was still taking milk; the *tushaua*'s old wife helped me while I gave milk, and took him away immediately afterwards. Every few days they washed my arm with hot water to make the swelling go down. When the *tushaua*'s old wife washed my arm, she said to her daughter: 'Daughter, pull the arm and don't ever let go of it; if you let it go, it might bend over. The arm is still soft inside; now it's in a good position, but if you let it go, it might bend and then it will never be put straight again.'

A long time afterwards, when my swelling had almost gone, the old wife said: 'Now it is hard; move it a little.' The *tushaua* wanted to come close; but he did not dare. They took off the arrow canes which surrounded my arm; but I could no longer bend it. Then the old wife began to pour hot water continuously over it, saying: 'You will see; by doing this with hot water, it will eventually become soft again. My mother's leg was like this and wouldn't bend, but with hot water massaging up and down all the time, it became soft again in the end.' In fact my arm began slowly to bend.

After they had taken off the bandage of arrows and as soon as the arm began to bend, they took a broad strip of bark and put it like a sling round my neck and behind my back to keep the arm in front near my breast. When I began to have my arm loose, because it was no longer swollen, the *tushaua* said: 'She can already bend her arm; tomorrow we will travel.' Now you can hardly tell where the arm was broken. From that time on, the *tushaua* has never beaten me again.

Fusiwe was very fond of dogs. For them dogs are almost humans. So many times I have seen women giving milk to dogs. When dogs die, they often weep and burn their bodies in the *shapuno*. Then they collect up the burnt bones and prepare them for the feast of ashes. Then they go hunting, as if it were for the death of one of their companions. They prepare the bones, but they do not eat them. They mix the ashes with banana *mingau* in an old *cuia*, pour it all into a deep hole dug near to the big posts of the *shapuno*, and fill it in. They then break the *cuia* and burn it. The master of the house offers the game and the rest of the *mingau* to those who have come to take part. He does not eat, just as though one of his relatives had died. Those who have been invited make a *mingau* some time later and return the invitation. Thus they remember their dogs; but they do not always make the feast of the ashes.

They rear many animals, but not to eat them. They have parrots, toucans, *japim*, and other birds. They also rear that small variety of wild boar; but often, when those boar grow up, they become fierce and run after people to bite them, but their masters do not kill them. Sometimes the others, if they find them in the forest, pretend not to recognize them and secretly kill them. They also take baby jaguars, but are much afraid to do so, for in the night the mother comes often in search of her young. If they kill a jaguar, they pull off strips of skin and tie them round their waists, especially of the children, so that they shall not pick up diseases, and so that the other jaguars shall not attack. When these animals of theirs die, they burn them, not inside the *shapuno* as they do with their dead and their dogs, but outside; and they do not pick up the bones, as they do in the case of the dogs.

CHAPTER 25

The Tragic Journey, The Reaho

Time passed and one day there came a younger brother of the *tushaua*, who lived in the *shapuno* of the Mahekototeri where he had a wife. He came into the square and went straight to the *tushaua*, who at that moment was tying the head of his arrow. The *tushaua* shouted: '*Pei haw*! He has come to tell us that the Mahekototeri want to attack us on account of the women whom we have taken!' Then the men seized their bows and arrows. The old father, who was in the hammock, got up and exclaimed: 'Where are my arrows? Mascohawe comes to warn us!'

Mascohawe said: 'Brother, you are older than I. The Mahekototeri are not angry with you, they are not angry. They have said: "There will not be war on account of women. Women are everywhere; young girls who grow up. Why must we fight for women who are worthless?" ' The young man continued to speak for a long time; he said: 'The Mahekototeri want to be friends with you again; you have killed no one, they have killed no one. They are sending to tell you to keep their women. Women, as soon as they have a son or two, grow old; they are no further use even for loading wood. They send me to tell you that you may certainly keep them. They invite you to their *reaho*.' He talked and talked. The *tushaua* answered: 'Yes, brother, I know that you have come to invite me, because you and they want to avenge yourselves, because you want to take our women. Then take them! I will come; I will come, because I do not want you to think I am afraid of you! I will come.' Thus he finished his speech. The next day the *tushaua* decided to set out with all the Namoeteri to go to the Mahekototeri.

We were already on the journey when a young man took another's wife by one arm; the husband saw them and they had a fight with *nabrushi*. I was at a distance with the *tushaua*'s other women; we heard the shouts and went closer. The young man had a great wound on his head and blood was coming out of his mouth and nose. He had fallen on the ground and could not get up again: they then made him comfortable in the hammock, which they tied to a tree-trunk, and carried him. When the *tushaua* saw him, he said: 'What has happened? A snake-bite?' 'No,' they replied; 'it was a vendetta; he has been struck on account of jealousy.' The young man looked, but did not speak; he could not speak. His relations picked him up and carried him forward.

The next morning the young man was dead: when we reached the *tapirí* where the relatives were with the dead man, we found the women weeping and collecting wood to burn the body. Fusiwe said to us: 'You stay here with these people and weep for the dead man.' Then he turned to me: 'You, who waste your tears by weeping senselessly for your relatives; you who enjoy wasting your tears, come now and shed them for this young man who is dead.' I left my basket and went there. The next morning they burnt the body; when the pyre began to burn, the heat made the white part of the brain come out of the hole in the head. Then they said: 'Put more wood on, cover him up well.'

The dead man's father with two sons, other relatives, Rashawe and an old man stayed to gather up the bones. The father said to the *tushaua*: 'Cousin, early tomorrow morning I will collect the bones and they will help me. When the sun is high, we will come; do not wait for us, we will catch you up.' They waited until the next day to let those bones grow cold.

The next evening, a young man, Fusiwe's cousin, said to his mother: 'Mother, I am going to shoot parrots, the long-tailed kind, because I must get their feathers for the feast; all those which I had, I have given in exchange for arrows.' He was a big, strong youth, and was already friendly with a girl. He had seen a big tree, of the sort they call *namoi*, full of little fruit which the parrots go to eat in the evening. It seems that the Shamatari were already in position behind that tree.

The Shamatari had been deadly enemies of the Namoeteri. After a long time the Shamatari *tushaua*, Rohariwe, had sent to say: 'You, Namoeteri, have killed our relations, our brothers, but our chief is no longer angry; we can become friends again. We do not want any more war between us.' Three elderly men and three old women came. Then they almost became friends again. I remember that in the Shamatari *shapuno*, before they shot me, two Namoeteri had already come to look for dogs. When I was already living with

Fusiwe, some Shamatari arrived at the Namoeteri *shapuno*; they recognized me and said that they wanted to kill me and that they would be in position along the way, waiting for me to come out of the *shapuno*, but they did not do it.

That evening, it seems the Shamatari were already waiting, hidden behind the tree, to blow *aroari* on that young man. They say that a poison exists, which they obtain from the potato of a plant called *piripirioca*; that poison is called *aroari*. They scrape those little potatoes, dry the scrapings and then put them in bamboo canes. Bees which suck flowers of that plant die; birds which pass near that poison die. When they want to cause a person's death, they blow from a distance that poison which they keep in those bamboos and the person dies.

The young man returned weak and tired: 'Mother,' he said, 'I have a headache; I want to be sick.' He did not even have a bath and lay down at once in the hammock. The next morning he went out with his friends. We came close to a little *igarapé* surrounded by wild cocoa trees. The sick man was all the time growing weaker and we stopped to make the *tapirí*. The *tushaua* made a separate *tapirí*, where he went with one of his women; he said to his oldest wife: 'Send your daughter to tell her husband to make a *tapirí* for all of you together. One *tapirí* for all is enough, for tomorrow morning we will continue the journey.' So they built a big *tapirí*; I put my hammock highest; beneath me was that wife who had a small son, in front of me the other two women, one with a son. The sick man was alone in a *tapirí* near us. In the night he grew worse; he groaned all the time. The Hekurá met, spoke, and sang their songs.

The next morning the *tushaua* said: 'Let the men go ahead,' and only we women stayed behind. They then took a long pole, tied the broad cotton hammock to the pole and laid the young man in the hammock. Two women in front and two behind carried the pole on their shoulders. They carried the sick man for a good way and then said: 'Now that's enough, it's their turn.' We took over from them. I was the last in line and a very great weight fell on my shoulders; then I said: 'Now let me go in front, as I am shorter!' and I moved to the front. That man weighed like a rock: we passed a wood of *pataua* palms, we crossed an *igarapé*. At last I said: 'Now let us change; I can't go on any longer.' We left the pole to four new women and we rested. We were all sweating; we took a swim and again ran after the others. That night we slept by the bank of that river; it was broad, with white water and full of *pium*.[1] In the night the sick man grew worse and died.

During that night the dogs barked a great deal. We heard pluf, pluf . . . a noise in the water. The *tushaua* said: 'It is men; they have jumped into the river and are swimming.' His old wife also said: 'Yes, I too heard a noise in the river nearby.' The *tushaua* continued: 'Let us go and see. Call Napagnuma. She was not born in the forest, but she has more courage than you; she was a child and she lived alone in the forest!' I was in the hammock, listening; it was perhaps about midnight. His daughter came and said to me: 'Come with us; my father is telling us women to go and see. It seems that someone has run this way.' He was sending us, because, in general, the enemy do not shoot women. I answered: 'I am afraid to die. If they are Shamatari, they will shoot me; I have already felt the pain of an arrow!' But I got down from my hammock, left the baby to another wife and went with his daughter, two other women and the sister-in-law. Each one of us carried a firebrand to light up the way and to see who had fallen in the water. The bank of the *igarapé* was steep like a barrier in the water. Then we knew that they were indeed Shamatari who had come close to us. I went ahead, but I was afraid. 'You go ahead,' they said to me. 'Yes, I'll go ahead; but if they shoot me, do not let me fall into the river, bring me back, for I don't want to die by drowning.' 'I will bring you back,' said the *tushaua*'s daughter.

It seems that when those who were in the water saw us coming with firebrands, they hid under the branches, keeping above water only their heads. Along the bank we saw human footprints and we went back. Around the *tapirí* the Namoeteri were standing together; more than a hundred. 'We have not seen anyone,' we said. The *tushaua* asked: 'Have you also looked under that big tree? Perhaps they were hiding there and let you pass.' We went back to see; while we were approaching, I heard crak, crak; they had come out again onto dry land and had trodden on a dead branch. I was afraid and said: 'There's nothing; why do we want the serpent to bite us in these parts? We have been searching for so long and we have not seen anyone.' But I felt that there were people near. I had the impression that they were looking at me and I was afraid.

When I came back, I lay down in the hammock and said to the *tushaua*'s old wife: 'There really are people around; you will see that tomorrow they will be waiting for us along the path.' I also

[1] *Pium*: Amazonic name for small biting flies (simulids and culicoids).

said to the *tushaua*'s daughter: 'Tell your father that there are men near.' But the *tushaua* had gone close to the dying man and, when the man died, he stayed there weeping; he did not come to sleep in his hammock. The dead young man was the son of an old uncle of his. I sent word to him: 'There are enemy about; let him weep inside the enclosure of branches they have made around the dead man, and let him not go away on his own, because they will shoot him.' His daughter said quietly to him, so that the others would not hear: 'I think the enemy are near.' They had made an enclosure of palm branches to take shelter from the enemy's *aroari*: the man had said, in fact, that he was dying because of the *aroari* they had blown at him.

The *tushaua* and the relatives wept until morning. When daylight came, the *tushaua*'s mother called me and said: 'Let us go too and weep together with those people, over that dead body. We too shall die one day and then there will be someone to weep for us. If we do not weep over a dead man's body, at our own death we shall have no one to weep for us.' I went with the old woman who was weeping bitterly. The *tushaua* was no longer weeping. I went up and said to him: 'The enemy are near. Have you not heard the dogs, which very early in the morning have been barking all around?' Then the *tushaua* sent some men to see: they came back saying that they had found the tracks, clearly visible on the soft mud. They had followed them, but the tracks disappeared in the forest. The *tushaua* said: 'Let us make a fire at once and burn the body.' The men cut down trees and in a short time brought a mountain of wood, made a fire and burnt the body. We all waited until the next day to collect the bones: the dogs barked that night too.

The next day the *tushaua* said to us: 'You women, go and help to gather up the bones! I want to leave here quickly; I hear blows in my ears, which tell me there are enemy about.' While we were walking, the *tushaua*'s old mother asked: 'Where are you going?' We replied: 'Your son has sent us to help those people to pick up the bones.' The old woman said: 'Son, your daughter must not go.' 'Why?' asked the *tushaua*. 'Because she is pregnant. You know that she is pregnant and that it is bad for a pregnant woman to pick up bones. Why did you have to choose her? You should have sent your son-in-law.' 'You go, mother, and tell him.' Then the old woman went to her son's son-in-law and said: 'You who are a man, go and help them to pick up that dead man's bones.' Thus the old woman sent the son-in-law and two other youths in our place and forbade us to go. They say that if pregnant women go to collect bones, their babies are born weak and then they will have pain in their eyes. That day they collected the bones, sifted them well, and threw the ashes in the mud of the river.

Thus we continued our journey: after four days some young Kashoraweteri arrived to invite us. They wanted us to go and dance anad sing in their *shapuno*. Soon after came some Mahekototeri to tell us that they too expected us. Then the *tushaua* called his brother Shamawe, his old father, and his uncle, and said: 'Father, and you who are old, tell me: shall we go to the Mahekototeri or to the Kashoraweteri? The Mahekototeri have invited us first; I think we ought to go to them. Tell us your opinion.' The old chief of the Gnaminaweteri also came. The old men did not answer; then the *tushaua*'s brother said: 'The old men do not know where to go; neither the father, nor the uncle, nor your father-in-law, nor my father-in-law. You, who are a chief, must decide and I will follow.' The others said: 'Wherever you drag us we will come.' Then spoke the old mother: 'Let us go to the Mahekototeri.' She had a sister and a niece with the Mahekototeri. We loaded our things and the baskets with the dead man's bones and set out.

That day we reached a spot near Mahekototeka, which the white men today call El Platanal. The Namoeteri men were talking a great deal among themselves. Shamawe, the *tushaua*'s brother, said: 'Perhaps the Mahekototeri have invited us to avenge themselves for the women we have stolen from them; we did it on account of this woman here, Napagnuma!' While we were standing still near Mahekototeka, that young man came back who lived with the Mahekototeri; he too was a brother of the *tushaua*. The Namoeteri were afraid and said: 'Why don't we go and call the Hasubueteri too, so that they may vindicate us? We believe they will kill us.' But the young man said: 'Come tomorrow morning to the *shapuno*; the Mahekototeri wish to hold a *reaho* at once, because they are expecting the enemy. The Hayatateri (*haya* is the deer) want to attack us and also the Shipariweteri; so we have been warned.' But the Namoeteri were suspicious. I was not afraid and said to the *tushaua*'s other wife: 'These men are afraid, but I do not believe the Mahekototeri will do anything.'

The Mahekototeri women, who had been stolen and were coming with us, were happy, because they were returning to see their mothers again after such a long time. Meanwhile the old Namoeteri women said to their daughters: 'If the Mahekototeri capture you, do not like these women of theirs, who have not run away; only one has escaped. You must escape!' 'Yes,' replied the young women, 'we will run away, we will cross the big river and follow you.' The young man, brother of the *tushaua*, concluded: 'They do not want the enemy to kill any one of you, because they do not want to be given the blame for it. However, come at once, for the bananas are getting spoilt.'

Early in the morning the *tushaua* Fusiwe said: 'Cut down *assai* palms.' They felled many trees. The *tushaua* chose the straight young branches; the men began to prepare the fringes, while the women helped. They took the pale, scarcely yellow, inner branches; with a little stick they opened those leaves which grow on both sides and thus they made a fringe which stayed hanging down. They continued to prepare these until the sun came up about ten o'clock. When the young men entered the *shapuno* to dance, they carry in their hand those branches with all the light-coloured strips; sometimes they have in one hand one of those branches, in the other hand bow and arrows, sometimes a branch in each hand. Some of them tie those branches around their stomachs, letting the leaves hand down like a long fringe.

Later, in the morning, the Mahekototeri returned to invite them, telling them to hurry, because they knew that the enemy were near; they had left their *shapuno* two days before to come to the attack. The Mahekototeri *tushaua*, Kashihewe, sent word to say that once they had entered they must all stay in the *shapuno* and no one must go out.

It was only just after midday and we were already painted with red *urucú* and black lines. I did not want to enter; I wanted to stay outside in the *tapirí*, because I was ashamed and I said: 'They will say that it is my fault that you have stolen their women and they will give me poison.' 'No,' said the *tushaua*, 'they will not harm you. How can you stay behind?' I answered: 'I have been by myself so much, I am not afraid, no wild beast will eat me; I will take the baby and the fire with me. During the day I will stay near here, and at night I will go into the forest.' The old mother said to me: 'No, no, come; if you don't stay with us, they will look for you and say that my son has not brought you because he was afraid that they would seize you.' I too thought: 'It's true; then they will say that he was afraid they would take me.' I took my hammock, put it in the basket, and went with them.

When we entered, the Mahekototeri were shouting with joy; '*Ha*, *hai, hai, ha* . . . Here is the *waiteri tushaua*!' they shouted. All the men were standing up with bows and arrows in their hands; even the man whose pregnant wife they had stolen was standing with bow and arrows; he was silently looking on. Meanwhile the Namoeteri with painted bodies, with white falcon's down on their heads and feathers tied around their arms, began to come in a line. They performed their dance, turning around on one side and the other, showing their bow and arrows and going right round the great square. Then they stopped and stood their bow and arrows up on the ground. We women with the children stood still some distance away to see where our men were going. Then each man went with his friend from there and we all split up. The *tushaua* Kashihewe shouted soon after: 'Get the banana pap.' They all stood up with their *cuias* and went towards the big vessels made of tree-bark, tied at the ends, which were already filled with banana *mingau*.

The Mahekototeri carried out no vendetta; they did not fight with hands or with *nabrushi*. In the night, the *tushaua* Kashihewe of the Mahekototeri, who had a twisted mouth due to a blow received on the head a long time before, said: 'No, do not be suspicious; I have invited you because I must finish the last *cuia* with my father's ashes. It was neither to take vengeance nor to do you harm. I asked you to come only for the best reasons. No one is dead and no one of us is angry with you. You have come with our women. None of them must say: "I want to stay with my mother"; they must all go back with you, because they have learned how to live with you.'

Then Fusiwe replied: '*Ehe* . . . I have come to you, for you have a machete from the white men; give me a machete that I may carry it with me, for it is very hard work for me to break the tree-trunks with my teeth to make my *shapuno*. You, who are a friend of the whites, have received those necklaces from them; put them round my neck, that the young ladies may say: "He has been there, where the white men's friend is; on his neck is a beautiful necklace; he has a lovely thing in his ears; he too is becoming a friend of the white men." Put those necklaces round my neck, because, when I go running through the forest, the monkeys will see me; they will stand looking at me in enchantment, and I will shoot them.'

They talk and talk always in a high, singing voice: he who arrives speaks first and, when he begins to grow hoarse, a companion shouts: '*Ehe* . . .' and carries on. At those feasts the old men recount ancient things: 'My nephews, when of old I lived a long way off, the enemy used to come and shoot. I went back to fight. You, young men, always talk of fighting, but you do not yet know how to fight. . . .' In the evening, they performed their dances with palm leaves and arrows. Before they began their songs, the *tushaua* of the Mahekototeri said once more: 'Let no man take *epená*. At night, while we are singing, it is possible that the enemy may listen and come near. Nobody notices while singing. You go and sit down on the path at a distance,' and he sent some men to guard the *shapuno*. No one took *epená*. When night fell, the *tushaua* Kashihewe shouted: 'Sing, sing, Namoeterignuma; I want to listen to the song of Namoeterignuma.' But the young women were afraid to sing. After a little while, the *tushaua*'s sister stood up and went to sing: she called other friends too. I did not want to sing, but she said: 'Come; otherwise they will say that you did not want to come because you were afraid.' She took me by one arm and said to me: 'You will always stay with me; I will not leave you with other women.' She went into the middle of the square; I was on one side and the eldest daughter on the other. First she sang a long song, a beautiful one, which I do not remember. She said she had heard that song as a child, when Waika women sang it. They wanted her to repeat the song many times. Then they asked me to sing; but I was too shy. Their women said: 'If you sing, I will sing too.' I answered: 'I don't know how to sing; I have never sung!' But they insisted: 'Daughter of the whites, sing for us; you must know many songs. The whites sing a great deal!' But I remained silent.

The women sing women's songs and the men sing men's songs. Every tribe has its favourite songs, and the men are never too shy to sing; but the women are often too shy. Generally the woman who sings is alone; sometimes she has under her arm two other young girls and, while she is singing, she goes to and fro with the two companions. When the woman has finished her song, all the others answer in chorus. When a man sings, he often stands alone in the middle of the square, leaning with both hands held high on his pointed bow upright on the ground; sometimes he places his hand on the shoulder of another man. Around him, the others listen in silence, standing still; when he finishes his song, they intone the chorus, dancing with steps forwards and backwards. In the night, the braziers remain lit all around the great square, while the Indians, lying in their hammocks, listen to the songs. A Kashoraweterignuma, wife of one of them, sang; but they didn't like her song. The woman replied: 'My song is ugly; but this is the only one I can sing.' They all then laughed. Again the *tushaua*'s sister sang:

she had a pretty voice and the song said: 'The *samaia* leaves go tan, tan, tan, when the wind blows'; the other women repeated the chorus.

Meanwhile they continued to ask me to sing. I answered: 'I cannot sing; I was little, I lived near my mother; I never sang, I did not dance.' But the old Mahekototeri replied: 'Because of you, daughter of the whites, we have lost our nieces; sing at least one song for us. When we invite the Kashoraweteri, we shall say: "This beautiful song which our daughters and our nieces are now singing was taught by Napagnuma."'

The *tushaua* of the Mahekototeri also came up to me with his arrows and said: 'Sing, so that I may listen to Napagnuma; we all know her by this time.' Then I sang that song which I had heard as a child at Cucui: a Brazilian soldier on the frontier used to sing it:

Fui eu, fui eu que matei,	It was I, it was I who killed him,
Fui eu, fui eu que matei,	It was I, it was I who killed him,
A cobra de Boropa	The serpent of Boropa
Quem matou fui eu.	Who killed him was I.
Eu ero pequeninha,	I was only small,
Carregada de botão;	All covered with buttons;
A menina quando dorme	When the little girl sleeps
Bota a mão no coração.	She puts her hand on her heart.

They all answered in chorus: 'Opugnuhén, Opugnuhén . . .' While I sang, the old men and women came down from their hammocks and came to sit around me, in the great compound. Behind the old men and women, stood the young girls. They were happy because I was singing.

Then the other women began again. I remember many of those songs, which I have heard over and over again. The *tushaua*'s sister sang: 'The toucan on the branch sings Iaokoekoeke . . .' and the others repeated in chorus. Then another Namoeterignuma sang: 'The stars are all shining high in the sky.' Later, the Mahekototerignuma began; one of them intoned a long song: 'The *ieisiḳi* leaves beat with the wind, tan, tan, tan; when the wind stops, their eyes grow sad . . .' Another sang: 'The whites on the river travel high, travel low, far away . . .' Thus they continued to sing, their companions repeated the chorus every time, one beginning first, then another, like a distant echo. When the song was beautiful, the *tushaua* and the other men said: 'This song is beautiful. Repeat the same song, so that our women may learn it.' There was a Hasubueterignuma, the wife of a Namoeteri; the *tushaua* shouted: 'I want to hear the song of Hasubueterignuma'; but the woman replied: 'I am tired; I want to sleep.' Her husband shouted at her: 'You cannot say no; it is the *tushaua* who has asked for your song. You cannot be mean with your song; you must give it to whoever asks for it, so that all may learn it and sing it everywhere.' Then the woman sang. Many were too shy and would not sing, because often, the next day, the youths who had listened while lying in their hammocks, jeered at them saying: 'You had a little voice, a wretched voice. How ugly your song was!' For this reason some of the young girls used afterwards to cry.

Towards midnight, the women stopped singing and returned to their hammocks. Then the men got up and began their songs, as the women had done. They too first began singly, then in chorus, when they repeated the same words; but the men's songs had different words. 'The *guariba* monkey jumps among the *inajá* palm and goes *tanana* . . .' Then another song: ' *Mamo* leaves are falling and swirling round as they fall . . .' The young men sang all night, while the old men chatted amongst themselves.

The next morning, the *tushaua* Kashihewe spoke thus: 'I have called you here, to finish with you the *cuia* containing my father's ashes. When I have finished it, I shall be free; the enemy will then even be able to kill me. I was anxious about this *cuia*; for some time I have been travelling and carrying it with me. When I have emptied it, I shall be satisfied.' The women take care of the bones and carry them on journeys. They said that for some time they used to preserve part of the ashes, because two relatives of the dead man, who had to take part in the last journey when they took the last ashes, lived with the Namoeteri. They could not finish those ashes without inviting them.

They broke the dead man's bow and arrows, which they had still kept; they took the feathers, which he used as ornaments and which were in boxes made of *pashuba* wood, well sewn with slender lianas, and burnt them all, saying as they wept: 'It is the last time; nothing of him must remain.' Then all the relatives squatted down around the banana *mingau*. The other men stood around, on foot, leaning on their bows and arrows; behind them again the women. Some wept together with the dead man's relatives. The *tushaua* of that tribe took the *cuia,* which a woman gave him, stopped up with resin and covered on top with those little white feathers like cotton, opened it, stirred and poured out the ashes, mixing them in the banana *mingau*. He drank a little, passed the *cuia* to another relative, and he to another; the *mingau* was in a big *cuia*.

All the relatives were weeping; one son said: 'Father, father, come back along this road which you used to tread. Why do you not come back? To which tribe have you gone?' The niece repeated: 'Have you perhaps got lost in this dark night? Do you perhaps feel the cold of the night and of the clear sky? Why are you not with us? Why are you no more with us? When you were alive, you never went wandering in the gloom of the night; only by day you went in the forest to find game and to eat it with us.' The brother-in-law said: 'O brother-in-law, you are dead. All is finished! You were our companion, our guide. You went hunting, I came with you, we returned together; you used to kill wild boar and monkeys; you picked them up and brought them back with me.' The old women wept and exclaimed: 'Come back to the *shapuno*; as you once did! This is the last day of your life, which ends with the remains of these bones. Come back, come back now to us, this very moment!'

At last the *tushaua* Kashihewe made them give bananas to the Namoeteri and said: 'Take these and go; sleep far off, while my men guard the path. Go a long way off, because, if the enemy arrive and find your footprints, they may come behind you and attack you.' The men went out, then we women with the children, then other men. Those stolen Mahekototeri women also returned with us; by now they were used to us. They had wept much, because their mothers had reproved them, saying that they had not run away because they did not love their mothers.

CHAPTER 26

Betrayal

We crossed the great river. I remember that I was walking near to the *tushaua*: I saw on the ground the nests of those small spiders which, when they are frightened, flee into their holes and close the entrance: they are called *waikushihemu*. One of the girls' songs among the Mahekototeri said that *waikushihemu* was standing at the door of his little house, and the jaguar had put his foot over him and had then devoured him, poor *waikushihemu*. I told him that I found it funny that the jaguar should eat so tiny a spider. The *tushaua* replied: 'Who knows; he was hungry and he could find nothing else!' And he laughed.

The men then found the tracks of the wild boar, and at length heard from afar where they were eating, because wild boar grunt. Then the hunters put the poisoned heads on their arrows and approached slowly; one group stayed put where the tracks passed by, and another group tried to surround the herd on one side and a third group on the other. When the men, who had approached from the side, began to shoot arrows, the boar ran along that same path by which they had come; thus they passed grunting through the hunters who were lying in wait, and who took advantage of this to shoot them again. If the wind, even a light breeze, blows in the direction of the animals while the hunters are approaching, even if they are two or three hundred yards away, the boar smell them and flee; then the hunters can no longer catch up with them, even if they pursue them all day. Wild boar fear the smell of man worse than the smell of poison.

The next day the dogs found two big tapirs which were eating under a thicket of *buriti* and pursued them; the hunters ran after them at great speed, but the tapirs reached an *igarapé* and threw themselves into the water. The dogs were barking all around and the tapirs snorting at them; the water was low. The *tushaua* shouted to the dogs: 'Catch them, don't let them escape,' and he ran together with his son-in-law, while the other men ran from the other side in the direction of the dogs which were baying. When Fusiwe arrived, his brother Shamawe had already shot a tapir, which was struggling and crying fio, fio . . . The animal was trying to get out onto the bank, but the dogs leapt on him and pushed him back into the water. Meanwhile the other tapir, which had not been wounded, after escaping along the *igarapé*, when the first wounded tapir stopped moving, came back close to the dead one; thus the men succeeded in shooting it in the neck. Then the animal ran away with the arrow stuck in it and with the dogs in pursuit, passing in between the hunters. One could hear the baying of the dogs and see the traces of blood. At last the sound of the dogs remained in one spot, for the tapir had hurled himself again into the water and all the dogs were standing still on the bank, barking; the men ran up and killed the second tapir too. They did not shoot the tapirs with poisoned arrowheads, but with spearheads, because they make big wounds; the animal wounded in this way leaves much blood and they can easily find it. If they use poisoned arrowheads, the blood does not show in the tracks and the animal dies a long way off, because the poison acts slowly on the tapir, which is so fat.

After a long walk we came to where the young man poisoned with *aroari* had died. It was evening and the men started to make *tapirí*; I and the *tushaua*'s eldest wife went to cut wood. The woman said to me: 'You, who are stronger, cut the wood; I will carry it.' I answered: 'I will beat upon the trunk with the axe; let us tie the top with lianas and then pull.' The tree broke nicely in the middle; while we were picking up those branches, we heard shouts from the *tapirí*: '*Au, au, au, pei haw, ai, ai* . . .' It was the *tushaua* and all the men shouting. Other women came running to where we were, thinking that it was the Mahekototeri who had pursued us and were shooting. 'Let us hide,' we said; 'if we run, they will see us and capture or shoot us.' Then we heard our men saying: 'Shamatari, our brothers-in-law.'

Five men had arrived with one woman and one small boy. They were all well painted with *urucú* of a brown colour on their bodies and faces and with black, snake-like lines. On their heads they had white harpy down and around their foreheads the crown of *wishiasina*. There is a monkey which they call *wishia,* which has a long, dark tail: they pull off the skin, let it dry, make a hole in the end and in the base, and tie that fine tail round their heads, from which hang big pieces of cotton, at the bottom of which are coloured feathers in a beautiful bunch. They were three brothers and two cousins of the Shamatari *tushaua,* Rohariwe, the one who had defended me. The woman with the small son was the wife of the eldest brother, whose name was Sherekariwe, head of a small group, still Shamatari, who lived apart from the others. After night had fallen, they approached the *tushaua* Fusiwe and began to speak in that singing way of theirs. The Namoeteri were very numerous and not all of them listened.

Sherekariwe said: 'What we have to say now is a secret, which we come to reveal to you. My brother (Rohariwe), that headman who is now in our *shapuno* over there, has said: "I went close to the Namoeteri, I blew my *aroari* poison on the Namoeteri, but I did not hit anyone."' Those men had come because they wanted the Namoeteri to kill Rohariwe. The one who was speaking was brother only on his father's side, for he had a different mother. The man continued: 'What I am telling you, no one knows. Once the *tushaua* Rohariwe was hiding in the wood; one of your young men had jumped up onto the tree to shake down some *caju* fruit, which the women were picking up. The *tushaua* was spying and threw his poison, but did not hit anyone, because there was too much wind. The dogs began to bark all around and the women said: "Come down, perhaps the jaguar is near and wants to eat the children, and so the dogs are barking."' (Jaguars also eat *caju.*) 'The young man came down from the tree and the *tushaua* from afar continued to blow *aroari,* but could not hit him on account of the wind. When he returned to our *shapuno,* he told us: "It is a secret. I have been there to the Namoeteri, I have drunk their *caju* juice and thrown poison, but nothing happened. Their *tushaua* did not notice; he considers me a friend, he embraces me and is well disposed towards me. I want to do just this: I want to kill one of their men and I want them to continue to think of me as a friend."'

While Sherekariwe was speaking thus, those Namoeteri men who were standing nearby began to grow furious. 'I came to you to tell you this secret, because a few days ago he also killed my father-in-law. In the morning the old man said to this woman of mine: "Daughter, I am going to get tobacco to share with everybody; prepare a nice little basket separately for the *tushaua.*" Then the *tushaua* Rohariwe got up from his hammock, took his bow and arrows and said: "I am going to kill an old *cotia.*" No one guessed: the *tushaua* went to the *roça* and while the old man was gathering tobacco leaves he shot an arrow into his back which came out in front. The old man fell and the *tushaua* drew another arrow; one had a hooked point and the other a poisoned head. Then the *tushaua* pulled the arrows out of the dead man's body and calmly came away. The old man's wife was nearby in the *roça* digging *uhina,* together with a small girl. The child said: "Mother, look at the *tushaua,*" but they were afraid to let themselves be seen, because, if they had spoken, he would have killed them too. He has already killed his own brother-in-law, and he has killed one of our women. Yes, it is true, he is my brother, it is true that we grew up together, but I don't want to have anything more to do with him, I am too angry with him.'

Then he turned to everyone and said: 'Now, listen; I will tell you something that happened right here among you, not long ago.' When he said this the women whispered amongst themselves: 'What can it be? What can it be?' He went on: 'A few days ago, in the forest, while you were going to the Mahekototeri, the *tushaua* Rohariwe was following you. He saw when that man killed that youth out of jealousy; he was following you secretly. He saw when that other young man went to shoot parrots under the great tree. It was evening; he was waiting for him in hiding and he threw poison on the young man. It was he who killed that brother of yours. It was he,' continued that Shamatari, turning to the *tushaua* Fusiwe, 'it was he who broke your arrow, that arrow of yours, the best you had, that brother who was your best arrow! It was he, it was my brother, who broke your arrow!' When one is dead, they never call him by name, and thus he called him arrow. The Shamatari went on: 'He came behind you; when at night you went to see from where those noises came, it was he who threw himself into the water. He was in the water up to his neck and you did not see him! Yes, it was he, Rohariwe, who broke your best arrow!' While that man was thus speaking, the women began to weep. 'It was he, and now you must kill him, kill him, kill him . . .' He repeated that word so many times: *'Shere, shere, shere . . .'* Then still turning to Fusiwe he said: 'And don't ever think that I want to make you kill my brother in order that I may afterwards avenge him. Never will I come against you; never, behind your *shapuno,* will my footprints mix with theirs. Another of his brothers might come, or a brother-in-law, but I will never come against you.' The man talked and talked, and then fell silent.

Then the youngest brother, whose name was Hohosiwe, came down from his hammock and said: 'Yes; as this brother of mine has said, so it was!' And he repeated the same things: 'Kill him; we cannot because he is our brother. We have not the courage, because he is our brother. He has already killed four of our men, and now he has killed yours. After he had killed that brother of yours, when he returned to his *shapuno,* he spoke thus: "Be on your guard; perhaps the Namoeteri will discover my tracks." He also said to us: "You too be on your guard, for you are separated from the others. The Namoeteri will notice this. Their *tushaua* Fusiwe is *waiteri* and is Hekurá; perhaps he already knows. I have tried my poison, my *aroari,* on his younger brother; it is an *aroari* which I have in my *roça,* and I wanted to try it out on that young man. I have broken his beautiful arrow; now I can certainly say that my *aroari* kills!" '

They talked so much. They told how the old woman, who had seen Rohariwe while he was shooting the old man in the *roça,* had gone to those who lived nearby, saying: 'If I were you, I would go and tell everything to the Namoeteri *tushaua.* No one here has the courage to kill him; make the Namoeteri kill him, otherwise he will kill you too, who are his brothers.' They said that they had gone to the *tushaua* Rohariwe and had found him with the little smooth sticks on the inside of his wrists and in the holes in his ears, as a sign that he had killed. They had asked him: 'We should like to go to the Namoeteri; where will they be now?' Rohariwe had replied: 'They have gone to the *reaho* of the Mahekototeri, but now they must be on the way back. Do not tell anyone that you have seen my footprints in those parts.' 'No,' they replied, 'we, your brothers, how could we, who are your brothers? Then again, we are afraid of the Namoeteri and they would come and kill us too.' But they were lying to their brother Rohariwe.

The woman also, Sherekariwe's wife, spoke and said that, while the Namoeteri were burning the body of the young man who had been poisoned by Rohariwe with *aroari,* he was still there, hidden, trying to poison another, but he had not succeeded, because all were weeping within the enclosure of *pataua* palm leaves. In fact, the dying young man had said: 'I am dying because they have thrown poison over me.' This is why the Namoeteri had surrounded the place with *pataua* leaves tied well together with lianas; so that the enemy should not see where they were weeping and should not be able to hit them with *aroari* poison. The dogs were barking, because they had heard the *tushaua* Rohariwe; so said the woman.

When they finished speaking, the *tushaua* Fusiwe said: 'I will kill him; if I say that I will kill him, I will kill him. The ashes of the dead man have not even been hung up, not even prepared. For me this is a cause for great wrath. If they had poisoned him some time ago and if we had finished the ashes already, my wrath would be not so great.' Then, turning to Sherekariwe, he continued: 'Tell your chief that I am sending to invite him. Tell him that the Mahekototeri have given me machete and axe. Let him come to me in my *shapuno*, let him bring me a dog and I will give him the machete and the axe.' 'Yes,' they answered, 'we will tell him.' 'You, however, do not come with him,' Fusiwe went on. 'If you dare to come, you will lie dead on my *shapuno* square, together with him.' Shamawe also, the *tushaua*'s brother, repeated to Sherekariwe: 'Don't you come, don't come with your brother; you have warned us; therefore I am your friend. Neither you nor other of your family must come. If I see my men kill you, I don't know what I shall do.' But they did not listen and died with the others.

The younger brother of the *tushaua* Fusiwe said: 'I too want a dog for myself and for this other brother. Tell your *tushaua* that I too have machetes; tell him to bring three dogs and to come with his women.' The Shamatari replied: 'Yes, we will say just that.' Then Shamawe took a machete, which he had had from the Mahekototeri, and gave it to Sherekariwe, who had told the whole story; the *tushaua*'s younger brother gave another machete to Hohosiwe and a brother-in-law of the *tushaua* gave one to the third of the Shamatari brothers; thus the three had machetes and the other two had only arrows. As they were taking their leave, those five Shamatari were happy; the Namoeteri repeated, 'We will make a feast and we will kill him.' While they were going away, the *tushaua* again said: 'I will kill him. Tell him to come as soon as I have repaired the great *shapuno;* tell him that I have many machetes.' The Namoeteri gave bananas and meat to the Shamatari, who went away. Their *shapuno* was a long way off, on high ground, I believe about eight days' march away.

CHAPTER 27

Yanoáma Assault

When the five men had left, the *tushaua* shouted: 'Let no one go hunting today. Let us go straight to that great *shapuno* of ours.' All the Namoeteri, of whom there were very many, had assembled together; Fusiwe was in command of them all. 'Let's go, let's go,' shouted Fusiwe, 'let's go, for Rohariwe is coming.'

Thus we came to the biggest *shapuno*, the round one, with only two exits; we built our *tapirí* near it so as to clean it for the *reaho*. The men changed the old palm branches on the sides of the roof very carefully, because sometimes snakes hide among those dry leaves. We brought new branches and picked big *miuma* leaves, which are used to cover the roof. Each of us women brought bundles of them. Meanwhile the men had cleaned the square as well, and thrown away all the weeds; they had replaced some trunks and collected so many lianas for tying them up. They covered them again with the leaves which we brought and put *inajá* branches over the leaves, so that the wind should not blow them away; the wind sprang up and scattered them, but the next day they put them back. They burnt all the undergrowth and the old leaves. Each man cleaned around his hearth. After only three days, the great *shapuno* was ready, because there were so many men.

One evening, while I was in the forest with the other women cutting wood, I saw many people pass by. I recognized the *tushaua* Rohariwe with about twenty Shamatari. Many of them were the same ones who wanted to kill me, when the young girl died who had eaten the toad's eggs. They too recognized me, but said nothing, perhaps because they were afraid of the Namoeteri. With them came two boys and also two women: the *tushaua*'s wife with a little girl and the *tushaua*'s older sister. They were painted as friends, with red lines and black lines; all the men had around their heads those hairy monkey tails.

I recognized the wife of the Shamatari *tushaua*. She had been so good to me, when they shot me; she had wept so much. Then I said to my comrades: 'Let us warn that woman! It upsets me so much to see them kill in my presence; let us tell that woman that they will kill them.' There was myself, the *tushaua* Fusiwe's daughter, the Aramamiseterignuma wife and the Shamatarignuma, wife of Fusiwe's brother. The Aramamiseterignuma said to the Shamatarignuma: 'Go, warn your relations,' but she did not wish to warn them, because she was afraid of Fusiwe. Then we came up to a small group who were coming behind and asked: 'What are you carrying?' 'They are wild boar,' they replied. 'Give them to us and we will carry them; you go back, do not come.' I also said: 'Go back, because here they are waiting to kill you!' The other wives of the *tushaua* said so too: 'Go back; tomorrow we do not wish to weep for anyone. Go back!' The men looked at each other. One asked: 'What? They wish to kill us?' We answered: 'Yes, they do.' The man then added: 'No man kills me! Look at my arrow; I can kill them.' I said: 'Many are the *waiteri*, but no man avenges himself when the arrow has entered his body.'

I heard two talking to each other: 'It's a lie! Those women are saying that the Namoeteri want to kill us, only because they would like to take our game.' Then we said: 'Go then; but tomorrow we don't want to see anyone run, leaving his blood behind and thereby soiling our *shapuno*.' The wife of Shamawe, Fusiwe's brother, who was a Shamatarignuma, did not speak; she merely wept, looking at her relatives. One man replied: 'I am a Shamatari; everyone is afraid of me!' Another added: 'These women say that they want to kill us; perhaps they are telling the truth,' but his neighbour interrupted him: 'The others are already in front, let's catch up with them.' One of my companions said: 'Let us run inside the *shapuno* too. If they shoot, they will run out; our men will continue to shoot them and they might hit us.' Another added: 'Who knows, perhaps they will not kill them today.'

The Shamatari had come with three dogs; on the way they had killed wild boar and all day they had smoked the meat. It seems that the *tushaua* Rohariwe had said: 'Let us take these wild boar, so that Shoriwe (he called Fusiwe brother-in-law) may eat them; he is waiting for us to come with our dogs.' He did not know what was awaiting him. His brother, who was sending him to his death, knew. One of the brothers of Rohariwe, who had come that evening to give warning, did not accompany him. They said that when Rohariwe left to come to the Namoeteri, he remained sad, lying in his hammock. Many Namoeteri did not know that Fusiwe wished to kill the Shamatari; many Patanaweteri did not know, not even Fusiwe's old uncle, *tushaua* of the Patanaweteri knew it. This is why afterwards that old man was so angry with Fusiwe.

Thus the Shamatari entered the *shapuno* and we heard the shouts of the men. They told me afterwards that Fusiwe, when he saw them enter, did not come down from his hammock: he put his hand in front of his mouth, took the arrows which he had prepared and threw them with force under the hammock. He did this because he was angry. His brother Shamawe came up to Fusiwe and said: 'Brother, come down from your hammock. If these Shamatari see that you are angry, they will shoot you in the night and run away.' Fusiwe, they told me, replied thus: 'I now feel the urge to cut off that Shamatari chief's head with the axe; I don't do it because it is daytime, and if they shoot, they might hit these women.' But Shamawe continued: 'You must not show your own anger. You should get up, ask when they are leaving and where they will sleep. I too want to kill them tomorrow, but I am not angry, I do not show anger. I think only of my arrow and I do not let my hand go from the arrows.'

Meanwhile, while the Shamatari were entering, some Namoeteri were shouting with joy, and others were looking at them in silence. Shamawe and those who were nearby said joyfully: 'Our Shamatari brothers-in-law are arriving and are hungry! Hurry up and get ready the banana *mingau* for them. After they have devoured us, they are already hungry again!' Thus they spoke, for thus Fusiwe wished them to speak. But the Shamatari did not understand. The braziers of Fusiwe and his men were a long way from the entrances; on our side the Patanaweteri, further off the Gnaminaweteri; on the other side of the *shapuno* the Pishaanseteri. The *tushaua* said to us women: 'All of you go and get water, to cook this banana *mingau*, for the bananas are nice and ripe. Tomorrow morning early I want to kill these people!' He spoke in a loud voice, but the Shamatari did not hear since they were a long way away. One man nearby asked Fusiwe: 'Why do you wish to kill them?' A woman added: 'If you kill them, we too shall be blamed. Do you not know that this Shamatari *tushaua* kills everyone, woman, man and child?'

Night fell; many men came around Fusiwe's hammock and began to say: 'Let us kill them at once!' Shamawe, Fusiwe's brother, had a Shamatarignuma wife, whom he had abducted when she was already pregnant; the daughter had been born with the Namoeteri.

This small girl came to ask us for *bacaba,* just at the moment when Rashawe was saying: 'I am *waiteri,* no one will escape from me.' 'Be quiet,' said Fusiwe, 'there are too many people and they might warn them. Tomorrow we will decide.' 'No, today,' they answered. Then those men got up, went towards the gate of the *shapuno* and began to paint the whole of their bodies with black coal. The little girl ran to her mother and said: 'Mother, these men are painting themselves black, because they want to kill the Shamatari.' They later told me that the mother answered: 'What have the Shamatari done to them? Why do they wish to kill them? I always hoped that they would not come, but they wanted to come!' Then the Shamatarignuma wept and when her husband Shamawe came back she asked: 'When will they kill the Shamatari?' 'Not this night,' he replied. Near them that Shamatari had hung his hammock who had come to warn them and whose name was Sherekariwe. The woman said to him: 'Why have you come? They will kill you too; the poison on the arrows is ready. They warned you not to come and they will indeed kill you; you should have come a month later, in order to be a friend. Escape tonight.' But that man did not listen. No one warned Rohariwe, the *tushaua* of the Shamatari.

During the night the Shamatari had cooked the wild boar and divided and shared them out. In the morning Shamawe came up to the *tushaua* Fusiwe and asked: 'Brother, have the Shamatari offered you game?' 'They have given me some, but I don't want game killed by my enemy. I don't want it; it would give me a stomach-ache.' He stood up and gave a piece of that meat to his oldest woman, saying: 'The Shamatari think that I will weep tomorrow for them! I shall not weep tomorrow for them!' The Shamatari were nearby; they heard this, they heard other things, but they did not flee. Perhaps they were afraid to run away, thinking that they would be pursued. Meantime many Gnaminaweteri and Patanaweteri, who did not know that the others wanted to kill, left the *shapuno*.

In the morning, the guests usually make a tour, asking for tobacco, arrows and other gifts. It must have been seven o'clock and still the Shamatari had not moved. Fusiwe's Aramamiseterignuma wife said: 'The Shamatari are still silent; they ought to leave at once, before they kill them.' Fusiwe was still lying in his hammock; about eight o'clock Rohariwe, the Shamatari *tushaua*, came up to him and asked him for tobacco. He did not answer, but made a sign: I got up, took a little tobacco from a box, put it in a piece of banana leaf and gave it to him. Fusiwe passed it to his enemy, still lying in the wide cotton hammock. Rohariwe asked him: 'Shori, brother-in-law, are you ill?' 'A little,' he answered. 'Your Hekurá are sad, and is this why you feel ill?' and he began to blow upon him. Fusiwe looked at him: 'Get up, Shori.' 'No,' replied Fusiwe, 'I am very ill.' I was alarmed; I kept my head down low.

Another Shamatari came up to Fusiwe asking for arrows. Fusiwe's younger brother answered: 'I don't give my arrows; with this I will kill you and keep the others to avenge myself if any one of our men dies.' The Shamatari did not answer and his other companions looked at each other; perhaps they thought he was joking and they laughed. Fusiwe's Aramamiseterignuma wife said: 'Do not speak like that. Even though he may be an enemy, you should not say that to his face,' and she began to cry. At last Rohariwe said: 'Go there all of you, on the other side of the *shapuno*, where they told us they would give us the machetes.' He too went; he was tall and strong, well painted all over and adorned with feathers; he had his son near him; his dogs followed him.

They told me later that Rohariwe, before leaving his *shapuno*, had said to that young boy, his son, who was afterwards killed: 'Son, come with me to the Namoeteri; let us go and take these dogs. I know that I shall not return. They want to kill me, but you come too; let them also kill you. It will not be good for you, if you then have to live without me.' Who knows how he knew; perhaps he had dreamed it, for no one had warned him. Then he told his old father, that old man whom I used to know, with the beard and white hair: 'Father, the Namoeteri have sent to invite me; they want these dogs. I will take these dogs, but I don't think I shall come back. I think they will kill me. I am going so that no one may believe that I am afraid. I am going so that they may kill me. I am killing many people; even the women and old ones are angry with me. It is better that the Namoeteri kill me. Father, I shall not return. When you listen to the Thunder, think: "They have killed my son! It is my son who is making his signal!" ' Then, they said, Rohariwe turned to his son: 'You, come with me; what would happen to you after my death?' He took his son with him and they died.

Meanwhile, in the night, many Namoeteri had painted themselves black and had gone behind the *shapuno*. I had seen them and had said to the *tushaua*'s other wife, the Aramamiseterignuma: 'They have painted themselves black, they will kill them; I am terribly sorry for them.' She replied: 'What? You are sorry for the Shamatari, after they have shot you? They wanted to kill you and they have made you spend so long in the forest?' 'It's true, but I am not dead.' The *tushaua*'s daughter added: 'Yes, it's true, she isn't dead.'

The *tushaua* Fusiwe took black *urucú* and rubbed it on his forehead and his chest, then said to my companion: 'Rub plenty of black on my thighs and calves.' The Shamatari were on the other side of the square, squatting down, waiting for the machetes. Fusiwe approached them and said: 'Here are the machetes,' and he threw them towards them. 'Now give me the dogs.' He took the first and second dog . . .; at that moment the *tushaua*'s younger brother struck Rohariwe with a heavy axe-blow on the head. The axe did not cut, but split open his head. Beside him, the *tushaua*'s brother-in-law struck on the head with another axe Rohariwe's brother, the very one who had come to warn them and whose name was Sherekariwe. I was bending down, cooking something on the fire and I heard the shout of the Shamatarignuma, wife of the *tushaua*'s brother: 'Ahi! They have killed him, my father!'

The two men fell. While their companions tried to take their bows and arrows, the Namoeteri were ready and shot them. I saw a youth running with open arms and I saw an arrow transfix his back and quiver there, while he was running. Then another, with an arrow sticking in his chest, and yet another with an arrow in his flesh. Meanwhile an arrow shot from the other side came and fixed itself in the trunk on which I was resting my foot. I cried out for fear, I embraced my child, I spread out the palm branches of the roof, leapt out and hid by lying flat on the ground, behind a *pupugna* tree. No wounded man shouted; only falling arrows and running people could be heard. The wife of the Shamatari *tushaua* was shouting: 'You have invited him in order to kill him! He had come so far to see you; he had crossed difficult mountains on the way to come to you, and you kill him!' she shouted and shouted; I no longer remember what she said. Rohariwe's sister was shouting too. The two Shamatari boys who had come with the men ran away; the smaller one was perhaps not yet ten years old. Almost all the Shamatari fled wounded; Fusiwe pursued them out of the *shapuno*.

Slowly I came back inside and lay down in the hammock. Rohariwe was not yet dead: he was full of arrows, he stood up, fell, stood up again. Fresh arrows, tak, pierced his flesh, which trembled under the blows; but the man did not die, and did not shout. They pulled the arrows out of his body and continued to strike him. He had arrows in his stomach, his chest, his face, his neck, his legs. I looked and wept.

Meanwhile Sherekariwe, whose head was split open, was not dead and tried to stand up. Fusiwe's other wife also looked on and wept; she saw him and said: 'Finish him off, don't make him suffer!' I went close; the dying man looked at me, recognized me and said: 'Aunt, what is becoming of us?' 'What is happening?' I answered. 'You are the guilty one. You have sent men to kill your brother. The *tushaua* had told you: "You are sending men to kill your brother! We shall kill him; but if you come, we will kill you too." ' There were two women nearby; the Shamatarignuma and a girl. I said: 'Take him out into the woods; soon he will lose his senses.' He tried to get up and run away. An arrow came and hit him in the stomach, passing through from one side to the other; the man fell again. It upset me so much; I wept for him too and I went away.

On the square everywhere was soiled with blood. The *tushaua* Rohariwe did not die; he fell and got up again. He tried to pull the arrows out of his body, but he was no longer able to do so. When a new arrow hit him, he only cried: 'Ahh!' A man came up and stuck his bow into Rohariwe's body, as if it had been a spear. Rohariwe then slowly, very slowly, stood up; his body looked like a trunk with many branches. He walked ahead swaying, gave a horrid growl like a mad dog, lurched and fell forward on top of all those arrows. And so he died. They said afterwards that that growl was his Hekurá escaping from his body. It must have been about ten o'clock when he died.

Fusiwe meanwhile had run in pursuit of the Shamatari who were fleeing. He told later how he saw a wounded youth under an *embauba* tree; it was the son whom Rohariwe had brought. The youth said to him: 'Do not shoot me,' but Fusiwe shot him. The youth repeated: 'Do not shoot me again, father; let me die, for you have already struck me a death blow.' He shot him again and killed him. Then he killed another in the forest. A few days later vultures could be seen circling round: it was the corpse of another which smelled.

Sherekariwe had got up again and gone out staggering towards the forest. I had not looked at him, because it upset me too much. The Namoeteri went to look for him: he was not yet dead and he was all red with blood. They put huge leaves around their arms so as not to get dirty. They lifted him up and dragged him a good way off. I heard them saying to him: 'We are carrying you along the way to your *shapuno*,' but they were deceiving him. Two held him up by the arms, while the others followed with the intention of finishing him off. I had gone out into the forest and I could hear: they kept asking him so many questions: 'Were you also there that time when Rohariwe threw *aroari* over our brother?' The man replied: 'I was not there! I saw nothing. If I had been there, I would not have come to warn you!' 'Tell us everything; if you tell us everything, we will not kill you; otherwise you die at once.' I was passing by with another woman; we were going to wash the bloody hammocks and to scrape the blood off the ground, because they do not like to see or to walk on the blood of dying people. I went close and saw that the Namoeteri were preparing the short sticks to strike him better. 'Why do you ask this unhappy man so many questions?' I said. 'Don't you answer: they will kill you with the sticks. Why do you answer? I would not give even one single word in answer.' I was so sorry for him; I wept and went with the other women to the *igarapé*.

About one o'clock, Fusiwe, who had pursued the fugitives, returned and said: 'I don't want children to come near me; I have killed Shamatari. Yes, I have now killed them; yes, they will all be raging against me.' He entered the *shapuno* and returned to his hammock; his uncle, who was chief of the Patanaweteri, came up shouting: 'You have killed the Shamatari! Your brothers have hit them on the head with the axe and you are the guilty one. I shall go away: I don't want to die for you, shot by the Shamatari. I shall cross the great river and go far away.' He shouted and shouted to the *tushaua* who did not answer. 'You will be alone in this great *shapuno*; now we shall see whether you are really *waiteri*. Yes, you are *waiteri*, but you know that the Shamatari too are *waiteri*. You know that they are running away right now, but soon they'll be here again; within one moon they will be here again to take vengeance. I want to see if you can resist their attack.' The old man shouted so much. The *tushaua*, who had remained silent, at last said: 'He had killed my brother and has even said so. This is why I was angry and killed him; my companions have urged me to kill him. I too still have arrows; if anyone comes, I'll know how to defend myself. Don't think that I rely on the arrows of your sons or on your own! I am a man; my brothers have arrows as your sons have. They are not women!' Then the *tushaua*'s father, old and white, who always sat down on account of the ancient wounds that he bore upon his body, said: 'Son, be silent; he reproves you rightly. You have killed Shamatari, who are *waiteri*, and we are few; they have many friends and will invite them, they will come to attack us and will kill us. Be quiet, do not answer!' The *tushaua* was silent and lay down in his hammock; he was sad.

Evening was coming on when the son of the old man who had shouted so much said in a loud voice: 'Let him who has killed the Shamatari take a liana and drag the body out of the compound, as far as the *roça*, to burn it.' Then those who had killed him took lianas and tied the dead body. So they dragged it out; you could hear the arrows which went tr, tr, trr as they scraped along the ground. The *tushaua*, sitting in his hammock, watched. The designs on that bloody body were still perfect; the ornaments had stayed in the ears and on the arms. No feather had fallen on account of the arrow-shots. Going out of the big entrance they dragged the corpse and took it hundreds of yards away.

The *tushaua* Fusiwe was in his hammock. Then the sister of the dead *tushaua* Rohariwe came up and said amid tears: 'I am old, I am no good for living with a man; I will stay here three days, I will wash the blood, I will burn my brother's body, and then I will go away. If I had been young you could have kept me, but I am old and I am useless; let me go.' She spoke and wept. Fusiwe replied: 'Stay here, go away, do as you please.' The wife of the *tushaua* Rohariwe, on the other hand, tried to escape with her little girl. A man ran after her, took her by one arm and brought her back to the *shapuno*: she was still a young woman.

Rohariwe's old sister came with us to the *igarapé* to wash the hammocks which were covered with blood: Fusiwe allowed her to come. Nearby there was hidden a son of hers, nephew of Rohariwe; he had a wound on his chest and held a stone over the wound, because without that stone he could not breathe. He saw his mother and called her: 'Mother, how many days will you stay here?' 'Today, my son, I will try to burn your uncle, and tomorrow or the day after I will go away.' 'Mother, I will wait for you, and I will hide in that old *shapuno* of the Namoeteri, on the way to our own *shapuno*.' Some of my women friends saw and listened; then the old woman said: 'Don't tell anyone that my wounded son is here.' The youth slowly crossed the path and went into the wood, holding that stone on his chest: his name was Ioinake—it is the name of a bee; he was a strong man, but short.

The following day many Namoeteri went to Fusiwe, full of anger, because he had killed the *tushaua* of the Shamatari. They said: 'Now we are leaving you; we are separating and going another way; we prefer to die of sickness, of snake-bite, but not of Shamatari arrows, for they are the most *waiteri* of all the Yanoáma.' The oldest wife defended Fusiwe and said: 'You are cowards; you are afraid!' The mother too shouted: 'You are scared, now you are trembling, because he has killed; it was not his wish to kill. The fault was with the Shamatari.' There was a great confusion in the *shapuno* that day.

The Gnaminaweteri women, who lived on the opposite side of the *shapuno*, went the next morning to pick *pupugnas* with that old headman who had always been kind to me. In the forest they found the other son of Rohariwe's old sister, badly wounded: he had had an arrow with hooked point in his leg and a poisoned one higher up. He had succeeded in pulling out the hook, but he was all swollen and trembling. He called the old Gnaminaweteri and said: 'Uncle, make a fire for me.' The old man rubbed his sticks together and made fire. 'Are they still looking for us?' asked the wounded youth. 'No, since yesterday they are no longer searching for you.' Then he asked: 'How many of us have been killed?' The old man answered: 'The *tushaua*, the *tushaua*'s brother, and it seems also that young son of his, over there on the edge of the *roça*.' 'And my brother?' 'He is alive, your mother has found him.' Then the wounded man asked them to tell his mother to wait for him too, because he could not go alone. The Gnaminaweteri women, they told me some time later, cooked the *pupugnas* and put them in leaves for him. Nearby there was another Shamatari youth, and he too was badly wounded. The old Gnaminaweteri said to the two: 'Continue along this path, and you will find an *igarapé*, then the path will become smaller and eventually you will come to Naritimateka. Wait there.'

The two little boys were perhaps the only ones not to be wounded. They ran away; one was very small and I could scarcely believe that he could run away by himself, but when one is very frightened then one really can run. Later the Hasubueteri (*hasu* is that small toad with red spots), who in those days had gone to the Shamatari, told us that that brother who had sent word to the Namoeteri to kill Rohariwe and who had not come, was in the *shapuno*, invoking his Hekurá; he was saying: 'Times are very sad; my heart beats fast within me; I think they have killed my brother.' He knew well enough, because it was he himself who had made him go so that they could kill him. 'Yes!' he chanted, 'You are killing my brother, but I am still alive; I have my arrows!' They said that, while the man was chanting, they heard from a distance the bigger boy who, while running down the path, was shouting and crying. Then in the *shapuno* they began to say: 'They have killed them all.' That treacherous brother exclaimed: 'Do not weep! My arrows too, like theirs, have heads. I will go and trample on the ground behind their *shapuno*. My bow too is hard; it can enter from one side and pierce the body right through.' The boys told how, as soon as they saw the *tushaua* hit on the head, they fled; they ran by day and by night climbed up into the trees to sleep. The men who were listening to them said: 'Perhaps the shade of the dead *tushaua* has accompanied them and so the jaguar has not devoured them.' It seems that the boys arrived after six days.

Then, said the Hasubueteri, came a man with a wound in his back; soon after came the one who carried the stone on his chest and who was still holding the stone over his wound. There came also one whose intestine was hanging out of his stomach; the intestine was dry, full of leaves stuck on to that yellow fat. His companions cut off that piece of intestine, but shortly afterwards the man died. Thus, one after the other, the wounded arrived. Rohariwe's brother continued to say: 'They have killed our men; I will avenge them.' The Hasubueteri, who stayed behind a few days longer, saw other men die who were wounded in the stomach. Those who were wounded in the legs and on the face were saved.

CHAPTER 28

The Funeral Pyre and the Old Women

Meanwhile the Namoeteri cut wood to burn the bodies of the dead. They made a big pyre outside the *shapuno* for the *tushaua* Rohariwe; near the *tushaua* they burnt the body of his brother, who had caused him to be killed. The *tushaua* Fusiwe said in a loud voice: 'Let all the Shamatari women, who are with us, go and weep with that poor old woman. You are of the same people; go with your sons, it is your duty to weep.' And all the Shamatari women, wives of the Namoeteri, went with the old sister of the *tushaua* Rohariwe to weep. We too approached them. That body did not want to burn. The *tushaua* saw us and said: 'Go back home quickly; there could be some men around who are not dead; they might shoot you.'

The *tushaua*'s body would not burn: among the wood could be seen the legs and the stomach and the liver which would not burn. They put more wood on top, but still that flesh would not burn. Then the men began to say: 'It doesn't burn, because when he was alive he did not even respect his sisters: Shamatari *yawere*.' Yawere is a man who misbehaves with his own sister. An old man began to shout. 'Go and see! This is what happens to any man who takes his own sister as his own woman! This is what will happen to you, if you do as he has done.' Four times they put more wood on top, but that body did not burn completely. The next morning they lit the fire again. That smoke had a horrible smell and the wind carried that smell to the *shapuno*. Then the Namoeteri said: 'Make a hole and throw that body in it, so that the evil-smelling smoke shall not enter our *shapuno* any longer.'

The women burnt the body of the youth, Rohariwe's son, whom Fusiwe had finished killing in the forest, but rain fell and put the fire out. I wanted to go, but the *tushaua* said to me: 'You must not go, let the others do it; you go and carry wood.' The next day, after the rain, the *tushaua* said: 'Go and finish burning those corpses, so that they do not rot.' Fusiwe's brother, son-in-law and another man went.

Then Rohariwe's wife went alone to collect the bones. In the *shapuno* they said: 'Now she will run away.' Then they took her little girl, who was two or three years old, and let her go: the woman put the bones in a bag and came back. The old sister also collected the *tushaua*'s bones; she picked up only the big ones and covered the other remains with large leaves. She put those burnt bones in the round basket, and then placed it in the big basket. She would not pick up the bones of the other brother: the Namoeteri women had said to her: 'This brother came and told everything; it was he who caused your *tushaua* to be killed.' Those bones were collected by a Shamatarignuma, daughter-in-law of the uncle of the *tushaua*, headman of the Patanaweteri.

Then Rohariwe's old sister decided to leave: the Namoeteri took the little girl, daughter of the dead *tushaua*, and handed her over to the old woman to take with her. But the mother, who was still young, had to stay with the Namoeteri. Then they gave bananas and fire to the old woman, who went away weeping. The old Gnaminaweteri came up to her and told her where the other wounded son was waiting for her.

Some days later Shamawe, Fusiwe's brother, said: 'Let us go and get the bones left over of that Shamatari chief which the old woman did not collect. We have no bones for our *reaho*; when we hold a *reaho*, we will make a hole on the edge of the fire, throw those bones in it and take banana *mingau*.' This is what they do with the bones of dogs. They prepared those bones and filled four *cuias* with them, putting them in a basket. A Shamatarignuma painted the basket red with wavy lines, lined it with leaves and closed it.

Meantime the Namoeteri separated: the Gnaminaweteri went towards their *roça*; the Patanaweteri went towards the banks of the great river. The Pishaanseteri also went away, and with them Rashawe, who was their chief. Few remained with the *tushaua* Fusiwe, about thirty men. They said that it had been Fusiwe's fault; but others also had killed the Shamatari. The son of the old uncle, who had gone towards the great river, had killed; the same Rashawe had helped to kill. They split up because they were afraid of Hohosiwe, the other brother of the dead *tushaua*. Two brothers had been left behind: Hohosiwe and Sibarawe. Fusiwe said: 'Yes; you are parting company through fear. Well, I will go along the path that leads towards their *shapuno*. You say that only I have killed Shamatari; I will go towards them, so that they may kill me. I do not run away for fear.'

One day, as I was returning with my women friends from the forest, I heard women's voices; I recognized the voice of a Shamatari, who was the sister of Sherekariwe. She was carrying a small monkey that Sherekariwe had given her. With her came four other women: the mother-in-law of the dead *tushaua*, mother of that woman whom the Namoeteri had taken; the old mother of Rohariwe, another sister of Rohariwe and another old woman. The woman with the small monkey saw me and recognized me. 'Napagnuma,' she said. 'I have come to take my brother's bones. I have been told that that Shamatarignuma, my niece, has collected them.' She wept as she told me this. I answered, 'These people say that many bones are still there, covered with leaves.' The old woman was weeping. I went on: 'Let us not stay here; let us go to the *tushaua*; he knows where the bones are and he will have you taken there.' In the meantime my friends had run to warn him.

So they came to the *shapuno*. Fusiwe was sitting in his hammock. The woman said: 'I have come for my brother's bones.' The other woman said: 'I am looking for my son's bones.' The other said: 'My brother's'; they all wept as they spoke. The *tushaua* looked at them, then said: 'I have had the bones collected up; I have had them prepared, not to eat them, but to throw them in a deep hole, near the fire! Now you have come to ask for them; go, take them. There too, on the ground, are still some bones; when the rain falls, a few appear.' The women asked: 'Send someone to show us the way.' The *tushaua* called his oldest wife and said: 'Go with these women and show them.' But the woman was afraid that there were Shamatari behind. 'What would they do?' said an old woman. 'All the Shamatari today are afraid of the Namoeteri and are saying that they are about to join up with the Karawetari, for fear of you. You have killed the *tushaua*, who was the most *waiteri*; how can you be afraid of them? Only that timid brother is left behind.' All those five women wept.

Fusiwe said: 'Who has ripe bananas?' We all had some; the *tushaua* took some from one side and some from the other and divided them among the old women. 'Now eat these bananas and give yourselves strength, for you arrive hungry from a great distance. Go; come back later to sleep here.' The women ate; then the *tushaua*'s oldest wife accompanied them. Of Sherekariwe, brother of the *tushaua* Rohariwe, they found only small bones; those of the hands, and the teeth. The *tushaua*'s wife told how that small monkey helped the old woman to seek the bones; perhaps it had understood. It sought them among the leaves, found them and gave them to the old woman; it found them in the water of the little *igarapé* which flowed nearby, and gave them to the women.

Those old women stayed three nights with us; they gathered up all the remains, even the smallest. Of the *tushaua* Rohariwe, they found many bones. The Shamatarignuma, who had collected the bones of Sherekariwe, had gone with the Patanaweteri. The *tushaua* Fusiwe had the women accompanied and sent word to give them all the bones they had. The next day, the old women came again: the *tushaua* gave orders that all the bones of their dead, which were still with us, should be handed over.

The wife of the Shamatari *tushaua* wished to return with the others, but an old man kept her in his *tapirí*. That old man already had a wife and the Shamatari woman had said that she would run away. 'My husband was not old; how can I stay with an old man?' The other women had listened when she spoke thus and had referred the matter to the old man's other wife. The Namoeteri did not let her go; then she gave to the old mother the bones which she had picked up.

When the women were leaving, Fusiwe said: 'Aunts, they have urged me on to kill; then, when I have killed, the others have gone away for fear. Tell the Shamatari that I am going along their path; they may come and kill me. They will find me in the middle of the road which leads to their *shapuno*. Tell the Shamatari to come: we are alone.' This was the message he sent.

After the old women had left, we followed their footprints for three days and came to the edge of a wood of *buriti* palms, near an *igarapé*. The *tushaua* said: 'Let us build our *shapuno* here; here we will wait for the Shamatari. The women will carry the news that we are alone and they will come to kill us. As I have killed their chief, so they will want to kill me: I am not afraid.'

They cut down the big trees and built a small *shapuno*, with a circular open space within; it was well made and the roofs were joined one to the other. Fusiwe made them plant all round the *shapuno* a palisade of *pashuba* trunks. When they decide to stay for a long time in a *shapuno*, they make palisades with big and very hard poles, which do not go rotten; they tie them tight with lianas, and when the lianas begin to rot, they renew the knots. But if they have to build a palisade in a hurry, they make it of *pashuba*. The palisade was about four yards from the *shapuno*. They cut down the bush for about a hundred yards all round, then burnt the fallen trees, in order to make a very thick growth of shrubs spring up, which the enemy cannot penetrate. At night the men sat down to guard the ground between the roof and the palisade. Among the trees which they had cut down the enemy would make a noise, by stepping on the dry, burnt branches and the men would hear and so shoot them.

We stayed a long time in that *shapuno*, on the road leading to the Shamatari. We arrived when the *pupugnas* were not yet ripe and they ripened there. When they were not yet ripe, the men went one day to hunt in the direction of the Shamatari. The hunters smelt smoke and approached it. They found the remains of the food and the embers in the hearths. The Shamatari afterwards told the Hasubueteri that they had come to kill us; in the night one of them woke up and said: 'I have had a bad dream; I have seen a lot of worms crawling up here into my mouth, onto my chest.' The others replied: 'Then they will kill you and will not burn you; it is better that you go back!' So they went back.

One afternoon the airplane passed over again; it also saw the new *shapuno* and began to circle over it. The men said: 'Let us call it, let us make it come down and, when it is close, let us shoot it.' They all went out with bows and arrows onto the *shapuno* open space and began to shout: '*Shori*, *shori* (brother-in-law, brother-in-law) . . .' The airplane came low and circled; they already wanted to let fly their arrows; but the *tushaua* shouted: 'Let him come even nearer.' The plane came very low, perhaps observed that they had arrows ready, and let out a great mass of smoke. Then they all fled; they fled, because they were so afraid.

CHAPTER 29

Invitation to the Mahekototeri

One day two sons of the old Patanaweteri chief arrived to say that all the Namoeteri must unite again, because they had too many enemies on all sides. Then we all returned to the great *shapuno*, near the big *roça* of Patanaweteka. They decided then to invite the Mahekototeri in order to be more friendly. The next day the men already began to bring into the *shapuno* bunches of bananas which they hung up in front of their braziers.

Then the hunters went hunting for the *reaho*. Before leaving, they invoked Sohirinariwe to kill much game. 'When the Moon was climbing in the sky,' said Fusiwe, 'many Yanoáma joined together to shoot her; they shot so many arrows that they obscured the light of the Moon. At last Sohirinariwe said: "When the Moon was low, you were not capable of hitting her; now she is high and you will never succeed." The Moon appeared between the clouds; Sohirinariwe shot her and the arrow hit the Moon. Blood began to fall; the Moon's blood. This blood gave birth to many people; the blood which fell first gave birth to the strongest. The Hekurá then took Sohirinariwe with them.'

When the hunters returned with so much game, Fusiwe called Rashawe and his brother Koroiwe and said: 'Go quickly and invite the Mahekototeri; sleep only once in the forest; the day after be there. You go, Rashawe, because you are a good speaker.' The two took feathers to put in their ears and around their arms, the monkeys' tails for their heads, made packets with *urucú* and set out.

Those who go visiting approach and, to make themselves recognized, whistle, fio, fio, fio, like an otter. Those of the *shapuno* reply: 'Pei haw, Tesamunu he.' Tesamunu is he who goes to invite. They said that Rashawe spoke thus: 'The *tushaua* sends us to invite you and desires that you go soon, because he wishes to converse; if you arrive late, there will be no time to converse.' Then their *tushaua* gave orders to set out.

Meanwhile the Namoeteri women began to say that the Mahekototeri had many things, many machetes, but that they did not give them away; that when they came, they ate so much and their stomachs were never full; that the more they ate the more they wanted to eat; that they themselves were angry with them. Fusiwe answered: 'It is not true; you women always talk like that, but they have always given us the machetes that they had. With those machetes we have cleaned our *shapunos* and prepared our *roças*.'

The Mahekototeri arrived and made their *tapirí* in the forest near the *shapuno*. Together with the Mahekototeri came also an old woman: she was the mother of Akawe, he who afterwards became my second man. She did not go to live with the other Mahekototeri in the *tapirí*, but came with us. That old woman remained alone, and told me to flee from the Mahekototeri, along the great river where the white men passed; but I refused.

Some Namoeteri of the group of the Gnaminaweteri, meanwhile, went to tell the Mahekototeri that Fusiwe had decided to attack them during the return journey after the *reaho*, and to seize their women, as he had done the other time. It was not true; Fusiwe knew nothing about it. The Mahekototeri, for fear, fled without saying anything. The next morning Fusiwe asked his brother: 'Yesterday, coming back from the hunt, I felt a silence on the side where are the *tapirí* of the Mahekototeri; go and see what has happened. Who knows whether the Shamatari have not come and they have fled!' Many men went and saw that the Mahekototeri were no longer there. 'What can have happened to them?' asked Fusiwe. But no one answered.

CHAPTER 30

The Burning Firebrands

After the Mahekototeri had fled, Fusiwe decided to hold a feast just the same, for the Namoeteri only. There the trouble began. Fusiwe shared out the game; it seems that scarcely any was left for the Pishaanseteri. In the evening the children began to play, throwing embers at each other; the same ember which one threw, another picked up and threw back. The *tushaua*'s old father shouted: 'Look, these children are playing; let no one of you men get in between them. When they start these games and grown-ups also join in, it ends in a fight.' Thus shouted the old man, who was eating bananas. The boys too began to throw pieces of embers which fell here and there. One burning firebrand fell on the roof of the *tushaua*'s brother, who was lying in his hammock. 'Who has thrown that fire on the roof?' he shouted. 'Is it perhaps the sons of the Pishaanseteri or the Gnaminaweteri, who are taking advantage of the game to throw fire in our direction? I want to see.' With other men he climbed up from the back and managed to put the fire out.

Then Fusiwe said to me: 'Take that cooking-pot off the fire and pass me all the embers!' The oldest wife added: 'Are you too now going to join in this game? You of all people, who lose your temper at anything? Before long we shall have a fight; I don't want to hold anybody's *nabrushi*. Only the other day I had to run to stop your *nabrushi* and all through you I got a blow on the head.' When the others saw the *tushaua* get up, they said: 'The *tushaua* himself is there.' And thus the grown-ups also began to hurl embers and firebrands. The old father shouted: 'Son, come and lie down; you are old, you have so many women, leave these games to the children!'

It was very dark. It seems that it was Fusiwe who hit a Pishaanseteri on the head with a piece of burning wood; much blood was shed and the man fell. They all threw lighted wood: toh, toh . . .; there were firebrands on all sides. I embraced my little boy, put him on my back and ran out, hiding behind some *pupugna* trees. The other women also began to run out shouting. It was about nine o'clock at night; the firebrands were falling on all sides and it looked like rain. They threw them from one side of the *shapuno* to the other; at first they were embers, then they were those big pieces of wood which are kept under the roof when there is danger of the enemy. You could hear them falling on the cooking-pots and on the *cuias*.

After a short time came silence; the *tushaua* ran out and called me: 'Napagnuma, blow on the fire, make some light, and see what I have here.' I looked for a firebrand, blew, and burnt a few dry leaves. 'Look here in my eye.' A firebrand had hit him on the edge of his eye and had made a deep hole. A piece of coal was stuck in the corner of his eye. The oldest wife, who had more courage, tried to pull it out while I blew on the fire to make light, but she could not. At last her daughter succeeded in pulling out that piece of burnt wood, which had stuck in deep, by the side of his eye. Much blood came out. 'Now,' said Fusiwe, 'yes, now I will kill these people with my arrows.' We wept for fear.

Meanwhile, in the *shapuno*, many men had got burnt. One Gnaminaweteri was shouting to the *tushaua*'s brother: 'You have burnt my son; he is all wounded in the chest; you do it because the *tushaua* is with you!' The *tushaua*'s brothers answered: 'It was you, Gnaminaweteri, who started it!' They were almost all against the *tushaua* who said nothing. Then all of a sudden he shouted: '*Watatie*! Silence! That's enough, or I shoot you tonight! If you wish to live, shut up, all of you.' The uncle's son replied: 'My father sends word to tell you that he will not be quiet.' Then the *tushaua* began to look for wood again to start up the fight once more and we women fled outside once again. Fusiwe's mother shouted: 'You who have tried to blind my son, by throwing a pointed stick in his eye, just wait now for his blows! I shall not flee with the other women; I shall stay near my son!'

All those Namoeteri who were opposed to him lacked the courage to rebel. The *tushaua* called them by name, and insulted them, but they did not answer. The old chief of the Patanaweteri then said to his men: 'The *tushaua* is very angry; it is better not to go on; it is better to leave.' So he went out with his men; others went after them. At length the *tushaua* also fell silent. We women silently went inside again and returned to our hammocks. From that moment Rashawe became an enemy.

The day after, all had come back to the *shapuno*. Fusiwe said: 'So I give trouble to the others in this *shapuno*! I will go away.' He said to us: 'Get everything ready and let's go; leave the bananas.' We put in our baskets the cotton, the earthenware cooking-pots, the arrowheads, the hammocks and the rest, and departed. We wept as we walked, because we thought we should never come back. Behind us women came the *tushaua* with his brothers, his son-in-law, his parents and his group of Namoeteri.

The following day we came to a mountain where lived the relations of the *tushaua*'s oldest wife; they were called Teteheiteri. There were few men with their women. They had separated a long time before, but previously they belonged to the group of the Patanaweteri. They lived high up, in a flat area, with a path which was difficult of access. We stopped in a small *igarapé* of clear water and some men went ahead to warn them; those who lived there sent word to tell us to enter at once and not to stay in the forest. We took a bath, but we did not paint ourselves.

It was a round *shapuno*; one side was unoccupied. They had prepared banana *mingau* and gave it to us. Fusiwe asked us: 'Do you prefer to make the *tapirí* outside, or to live near these people?' I replied: 'I don't know,' and I asked the oldest wife, who said to me: 'Let us two stay here, near my brothers; the other women of the *tushaua* can stay at a distance, since they give us little enough help.' Then she called Fusiwe and said: 'Build three *tapirí* for the three other wives and stay with them. I and Napagnuma will stay with my brothers. Nothing will happen to us.' I was already expecting my second baby and beginning to show a big belly. So I stayed with the oldest wife; we went into the forest, into the *roça*, gathered *pupugnas* and *urucú*, and shared them between us.

A little girl of theirs had died: they crushed the bones for the *reaho*. I saw for the first time the bones being crushed inside those big Pará nutshells, as I had seen them do for the dogs.

Fusiwe asked the Teteheiteri if there was ground for making a *roça*. The oldest brother-in-law, who was in command, said: 'Yes, quite near here on the mountain.' 'I don't want it near here,' answered Fusiwe; 'because the other Namoeteri will perhaps want to assemble again and I want no more of it. I want the *shapuno* and *roça* to be at a distance.' After some days the oldest brother-in-law with his men accompanied us to show us the ground where we should make our *roça*. It was a long way off, in a clearing with a wood of slender trees. Fusiwe and his men cut down the biggest trees, lopped the smallest and made a large, empty space. It was not necessary to burn, because the big trees were few. There remained only, in the middle of the *roça*, two large trees. The Teteheiteri helped to make the field and, after seven or eight days, we all returned together to their *shapuno*. Fusiwe said: 'Now give me banana seedlings, so that I can plant them straight away in that field that we have prepared.' We women went with the men to pull up those seedlings in the *roça* of the Teteheiteri. Many of them will go into one basket, but they are very heavy. Fusiwe said to me: 'I have a son; I do this work so that my son may stay a long way away from the other Namoeteri and may never go back to them.' So we took those seedlings: it was very hard work on those mountains. I walked carrying the burden on my back, with the strip of bark across my forehead, leaning on two sticks so as not to slip. The *tushaua* carried an enormous basket, full. Thus we walked for three days in order to get to the *roça* that we had prepared.

We did that journey often; we also took those roots which they call *uhina* and which produce broad leaves; we took cotton and tobacco, we took seedlings of arrow-canes and of manioc. We planted all those things in that *roça*. We were terribly tired when we arrived. That path had grown wide through all the coming and going with burdens. We also planted *pupugna* palms. We used to scrape the seeds on the rock, until they became nice and smooth on the side where there is a little hole from which the plant grows: they said that in this way they got a tree without thorns. Fusiwe's old mother used to tell me that it was the bird Agnacoremasiki which showed the first *pupugna* to the Yanoáma.

One evening the *tushaua* said: 'I will try to kill a crocodile.' Along the *igarapé* lots of tracks of crocodiles could be seen. Later he came back with his brother. They had caught a *mutum* and a big crocodile; they had cut it up because it was too heavy. Fusiwe gave the crocodile to the women to cook. The women may cook birds, fish, crocodiles; but the men must cook the big game. The Teteheiteri brother-in-law said: 'Here you will eat many crocodiles, because there are so many of their footprints in the mud.' So we built a *shapuno* near the big *roça* which we had prepared, and there we lived.

CHAPTER 31

Karyona

Then my second baby was born. He too was born by himself. I picked him up and left the placenta and the umbilical cord in the forest: they put the umbilical cord high up on the *pupugna* tree. When I came back to look for them, they were no longer there; perhaps an animal had eaten them. When Fusiwe saw the infant, he said: 'He has big eyes like *Karyona*, that beautiful bird with the big eyes. His name shall be Karyona.'

It was at that period that there came a terrible epidemic. Fusiwe did not want us to take the children into the sun; he said that when it is very hot, Hekurá of the Sun steals children. 'When you go to the *roça*, do not wait for the Sun to be very high; when he is high, it is bad.' Thus he would not let the children stay outside in the evening, because Night, the dark Titiri, might steal them. He knew the path of Night, of the Moon and of the Sun.

My first child was ill and was dying. The old Shapori started to seek the little boy's shade. They took much *epená*, lay down on the ground, listened and said: 'The Amahini have not stolen him; there is nothing to be heard.' Then they squatted down in a row; the *tushaua* went in front and said: 'Let us look at this path; this is the path which leads towards the white men; there are no footprints, you see, for this path is closed. I'll go first because I know the paths: I know the way for the Sun, the Night, the Moon, for Titiri, for the whites, for the Amahini.' He went forward squatting down in another direction and repeated: 'This is the path which leads to the Amahini, but there are no tracks. On this road towards the Moon, the tracks are old. Here is the path of the Hekurá of the Shamatari: was it they? See, here go their tracks; they climbed up onto the roof of the *shapuno*, here they hid! Look, here are the signs of two Hekurá.' The others looked and said: 'It is true, from here they went away!' Thus they next moved round in a circle, still squatting down, and repeating: '*Hai, io, hai ioroma*.' Then the *tushaua* said: 'There is no doubt that it was Hekurá of the Sun who stole him!

Let us go along the path of the Sun. The child is weeping up there; the Sun has shut him in, and so he is crying. Let us see whether we can get him back.' Fusiwe was a great Hekurá, and knew everything.

They then went to inhale some new *epená*; they inhaled four or five times, then said: 'Let us get well and truly drunk in order to visit the Sun and not to burn!' They began to beat their arrows amongst themselves and to run. The *tushaua* went in front and said: 'Careful, careful, don't run! Follow me; I am rising up into heaven, I am rising up into heaven towards the Sun.' When they are drunk with *epená* they really believe they are rising into the air. Then a man shouted: 'The Sun has struck me hard in the eye!' He began to run and fell. Another remained hanging by one arm on a high tree-trunk, shouted '*Ua, ua . . .*', let go his hand and fell down like one dead. They said the Sun had blown upon him. The Sun blew fire on them and with that fire they burned; they ran, fell and lost their senses. The *tushaua* went forward and did not fall. At length he said: 'Thou, O Sun, dost burn, and art greater than I, but I have come into thy *shapuno*. Thou hast taken my child, and now I come to reclaim him.' He took things and carried them away; he came running towards the little sick boy with that basket.

Then he began to sing, sucking in the child's throat. He said: 'Magnebiritawe, Hekurá of Tukano, come, suck in his throat, so that his throat may grow fresh again. Come thou, Pregñiuma, daughter of Hekurá of Toad. Thou art beautiful, sit down nearby and cool the body of this sick child with thy cold hands, with thy tiny hands like the hands of a fly. Pregniuma comes, and is beautiful, with a face painted with coloured lines. Look, she sings with the voice of Hekurá: "I am Pregniuma, it is I who live along the *igarapé* and sing my song *pri, pri, pri . . .* Now I will refresh your body." ' Thus spoke the *tushaua*, then sprinkled over the child's body water of Hekurá, water that was invisible. 'Now comes also Hasuburignuma and sings thus. She is young, tall, beautiful, she comes dancing and approaches close. All night she will stay near the patient to calm his pains and will never leave him. Magnebiritawe also arrives with her little packet, singing: "*biri, biri*"; in her packet she has the curing remedy; the remedy of the Hekurá. Look, she passes it over the body and the patient will grow well again. Thou, Arariwe (Hekurá or *arara*) go away, thou makest too much noise, dost disturb the sick, so stay away. And thou Ignamariwe (Hekurá of the sloth), art too slow, thy hand is too slow to seize the sickness, so go away too.' Then the *tushaua* continued in his chanting: 'I am Heheriwe (Hekurá of the bat), I have come here to bite the sickness and draw it out. With my wings I blow upon the sickness. I am a bat; when I was a man, I loved my mother-in-law, and so now I am a bat.' Then Fusiwe went away saying: 'Stay here, Pregniuma, stay here, Hasuburignuma, let all the Hekurá stay here, that the sickness may not return.' The child had truly improved.

So many others fell sick and began to die. They said that they were dying, not because the soul or the shade (which they call *nohotipe*) had been stolen from the body, but because Shawara-wakeshi had come, a being that was all pale and entered into the body of people and killed the Hekurá.

I remember that I was standing near the *tushaua*, under a *bacaba* tree, when we heard a shout from a distance: '*Eheee* . . .' The *tushaua* said to me: 'Do not answer, it is the Mother of sickness, the Fever, who is calling. She has seen men's footprints in different directions and does not know where to go. She is shouting to find out where to go; if you answer, she will come here to you. Last night I dreamed of so many white men, all clothed and with a cloak over them; when they shook the hood, smoke came out, and that smoke entered into us. When the whites undress, they leave the illness in their clothes. We die because of Shawara-wakeshi; it is the whites. White men cause illnesses; if the whites had never existed, diseases would never have existed either.' Perhaps he was partly right. I have lived with them so long; I almost died under their arrows, but I never had any illness, never a headache. I have known illnesses only after I returned to the white men.

When the epidemic began, they all scattered; every family lived in a little hut separate from the rest. Even the old wife of the *tushaua*, who had always loved me very dearly, died. They suspended her body on a very tall tree in the forest, in a large basket. In the lower part of the basket they made many cuts to let out the putrid liquid and to allow the clean bones to remain inside. This is what they do when they are a long way away from their *shapuno*, on a journey or when they are ill and cannot burn the body. They put the body of the woman and of the children who died into the big baskets, covering them over with a panier so that the vultures could not see them. They tied them tightly up in the trees, so that the jaguars would not get them. One morning they had hung up the basket with the body of a small child; in the evening, when they went to see, it was no longer there. The jaguar had knocked it down and devoured it. On the other hand they wrapped up the bodies of men in tree-trunks woven tightly together and then pulled them closer. Then they suspended these trunks horizontally, with the corpse inside, on the top of tall posts crossed over each other, so that in time all the putrid matter would fall out and the skeleton remain. Sometimes I have seen them put the body of women in between the posts, instead of in the baskets.

The *tushaua*'s dead wife had recently had a small son, who cried all the time. The *tushaua* said to me: 'You who have milk, give it to this child.' Whenever the baby cried, the *tushaua*'s sister brought him to me, and I gave him milk. He wanted it all himself and he pushed my second son away. I brought him up; he grew into a big boy and I loved him.

The *tushaua* also fell ill. He walked leaning one hand on a long stick and the other on the shoulder of one of his wives. One day, in an *igarapé*, he bent his head to drink; he fell and lost his senses. His daughter ran up with another wife, lifted him and put him to sit down; that time he almost died. An old Namoeteri, who was a Shapori, came up and asked: 'What has he had?' 'I don't know!' answered the daughter. 'Last night he was very bad, now he has come to drink and he fell.' That old man, who was carrying earthenware cooking-pots on his back, put them on the ground and started to shake him and to chant. He inhaled *epená* several times, saying: 'The sickness has burnt the throat of the Hekurá of the parrot, his companion; therefore he has lost his senses.' He began to suck the throat, the chest, and the head of the *tushaua*. It must have been eight o'clock when Fusiwe fell; that old man continued to minister to him until almost noon. Then, when the *tushaua* revived, he said: 'Let us go.' The *tushaua* started walking again, leaning on two sticks: he walked very slowly.

One day Fusiwe, who was taking *epená*, said to that old Shapori: 'The Hekurá of the parrot, Hererehiriwe, exists no longer; with my illness he has disappeared.' The old man answered: 'Yes, it is true; that companion of yours is no longer here: he has gone away, he exists no more. I will invoke another Hererehiriwe to come to you; that one you had is no more. When you are well, I will call for you one of my Hekurá.' The *tushaua* wept for having lost Hererehiriwe.

The sickness passed and we returned to live in our *shapuno*. Fusiwe's son-in-law went to seek honey some way off. When he came back, he said to us: 'The *tushaua*'s uncle is awaiting us, and inviting us.' It was the uncle who was chief of the Patanaweteri. After some days, the same uncle arrived. He said: 'Why don't you want to come to us any more? The Shamatari are still enemies and you are as sons to me, bcause you are the sons of my eldest brother. Cousins (thus he called us), prepare everything and come!' The *tushaua*'s old mother said: 'We must obey this old man.' That *tushaua* had learnt that Fusiwe's first wife who was a Patanaweteri was dead and had wept a great deal. So we went into his *shapuno*; we entered without painting ourselves, because we were all Namoeteri who were congregating.

Fusiwe's mother, who was a sister of the old mother of that chieftain, the *tushaua*'s uncle, came happily to meet us. When the two sisters saw one another, they wept for joy: 'Come in, come to our *shapuno*,' she said. Fusiwe called her mother. That chief's sons called the *tushaua* 'elder brother' and the daughters considered us, the *tushaua*'s wives, as sisters-in-law. My sons were their cousins.

At that time they were going every so often to see whether the body of the old wife and the bodies of the other dead, which had been left on high in the forest, were still there and whether the bones were now clean so as to prepare them. First they brought back the bones of Fusiwe's old wife, who had so many relations amongst the Patanaweteri. They burnt on the spot the basket in which was the dead woman's body, and made a big parcel of bones, putting the biggest underneath and the smallest on top, inside bark which they then tied tightly with lianas. With their hands they had pulled apart all the bones: it had frightened me horribly. They returned with that parcel and did not enter the Patanaweteri *shapuno* at once, but hung it up outside. Very early the next morning they cut wood and made a fire in the middle of the open space, because it was a time of drought and they were afraid the fire might burn the roof.

Bones burn more quickly than when there is flesh on them; they burnt them in the morning and began to collect up the ashes in the evening; they finished picking them all up the next day. They already had ripe bananas; the *tushaua* sent his men to catch game. When they returned with young wild boar and monkeys, he said: 'I shall not make a feast for many people; only for those who cut wood and made the fire.' But many came; they came from other tribes. Many tears were shed.

We stayed a long time in that *shapuno* of the Patanaweteri. Those Namoeteri who were called Gnaminaweteri also joined forces and made a feast to which came the Hasubueteri too.

After a long time Fusiwe wanted to go back to live in the *shapuno* which we had built near the great *roça*; we found the bananas and the *pupugnas* had grown tall. Every so often Fusiwe said to all of us women: 'Let us go to see my old father.' Thus he called the *tushaua* of the Patanaweteri. On the journey he talked with us and with the small children, and gave advice. 'When we are in their *shapuno*,' he said, 'you little children, don't go running here and there, do not touch their things, take only what they give you and don't go asking for anything.' He was good with us; sometimes he said to me: 'Let us go together; bring the children.' If he had something, he gave it to us. When he went hunting and caught fine coloured birds, he called the children so that they could enjoy themselves. He was good to everyone: if people arrived from outside, who had nothing, he made them live in the *shapuno*, and sent them to his *roça* to get bananas and other fruit. He gave tobacco to the old men and women; even that tobacco which one keeps hidden when it is almost used up. He also took ours to give away as a gift. Sometimes I wept with resentment, because he gave everything he had and was left with nothing. He was never angry with anyone; he was angry only if they provoked him.

This old Patanaweteri *tushaua* always gave Fusiwe advice; he said: 'You have many women, Aramamiseterignuma, Hasubueterignuma, Namoeterignuma, Napagnuma; this last one is different, but she is like us. I call her niece, because she is human like us. Do not maltreat them, do not do as many do who beat them; women suffer more than men. Sometimes men beat them and the women flee into the forest with the children; then a jaguar appears, kills them, and he who loses is the father himself.' 'No,' answered Fusiwe, 'I never beat them; if they quarrel among themselves I do not stand for it, and then I must beat them all, not only one. Now they hardly ever argue at all.' The old man then said to us: 'You women must not quarrel among yourselves, but you must love each other as though you were sisters. You must think of these children as if they were all your sons, and not be jealous of them.'

During that period Fusiwe's old father also died. He died while we were returning from a journey. His body remained four days without being burned to give time to the relatives to come and help with the funeral pyre; it remained hung up in the hammock under the roof; it swelled and became large. Then it was burned.

CHAPTER 32

The Provocations of the Pishaanseteri

After the battle with fire, the Pishaanseteri were no longer our friends. While we were together with the Patanaweteri, they went into our big *roça*, near to the Teteheiteri, and broke the tobacco plants, because of the anger which they still felt against the *tushaua*. Meanwhile, the *tushaua*'s eye had healed, but underneath it there remained a deep scar. Fusiwe knew nothing about what had happened, and one day said to his uncle, chief of the Patanaweteri: 'In the *roça* that I have planted, the tobacco is growing very well; you can send men to gather it.' The uncle answered: 'Our Hekurá have seen two young men, who used to sleep in the *tapirí* near your *roça*; they had hung tobacco leaves over the fire. Perhaps they have gone to get your tobacco.'

Then the *tushaua* sent his son-in-law to see; the man set out in the morning and came back in the evening of the following day. When he returned, he did not speak directly with Fusiwe, but said to his wife: 'Tell him not to have any more hope in the tobacco; only a few leaves are left, which I have taken,' and he deposited a packet of tobacco leaves. 'In the *roça* the bananas are pleasant to look at, with all their seedlings around; three plants for arrows have already started to form canes. But they have ruined all the tobacco!' Fusiwe's daughter said to him: 'Father, those people have taken all your tobacco; out of mischief they have stolen the plants, because our *roça* was too beautiful!' The son-in-law continued: 'It was the Pishaanseteri; all the footprints went towards their *shapuno*; their *tushaua* is Rashawe.'

This was the beginning of Fusiwe's wrath and was the cause of his death. When it began to grow dark, the uncle, *tushaua* of the Patanaweteri, shouted: 'All keep silent; let us listen to what my son wishes to say.' He called the *tushaua* his son. Fusiwe spoke slowly; all stood listening in silence: 'I have planted much tobacco,' he said, 'and the Pishaanseteri have broken down the leaves and torn up the plants. What do they want from me? They want me to kill them. They are acting like this because they are all still alive. I will kill one of them, so that then they may have cause to be angry with me; it was I who should have been angry with them, because they have wounded me in the eye, but I was not angry.' He spoke a lot: 'They are lazy; they have no tobacco and they go treading in my footsteps to take mine.' He spoke; he spoke until late at night.

When Fusiwe finished, his old uncle replied: 'Oh my son, you must not shoot. You have two male children; one is growing up, the other has only recently appeared. Why do you think of killing? Do you think that killing is a joke? If you kill today, tomorrow your sons will be alone and abandoned. When a man kills, he often has to flee far off, leaving his children behind him, who weep for hunger. Do you not yet know this? I know it, because I am old. When we used to live on the other side of the great river, we used to fight with the Kunatateri, who had killed one of us. We fled, carrying with us the bones of the man who had been killed; on the journey we found no bananas and so much time passed before we could prepare the banana pap for the ashes. We ate only *inajá*, the fruit of *balata*: sometimes not even that. The children wept and I wept for the pain of seeing my sons go hungry. Your father wept with me and you yourself, who were then a child, used to weep for hunger. So would you now wish to do the same? If you kill those people, you yourself will suffer for it with your sons. Wait; soon the tobacco leaves will sprout again and be like they were before. Do not remain angry; if they had killed a brother of yours, you would be right to kill them, but not for a plant. A father, a son, a brother we can never replace; a broken plant we can replant when we please. Do not let yourself be conquered by anger; let us sow tobacco seed. When the seeds germinate, we will take the little plants and transplant them in the same *roça*; thus you will have the same tobacco as you had.' He spoke; he was a good speaker, that old man, who was kind to everyone. He was a calm old man, who did not believe in killing. When my sons' father died, he brought me pieces of meat; he took my young boy by the arm and said: 'It's your old grandfather who is giving it to you,' and he gave him bananas and meat, to bring to me; he was the kindest man of all. Then the *tushaua* calmed down.

We returned to our *shapuno* and found that they had broken the tobacco plants.

Some time later, the old Teteheiteri chief sent to invite us and we went. My second child was already growing bigger. While we were still with the Teteheiteri, the husband of the *tushaua's* half-sister, who lived with the Pishaanseteri, arrived. He was painted, and he looked sad; the men were out hunting. The Teteheiteri women said: 'Here is a Pishaanseteri; is there some bad news?' The *tushaua* was lying in his hammock; he had taken *epená,* he had chanted and spoken with his Hekurá. Before the man arrived, he had already said: 'People are coming, I feel it in my legs. I feel my heart beating: they will come along that path.' The women had replied: 'Nobody is coming; who can come to us? No one knows where we are.'

But the *tushaua*'s mother said: 'You will see that before long someone will come'; in fact that man came, hung up his hammock and lay down. The *tushaua* got up and went to squat down near him; the man came down from his hammock, took his arrows, squatted down opposite him, and began to say: 'Don't think any more about your fruit; the Pishaanseteri have made their *shapuno* near your *roça* and are ruining everything, breaking the branches of the *urucú*. My woman shouts, but they answer that it is you who wish them to act thus. They have ruined the tobacco, they have broken down the maize plants which were about to produce their crop; everything has fallen to the ground. They do this because they want you to leave them your *roça* and go back to live permanently with the Patanaweteri; this is why they provoke you.'

His other wives began to protest. The Namoeterignuma, whose name was Tokoma, said: 'We have worked so hard to plant that crop; they provoke you, so kill them. First they have ruined your tobacco and you did nothing about it; now they are ruining your still unripe fruits, the cotton, the *urucú*. It's time to reply.' That woman had much to say; at last the *tushaua* answered: 'Yes, woman, you incite me to kill. You want me to kill the Pishaanseteri and I will kill them: remember that it is you women who will suffer for it!' He was angry, because that woman spoke in such a way. I said: 'You incite him to kill the Pishaanseteri, because you have a father. I and this other woman, the Aramamiseterignuma, shall stay here, alone, in the hands of others. Not you, you will stay with your mother, and so you want him to kill. I don't wish him to fight with the Pishaanseteri, for I am afraid of their chief, Rashawe. He is very strong; in every fight he goes to the head of his men; they are all afraid of him.' Rashawe had been kind to me; but I was afraid of him, if they became enemies.

Fusiwe said: 'Let us go back and have a look at our crops!' On the way towards our *shapuno* the *tushaua* said: 'When my father was alive, he always used to say to me: "Do not kill." Now the old man's no longer here.' So we came to our *shapuno*. In the evening the *tushaua* took his *epená*, squatted down, called my little boy, the elder one, and said: 'Son, these people are provoking a fight with me; if one day anger takes hold of me, I will kill them; but then you too will be left without a father!' He looked at the child: the child looked at him and laughed: 'You, son, laugh today; but you don't know how much you will suffer one day with your mother, when I am no more.' He went on taking *epená*, while the boy looked at him all the time. The other child at that time could still not walk, but crawled along the ground on all fours.

Then Fusiwe began to sing his Hekurá chants; he said: 'Go tomorrow into the *buriti* wood; I see many wild boars; they are making a noise; they are eating the fallen *buriti* fruit. Let us kill and eat them for the last time. We shall then fight and these people will exterminate us; as they break down our plants, so they will do with us.' While he was chanting, an old Pishaanseteri woman passed behind our *shapuno* and listened; she went back to the Pishaanseteri and said that the *tushaua* was insulting them, treating them like wild boars, monkeys, or wicked men.

The next day, the men wanted to go hunting. Fusiwe decided to go with us women into the forest to see whether the Pará nuts on two big trees had started to fall. We passed through the *roça*; the *tushaua* saw his beautiful plants of arrow-canes ruined and said: 'They really want a fight. Do they want to kill me or do they want me to kill one of them, what do you think? When anyone wishes to be enemies, this is exactly what they do; they break down the arrow-plants.'

Behind us came the brother, the son-in-law and the brother-in-law. We came near to an *igarapé*; the *tushaua* looked on the ground and said: 'There are fresh human tracks; it must be the Pishaanseteri; if it is they, I will shoot them.' I was afraid and said: 'Why do you want to shoot them? They will be hunting and then they will say that you had hidden in the forest to kill them, because you lacked the courage to kill them in their *shapuno*. Don't kill them, because otherwise they will attack our *shapuno* and kill our children.' 'No,' he replied, 'I will kill them;' he took two poisoned arrowheads out of his quiver and fitted them onto the arrows. The other wife also repeated: 'Don't kill them,' and we went on walking.

At the end of the path we saw some Pishaanseteri; Washawe (which means bat), Nimotawe, Xotonawe and others; they were sitting down, making heads for their arrows, talking and laughing. Together with them were seven women. They had not seen us; when we came near, they were confused and lowered thir heads. After we had passed by, one of them gave a great laugh. The *tushaua* stopped, looked at them, then said: 'Yes, this Xotonawe, who has a face like an ugly monkey, laughs loudly after I have gone by. Do you think perhaps that I am an animal like each one of you, so that you may laugh at me when I go by? You know well that all are afraid of me. So would you like me to kill you?' and he beat heavily upon his arrows. I caught hold of his arrows and said: 'Let us go; they were not laughing, they were here for hunting.' Fusiwe listened to me and continued the march. When we were at some distance away, he said to me: 'You wanted to spare my arrows: I was just about to shoot that man who was laughing.' 'It upsets me that you should kill people with whom we used to live; I consider them my relations.' 'Then you will weep when I kill them?' 'Yes, I will weep.' They did not answer, but returned to their *shapuno* to call their companions. They took their *nabrushi* and ran to our *shapuno*, where there were only three women.

We were in the forest gathering nuts: about midday Fusiwe said: 'Let us go back; they have not pursued us, but have gone back. Perhaps they will want to do something in our *shapuno*; you will see.' I collected the nuts without opening the big shell and put them in my basket; he opened some and we hid others. While we were passing near their *shapuno*, we heard loud voices, and then on the path we met an old woman, who was running to warn us; 'Nephews,' she said, 'lots of them have come with *nabrushi*, ready for a fight; they have found nobody and have said: "There are no men here, so we'll come back tonight."' The *tushaua* answered: 'I don't want a battle of *nabrushi*, I want a battle with arrows once and for all; I want to draw blood in earnest, because blood which is drawn by *nabrushi* does not kill.' I kept saying to Fusiwe: 'Do not kill, for they have not killed anyone; I am afraid for our children.' But the other Namoeterignuma wife said: 'No, he must kill them; why do you protect them?' 'Because I don't know where to go if the *tushaua* dies. If he kills, the others will kill him and I cannot escape with these children.' While we were arguing thus, he shouted and told us to keep quiet.

In the afternoon we heard the dogs barking behind the *shapuno*; Fusiwe said to me: 'You have courage; go and see.' I was very much afraid, but I went out slowly to spy around and I came right to the *roça*. I saw all the Pishaanseteri painted black, brandishing their *nabrushi* as they came, with both hands high above their heads. Behind them came the women with bows and arrows. I went running back to the *shapuno* and told him: 'The Pishaanseteri are coming with *nabrushi*.' The other men meanwhile had come back from hunting. Fusiwe shouted: 'Take the *nabrushi*. Don't you hear how they are stamping the ground with their feet? *Rahaķashiwa*, my arrow, is good enough for me.' 'No,' said his brother, 'don't shoot straight away, but take your *nabrushi*. If you don't take the *nabrushi*, I too will take my arrows.' The Pishaanseteri were coming nearer and making a noise by stamping loudly with their feet on the ground.

Meanwhile the Pishaanseteri wanted to enter the *shapuno*; the Namoeteri of Fusiwe were shouting: 'We are few, but you shall not enter; no one will enter.' When someone tried to enter, the men inside struck him hard with *nabrushi*. The *tushaua*'s son-in-law gave a great blow to a Pishaanseteri on the head and he fell down; then I heard them shouting: '*Pei haw*! One of us has fallen; women, give us our arrows!' When they want to fight with *nabrushi*, they make the women carry the bows and arrows; if those at home defend themselves with *nabrushi*, this is how they fight, but if they draw arrows, then they take their bows and arrows from their women, who are close by. Fusiwe, his brother and his nephew were the only ones who had their arrows in their hands. Fusiwe shouted: 'He has fallen on account of a *nabrushi*, not an arrow!'

The man who had fallen was losing so much blood from his head; some companions carried him away. Then Rashawe shouted: 'Today the *tushaua*'s son-in-law is *waiteri*, because he sees his father-in-law; if he had been alone, he would not have done anything. Today we will make you weep; we will make you weep!' The *tushaua* replied: 'Come, come, Rashawe; I want to weep!' And he seized his bow like a spear. 'Let go of your bow,' shouted Rashawe 'and take your *nabrushi*.' I went up to Fusiwe and took his arrows, because he was about to shoot; 'Let go of your arrows,' I said, 'and take your *nabrushi*.' 'You are afraid for me,' he replied; 'do you think I am not a man?' 'No, they are without arrows.' I snatched his arrows and ran away. He came after me, but I continued: 'You have prepared your *nabrushi*, so take it.' It was a nasty *nabrushi*, heavy and short; it was thin where he held it, but big at the top end, with knobs.

Fusiwe took the *nabrushi* and stood near the entrance, waiting. When Rashawe tried to enter, he gave him a great blow on the head and tore the skin, which remained hanging with the hair mixed in with blood. Rashawe did not fall, but shouted: 'Ihhh! Now I really will grow angry, since you have cut my head open.' He called his brother and said: 'This arm of mine has become soft; pull it, for I want to avenge myself.' We were watching; the brother pulled his arm hard; Rashawe said to his other brother: 'Give me your *nabrushi*, which is bigger.' Meanwhile Fusiwe was calling him: 'Come, come, come at once and avenge yourself, instead of leaving the boys to face me. You want a fight with me, so come on.' 'Yes, here I am; do you think I am afraid of you who have hit me over the head with that horrible *nabrushi*?' He came running and gave a blow on the head to the *tushaua*'s son-in-law; the *tushaua*'s brother answered him with a blow on the arm and made him drop his *nabrushi*. The *tushaua* went on: 'I don't know a *waiteri* who drops his *nabrushi*!' 'Come, come and avenge yourself!' Rashawe was losing much blood. 'I cannot avenge myself now, because my arm is soft; I will come and avenge myself with an arrow.' 'How?' said Fusiwe. 'When a man has a fresh wound, he is angry and seeks revenge; so come along, at once.'

Some Pishaanseteri had hit the *tushaua*'s brother on the head. Rashawe was wounded, many other Pishaanseteri were wounded, and it was beginning to get dark; their women were shouting, saying: 'You, *waiteri*, are spilling the blood of our brothers.' We were weeping and shouting. The *tushaua* continued: 'What? You are more in numbers and yet I see you retreat; come on, then, come on.' Then a Pishaanseteri, a tall man named Tukumapahawe, ran in front and said: 'Here I am, it is I; do you want a fight with me? My sons are all in the fight.' The *tushaua*'s son-in-law, who was irritated because of his wound, ran to face him. The man took fright, threw his *nabrushi* and tried to flee; the *tushaua*'s son-in-law hit him from behind and knocked him down. A son ran up and said: 'Father; you should have stayed behind and left us in the fight.'

Those of the *shapuno* were fewer, but knew how to defend themselves better; the *tushaua* saw that the Pishaanseteri were retreating and shouted: 'Let us take advantage of this; let us go out and chase them.' It was by now dark; those of the *shapuno* joined forces and started to stamp loudly and threateningly with their feet; the Pishaanseteri then began to flee, while the others pursued them. At length Fusiwe shouted: 'No, I am not angry; you have struck me and my blood is flowing, but I bear no wrath against you. Now it is enough, go back and sleep; I too am going back to sleep.' Mirahawe, Rashawe's brother, answered: 'You must go away; you must leave us this *roça*; here we must live. Go and live with the Patanaweteri; we must be the masters of this place.'

The *tushaua* recalled all his men and made them close the entrances to the *shapuno* securely, saying: 'Close everything; when Rashawe is angry, he does not know what he is doing; he takes fire with his hands. Perhaps he will try to come back tonight with arrows and shoot one of us.' During the same night, the brother and another man went to warn their uncle, *tushaua* of the Patanaweteri. The next day nobody went out; only I took leaves to squeeze out *urucú*. While I was collecting those big leaves, I heard the little birds singing, as they sing when they see someone; it was the Pishaanseteri. They told me afterwards, when I went to them a long time later, that they saw me that time: 'Let us shoot her,' said one of them, 'she has two male children. If she dies, the sons will also die; those sons whom the *tushaua* loves so much. We must kill the sons too, otherwise, when they are grown up they will avenge their father.' But another replied: 'No, don't shoot; she is a woman and she has no one here with her.'

CHAPTER 33

The Young Tokoma and the Wrath of Fusiwe

The following evening more than twenty of the uncle's men, all painted black, already arrived in our *shapuno*. They had painted themselves before setting out; they had black around their neck like a collar, black on the forehead, cheeks and body. Our *shapuno* filled up with men, who were carrying only bow and arrows, not even hammocks. While they were entering, one let out a shout, but the *tushaua* made him keep quiet: 'Do not shout; if they hear shouts, they think we have sent to call for help.'

The eldest son of the Patanaweteri *tushaua* came up to Fusiwe and said: 'I have come by this road; by this road I wish to carry you back with all your men on my shoulders. The Pishaanseteri, who are *waiteri*, want to kill you; therefore I have come to load you on my shoulders and take you with all your men into our *shapuno*. I want to see whether the Pishaanseteri are truly *waiteri* and whether they have the courage to enter our *shapuno*. They have told us that the Pishaanseteri have been to the Hasubueteri and have said: "We wish to kill the Patanaweteri; we alone will remain, we, the Pishaanseteri, the most *waiteri* of all." "O Pishaanseteri, do not speak of us, do not name our name thus! Go into the forest, seek the tracks of the tapirs, kill them, drink their broth and remain satisfied, but be silent in your *shapuno*. If you continue to provoke us, I will invite the Hasubueteri, I will invite the others and all together we will come and destroy you. Today I have come, I have brought nothing, only bow and arrows and my quiver with poisoned arrowheads. These two poisoned arrowheads my father sends you, so that when yours are finished, you may throw his." The *tushaua* replied: "That is what I like to hear; tell me that, tell me that! That is what I want to hear."' Then the man continued: 'Start, all of you, with the women, go back to our *shapuno*; we will stay in here, and make a fire. The Pishaanseteri will think that it is still you. Afterwards we too will come.'

We set out in silence; the Pishaanseteri did not notice. During the journey those Patanaweteri who had stayed to guard our *shapuno* caught us up and told us that they had made a fire, that they had whistled, and made a noise in the *shapuno* while they were keeping watch on the paths all round. It seems that in the night the Pishaanseteri had come close, but they had drawn arrows from a distance to frighten them, as soon as they had heard the whistles which they were making to call each other.

On the journey Tokoma, that young wife, wept and said to Fusiwe: 'You are afraid of the Pishaanseteri, and so you are going away.' She was upset and often beat her small daughter. She was dark and young, and the *tushaua* loved her. They said that when she was still in her mother's stomach, the *tushaua* had already begun to bring game to his mother-in-law. The mother-in-law was also very anxious that the *tushaua* should be her son-in-law, and used to send him roasted bananas. The *tushaua* was coming with us, because they had told him: 'You go among the women, so that you can defend them if they are attacked.'

Before reaching the *shapuno,* the *tushaua* painted himself red and said to us: 'Paint yourselves also, you people! If you enter without painting yourself, it is as though a relative has died!' We all painted ourselves; Fusiwe took black *urucú* and told me: 'Rub it on my sons; they will be *waiteri,* they will fight when I am dead.' The *tushaua*'s brother also painted his sons black and his daughters red. When we entered, the old uncle was sad and said: 'I had warned you not to go; stay with us. The *roça* you have planted here is already beautiful; leave them the old *roça* and don't ever go back there.' They were all full of rage against Rashawe.

So we stayed with the Patanaweteri. The uncle kept giving Fusiwe advice: 'My son, do not think of killing the Pishaanseteri; you have small children. After they kill the father, the little children go sadly looking for him. They hear the others calling their father. They too repeat: "Father," but their father is no longer there. Do not think of killing the Pishaanseteri. We used to live all together; call them once more to come with you. Do you perhaps think it is easy to kill the Pishaanseteri? Do not think of arrows merely in order to kill, but think of hunting. Kill birds, wild boar, tapirs; then invite the Pishaanseteri to eat them. Remember that we are all in this world to die. You sleep, you dream something horrible in the night, get up and want to kill the Pishaanseteri; you think: "I have a bad dream, because they think evil things of me," and this is why you want to kill them. You must not think of this, my son, but think of your small sons, of your daughters, who will weep for hunger; after death the sons weep. You do not know who the Pishaanseteri are: of old their fathers used to fight against the Kunatateri, against the Waika, against others, and they used to kill on all sides. Their fathers were truly *waiteri*. They are the sons of those who used to pull out from the back the intestines of those they killed, and tear off their arms and cut off their heads and hide them in the woods.' The *tushaua,* filled with rage, answered: 'Father, do not talk to me like that; I will cut off their heads, put them in a pot, cook them, and drink the broth of their heads!' The uncle replied: 'You answer me thus, but do not think that our men are afraid; even of old, when we used to go to war, it was the Pishaanseteri who were always in front; I know what their grandfathers and their great-grandfathers have been as slayers of people; this is why I do not wish to kill the Pishaanseteri.' I listened.

A short time after our arrival, the Mahekototeri sent word to say that many white men had passed by and left machetes, axes and clothes, in exchange for bananas. All the Patanaweteri said: 'Let us go; we want the machetes.' But Fusiwe did not wish to go, for he had wicked intentions; he had decided to kill those men.

In the evening he came close to me and said: 'The Mahekototeri have come to invite us; the Patanaweteri have said that they will go to get machetes and axes; I shall not go.' 'Why?' I asked him. 'I wish to kill the Pishaanseteri.' I was afraid and asked: 'Where then shall we go to kill them?' 'We shall go to where my brother-in-law has his *roça*. He arrived yesterday and told me that at his place there is plenty to eat. There is much manioc: it is a large *roça*; there is tobacco, there are arrow plants.' It was a brother-in-law, brother of Tokoma, that young and beautiful wife, who lived apart, together with his father-in-law, his brother, his cousin and a few other relatives, with their women. I said: 'It is better to stay here; we are all right here.' 'Have you arrows like me,' he replied, 'to shoot the Pishaanseteri, when they attack us here too?' 'No, I have no arrows, but I don't want to go there; it is too far.' He looked at me and said: 'Then stay, I will go.' 'Go then,' I replied. He was crouching down and holding my second child between his legs; he stood up, put the baby in the hammock and went away.

After some days the old uncle called him and said: 'My son, the Mahekototeri have invited us, because they have machetes and axes; you come too with me, let us all go.' 'Yes,' answered Fusiwe, 'I'll come too.' The next morning, while they were all leaving, Fusiwe went to the old man's son and said: 'Ask for a machete for me too, and tell them I will send later some cotton prepared by my women.' 'Are you not coming, then?' 'No, I will wait for you here.' He was lying; I would have liked to say so, but I lacked the courage. When the old man learnt that he no longer wished to go, he said: 'We must cross the great river; at this time it is full and perhaps we shall stay some days on the bank, before the tree-trunks are ready, which we shall have to tie together to pass over. Often, when the river is full, the trunks become untied and the current carries them away.' 'Yes, I will wait for you here.' 'Will you wait for us here and not go once more to challenge the Pishaanseteri? Let them calm down; when the *pupugnas* are ripe, I will send and invite them to try them with axe-blows or *nabrushi* so that their anger may pass.' 'No; I have no further thought of challenging the Pishaanseteri.' But it was a pure lie.

The old wife of the Patanaweteri *tushaua* came up to me and said: 'You, who always go to our *roça,* look at my tobacco. There are already those grubs that eat the tobacco and, if I do not kill them, in a few days they will have finished the leaves. Use the big tobacco leaves too. I am telling you, for I don't trust the others.' I answered: 'Yes, I will go, but I am afraid we shall be leaving at once. The *tushaua* has told me that he wants to go to that brother-in-law of his, because he wishes to kill the Pishaanseteri; this is why I am afraid.' We were standing there, behind the *shapuno*; I started to cry. The old woman exclaimed: 'He no longer listens to advice,' and she went away weeping too.

As soon as the Patanaweteri left, the *tushaua* said to us: 'Let's go; let's go away at once, because I want to reach my brother-in-law quickly. Let's go and see that herd of wild boar which I want to kill.' The Aramamiseterignuma wife said: 'You think all the time of killing and do not think of your sons.' The *tushaua* replied: 'Yes, I must kill the Pishaanseteri, because this woman here,' and he pointed to the youngest Namoeterignuma wife, 'says that I am afraid of them. I will kill them; then she will remain calm, after they have killed me for vendetta. Only for this reason will I kill them and she is responsible. I would like to see her, when they have killed me, with her white hair next to her mother, having no longer a husband.' That woman replied: 'I shall say that you are going to kill the Pishaanseteri only to get my brother killed later.' The *tushaua*'s brother-in-law, to whom we were going, was in fact her brother. 'I am not saying that I want to kill the Pishaanseteri, so that they may kill your brother; you are already making this story up; you always make things up!'

We walked on, but Tokoma did not wish to come with us. 'Let him go with the women whom he loves more than me,' she said. 'Can it be me whom he loves more?' I asked her, 'and is that why you are saying this?' The *tushaua* said to me: 'Be quiet; this discussion is with me, not with you. Go ahead with the children.'

I had gone a few steps when the *tushaua* took his bow, fitted a hooked arrow and shot it straight at her leg. The woman shrieked with pain and called me: 'Mother of the child . . . Come . . . Pull this arrow out of my leg!' I wanted to go back, but the *tushaua* stopped me and said: 'As she has the strength to speak, she must have the strength to pull out the arrow; I will shoot you too if you go to her help!' I was afraid, I started to cry and I went on walking. Tokoma was weeping and shouting; the *tushaua*'s daughter turned to her father: 'What? You shoot a woman? A man may not shoot a woman; you think only of killing and shooting, of causing pain to women!' She tried to approach the wounded woman, but the *tushaua* would not let her pass. Then came another of the *tushaua*'s wives and said to us; 'You have no courage, but I will go and help her,' and she ran to Tokoma. The *tushaua* was standing near the wounded wife and saying to her: 'Loosen the hook and do not break the arrow; I will not pull it out for you. You have a big mouth for talking and you will be the cause of my death. I will kill the Pishaanseteri, so that they may kill me and you may at last be at peace. We shall see whether you will find another good man who will treat you as I used to treat you!' Then he said to his other wife who had come up: 'You take the little girl and carry her; she must come by herself, leaning on her sticks.'

Weeping, Tokoma untied the long thread which held the hook, removed the arrow which had passed through her leg and left it on the ground. He picked up the arrow and, when he came near to us, said: 'Wait for that gossip of a woman; I don't think she can walk.' The woman was coming slowly, weeping and walking all twisted. I exclaimed: 'So you shoot women? We had not asked you to do this; we had asked you only to stay in the *shapuno* of the Patanaweteri, but you had resolved to shoot women! You think of shooting women, of killing Pishaanseteri! So kill them all and you'll see that you end up dead yourself! He who draws the arrow does not feel the pain, but he who receives the wound feels it! It grieves me to look at this woman and I know how much it hurts!' 'You are protecting her then?' Fusiwe said to me. 'You protect that very woman who is always shouting against you?' 'Yes,' I replied, 'I am not angry with her; she shouts against me, but she has never come against me with a stick, as she has with the other wives.'

Meanwhile Tokoma came up to us in tears; she seized the *tushaua*'s quiver, filled with poisoned arrowheads, and threw them a long way off. 'You must not throw them away,' I told her, 'it was not the arrows which caused you pain, it was their master.' Weeping all the time, she answered me: 'Be quiet; it was I who received his shooting, not you!' 'He shoots and beats only wicked women. If I spoke like you, he would strike me too! I have never received blows from him, because I have always done as he wished.' Once, however, I too had received that blow from his stick which had broken my arm!

We slowly continued our journey. The *shapuno* of those people was on a beautiful hill, surrounded by other hills; they lived alone, near their *roça*. The Pishaanseteri lived a good distance away. Fusiwe had decided to leave us women there, without the enemy's knowledge, in order to go and kill the Pishaanseteri. We travelled on, and at night we slept in the forest. The wounded wife could scarcely walk. So we came close to that *shapuno*. Her brother, headman of that small group, was a little man; he walked lame because he had been shot with an arrow in his behind, and the arrow had come out from that part of the buttock where the bone moves. At last we saw smoke; it was their *shapuno*. Nearby there was some lovely clear water which was bubbling from the rock and then disappearing.

The *tushaua* told us: 'Paint yourselves!' We all painted ourselves and went into their *shapuno*. When the lame brother-in-law saw us, he shouted for joy: 'Our *shapuno* is large, because some other people used to live with us who have gone away; tomorrow clean that part and stay with us.' He called the *tushaua* his elder brother. Fusiwe replied: 'I have come to leave these women of mine here.' Then the brother-in-law turned to his men and said: 'This very day you will go and cut *pashubas* to make a palisade all round immediately.' Fusiwe said: 'Let anyone who wanted me to kill the Pishaanseteri go and break down tree-trunks to make defences around here.' I replied: 'I have never told you to kill the Pishaanseteri; I have always been in their favour.' 'But I will kill them, just to see the face of a certain person.' He had made up his mind to kill them.

CHAPTER 34

The Human Sacrifice

A young Pishaanseteri, half-brother of Rashawe, had always come with us. When my first son was about to be born, he was still a boy. He thought that a female would be born and he wanted to become her husband: he brought us game, which his old father made him give us. He was afraid of me and of the *tushaua,* because he already considered us his parents-in-law; he lived with us at a separate hearth, but he ate with us. When my son was born and he saw that he was a male, he continued just the same to bring gifts. I told the *tushaua*'s other wife: 'Cook bananas for him; I have no daughters and I cannot look after him.' The other wife said: 'Yes, I will cook bananas, but he thinks it is you who are doing it.' So she cooked bananas and prepared *bacabas* which he brought. Then the father and mother of that boy died. My second male child was born too and the youth continued to live in our group, always apart, but with us. The same Rashawe, his step-brother who loved him very much, had told him: 'Kill game, tapirs, wild boar, and send it so that your father-in-law may eat it; two sons have been born, so now a daughter will be born and she will be yours.'

That young Pishaanseteri came with us as far as that small *shapuno.* The men then said to him: 'Go to your brother; the man who must be your father-in-law will kill your brother.' The youth wept and said: 'I don't want to leave him; why must I go away? I was a child when I began to live with them. The man who will be my father-in-law has always treated me well, and has given me arrows; he has never allowed me to go to sleep hungry. When I come back from the forest, everything is ready for me; the banana *mingau,* the bees' honey. I have grown so used to him that I consider him my father; it is a great grief to leave him.' They accompanied him along the path and told him: 'Go, for he will kill your brother and then he will kill you.' Fusiwe had never said this; he had simply said: 'I want to kill his brother Rashawe; will this boy then want to avenge him and kill me?'

In the evening, after the men had sent the young Pishaanseteri away, Fusiwe asked me: 'It is already late; has that youth not yet come back from the forest?' 'No,' I replied, 'that other woman of yours has told me that these relations of yours have sent him away, because you wish to kill him.' 'No, it's not true; I do not wish to kill this youth. He does everything I ask him and I haven't even a daughter for him. When I was sick to the point of death, he always brought me bees' honey; without him I would perhaps have died.' Then I said to him: 'I beg you, if you go to fight the brother, for heaven's sake do not kill him; he is like a son to me. When my little ones were weeping, he used to send a woman to take them, and he took them with him to bathe, as though they were brothers.' Fusiwe answered: 'I shall go against them; the first one who comes out of their *shapuno* I shall kill.' All we women, even the one who wanted to kill the Pishaanseteri, begged and begged him not to kill the boy. His daughter said: 'Father, that youth has always been one of us.' 'Daughter, I shall have to kill the first man who comes out of their *shapuno* and stands before me; I must not think whether he has been my companion.'

Fusiwe said to that lame brother-in-law of his, who was chief of the small tribe: 'Brother-in-law, give me some manioc; these women will prepare it and I shall take it on my journey. On the way I shall look for wild boars, kill them and smoke the meat, which I shall carry with me until I come to where those friends of mine are, the Pishaanseteri friends. I want to prepare poison for hunting.' The brother-in-law said: 'I have some very strong poison, which I made the other day. All my men have quivers full of poisoned arrowheads; each one of them will give you three heads.' He gave him about ten; they were beautiful, new and red. The *tushaua* smelt them and said: 'Yes, that is how I like them.' In the evening the men gave him the others and he filled his quiver.

We went to the *roça*; Tokoma could not come, because her leg was very swollen. We were in the *roça* when that lame brother-in-law arrived and asked us: 'What does he think of doing there with the Pishaanseteri?' One of the wives said: 'He wants to kill them.' I continued: 'He has come here to leave us women in safety and go to kill the Pishaanseteri. He wants to kill them for a challenge; he has said: "They all say that the Pishaanseteri are *waiteri*: I want to see for myself whether they are *waiteri*. All the other Namoeteri live apart; I want to kill the Pishaanseteri so that I can see whether all those who live apart join together for fear, in one single *shapuno*."' 'Perhaps he wants to go back to being chieftain of them all?'

The next day we prepared the manioc and made those little *bejú*. I went up to Fusiwe: 'Do you still listen to me? Do you remember that the Patanaweteri had told you that on their return they would invite the Pishaanseteri to have a fight with *nabrushi* and axes, so that they might grow calm again? So you have lied with them, saying that you were not going and now you are going! If you kill the Pishaanseteri, they will pursue you, they will meet the Patanaweteri and kill those poor creatures, while we remain hidden.' 'Yes,' he answered, 'I shall kill them; why do you defend them? Are you not then sorry to see the plants which you planted under that sun, and those fruits which, when you planted them, made you weep for fatigue, that now neither you nor your children will eat?'

Then he answered no more. He took his arrows, tied them up and put them on his shoulders. He took the basket of *bejú* and had it brought to his son-in-law. He had painted himself black, all black on the neck, chest and legs, with broad black stripes. The son-in-law and three other men left with him. All the women were weeping, but he set out. They shouted: '*Hai, ai, ai, ai . . .*' They beat their arrows amongst themselves; the *tushaua* went first in the line.

The *tushaua* afterwards told me the whole story. They came to where our old *roça* was. The Pishaanseteri had changed *shapuno,* but they saw their track. Night was falling and they sat down in the forest. When it was dark, Fusiwe spoke as follows: 'Let us go along the path. Tomorrow morning early we shall meet people; I feel that there are people thinking about this path so we shall keep watch!' It was a clear night with a moon; while they were going towards the *shapuno,* they heard a bird, the *mutum,* which was crying out its song in the night. Fusiwe said: 'Let us wait here; they will hear the *mutum* bird and they will come to shoot it in the moonlight.' During the night, attracted by that song, there came a Pishaanseteri, but he did not come right to where they were lying in wait; when the man came close, the bird fell silent.

As soon as dawn began to break, Fusiwe said: 'Let us go towards the path which leads to our big *roça*; that is where they will come.' So they came to the edge of that old *roça* of ours. They said there were many bamboos felled to the ground; the path rose steeply uphill. The *tushaua* crouched down in front of them all, behind a big tree-trunk. The others remained hidden further back. The day was not yet light and the *tushaua* heard the youth coming, calling the dog: *'Au, au, au.'* He recognized him. 'Why must it be you who comes?' he thought. 'Yes, now I must kill you!' It was he; he was coming with a younger cousin. The *tushaua* regretted it very much, but then he thought: 'I must kill him; he is Rashawe's brother. When this young man is dead, then Rashawe will be quite right to bear me a grievance.' The youth was coming; the *tushaua* aimed his arrow at him; it was an arrow with the head of a black spear which, they say, is so poisonous. The youth saw him and shouted: 'Do not shoot me!' and he lowered his head. Fusiwe shot the arrow straight into his stomach. He fell down and said again: 'Do not shoot me again, let me die as I am. You have shot me right in the place where death is.' Thus he spoke, and while he was speaking, the tears were running down his cheek. 'I did not want to kill you! This was not what I wanted! Why did you come? I was expecting your brothers; you knew well that I should come to kill!' The *tushaua* did not shoot again, but the tears were running from the young man's eyes as he looked at him. His cousin ran to the *shapuno* to warn them: they came and carried the dying boy away. The Pishaanseteri afterwards told me that he wanted water, water, water, and then he died. His liver could be seen through the wound. Those bamboo arrows do not remain inside; they cut and then they come out.

Shortly after Fusiwe heard the Pishaanseteri running from both sides to surround them. They had found their tracks at once. The companions hid in the bush and split up. He ran down towards the *igarapé*; he heard the noise from both sides. He found a thicket of bamboo, went inside and squatted down; he scratched himself all over and got covered with thorns. When he no longer heard any noise, after some time he slowly made a path with his bow between the bamboos and came out. He walked in the forest, away from the path. Night fell; he climbed a tree, tied three lianas together, and made himself comfortable. During the night it rained heavily; he remembered that youth and wept. He told me: 'Up there, on that tree, that night, I wept so much, but I could do nothing more. I remembered that he had always done what I had asked of him without protesting, but happily. I used to send him to collect *pupugnas* for me, and to hunt a long way off; he was like a son to me. All this I remembered and I wept; I wept that night. Then I fell asleep; when I awoke, I felt tired all over and I thought "The young man is dead."' He told how, when he came down from the tree and began to walk, he did not recall even having killed; he came running along the path and saw smoke at a distance: he took fright.

During the night the Pishaanseteri had passed in front; he had not noticed them. They had made their *tapiri* for the night; he found their remains. They had painted themselves black and on the ground were to be seen *urucú* seeds crushed on those big leaves, together with coal for making a very dark colour. They had already departed. Then he left the path and took to the woods, for fear that they were watching the track.

The next evening his companions began to arrive in our *shapuno* and told us that he had killed. It was already night, but the *tushaua* did not come. The lame brother-in-law then said: 'My brother-in-law thinks only of killing; perhaps they have caught up with him and killed him.' Fusiwe came back the next day, in the evening, after the rain. On the journey he had put the small sticks in his ears and on his wrists; the rain had washed the black off his body. He asked us: 'The others who were with me?' 'They are already here,' answered his brother-in-law. 'They spurred me on; now that I have killed a Pishaanseteri, they are all inside the *shapuno* and no one thinks of keeping watch over the path. I followed the Pishaanseteri tracks as they pursued them; they were coming in this direction and I believe by now they will be quite close.' They all took fright, picked up their arrows, and many went to guard the paths. Almost all the Pishaanseteri had come behind; we afterwards learnt that only Pohawe and a few others had stayed behind in the *shapuno*, near the dead boy.

The lame brother-in-law, owner of the *roça* and chief of that small group, said: 'There is much tobacco in my *roça*; if you want to pick any, go at once, because tomorrow no one will go out. The Pishaanseteri might be nearby.' The chief of the *shapuno* gives orders to everyone, even if those who arrive are more than his men. I and another of the *tushaua*'s wives went. We passed in front of the pile of wood I had made on the previous days, and made our way towards the tobacco. I saw two big tobacco leaves broken off, near a small leaf. I picked up this tobacco and felt that the stalk was still wet: it had only recently been broken off. I was terrified and said to Shereko (this was the name of that Aramamiseterignuma): 'Now they have broken the leaves.' She looked, saw the fresh leaves and said: 'Let us go away!' I shouted: 'Pishaanseteri, Pishaanseteri, I am alone, do not shoot me, do not shoot me!' When we arrived, the men had heard the shouts and came running out. Fusiwe too ran out and passed near me. 'Why are you going?' I asked. 'You say that when one has killed, he must remain hidden and must not come out of the *shapuno*.' 'I am going,' he said, 'because there is no one who can defend these people. These men do not yet know how to fight.'

Two old women followed our men to seek the tracks of the Pishaanseteri. The Yanoáma never shoot old women. They found the place where they had sat down, where they had prepared the tobacco and where they had thrown all those hard tobacco stalks which are in the middle of the leaves. I think they were preparing the tobacco just when we arrived at the *roça*. Their tracks were then lost among the rocks, where it is easy to hide one's footprints. The sun was still high and the men were already returning.

Two days passed; early in the morning, the lame man's father-in-law said: 'I am going to get two bunches of bananas.' 'Be careful how you go,' said Fusiwe, 'keep your arrows ready.' Fusiwe's son-in-law added: 'I know where there is bees' honey; while he gets bananas I will get the honey. When we were cutting the tree-trunks in the forest for the palisade, I saw the bees in a big tree.' 'What kind?' asked Fusiwe. 'Those black ones.' 'Of that honey,' added the *tushaua*, 'I think there must be a great deal; but it is better not to go.' But the old man, the *tushaua*'s son-in law and two other men went to get the honey, carrying an axe. I was very frightened and got up from the hammock. 'I am so afraid,' I said, 'that my hair is standing on end.' 'Afraid of whom?' asked Fusiwe. 'Afraid of people; I think the Pishaanseteri are standing around here ready to attack us.' I sat down in the hammock again; very little time had passed when he heard a raucous shouting of voices: '*Haw, haw, haw* . . .' Then I really trembled and wept for fear. 'They shouted from over there. I had told them not to go, but they did not want to listen to me!' exclaimed Fusiwe. I said: 'They think Rashawe is afraid; they have actually said that he does not even kill ants!'

The *tushaua*'s brother and the lame brother-in-law ran out with bows and arrows and met their companions who were carrying the *tushaua*'s son-in-law. An arrow with a spearhead had gone right through his thigh in front and come out from his buttock. They said that the blood was spurting out, pouring from the wound both in front and behind. They carried the man into the *shapuno*; I was terrified at all that blood. The man had become all yellow and was trembling. His wife, who was the *tushaua*'s daughter, started to cry; but the wounded man said to her: 'Don't cry, I shall not die; I have already received other wounds from these arrowheads.' He had a huge scar from being shot by the Hasubueteri, his relations, and he was not dead. His little daughter also wept, but her father told her: 'Do not weep, do not weep!' He remained on his feet, trembling and very pale; the blood would not stop. Then they made him lie down in the hammock.

Meanwhile the Pishaanseteri, pursued by the men of the *shapuno*, had gone round in a circle and, without our men noticing it, were now behind our palisade. I went close to peep through the posts and saw them coming on all fours, holding their arrows ready on their bows. I recognized Rashawe, who was tall and strong, with his enormous arms, in the midst of all those men. I went back to Fusiwe and asked him in a whisper: 'What are you doing? Don't you see the enemy?' He looked at me: 'Where?' I took him to the palisade and said to him: 'Look, behind that tree I have seen Rashawe; I recognized his great arm.'

Then the *tushaua* slowly tried to go out of the gate of the *shapuno*. He had hardly gone out when, *tak*, Rashawe's arrow was off; the *tushaua* avoided it. If they are careful, and hear that the arrow has been shot, they can avoid it. The arrow buried itself in a tree. Rashawe thought he had hit him and shouted: '*Prr haaau*! That's what I wanted to do to you!' The *tushaua* answered: '*Hai, ai*. No, you haven't hit me.' 'You are lying; my arrow has entered your body.' 'You have not hit me,' replied Fusiwe, who pulled Rashawe's arrow out of the trunk and went back inside the *shapuno*. He leaned close to me in the hammock and said: 'Yes, it is Rashawe; he has not run away, he has not hidden, he has stayed there. You go on looking through the palisade.' Then I saw that next to Rashawe were his brothers, his cousin Totoiwe and another youth.

Fusiwe took the head off Rashawe's arrow and put a head of his own on it. They say the head of an arrow does not wound its master, and therefore Fusiwe changed the head on Rashawe's arrow. He told me: 'On the way I used two arrows and one I have used here; I am left with only four; now I'm changing the head of Rashawe's arrow, because I shall need it.' He went out again to met Rashawe, who was hiding between two tree-trunks. The *tushaua* had tried to see him through the palisade, but could not shoot the arrow between the trunks. His lame brother-in-law followed him and hid behind a tree, near the palisade, saying: 'I will not let the *tushaua* be killed; I will wait for them to come closer and then shoot.' I was looking at Fusiwe; he had only gone a few steps when another arrow from Rashawe came . . . *taha* . . . *taha* . . .; then a second fixed itself in the stockade. Fusiwe shouted: '*Chia, chia, chia* . . . you haven't even hit me this time!' Then I saw the *tushaua* shoot an arrow at Rashawe, who avoided it; the arrow fixed itself in the trunk near him: '*Prrrraua*!' shouted Fusiwe, 'I've got you this time!' '*Ehe*,' answered Rashawe. 'Yes! You've hit the tree neatly!' Then the lame brother-in-law, from behind his tree, hurled an arrow at Rashawe. I saw Rashawe run away and squat behind a big tree of red wood which my father calls *pau Brasil*. Fusiwe shouted: 'Rashawe, don't escape, don't run away; I am alone and you are many and you run away!' 'No, I am not running away, I am not escaping, I shall not return to my *shapuno* until I have killed at least one of you! You came to attack me when I was sleeping peacefully! I would never have expected you to come to kill me!' 'The fault is yours,' shouted Fusiwe. 'You have destroyed my plants and my arrows; now is come the last day of your life!' Rashawe shouted to him: 'You have killed my brother! Why have you killed him? As my brother died by your arrow, so shall you die by mine. You do not make me afraid.'

So they were saying to each other while I listened. I recalled the time when Fusiwe and Rashawe were such great friends and everyone was happy. When Fusiwe used to say to me: 'I will prepare a beautiful bow with *pupugna* wood; I will make arrows and tie them well together, and give them to my sons when they grow up and say to them: "Carry these bows and these arrows to your mother's relations; go and meet them." You too shall go!' Then the other women used to answer: 'You will send her and she will not come back; they will take her with her two children.' But I used to say: 'No, they will not take us; we shall come back.' 'Yes,' said Fusiwe, 'I will send them all to meet their relations and they will come back.' I would in truth have come back. He always used to talk like this; Rashawe used to add: 'Yes, it is well, it is well that we become friends of the white men. You have two sons, grandchildren of the white men; they can go and bring back machetes for us.' When they spoke that way, they were all happy. All this I remembered at that moment.

The *tushaua*'s son-in-law continued to lose blood. He was dying; he trembled all over. The Shamatarignuma, wife of the *tushaua*'s brother, said: 'We must stop the blood; you go and get water from the *igarapé*.' 'I am not going,' I replied, 'I am afraid.' Then she herself went to the *igarapé*, collected that white mud like milk and came back; they did nothing to her. She dissolved that white mud in water and put it in the dying man's mouth. He took it. The mother of the lame brother-in-law, who had been made accustomed to war by her dead husband, said: 'Rub the white mud over his body, on his head, so he won't die.' 'I shall not die,' the man went on saying; 'I shall live a long time yet; do not weep'; but he was very pale and trembling all over. So the old woman began to rub his body with that mud.

Outside they continued to shoot at each other; at length Rashawe shouted: 'My arrows are finished; now you can be satisfied; if you come after me, I shall have nothing to shoot you with.' The *tushaua* answered: 'You and your men have taken my *roça*.' Shamawe also said: 'You have provoked us and attacked us just so as to take our *roça*, but you will not be happy: soon it will be an empty space.' 'No,' replied Rashawe; 'it will not be an empty space, it will not become empty. Do you think perhaps, O Shamawe, that I am a woman and that I will abandon the *roça*?' 'You are making a mistake, O Rashawe; soon the *roça* will be an empty space and the tapirs will come to eat the *embauba* leaves.'

While on this side of the *shapuno* they insulted each other and hurled arrows at one another, on the other side a woman, who had been left without wood, sent two children out to get some. They said that it seemed exactly as though she wanted to get them killed: in fact an arrow came and passed right over the head of one child. We heard the mother shouting: 'Oh my son; do not shoot him!' The child, too, shouted with fear. The Pishaanseteri thought they had hit him: '*Prrrha . . . hi, hi, hai, ai . . .* now cook the child and eat him!' This was their cry. Then one of the men of the *shapuno* hurled an arrow in their direction and we heard a frightening shout; the Namoeteri said: 'This time, yes, we have hit one of them.' The man who had sent the arrow continued: 'Do not shout; rake away all your footprints, for you will live no longer, the arrowhead that has hit you is so poisonous!' The Pishaanseteri fell silent; it seems that that man who shouted had his hammock slung over his back; the arrow had stuck in the hammock and the man had thought it had entered his body.

It must have been eight o'clock when they wounded the *tushaua*'s son-in-law; the sun was now at noon and the Pishaanseteri had not yet gone away. Meanwhile an old Shapori had come up to the wounded man and was saying: 'You will not die, you will not die: the Hekurá have come, they are taking away all the poison from the bamboo head and washing it with Hekurá water.' Then the Aramamiseterignuma said: 'Now that not much blood is coming out, let us burn cotton and put it over the wound.' They took cotton, cut off the seeds, burnt the cotton all around and placed it over the wound; they then took more dry cotton and bound it up with the thin bark of a tree. Thus it was that the blood began to clot. The cotton became all saturated; then they burnt more lumps of it, put them in place of those which were full of blood and bound them up again. No more blood was then flowing from his leg, while behind it continued to drip, but always less. It seemed that the man must die, but he did not die.

Rashawe and his men were still around the *shapuno*; Fusiwe shouted: 'Rashawe, you must be hungry; for two days you have been pursuing me without eating.' The other did not answer. Then we heard Rashawe's cry: 'Do not be afraid for much longer; we are returning to our *shapuno*; now we are leaving. . . .' Fusiwe was still hiding among the tree-trunks outside the *shapuno*, trying to see Rashawe; Fusiwe's men and those of the small tribe were in position near the palisade, some here, some there. After Rashawe had shouted, all the men began slowly to move to see whether the Pishaanseteri had really gone away.

When it began to grow dark, Rashawe returned once more to attack us. The wife of that lame man was saying to her daughter: 'Go and get water to make *mingau* tomorrow for your father.' The daughter was afraid to go out and at that moment an arrow arrived and fixed itself on top of a post of the defending stockade. The *tushaua* jumped on his hammock, shouting: '*Hochia*!'—this is what they say when arrows fall—'You, women and children, go, all of you, behind the low tree-trunks under the roof! They are not letting us sleep today.' He took the heads of his arrows and began to sharpen them better, then said to his brother-in-law: 'Let us prepare more arrows; cut the canes and give them to these boys, so that they can fix them to the base of the arrow-canes; we are being left without arrows.'

The brother-in-law took his big bunch of canes and began to choose them. 'These longer ones are for hunting,' he said; 'with short arrows one shoots people better!' They say that with a long arrow it is easier to make a mistake; the arrow flies and shakes, because sometimes its passage is a little twisted; the short arrow flies straighter. The *tushaua* chose the straightest and shortest canes, then said to me: 'Where are the *mutum* feathers?' 'Here they are,' I replied; I took that receptacle made of *pashuba* wood, in which they keep feathers, and passed it to him. He asked for resin and cotton thread; he divide the feathers in two and cut them around with those sharp leaves which they call *sonamacasi* and which they cultivate in the *roça*: he rested the feather on a banana to cut it better. The boys then started to tie those half-feathers to the base of the arrows. Meanwhile the women of that small tribe were weeping and said: 'Now we shall no longer live in peace: the Namoeteri have come and that is the beginning of our ruin!'

In the night we heard, behind the palisade, *crak*—a branch breaking underfoot: the dogs started to bark. They said it was a Pishaanseteri who was trying to see through the palisade, where there was fire, so as to aim his arrow; he did not succeed because the palisade was very thick. We heard him throwing pieces of earth at the dogs; the men inside shot some arrows in the dark in his direction. Then we heard a noise on another side of the *shapuno*. 'Shoot from inside towards the noise,' said Fusiwe, 'so that they don't come too near to the palisade!' The Namoeteri were shooting; then we heard people running near to where the arrows were falling. No one slept that night; in the morning we heard that the Pishaanseteri were calling each other to go away.

When it was light, Fusiwe said: 'Women, go and pick up the arrows around the *shapuno*.' We walked very slowly; I found an arrow headed with a bone-hook stuck tight in a tree; I pulled it and the bone broke. In the night they do not shoot with poisoned arrowheads, so as not to waste the poison, because in the night it is difficult to hit. I found two other arrows with bamboo heads, then still more arrows. We found many and then we went back. That day, however, no one else left the *shapuno*.

Meantime the Patanaweteri had returned from the feast which they had held with the Mahekototeri; a Patanaweteri related to Fusiwe came to meet us. He saw those little sticks which the *tushaua* wore in his ears and on his wrists, and he went back full of fear to warn his men. The old uncle, *tushaua* of the Patanaweteri, sent men immediately to fetch us. That son whose name was Komaiwe, Hekuraiwe, and others came; they said: 'Our father sends us to tell you that you are too few to be able to fight against the Pishaanseteri, who are so many. Our father sends to tell you to come and live with us, in our *shapuno*.'

The next day we set out to return to the Patanaweteri. When we arrived, the old chief said to Fusiwe sadly: 'Why have you done it? I had asked you not to move, not to kill, and you have not listened to me.' The old man spoke for a long time; the *tushaua* listened in silence.

The *tushaua* had suffered so much; he had bitterly repented having killed the youth. He told us: 'I feel so much pain for having killed him; while I was killing him I felt as if I was killing a brother of mine, or one of my own sons.' When Fusiwe had returned to the *shapuno* and had seen us women weeping for that young man, he had said to us: 'Women, do not make me weep, do not make me too weep; the fault lies with his brothers.' The *tushaua* had remained sad, so sad.

After a moon, the Patanaweteri *tushaua* said to the father of my sons: 'It is time to take those little sticks out of your ears and off your wrists and to hang them up in the forest.' After perhaps another five days, the *tushaua* went to have a swim in the *igarapé*. All the young men went to accompany him, to keep watch. Then the other wife shaved his hair. Immediately after, that young wife, who had thought only of war on the Pishaanseteri, began to paint his body with brown lines like a snake on a red background; she made designs around his mouth, on his cheeks and his forehead, with thin, wavy black lines. Then the men took his hammock and went to fix it high on a tree in the forest; they tied the little sticks together, and the *cuia* with which he collected honey, and hung them all up. They then gave him a new cotton hammock. His penitence was over.

While the wife was shaving his head, I had seen people arriving and had asked: 'Who are they?' It was an old Hasubueteri, painted with lines and red designs. When it was dark, the old man began to speak, so that the Patanaweteri *tushaua* should listen to him: 'I have come to invite you, because the *tushaua* of the Hasubueteri has many *pupugnas*. He is inviting you all to go to him; he expects you in four days. He has said that he will send his men hunting at once.' The Patanaweteri *tushaua* replied: 'Take me, take me with you, since you want me. The way is long, but we will walk until we get there.' Having finished speaking with the old uncle, the man came to where Fusiwe stood and said: 'I have come to pick you up and take you to the Hasubueteri. Your brother-in-law sends to invite you for a feast; he does not want you to remain alone; he wants you to join up with him, because he has heard tell that the Pishaanseteri are now your enemies.' 'Yes,' answered Fusiwe, 'I will come.' The majority of the Patanaweteri were against Fusiwe; almost all of them were relations of the Pishaanseteri. The men were serious and spoke little; the women showed themselves more hostile. Sometimes I heard them speak and protest. The only friends were the old uncle, *tushaua* of the Patanaweteri, the three sons and the four brothers-in-law.

They say that early in the morning, after that old Hasubueteri had invited us, a woman went out of the *shapuno*; she was the aunt of that young man whom the *tushaua* had killed, the son of her brother. That woman went to warn the Pishaanseteri. They said that she told them: 'An old Hasubueteri has arrived to invite them to a feast of theirs; we shall go by the big path. You, Pishaanseteri, come and follow us on the sides, until we are near the Hasubueteri.' They said that that woman explained carefully what they must do to kill Fusiwe; this they afterwards did. After three days the woman returned: no one asked where she had been, because they were all against us. The next day we set out. Later the Gnaminaweteri caught up with us. That time it was the old Patanaweteri *tushaua* who was in command of us.

CHAPTER 35

The Warrior and Death

We slept the first night; the next day we women went to catch fish in an *igarapé*; the *tushaua* came with us. While we were fishing, our dogs began to bark. It seems that that woman who had warned the Pishaanseteri, when she heard the dogs bark, ran away and said to the Pishaanseteri: 'You cannot kill him here, because there are too many women, and you cannot see him well. Hide and wait further over there.' None of us noticed because we were in the water catching fish. But the *tushaua* guessed and said to me: 'Never stay behind with the children, but go ahead with the others. The Pishaanseteri will come hiding behind us. Do you think perhaps that they won't come? No, they certainly will; they are already nearby and I know that on this journey they will kill me. I know, because I am feeling very bad; you cannot understand how bad I feel.' I answered: 'You know, because you wanted to kill Rashawe's brother! This is why you know that he will kill you.' He wanted me to go close to the others and he went away from us. In the night the dogs barked again; the Namoeteri were shooting arrows from the small *tapirí* towards the dark forest, where the dogs were barking.

The next morning we left early; the others tried to walk more quickly, leaving us in the rear; in the evening, the others made their *tapirí* in front. I said to Fusiwe: 'You see, they are making their *tapirí* in front and not with us, because in that way we will remain alone behind.' 'Yes,' he replied, 'they have obviously arranged with the Pishaanseteri to leave me at the back, so as to be able to kill me. I have already told these people: "You go and make your *tapirí* in front, so that mine, that of my brothers, and of my son-in-law, shall be apart from yours. After my death you will be sorry for it. Do you believe that the Pishaanseteri, after they have killed me, will be your friends? No, when they have killed me, they will be your enemies, even if today you are opposed to me." This is what I said and no one replied.'

That night we slept and nothing happened; the next morning we continued the journey. When evening began to fall, we were already in the territory of the Hasubueteri. Near us ran an *igarapé.* The *tushaua* made our *tapirí* where the ground began to rise to go up to the Hasubueteri. Shamawe made his close by and the son-in-law with another brother on the other side of the *igarapé.* The other *tapirí* were about a hundred yards from us.

Very early in the night we heard a bird singing: Curi, curi, curi; the *tushaua* said: '*Pei haw*, the Pishaanseteri are nearby; the bird has sung!' Immediately afterwards the same bird sang again. That night much rain fell. Karyona, my second son, had severe sore throat and fever; he groaned and wept. The *tushaua* got up, took his *epená* and began his chant. I remember the chants of the other Hekurá, but I cannot remember his. He sucked the boy's breast and throat to draw off the evil, and chanted; he did not know that the Pishaanseteri were squatting down in the darkness nearby, under that great rock. They said afterwards that the Pishaanseteri recognized him and said among themselves: 'The one who is chanting is the *tushaua*; he is here, at the entrance to the path. We cannot hear the others, only him.' Fusiwe chanted, then said: 'My son, after they have killed me, then no one at all will look after you when you are ill.' He made me heat the water and he washed the little boy's head with hot water; I washed him, lay down in the hammock and went to sleep. I woke up and the *tushaua* was still chanting his songs to cure his son. Then he said to me: 'It is almost daybreak; I will keep quiet now; perhaps the Pishaanseteri are listening to me. Let them listen to me! They are all against me, even the Patanaweteri. So they'll be happy when they have killed me!' Then he stretched himself out in his hammock and slept.

Soon afterwards rain fell and we woke up. Fusiwe said to me: 'Tomorrow morning, when you get up, take five tobacco leaves from that basket; rub them in hot ashes, and make the tobacco really hard and big. When I am dead, put it in my mouth. That tobacco,' he went on, 'I shall never use again. That tobacco shall all be burnt.' I did not answer; it seemed that someone was telling him what was going to happen or that he foresaw it. I took those long leaves of tobacco and prepared them.

It was scarcely light when four Patanaweteri children passed by, whom their mothers had sent to prepare *bacaba* juice. Soon after, we saw them run by again. They told their mothers that while they were getting water, some Pishaanseteri had come up to them, all painted black, and had asked them: 'Children, where is the

Namoeteri *tushaua,* that one who used to live with us?' The children had replied: 'He is here, on the path; he is not with the other Patanaweteri.' The Pishaanseteri had further said: 'Go away quickly and don't say a word to those who are here.' The children told all this to their mothers; they, instead of preparing the *bacaba* juice, threw away the water, put their things in order at once and left without a word to us.

It was beginning to drizzle; I got up and looked where the Patanaweteri *tapirí* were; I saw no one and heard nothing. The *tushaua*'s other wife said to me: 'Make your husband get up, for he's still asleep; almost all the others have gone away and are climbing the mountain.' I shook his hammock, saying: 'Get up, the Patanaweteri are almost all on the march already, and only we are left here.' He sat up in his hammock: 'I have had such a bad dream,' he said. 'I have dreamed that these people had taken boiling ashes and were rubbing them on my face; I was being burnt all over. I think it was that fire with which they intend to burn me. I have had such an evil dream; I believe they will kill me.' I replied: 'You think only of death; you have sought a fight with these people and now you think only of death.'

Meanwhile my son started to quarrel with his small half-brother, the son of that wife who was dead. It seems that the little one had given my son a bite; my son had given him a push and made him fall down. Then the *tushaua* said: 'You are quarrelling all the time. I'll take your heads and knock them together, one against the other, and then I'll knock you to the ground: be careful, for I am upset. When they have killed me, you will then continue to quarrel! You who ought to love each other, you who will soon have no father.' Then he asked: 'Where is the basket with the bitch's babies?' The bitch, which he loved most, had had puppies; my son Maramawe used to carry them in a basket during the journey. The other wife took the basket and passed it to him; he tied the bark strip tightly to the basket, so that the child could carry it. While he was tying it, he asked me: 'Is it long enough?' 'Make it a bit longer,' I answered.

Suddenly, tak, an arrow arrived. I did not see the arrow; I only heard the young wife shouting: 'Ah, father of my daughter!' The arrow had passed over the head of my child and had entered the *tushaua*'s belly. Nearby, all painted black, I saw the Pishaanseteri running. The *tushaua*'s brother, lying calmly in his hammock, had not even noticed. I ran, shook his hammock and shouted: 'Look at the Pishaanseteri running! They have hit your brother! You don't move when they hit your brother!' He leapt from the hammock and hurled an arrow at the Pishaanseteri, who were running away. 'Run,' I shouted, 'follow them; today is the day for running; you only know how to run well after women!'

Another arrow poisoned with curare had meanwhile hit the *tushaua* in the shoulder. The *tushaua* did not utter a shout; only the small boy was shouting with fear. He was standing upright; from that great wound in his stomach, made with a bamboo arrowhead, protruded the long intestine with that yellow fat. He walked a few steps, tried to stand up, but fell. 'This time they have killed me!' he murmured. His brother embraced him; the son-in-law came running with his daughter and carried him under a *tapirí*. The other brothers ran ahead to warn the old Patanaweteri *tushaua,* his uncle.

The old man came running; he was beating his hands and weeping as he said: 'Oh my son, my son, they have killed my son!' The daughter was trying to put back the long bowel with the fat, pushing it with her fingers. She pushed and pushed. They took the bark of a tree and tied it over the wound so as not to let the intestine come out again. The old man was weeping and beating his hands. 'Father,' said Fusiwe slowly, 'this time the arrow has found where death is!' Meanwhile the daughter continued to hold her hand over the wound so as not to let the intestine protrude. That old chief of the Gnaminaweteri came running also and set about pulling out the arrowhead with the curare on it. 'It is not this one which is killing me,' said the *tushaua*; 'the other one has already killed me.' Fusiwe looked around and said: 'Where is my son?' He was looking for my elder son, who was on my knees, next to his little brother who was ill; the other boy of that dead woman was also leaning against my back for fear. My son went up to his father: Fusiwe took his hand: 'Ah my son!' Then he said to me: 'Your people are still alive; look for them, go to them, for you will not live happily with our sons in this land. It grieves me to leave my sons.' Thus he died, with his hand clasped tightly in that of the child; not a single shout of pain. When the child realized that he was no longer breathing, he shouted out with fear. Thus he died, immediately.

Shamawe, the *tushaua*'s brother, said in tears: 'Cut down that tree; tie the hammock to the tree.' So they tied the hammock to the trunk, firmly fixed at both ends, and put the *tushaua*'s body in it; two men in front and two at the back took the trunk upon their shoulders. Sadly we began to climb that hill which was in front of us; the ascent was steep. I carried that sick child of mine on my back and the one who had no mother I took in my arms. The bigger boy went in front of me and carried across his shoulders that basket full of puppies; he wept and asked me: 'Now when will my father come back?' 'I do not know,' I replied, 'go on walking; you see that the Pishaanseteri are close by!' Then the poor little chap ran and ran for fear. So we came to a level stretch of ground. All those people who were hostile to us were already sitting there. That woman who had gone to warn the Pishaanseteri, when she saw the *tushaua*'s dead body, exclaimed: 'It's a good thing they have killed him today; he killed my nephew!' The other women, who listened to her, told me this afterwards.

Three Hasubueteri had arrived and were saying: 'Our *tushaua* sends us to tell you not to stay out here, but to go at once, all of you, into his *shapuno,* which is large; one part of the *shapuno* is ready for you. He wants you all to come in, because four old Pishaanseteri came some days ago and said: "You are inviting the Patanaweteri and the Namoeteri for a feast; very well, we will kill the Namoeteri *tushaua,* even if he is inside your *shapuno,* even if he is talking with you; we shall enter and kill him." ' While the three Hasubueteri were talking thus, the *tushaua*'s body arrived; the three took fright and went pale.

Shamawe said to the men: 'Take a rest; you are tired.' Those who were carrying the body stopped. I then remembered the tobacco; I said to Shamawe's wife: 'Here is the tobacco he asked us to prepare.' The woman spoke to Shamawe of it, and he came up and said to me: 'Since my brother asked you for it, give it to me.' I passed it over to him; Shamawe squeezed the leaves, beat them and went near to the corpse. He put the tobacco in Fusiwe's mouth. There were too many people around; we, his women, stayed at a distance. The three young Hasubueteri came up to us and said: 'Did you not know that the Pishaanseteri are *waiteri*? Why did you stay so far away to sleep? You should have gone further on.' We did not reply. Then the three began to walk towards the Hasubueteri *shapuno* and all the others followed them.

We did not reach the Hasubueteri *shapuno* that day, as it was too high up; the hill was high, always higher. The Hasubueteri *shapuno* was large, the biggest, quite enormous and round, and it stood up there, with two entrances. Nearby, a few hundred yards away, lived the Ashitueteri (*ashi* is a fruit of the forest, which has a thorn on top). When the *tushaua* was alive, we had been there once; the Hasubueteri are very numerous, more than a hundred men, with their women and children. They changed over the men who were carrying the tree-trunk on which was tied the hammock with the body; we followed behind. The men said: 'We cannot walk fast behind the others.' Shamawe answered: 'We will stay there, near the big *igarapé,* where are the *tapirí* which the Hasubueteri use when they come to our *shapunos*.' It must have been seven o'clock when they shot him; about midday the weather grew as dark as night. That day it rained and rained and rained. In the evening, when they halted, I cut *pataua* palm leaves to protect myself and stayed under them with my sons. The little one, who was sick, was crying and would not take milk; the bigger one was crying too because he wanted to see his father.

Meanwhile they rubbed resin on the trunk to which the dead man's hammock was tied, and fixed to the trunk some feathers that were white as cotton. Then the sister began to paint Fusiwe's body with red *urucú*; she called Tokoma, because she knew how to paint better than any other woman. With a little chewed liana, she drew brownish lines, using a colour made with *urucú* paste and ashes; she made a broad stripe on his forehead, thin lines like snakes on his face, and thin lines around his mouth. His brother asked me for the wooden receptacle in which his feathers were kept; I gave it to him and he opened it; he took the feathers and arranged them on Fusiwe's arms, in his ears, and in his lower lip. He was beautiful, and looked as if he were asleep. The small boy went up to his father's hammock, and pulled and shook it.

Not long after came some Hasubueteri women, weeping. A female cousin of the *tushaua,* who lived with the Hasubueteri, said: 'My brother, the Pishaanseteri are *waiteri*; they have eaten you! You used to walk gaily along this path to come to our feast with your sons. You were near our *shapuno* and the Pishaanseteri have devoured you, my poor brother!' The daughter of that cousin wept and said: 'My uncle was handsome and strong! Come again, enter once more into our *shapuno*, as in the time when you used to come to us. My uncle, you were strong and happy!'

Shamawe sent men to cut down tree-trunks to burn him; they felled a big tree and, in the rain, began to chop it up. I was on one side, sitting with my little ones; near me the Aramamiseterignuma wife, who had no relatives, was with her two small girls. I was very sad and I thought: 'Now where shall I go? What shall I do? I am more lonely than ever! When he was alive, I had somewhere to live, but now? I have no father, no mother, no relations!' I thought and I wept.

They prepared the pyre; it was the Gnaminaweteri, all painted black, who made the fire. They removed the hammock with the corpse from the trunk where it had been hanging and put it in the fire, covering it over again with lots of wood. Those men howled like monkeys. All around was weeping. Even the Patanaweteri women, who had been against us, were weeping. They were angry, but they wept. We wives, and the other women who were relations, painted our cheeks with tears and black coal: that black colour had to stay there for a long time. The wife of the old Patanaweteri uncle came to me and asked me for the bow and the quiver with the poisoned arrowheads. They also took another bow and the hooked points, which the other wife, that young one, had: they burnt them. There remained other bows and arrows of Fusiwe to be burnt later.

The *tushaua*'s sister took my elder boy by the hand, so as to go and weep with the others. The child had refused ever to leave the hammock of his dead father and his aunt said to him: 'Your father has gone away, my son.' Around the funeral pyre the sister was saying in her weeping chant: 'Oh my brother, you have left me; brother, if you meet our father, tell him: "Father, let us return together to the *shapuno*." My brother, you were Hekurá; you were the Hekurá who knew more than all the other Hekurá; you it was who taught them all to be Hekurá; today you are dead and no one has gone to avenge you.' The brother Shamawe said: 'My brother, where you went I followed; now I no longer have my brother, my guide, our guide!' That uncle of my son, the *tushaua*'s cousin, embraced my son, his nephew, and said: 'This chant which I possess, this Hekurá chant will show you, when you are bigger, the way of the Hekurá. Your dead father wanted to teach you himself; now he is dead and I will teach you to be a Hekurá.' That man kissed my son and his tears rolled down. He was Kumaiwe, son of that old man of Patanaweteka. They all wept and wept; the *tushaua*'s youngest brother wept less than the others and looked at me. I, by myself with my sick child, wept, while it rained. The rain was heavy, but the fire was high, and went hua . . . hua . . .; the flames leapt upwards. They began to burn the body about one o'clock; when night fell, it was all burnt; only a piece of liver and intestine were left. They then hung those organs at a certain height, above the flames, and all were burnt. Then they covered all the bones, in order to collect them up the following morning.

I and the other Aramamiseterignuma wife, who had no relations, did not know where to stay. The woman asked me: 'And where shall we go?' 'I don't know,' I replied. It was now night and a young man came up to us; he was the son-in-law of the *tushaua*'s sister. He asked us: 'Have you no *tapirí*?' I did not reply; the other wife said: 'No.' 'Then sleep in the little *tapirí* that I have made; I will sleep next to my woman.' He enlarged his *tapirí* and made us come into it. We, four wives, tied our hammocks up around the fire. The wife who had been shot asked me: 'Shall we now all be separated?' I answered: 'I don't know, you only thought of getting him killed, now you can be happy! You have a father and a mother, and so you wanted his death; now you are happy and you may look for a man who will not maltreat you.' She began to cry and said to me: 'I do not want to be separated from you. Later, very gradually, we will be separated.' I did not answer. I picked up my few things which were close to me, by the fire: my cotton hammock, my ball of cotton and my basket.

My little son who was ill would not take milk: the Aramamiseterignuma said to me: 'Take him to that old Hekurá, so that he may suck his chest; his throat is so hot!' 'Let him die, it's better for him! What shall I do with these two children? I have nowhere to go! The sickness ought to have struck me, not the child!' And I wept. The woman took the boy in her arms and carried him to the old Gnaminaweteri. She said that the man inhaled his *epená,* sucked the little boy in the head, and in the neck, and chanted his chants. Later the woman brought the child back to me. I took him in my arms. His little brother came close to me in my hammock. His tiny hammock remained empty.

That night Tokoma, the young wife, did not sleep. Poré had come; he pulled her, shook her in her net, and caught hold of one of her hands with his cold hand. I was not afraid; nothing happened to me; I felt nothing. Every minute she would come down from the hammock to stir up the fire, would wake me and say: 'Mother of the child, stir the fire; there are people here'; but there was no one. She would say: 'He has shaken me in the hammock, he has blown on my face, *sc* . . .; I opened my eyes and saw nobody.' Not even the Aramamiseterignuma with her small girls saw anything that night, just like me.

In the morning they collected the burnt bones: the three brothers, the sister, the brothers-in-law and the son-in-law collected them. They were in a hurry to finish before it started to rain again. We, the wives, did not collect any of them.

The next day, when they had brought together all the burnt bones, came the *tushaua* of the Hasubueteri, who lived nearby. He was a strong, tough man, and he said: 'I have come here; I want to know when you will prepare the bones, because I want a *cuia*-full for myself apart from the rest; it will be my souvenir of him. I will eat a little of them at a time, and each time I will take vengeance for him on the Pishaanseteri. Few moons will go by, and I will take some more and again I will avenge him. If you do not avenge him, we will do so. It is easier for us to find the Pishaanseteri again, to attack them and to kill them.' He then said that if they did not give him those ashes, he did not have the right to avenge the dead man and to kill the Pishaanseteri.

Shamawe said: 'We are on the march and we have no bananas. My intention is to prepare the bones there, in our *shapuno,* in his *shapuno*. I do not wish to prepare my brother's bones in other people's territory, nor in small *tapirí,* but in the great *shapuno*. He was our chief.' The Hasubueteri *tushaua* answered: 'You have no bananas; tomorrow I will send men to bring you all the bananas you need.' Then the old *tushaua* of the Patanaweteri said to Shamawe: 'He has asked for a *cuia* full of the ashes in order to avenge him. If we give him those ashes, when he eats them he will invite us, and we shall go together to avenge him. So, when we eat the ashes which will be left with us, we will invite him, and he will come. The Hasubueteri are many and they are *waiteri*.'

We did not go into the *shapuno* of the Hasubueteri, but stayed in those *tapirí* in the forest. The next day five young men arrived carrying bunches of bananas; two days later others arrived, again with bananas. Shamawe had the fruit hung up and said: 'Now we have enough; now we will prepare the ashes only, and we will not eat them.' The Hasubueteri *tushaua* replied: 'Prepare them at once and do not think of hunting for game, for you are in danger. Perhaps the Pishaanseteri are lying in wait around here, in order to shoot you. You can go hunting when you are in your *shapuno* behind the palisade, where your women and your children can hide.'

After six days, as soon as the bananas had ripened, Shamawe said: 'Today we will make the banana *mingau*.' He had wood cut up, and made them prepare three big *mingau* troughs, then sent to invite the Hasubueteri. The old Gnaminaweteri chief had prepared a tree-trunk well burnt inside; they painted it well, black inside, red outside, and attached feathers, white as cotton, to it all around. They also decorated the big cylindrical stick with which they would crush the bones: they drew wavy lines and put feathers on the top and in the middle. The Gnaminaweteri, who pounded the bones, painted themselves with black *urucú*. They beat hard with the thick stick inside the trunk and with every blow the bones all broke into fragments. They passed them many times through a kind of flat sieve, which they call *shotekeheke,* which the Aramamiseterignuma wife had woven; it was very beautiful, painted with wavy lines of red *urucú* with black spots inside each curve. While they were preparing the ashes, they all wept. Then they filled with those ashes the narrow-mouthed *cuias*. The Hasubueteri *tushaua* took a big one, which he had brought himself; the *tushaua* of the Ashitueteri, who was also a relative of Fusiwe, took another smaller one; Shamawe took two; the old uncle, *tushaua* of the Patanaweteri, took two more, and the uncle's son one. Four were left over; the Aramamiseterignuma, who, after the woman who died, was the oldest wife, took them into her charge. They said they would keep them until these two sons of mine had grown up, so that they might then avenge their father against the Pishaanseteri. But I thought: 'They speak in vain; I shall not stay with them; their father, when he was dying, told me to take them away.'

My son kept on saying to me: 'Mother, I want to go to my father!' But his father no longer existed. His aunt used to say to him: 'Do not seek him any longer, he has gone away'; but the child, weeping, called out: 'My father, my father.' A Hasubueteri woman came up and said to him: 'Don't weep any more; you are *wahati* (cold), but the sons of those who have killed your father will also remain *wahati*; their mouths will also say "Father" and they will seek their father, because soon their fathers will all be slain.'

PART THREE

CHAPTER 36

Yanoáma Stoicism

When they had finished preparing Fusiwe's ashes, the *tushaua* of the Hasubueteri, after taking his *cuia,* told them all to go into his *shapuno,* to the *reaho* which he had prepared. Those who were not Fusiwe's relations painted themselves red; I painted my children black. The *tushaua*'s Hasubueteri cousin said to us wives: 'You women will come and live with me; let the others paint themselves and dance.' We entered that big *shapuno* and hung up our hammocks near the hearth of the Hasubueteri *tushaua.*

In the night I heard the *tushaua* say to Shamawe and to the Namoeteri: 'Do not think that I have taken this *cuia* of ashes to waste them. After you have left, I shall go to the Shamatari, who are my friends, and tell them to invite the Pishaanseteri to a *reaho* to dance and sing together. I will tell them also to give the Pishaanseteri game and *pupugnas*. The second time I will have them invited for a maize *reaho,* and see that this time too they are well treated and given plenty to eat. The third time I will have them invited again by the Shamatari: on the third occasion the Pishaanseteri will no longer be suspicious. I will hide with my men, near the Shamatari *shapuno,* and when the Pishaanseteri enter, by agreement with the Shamatari we will kill them.'

While the elders were talking in this way, the young men were singing in the night: they were many, and I was afraid. We, the wives of the dead *tushaua*, and the women of his small group, did not sing. The other women sang; only a few of them were sad, and did not wish to sing.

The feast came to an end. After some days the Namoeteri decided to go away. The female cousin of the Hasubueteri *tushaua* came up to me and said, 'You and the children, stay with me.' But I decided to go away with the others. The Patanaweteri went into the big *shapuno,* while the Gnaminaweteri returned to their own.

There was a boy named Makakawe (*maka* is a small toad): his mother had died. I had looked after him; I had given him food. The *tushaua* said to me: 'Give this boy something to eat and look after him. His mother is dead, his step-mother and father take no notice of him. Let him come with us, and help him; when children are brought up by others, they always remain affectionate towards them. One day he will bring you bananas and catch game for you.' And the boy played with my children, who were younger than he was; he took them with him swimming. He was by now nearly grown up; the *tushaua*'s other wife called him and said: 'Take the bananas for Napagnuma; will you not bring them for your step-mother?' 'No; I will carry them for Napagnuma,' he replied. He tore off a long strip of bark from a tree and loaded four bunches of bananas for me. At night he went to sleep as usual near his father and step-mother, but in the daytime he got fish and game for me. The day after we left he brought me two big fish which he had caught in an *igarapé,* and said to me: 'Aunt' (that is what he called me), 'I have caught some fish; here are two for you. We are few, take them; I will eat the rest with my father.' He was a good boy; I remember that when the *tushaua* was still alive and I went to the *roça,* he often used to say to me: '*Kamigna esho,* I too,' and he carried wood and heavy baskets for me.

After travelling for three or four days, we came close to the big *shapuno* of the Patanaweteri. Shamawe wept and said: 'Where shall we go, now that my brother is no longer here, who used to guide us?' The old Patanaweteri uncle answered: '*Pei haw!* You come too into our great *shapuno*; you have been left alone; remember that the Pishaanseteri are enemies and are *waiteri.* That was not a dog which you killed and it is not a dog of yours that they have killed!' The Namoeteri men began to say: 'If we go now with the Patanaweteri, as soon as our children or our women have the slightest quarrels, they will say to us: "You used to live apart before; now that the *tushaua* is dead, you have no longer the courage to live alone, you are afraid!" ' The old Gnaminaweteri *tushaua,* who was listening, said: 'In the past quarrels used to take place between you and the Patanaweteri, and not with us, who are so few. Come and live with us; you will live more peacefully. If you remain on your own, they will attack you; if you go with the Patanaweteri, you'll soon be quarrelling.' Shamawe asked us: 'Do you prefer to remain alone, where we were when my brother was alive, or shall we go with them?' The Tokoma wife, the one who had been wounded with an arrow in one leg, replied: 'Yes, let's go with the Gnaminaweteri; if we stay on our own, the Pishaanseteri might attack us.'

My elder son continued all the time to look for his father; he wept and asked me: 'When will he return to this world?' He loved his father too much; when his father used to go hunting near the *shapuno,* he took him with him. If he killed a toucan, an *arara* or some other bird with fine colours, when they came near to the *shapuno,* he would tie it across the boy's shoulders as he walked with his little bow and arrows. But when he killed some large animal, a tapir, a wild boar or a stag, the father would load it, and after drawing beautiful designs on his son's body, would enter with him happily, saying: 'With these designs he will grow more quickly.' The little boy had grown too accustomed to his father's company.

So we went into the *shapuno* of the Gnaminaweteri; it was a fairly big *shapuno,* because all the men, even those without wives, had their separate hearths. Their *tushaua* immediately caused a strong palisade to be built all round, to defend us from attacks. I, with my two children, took up my position next to the Aramamiseterignuma with her small girls.

During that period the *tushaua*'s mother, poor good old woman, died. It was perhaps two months after Fusiwe's death when his younger brother wanted to take me for his wife. When I had first come to them, he was still very small; we had been children together, we used to play together. I looked upon him as my brother or my son. I told him that he meant nothing to me; he answered; 'If you don't want me and if you run away I will shoot you'; but I was not afraid and I refused him. Another wife was desired by another brother, but he had to wait a long time. My life had become sad. The men went hunting, but they scarcely gave me anything.

I recall that one day Shamawe killed one of those big anteaters called *tamandua*. The following morning I was going into the forest to look for big leaves when I heard the cry of a man from the direction of the *shapuno* of the Patanaweteri, who lived not far from us. The man was shouting: '*Au, au, au . . .*'; he had been shot. I heard the shout from afar, then the shout was coming nearer. I picked up the basket, took my child by the arm and ran into the *shapuno*; I said: 'There's a man shouting, and his shouts are getting nearer!' The old Gnaminaweteri *tushaua* asked: 'Who can it be? It must have been Rashawe who shot him, for he has sent word to say that he will attack us, come into the *shapuno*, take us by the hair and set fire to our hair!'

I put the children into the hammock and thought: 'I'm going to spy; if it was Rashawe, he won't shoot me.' So I came near to the palisade and saw on the path a young man who was running towards me and swaying as he came. He was the brother of Shamawe's Gnaminaweteri wife; I called her and told her: 'Look, it's your brother!' The women came out to meet him weeping and took him into the *shapuno*. He would not lie down in the hammock, but remained standing up in the middle of the *shapuno* square. 'I have run away, but I have not left my arrows: I wanted to avenge the *tushaua,* but I didn't expect to die like this! I wanted to die, but in battle, after having avenged Shoriwe.' He called the dead *tushaua* Shoriwe (brother-in-law). As he spoke he leaned on his bow and on two arrows. Meanwhile the women were weeping: they pushed the wounded man towards a hammock; the man let himself fall on the hammock, but the rope holding it up broke and the youth fell to the ground. He got up again, leaned on the long bow with his hands held high and remained standing. 'I want to stay on my feet!' He swayed as he leaned on the bow, but he would not lie down. 'I want to return to my father's *shapuno*.' 'No,' replied the old chief, 'stay with us; you cannot go.' The man fell again to the ground; he raised himself up, remained sitting and said: 'Now my Hekurá are abandoning me,' and slowly he chanted his Hekurá chant. Then he said that his throat felt dry; they gave him water and he continued with his chant. He then remembered his father and said: 'My father, the Hekurá have fled; their *shapuno* is empty.' Fusiwe had been the first to teach him to be a Hekurá, then his father, then his uncle; three times he had been re-initiated as a Hekurá. He had not yet had a woman; he was tall and strong: therefore he resisted all that day before he died.

He was sitting on the ground, then he stood up and leaned on a post of the *shapuno* and asked: 'Where is my father? Why is my father not here?' The old Gnaminaweteri *tushaua* called his Hekurá and said: 'This arm of mine has gone to sleep; it has been hit with the head of a bad, strong, black arrow; it was not a curare arrow which struck it.' All around the others, who were *Hekurá* were trying in vain to remove the pain from the wounded man's body. They wanted to give him bees' honey and banana *mingau,* but the youth replied: 'If it were in order to live, I would take it; but I must die and I will not take anything,' and he continued to ask, 'Where is my father?' He was shot about eight o'clock in the morning; about ten o'clock the old *tushaua* said: 'This young man will die; go and warn his father.'

I was squatting down and hiding some way off; I was afraid

to look at him, so pale was he, with that blood flowing. Slowly he came up to our hearth and exclaimed: 'Shoriwe, you have left two sons; now I am coming to you.' He was not shouting, nor weeping; only when he moved and felt such pain, he said: 'Father, my father'; his mother had been dead for a long time.

His father arrived in the afternoon. The old man's weeping could be heard from afar. It was painful to listen to him, as he said: 'Oh my son, you have passed along this path; here is your blood! Son, do not leave your father alone! Your mother has already left us and now do you too wish to desert me?' With the old father came also that uncle who had brought him up together with his father, when the mother died. They arrived, and amid their weeping they remembered when they used to carry him on their shoulders, when they gave him bees' honey and banana pap, because his mother was dead; then when he was bigger and used to follow them into the forest. All that had happened, they spoke of amidst their tears. Many other men came too: the father and the uncle painted themselves with big black spots on their body.

The young man had now lain down and every so often he groaned; when he tried to sit, the blood came out of his wound like a fountain. He said: 'They have killed me with *rahaḵashiwa,* that evil arrow of the Waika.' His father wept, but he said: 'Father, do not weep; your weeping is so sad, I cannot bear to hear it.' The other old man also wept and wept; in the evening, they scarcely had any voice left.

Night fell; I remained awake, listening whether I could hear the noise of the enemy. The Aramamiseterignuma, who had gone to see the youth, told me later that he got up trembling, leaned on the trunk which was holding up the hammock, and turning to his father murmured: 'Father, now the last Hekurá which was near me, which kept me alive until you came, Pashoriwe, the Hekurá of the monkey, is deserting me.' I heard the shouts from a distance; they say he clung to the trunk, grew stiff and fell dead. Then all began their shouts and their wailing.

I was alone and afraid; I thought: 'Will Poré now come here to me?' I was afraid of their Poré, then I thought: 'He was not my enemy; how can his Poré come against me?' I hugged my children. It was raining; all night long they wept in the *shapuno*.

The following morning, the old father said: 'I don't want to make the fire here. I don't wish to burn my son in this *shapuno*; I want him to be burned there, in that *shapuno* where my *tushaua* cousin used to live.' It was the *shapuno* where the Shamatari *tushaua* had also been killed. They wish to burn a dead man in the compound of the big *shapunos,* so that the undergrowth shall not grow over him; if they make the funeral pyre among *tapirí* in the wood or in small *shapunos,* which they then abandon, bushes soon grow on the spot where the body has been burned.

The dead man's old father came up to us and, weeping, turned to my elder son: 'Your father has left us; so too has my son left me.' I lowered my head; the tears were streaming down my cheeks. 'Now I will burn my son,' he continued, 'where we used to live together; you too may come. You, take the children and then come back here.' My companion, who was a niece of the old man, said: 'Yes, uncle, we will all come. We must come, because your son is dead on account of a feud for what our husband had done to the Pishaanseteri.' 'Then we will go at once,' replied the old man.

I took my bundle of bark to carry the smallest child during the journey and collected up my things. We women went out first to see whether the enemy were still nearby, but the Pishaanseteri had already gone away. The dead man's body was in a cotton net; four men, two in front and two behind, carried the body with the hammock tied on a long pole.

We quickly reached the *shapuno*; many men went to cut wood, while others with bows and arrows guarded the paths. Then all the Patanaweteri came to be present at the pyre. Heavy rain was falling and since the *shapuno* was old and the roof in bad condition, we all got wet. They made the pyre near the entrance of the *shapuno.* Those who prepared the fire all painted themselves black. When that dense smoke of burnt flesh formed, my companion said to me: 'Let's go outside, this smoke gives the children a bad headache when they breathe it.' Already the same evening they began to collect up the burnt bones, while many men continued to keep watch; the next day we women returned to the *shapuno* of the Gnaminaweteri.

CHAPTER 37

Endocannibalism and the Killing of the Widows

Three days after we had returned, I was with Fusiwe's daughter in the woods gathering fuel, when I heard shouts from afar: '*Pei haw, pei haw, hai, hai* . . .' The woman said: 'It's the Pishaanseteri; let us run away!' 'If it were the enemy,' I replied, 'it would be a different shout; the voice would be ranting.' Sometimes there are trained parrots which give warning by shouting loudly '*Waiucape, Waiucape,* enemy, enemy . . .' We went back and found the *shapuno* full of people. They were the Hasubueteri, accompanied by many women and by few Ashitueteri. They were coming into the *shapuno* of the Gnaminaweteri, where we lived, and not into the big one of the Patanaweteri, because Shamawe had said to the Hasubueteri *tushaua*: 'I do not wish to go into that big *shapuno,* because there is the woman who showed the Pishaanseteri where my brother was, before they killed him.'

When it was fairly late the Hasubueteri *tushaua* took his bow and arrows and went up to Shamawe: 'I have come here with my light hammock slung over my back. Do not think that I am here to eat banana pap and *pupugnas*; I am here simply because I have a desire for war. I want to see whether our enemies are men. All those whom I have chosen and who have come with me are those who are the first to hurl themselves into battle. I have separated those who are not the first to face up to battle. Tomorrow show me the way to Rashawe; I, I alone wish to kill Rashawe.' But it was not Rashawe who had killed the *tushaua*; it was Herikakiwe and Eramatowe; the latter was in fact the son of that Hasubueteri *tushaua*'s sister. I learnt this when I fled to the Pishaanseteri. Those two, and not Rashawe, had put the little sticks in their ears and on their wrists.

They talked all night; the oldest wife of the Hasubueteri *tushaua* had brought his *cuia* with Fusiwe's ashes. The next morning, Shamawe said: 'I will not touch my *cuia* of ashes: tomorrow we will break the other arrows and his bow which were left behind and we will burn them. We will renew the painting on the *cuias* which contain the ashes. This is all I will do.' We women still had all the dead man's things: three boxes made of broad *pashuba* bark well tied together, which contained the feathers, those white ones, and those coloured toucan feathers and those of every kind of bird. In one box there were only the black feathers to put on the base of the arrows. I had three bundles of bamboo arrowheads; my other companion had three bundles of bamboo heads and one bundle of little sticks ready to fix on the bone hooks, little sticks of very hard wood. Shamawe came up, squatted down close by and asked: 'Where are his things?' Another brother came too. That companion of mine got up, took the *cuias* with the ashes, which they wanted to paint again, and gave them to him; everyone was weeping. The brother then took the arrows, broke them, made a fire on the open space and burnt the arrows and the other things, weeping. Meantime the Gnaminaweteri had prepared the banana *mingau* which they gave to everyone.

When night fell, the men congregated in the middle of the square and shouted: 'Eheee! . . .' They say that from afar, when they go to kill and utter that shout, a raucous shout must answer: 'Auuu . . .' Three times they all repeated that shout together: 'Eheee!' No reply. 'Ahaaa . . .' they said, 'no one answers; our journey will be in vain.' Once, when I was in Punabuiteka, the warriors congregated and shouted; I too heard the reply: 'Auuu,' in a raucous voice. They say that it is the soul of the enemy whom they will kill, who is answering. If they hear that reply, they beat their arrows amongst themselves, *pah pah* . . . 'Good!' they say. 'He has answered! Good. He is dead!' And they go happily to lie down in their hammocks. My father now tells me that it is the echo; it is their own voices coming back.

That time no voice answered. The next morning they got up early and painted themselves black with a leaf which they chew and which stains as though it were a colour. Some gave themselves only a few large, black streaks; others painted their whole body black: only their teeth and their eyes were white. Then they placed themselves in two long lines in the midst of the compound; on one side the Hasubueteri, in front the others. All had bows and arrows held upright in their hands. They uttered their cry, then said: 'Let the women not look in what direction we go.' They say that, if their own women see which way they go, the enemy's women also see them as they arrive. 'Let all the women lower their heads and turn round.' We lowered our heads and they began to go out. The Hasubueteri *tushaua* shouted: 'Let half of my men go ahead; let those come behind from here and at the rear the other half of my men; I will go in the middle.' Ahead went the *tushaua*'s son-in-law, who was a Hasubueteri; at the rear, with the other Hasubueteri, went Shamawe and the sons of the old *tushaua*, who were great friends of Fusiwe, and a few others. The warriors who left were more than fifty. The *tushaua* shouted again: 'Let all men march close together; let none remain by himself.'

When the warriors had departed, about eight o'clock, the old Gnaminaweteri chief said: 'Women, go now and get wood, because in three days' time none of you will be allowed to go out of the *shapuno* any more. In three days the Pishaanseteri, who will come from the rear, will have attacked. I want no one then, woman, child or man, to leave the *shapuno*.'

All the women went to the *igarapé* and I stayed in the *Shapuno* with the other Aramamiseterignuma wife: we were the two wives who had no relatives, who had no one. Then two old Hasubueteri women, who had come with their men, came up to us and sat down: 'Oh nieces, do you know something? Yesterday, when you were in the forest, the Hasubueteri *tushaua*, that Patanaweteri and that Gnaminaweteri were talking with the eldest brother of your husband and with the other brothers. The eldest brother was saying: "Now we will go to fight; the second time we go to fight, when we return, we will prepare banana *mingau* and will take it with the ashes. As soon as we have finished taking the ashes, we will kill those two women. We will kill them because, otherwise, when the others attack us, they will take them and by them will have sons, who will be our enemies. It is better to kill them first." The old Patanaweteri *tushaua* replied: "Son, don't think of killing women; the woman remains with her son and rears him in the place where her husband was. Aramamiseterignuma has her relations far away; Napagnuma has no relations, so why do you wish to kill them?" "No," they replied, "no one will stop us; while they too are weeping over the ashes of the dead man, we will kill them." ' Thus we were told by the two old Hasubueteri women; then they went on: 'The Hasubueteri chief said yes, but then it grieved him to see two women killed while they mourned. Therefore he has called us to warn you. He has said: "After we have gone away, tell those two women to flee, if they wish to live." Flee, flee where you please, go into our *shapuno* before us; we will tell no one where you have fled.' When they stopped speaking, I started to weep and replied: 'Where shall I go? I will not go away; have I by chance killed my husband, their brother, and is this why they want to kill me? Am I at all to blame? I have done nobody any harm.' When they saw me weeping the old women also wept and continued: 'Go away at once, while the other women are cutting wood. We have warned you to save you.'

In the *shapuno* about fifteen Hasubueteri men had stayed behind to defend it in case the enemy came: one was rubbing poison over the head of his arrow, another was smoothing his bow, another fitting the hook on to the arrowhead. The old women said to us: 'Don't be afraid of them. They will not say anything to you and they will not come after you. The *tushaua* has told us: "If they are afraid to run away for fear that these men of ours will pursue them, tell them they may run away, for they will not pursue them." ' So saying, the old women went away weeping.

My companion asked me: 'What shall we do?' 'I shall not run away,' I replied; 'Where can I go? The Hasubueteri, with women, are worse than the men here.' My older son was looking at me while I wept; he asked me: 'Mother, why are you crying?' The Aramamiseterignuma added: 'When we were in the *shapuno* of the Hasubueteri, they told me that two Konakunateri, who had been to the Aramamiseteri, saw my mother and my brother; my father was killed a long time ago.' I said: 'I don't know the way: from here a path leads to the Shamatari, another to the Hasubueteri, another to the Konakunateri; here the Pishaanseteri, further over there the Mahekototeri. The path leading to the Aramamiseteri, I don't know. How can we get there?' But she insisted: 'Let's run away,' she said, 'let's go.' Then she took the basket in which were the *cuias* with the dead man's ashes and hung it well above the fire; she took a small parrot: 'It was he who gave it to me; I want to take it as a souvenir; I'll keep it until it dies.' Then I too took my basket with my things, took a piece of machete, which had belonged to Fusiwe, took the little boy in my arms and went out with her. While we were leaving, the dead *tushaua*'s sister, who always came with me, saw me and looked at me. We went out: she said nothing.

With us came Makakawe, that boy who had lost his mother and who always followed me. We had not gone far when the Aramamiseterignuma exclaimed: 'We have forgotten the fire.' I said to my elder son: 'Run and get the fire'; the other boy said: 'I'm going too.'

Then I added: 'If anyone asks you why you want fire, say that the women want it to get and burn an ants' nest and to give you the eggs to eat.' The children went; we heard from above the women who were beating to collect wood. Soon after the boys came back with the fire; in the *shapuno* they had in fact asked what they wanted to do with fire. The boy asked me: 'But where shall we go to get wood? The other women are down there.' 'Yes, let's go that way,' I said; 'you go first.' He ran ahead. I didn't want to take him with us, because I was afraid that, if I arrived among the Aramamiseteri with that boy whom they did not know, they would perhaps kill him. When he was at a distance, we left the path and went into the forest.

So we went running towards the thick forest: I, with my little boy round my neck and with my few belongings, the other woman with her two small daughters and her bird in her hand; my bigger son walked by our side. We walked ever so far; that same evening we reached a big clearing. I recognized it; it was the very one where I had been such a long time before with that old woman, when I was 'of consequence'. Then we found again the tracks of those who had gone to fight. 'We'll follow this path,' the Aramamiseterignuma said, 'but from inside the forest.' 'But where are we going?' I asked. 'Isn't this by chance the path which leads to the Pishaanseteri? Why do you say that we are going to the Aramamiseteri?' She answered: 'I know the way well. We shall pass close to the Pishaanseteri *shapuno*, always keeping through the forest and not on the path; we shall pass behind and carry on from there.' 'So you know the way well, then?' 'Yes, I do,' she said, but she was lying.

We walked a very long way; we passed, I think, through five groups of *tapirí*. In the end I sat down and began to cry: 'I'm not going on any more,' I said. I remembered that boy who wanted to come with me and who had no mother and I was so sorry for having left him behind. 'I'm going back; if they want to kill me, let them kill me in the *shapuno*. It's worse if they pursue us and kill us in the forest.' 'It's a bit late now to go back,' she replied. 'When you go back, they'll kill you.'

I got up and ran back towards the *shapuno*, telling my son to come with me. I was already quite a way off, when she came running up; she grabbed hold of my little boy, whom I was carrying on my shoulders, and said to me: 'Give me the child!' 'No, I'm going back with him to the *shapuno*. When his father was alive, I never ran away for fear; why should I flee now? Just let them kill me and bring up my sons.' She started to pull the small boy to one side, and I to the other; the child was crying. In the end she snatched him away from me and slung him up on the strip of bark, next to her smallest girl, and ran away. 'You go back with the bigger one,' she said, 'for it's he whom they love most.'

I set out with the bigger boy towards the *shapuno*; we passed by a group of old *tapirí* again, but my son began to weep, saying: 'Mother, let's go and get my young brother.' 'I shan't be able to get him back,' I answered; but the child was crying and wouldn't walk. He did not want to leave his brother. At last I said: 'Come on, let's go.' I started to run after her footsteps, which were beginning to dry up. We caught her up while she was climbing a hill. I tried to snatch the little boy: 'Give me my son,' I said. 'Why do you want him?' she asked. 'Because you are going to where the Pishaanseteri are. They have killed my sons' father and they will kill my sons in my presence; how can I go there?' I was pulling him, but she would not let go and I couldn't get him back. She was bigger and stronger than I; in tears, I followed her. We passed into an old *roça*, where there were still some bananas; she wanted to pick them, but I disagreed with her. We came to a clearing full of arrow canes; I saw footprints which must have been those of Pishaanseteri, perhaps three or four days old. 'Today or tomorrow we shall meet the Pishaanseteri,' I said; 'you will get my sons killed without wishing to.'

It was beginning to grow late and I asked: 'Where shall we sleep? If we sleep on the path, they may pursue us and early tomorrow they may catch up with us.' 'Yes, let's go and sleep in the forest,' she answered. We went into the thick part of the forest and started to prepare a *tapirí*. In the night a dog came up to us; it approached wagging its tail and I exclaimed: 'Look, the Namoeteri are following us!' It put its paws on the child and licked him on the neck and on the back; it was the bitch belonging to his father, the mother of the puppies.

I lit a nice fire: in the night the dog barked often; I was afraid, because they say that dogs bark if they smell the jaguar. It was still night and I woke up again; I looked at the fire and saw that it had gone out. 'Sherekuma,' I said, 'the water has taken the fire away.' She woke up terrified; the water of the *igarapé* had risen and was just beneath us. I put my small boy on my shoulders and we ran farther up. I shouted and shouted at her; but she didn't answer; at last she said to me: 'Is it my fault if the fire has gone out?' 'It's your fault that we are in this forest. Now light the fire if you know how.' 'If I were a crocodile that spits fire from its mouth, I would spit it out and no mistake; but you, who are a white's man daughter, why don't you do it?' 'My white father used matches, which you don't even know.' 'Well then,' she said, 'take rotten, dry wood and draw fire from my mouth.' 'I am not,' I replied angrily, 'that bird which your Hekurá say knows how to draw fire out of the mouth.' So we continued to quarrel, until I started to weep and said no more.

The children too then began to cry, in the dark, in the cold of the night. I said to my bigger boy: 'Your father's to blame for everything; he only wanted to kill, kill, kill. Now that he's dead, it is I who am left to suffer with you; I feel the desire to kill you both here and now.' 'You are very angry,' answered the bigger boy. 'Yes, I am angry and you be quiet.' The children continued to cry. 'Never have I urged him on to kill; she who sent him to his death is now enjoying peace and quiet near her mother, while I am suffering here. Never have I said: "Kill, for the Pishaanseteri have taken the fruit."' I prayed and wept until day began to dawn. Then I gave the boy a push and told him: 'Let's go.' The woman asked me: 'Where are you going?' 'You know by now,' I replied. 'I'll come after you.' So we climbed a high hill, then descended into a plain and entered a boundless *buriti* forest. At last we reached a big *igarapé*. I said: 'We cannot go along the path; people who are fleeing must not go along paths, because they get found and killed. You have to go through the forest if you are to be safe.'

So we walked along the *igarapé*. We didn't know where to go, we had no fire, we had found no fruit; the children were crying. I saw those leaves which they call *waruma*; they are big, round leaves. I did not knew whether they were edible; no one had eaten them. I thought of giving them to the children. I opened those leaves, took that hard, white, softish stem and chewed it; it was not bitter, it wasn't bad. I said: 'This cannot be poisonous. I've seen the monkeys eating this hard part of the leaf, so let's give it to the boys.' I prepared a large quantity, ate it and gave it to the children. When she saw that we were eating it, she too began to gather and eat it.

We carried on walking. I recognized the *igarapé*: it was the very one where I had been before I had any children, while I was accompanying the *tushaua* as he went hunting. There was a big tree-trunk which crossed the stream: I said to my son: 'I recognize it; our old *roça* used to be near here. We lived near this *shapuno* when you were born.' I asked her: 'Do you recognize the *igarapé*?' 'I think I do,' she answered. I saw again the place where I had been with my son's father, when I was still pregnant. At that spot he had beaten the water with a poisonous liana to catch fish: I saw the trunk of the liana that the *tushaua* had cut.

So we came, keeping all the time to the forest, to an old clearing, where once there was a *roça* belonging to the *tushaua*; it was called Mashiweteka (*mashiwe* is a rock). The Namoeteri had said before leaving: 'If we meet the Pishaanseteri in the forest while they have gone hunting, let us kill them. Then let us return by way of Mashiweteka.' I said: 'They said they would come back this way. I want to see whether I can find their tracks again.' But I found some recent tracks of Pishaanseteri; I recognized them because they went in the direction of their *shapuno*; all the toes were pointing that way, where the big *roça* of the *tushaua* was, which they had taken for themselves. If they had been the Namoeteri, the toes would have been pointing the opposite way. I was afraid: 'Can it be that they are not in these parts?' I walked a few steps and saw some of their fibre hammocks still hanging there, and, nearby, a bunch of bananas and three arrows.

I ran back and said to my companion: 'There are bananas and hammocks.' 'Perhaps they have had a fight and have been killed and that's why they threw down the bananas and left the hammocks. Let's go and see.' We went and had another look: 'Yes, that's what it is,' she said. We went further forward and found a bunch of *inajá*, and nearby, the fresh kernels of the *inajá* fruit which they had eaten. I climbed a tree, began to shake the bunch, and the fruit fell. 'Don't eat them straight away,' I said, 'let's put them together and take them away. Now let's hide our footprints.' We concealed our tracks and went away.

We found a grotto among the rocks; the children ate those *inajá* and we decided to sleep in that grotto. I said to the children: 'You must not cry tonight, because your father said that the jaguars go to sleep in these grottos. If you cry, the jaguars will hear us.'

In the morning, when the birds started singing, we went out. Then she said: 'Today we will go to them.' 'To whom?' I asked. 'To the Pishaanseteri.' 'Will you have the courage to take me there?' I said. 'Certainly.' Then I went on: 'I won't come; I'll stay hidden in the forest. At night you will come out of their *shapuno* and leave the fire near the big gate. I will come close and get the fire. You stay one day with them; the next night, run away to where your relations are.' 'Yes,' she answered.

We went into the forest until we found a path, where we saw some broken branches and, not far off, the spot where two men had been sitting. 'It's still warm, they've only just this minute gone away.' It was the place where they take up position to guard the path; soon the others would arrive to take over from them. I was very frightened. Some go on guard a long way off; others stay closer by, about a kilometre from the *shapuno*. If they see any enemy, when the first group come running and shout, the second hear the shout and run to warn those in the *shapuno*. So we came near to the *shapuno* of the Pishaanseteri. I said: 'I will go into that grotto, where I used to hide, when they burned the dead. Don't you warn anybody!' She went to the *shapuno* and the dog followed her.

Not long after I heard a woman's voice calling me: 'Napagnuma, Napagnuma'; it was one of the wives of Fusiwe's father. I did not answer and told the children to keep silent. With that old woman came her three daughters and two sisters-in-law. The old woman knew that grotto, because we always used to go there together to hide, when there was that fetid smoke of the dead. She found me, hugged the children and wept. One daughter, Fusiwe's step-sister, was weeping: 'After they have killed my brother' (so she called him) 'you run away for fear! Now you come into this enemy tribe! Why have you come with these children? Don't you know that male children cannot go among an enemy tribe, because they kill them?' All those women were weeping for sorrow. The old woman continued: 'I will not let them kill the children, no.' I said: 'I did not want her to warn you; she had promised me, but instead she has warned you.' Then the old woman's sister-in-law, whose name was Komishimi, took my older boy and said: 'This boy will stay with me; I will defend him, for his dead father was so good to me; he always treated me well; it was he who treated me best. After they killed the *tushaua*, my husband wept for a long time.' I thought: 'If the men here want to kill my children, I will get myself killed at the same time. I will ask them to kill me then too.'

So we entered the *shapuno*. Rashawe's uncle, brother of his father, was squatting down eating. As we passed, he stared at us, recognized us, and shouted: 'Who's coming? You who are young, take these children, cut off their heads and throw their bodies and their heads onto the same path by which they came. Thus may their uncle learn that we have cut off their heads with machetes, which we have.' I was not afraid and replied: 'Yes, you may cut off my sons' heads and throw them onto the path by which we came; I merely ask you not to leave me alive; you must kill me along with them. You are *waiteri* and you can kill; neither I nor my sons have a father to defend us.' My dead husband's step-mother said to me: 'Stop talking and walk,' but I went on: 'You have already eaten their father; now you may devour his sons and me. You must not ask the young; the old men also know how to kill; so come on, kill.'

So we came to the hearth of the old woman, who said to me: 'Sit down with the little boy in my hammock.' It was already evening, it was raining and cold; the woman took a *cuia* and passed us a banana, *mingau*. My elder son had gone with Komishimi, wife of the old woman's brother who was still young, to the other side of the *shapuno*. I asked the old woman: 'Go and fetch my son.' She went, but her brother replied: 'Leave him with me; it's better that he stay with me. At your place there are only women; if anyone comes here to kill him, I will not let them. It's true, his father has killed one of us, but the little boy did not know what his father was doing.' The old woman came back and said to me: 'My brother wants him to stay with him, because he will defend him.' I wept and would not even eat; I thought: 'These men will kill that son of mine before long.'

It was already nearly dark and Rashawe's uncle shouted again: '*Pei haw* . . . Faint-hearted Pishaanseteri, why don't you kill the children? Are you afraid by chance? Their uncles will afterwards say that you have not killed them because you were afraid.' The old woman's son, who was a step-brother of the *tushaua* on his father's side, said to me: 'Let him speak, let him shout; if he wishes, let him come and kill them. But if he comes to kill them, I have my arrow and my bow and I will kill him. Don't be afraid, they will not kill the child. I am a relative of the *tushaua* whom they have killed: I wished to avenge him by killing one of them. It was my mother who stopped me from doing it.'

After some time Rashawe came up holding his bow and arrows in his hand. I was trembling with fear, because he was the most *waiteri* of all. I did not even dare to look at him and thought of the time when he was so friendly with my sons' father, when they used to take their *epená* together. The *tushaua* loved him very much; whatever he ate, he would send part of it always to Rashawe and Rashawe would send some to him. All this I remembered at that moment; I lowered my head and started to cry. He came close, squatted down and said: 'You have come here?' 'Yes, I have come.' 'Did you remember this *shapuno*?' 'I did not remember; it was my companion who brought me, or I should not have come.' 'Don't be afraid; don't be afraid that anyone will kill your sons, don't be afraid of anything. It is I who ought to kill your sons. It is true, their father has killed my brother . . . But I feel so much pity for you and I have no anger against your children.' When he said 'The father of these children has killed my brother,' I was afraid. He went on: 'Don't be afraid, not one of these men has the courage to kill the children. They are waiting for me to kill them. They say: "It was not we who killed his brother; he is the one who must avenge his brother; we are other men"; that is what they are saying, that is what I have heard them saying here and there. But I keep my arrows tightly in my hands, so tightly that it hurts me. I will not shoot the children for your sake. I have saved you, when the *tushaua* wanted to kill you; now I think "How can I kill the sons of this woman whom I myself have saved? How can I now make her suffer all over again?" I wept when I saw you coming in and when I heard the old man wanting to kill the children. I come now to talk with you; now that I have ceased to weep. Do not be afraid. Only I could kill them, no one else would have sufficient courage; but I feel too much pity for you. Sleep here in peace, no one will molest you; I will not allow anyone to worry you. I was a great friend of your sons' father. If you had been another woman, I would have killed you all as soon as I saw you enter the *shapuno*.' He spoke even more, he spoke to the old woman and finally he said: 'Sleep in peace; not even my elder brother will say anything: he is like a woman'; and he returned to his hammock.

Three days later a young man came: he spoke to the old woman, saying that he wanted me. I was in my hammock, listening; the two were talking in the compound. The old woman was saying: 'I cannot order her, but I have heard her say as she wept: "I have not come to look for a man, nor will I follow a man; I come here because my companion has brought me here; I am here because I don't know where to go and I will leave here."' 'Yes,' I said, 'let this Washiwe go to the tribe of the Patanaweteri, where there are many young women without husbands. It is enough for me to have these two children and to be a fugitive; I am not here to live with a man, nor to seek a man.' Then I spoke, protested and wept. The next day he came again, but I shouted at him and he went away. The following morning Rashawe came and asked me: 'What did that man want yesterday?' I told him and Rashawe said in a loud voice: 'That man is shameless! A woman flees for fear of death, because they want to kill her, and that man wishes to take her as his woman, taking advantage of this. I will not let anyone take you. Don't be afraid! They speak thus, because they are young.' But they thought: 'She does not wish to come with us, so let us take her and carry her off. Here we cannot do as we like with her, because Rashawe is always on her side.'

At that time the Shamatari had already invited them once to a *reaho*, where the Pishaanseteri had gone to eat *bejú*: it was the first feast. The Shamatari had already arranged with the Hasubueteri to kill them at the third feast, but the Pishaanseteri still knew nothing and thought that the Shamatari had become their friends again. So they thought of taking me and fleeing with me to the Shamatari. After three days the old woman said to me: 'Let us go into the *roça* to get bananas.' I answered: 'I am very much afraid, but I will come.' With us went the old woman's two daughters, her sister-in-law Komishimi and other women. We got the bunches of bananas. The old woman and her daughters went in front; I came behind carrying the bananas on my back and my smaller son clinging to my head. The bigger boy, with two small bunches of bananas tied to him, walked ahead; behind him came the other women.

Suddenly a young man, who was hiding beside the path, came out with bow and arrows in his hand and seized me by the arm. I shouted: 'Let go of me, let go of me; or I'll bite you!' The young man shouted to the women: 'Go on, go on!' My bigger boy dropped his bananas on the ground and pointed his little bow against the man, saying in a child's voice: 'You have seized my mummy's arm; I'll shoot you,' while he took aim ready to shoot. Another man seized the bow and said: 'You, what are you doing?' 'Leave my bow alone, leave my bow,' shouted the boy. The old woman came running back towards me; meanwhile the young man who was holding me was saying to his companions who were standing around: 'Come and help me; can't you see all these women?' The old woman took my son in her arms; I, who had dropped the bananas, succeeded in seizing the man's hand in my mouth and clenched my teeth with all my might. The man shouted: 'Don't bite like that!' and let go of me. 'When these children's father was alive,' I shouted, 'none of you dared to touch my arm! Band of shameless men; you have the courage now that he is no longer with us. If he had been alive, you wouldn't even have passed nearby.' The man answered: 'It's not I who want you; it's that man over there in the forest, who wants to run away with you; but he won't hurt you.' Then another man tried to take me, but I shook myself free. Meanwhile the women were shouting; the old woman was saying: 'When he was alive, you would never have dared to touch her.' The men then went away. I returned towards the *shapuno*, shouting loudly: I went inside and continued to shout until I got to my hammock. When I am aroused I really do shout very much; I wept, I shouted, and I treated them as cowards.

CHAPTER 38

Vendetta without Hatred

I did not sleep that night; the following night the Namoeteri were already coming around the *shapuno*. My smaller boy was crying and would not sleep; I was sitting in the hammock and heard trak, trak. With their feet they had trampled on those dry bamboos. I was afraid and thought: 'It's the Namoeteri! If I try to run away, they will shoot me.' The Namoeteri were trying to come near and I heard them moving about in the undergrowth; it was very thick around the *shapuno* and they could not get through. All around, under the roof of the *shapuno*, which went right down to the ground, the Pishaanseteri had put wood about a yard high, to protect themselves better. I said to the man who was standing next to me—a lame relative of the dead *tushaua*: 'There are men all round us who are about to attack!' 'I've been hearing them for a long time,' he answered. 'As soon as the silence of the night descended on the *shapuno*, then I already heard them. One came near in the undergrowth; his arrow flopped to the ground: ta, ta, ta . . . then, it seems, he went back. Later I heard another one closer by, calling his companions with the song of a bird; I took my arrows, put them under the hammock, and now I am waiting. Stay in your hammock; don't worry; the wooden defences here are very large and their arrows won't be able to penetrate them; don't be afraid!'

But I was afraid and thought: 'Today someone will die.' They said that that man was lame because the enemy Hekurá had collected the earth where he had passed, had enclosed it in a packet of leaves, into which they had then pushed many thorns, and put the whole thing into one of those big ants' nests in the forest; therefore, they said, his leg had first become very swollen and given him great pain, and then it had become dry. The man could no longer walk properly.

Dawn was just beginning to break when I heard a voice: 'Father, give me some tobacco, for today I want to go hunting a long way off; I would like to kill a tapir before the Namoeteri arrive.' It was the son of that old uncle of Rashawe, who wanted to have my children's heads cut off. A neighbour said: 'Do you think the Namoeteri will come now?' Another answered: 'They won't come; they won't come for the time being.' In my heart I said: 'Oh, won't they come indeed! They are already lying in wait behind the *shapuno*!' The old man answered his son: 'I have no tobacco.' 'Then,' replied the son, 'keep your tobacco hidden; if the Namoeteri kill me, do not weep, but keep happy. Then you will be able to use your tobacco yourself. And do not burn my body either.' The old man replied: 'It pleases you to say to me: "The Namoeteri will kill me." All right, if they kill you, I will not weep.' 'I don't want tobacco,' added the youth, 'keep it for yourself.' He took some bananas, tied them up and went out hunting with another youth. I thought to myself: 'Soon he'll be dead; this young man will not come back.'

In the *shapuno* they were all still lying in their hammocks; only I was sitting down, with my ears wide open. I heard a shout: 'Waiucape, Waiucape haw . . .' It was the companion shouting. The Namoeteri aimed arrows at him as he fled, but did not succeed in hitting him. The dog could be heard barking furiously. The lame man, who was near me, exclaimed: 'The arrow has already entered!' The men jumped from their hammocks, saying: 'Listen to the shouts; listen to the shouts; they are Namoeteri!' The women ran towards the shouts; they do not shoot women. The Namoeteri were standing near the wounded man, but did not shoot. The women tried to lift the youth, who was still alive: they carried him a little, put him down on the ground and went back into the *shapuno* to get a hammock. As soon as the women came in again, the men left the *shapuno* running along the various paths; then the women returned to the wounded man, carrying a hammock, but when they arrived, he was already dead.

A man came running back; he was the dead man's eldest brother, and he said to his father: 'You did not give your son tobacco; your son is dead! Now I want to see whether you weep; I will no longer call you "Father"; you have caused my brother to be killed! If you had given him tobacco, he would have prepared it in the *shapuno* and another man would have gone out first and met the enemy! My brother was too young; he did not know how to avoid arrows!' The old man threw himself into the hammock and began to weep bitterly; his wife scolded him, his daughters scolded him. Meanwhile they arrived in the *shapuno* with the dead man's body in the hammock; all were weeping. Rashawe, with his brothers and all the strong men, ran behind the Namoeteri. In the *shapuno* remained only the women, the lame man, the old men and very few others. The lame man said to me: 'Come near me with your children; they have killed the son of that old man who wanted to cut your children's heads off; don't worry, I will defend them.' He took five arrows; they were arrows which Fusiwe had given him saying, 'I give them to you, because you cannot walk properly and you must defend yourself.' I recognized them.

The dead man's father, in his mourning, was saying: 'I wish to kill the sons of that Namoeteri!' I was afraid, because Rashawe had run to the fight; the old woman said to me: 'Let him speak; now he is right, now they have killed his son.' The husband of Komishimi, the man who had wanted to have my elder son with him, had also stayed behind in the *shapuno*, because he was afraid they might kill the child for vengeance; he had made them put him in the same hammock with his son so as not to be shot. Soon after, some men began to return, having gone by a path behind the Namoeteri but without finding any tracks. About midday some others came back and about three o'clock Rashawe's brother came with many men. Rashawe still did not return and I was very frightened. So night fell.

The old man wept and repeated: 'My sons, do not be afraid, kill, kill these two Namoeteri. You are afraid of the uncle, and so you do not wish to kill them. If I had been young like you, I would already have killed them.' The dead man's elder brother was weeping, chanting his death chant: 'Oh my brother, the Namoeteri have killed you! They have killed you because we had killed their *tushaua*, the greatest Hekurá they had! For vengeance they have killed you, my brother; for vengeance against us, who had killed the greatest, the strongest of all. Their Hekurá too had remained sad, and so they came to kill you. Now their Hekurá are saying: "They have chosen at once our greatest Hekurá; we have struck a young man; soon we will strike down a Hekurá." This is what they are saying, but I do not answer: "Let us kill these two children for vengeance for my brother"; I know how to think; a child has no guilt. I will avenge myself against the old Namoeteri; I know against whom I must take vengeance.' The other brother was chanting his weeping song: 'The Namoeteri are weeping and the birds also are sad, as they hear men's mourning. This is why they have come to kill you, Oh my brother . . .' The old man wept all night and begged them to kill my sons:

'Father,' answered the elder son, 'do not urge me on any further to kill these infants; what guilt have they? They have done nothing. I lack the courage to kill a child who cannot do harm to anyone.'

When day broke, others arrived who had found the tracks of the Namoeteri. They had followed them, but had not caught up with them and had slept on the road. Rashawe had not yet arrived and they were all waiting for him to light the funeral pyre. At last Rashawe arrived. The old man talked and talked; he tried to persuade him to take vengeance on the children. 'No,' said Rashawe at last, 'those little ones are in my hands; no one shall open my hands to take them away. I do not wish to hear their names; I forbid the children to be killed, I forbid the children to be killed! I protect them and consider them as my own relatives! Their father treated me well and their mother too. It is true, their father killed my brother, but I have no wrath against the children; I will avenge my brother against the old ones.' The old man replied: 'You too are afraid.' 'No, I am not afraid; I have pity.'

They wished to kill my sons, but Rashawe did not permit it; therefore, after they killed Rashawe, I wept bitterly. He saved me, then he saved my sons, and if today we are alive, it was Rashawe who allowed us to live.

The old man continued to weep. About three o'clock, Rashawe said: 'Let us make the fire; we must not wait for nightfall. They might kill another one of us; we must not let the corpse wait to be burnt.' They went to collect wood and late in the evening they burnt the body; in the night they dragged the embers and collected the remains. The next day they finished collecting the bones; then they all, men and women, went to get bananas. I did not know what to do. I thought: 'If I go back to the Namoeteri, they will kill me as soon as they find out that I have been with these people.'

CHAPTER 39

Riokowe, New Shamatari Chief

Meanwhile that Aramamiseterignuma companion of mine, wife of Fusiwe, what had she done? A few days after we had arrived, she had already joined a man from there; therefore I again had a quarrel with her. I found her in an *igarapé* taking a bath and I said to her: 'They have told me that you are living with a young man; you are a shameless woman. You said you wanted to take me to your brothers' tribe, but instead you have come to live with these people; you came after men while your husband's ashes are still warm. You already have a man here, and I thought you were a woman like me! Didn't you see how I defended myself when they tried to capture me? You are a shameless woman; you love my sons very much, but you will not see them again. I shall run away; at the first opportunity I shall go back to the whites.' I reproved her severely, I almost beat her; she began to cry. I did not beat her, because I thought she had suffered so much with me those days in the forest. She answered: 'It is true; I have stayed with a man,' and she wept for shame.

She did not know that one of her own brothers, whose name was Riokowe, was with the Shamatari. Riokowe was a strong man and by now was in command of the Shamatari. It seems that it was the Hasubueteri who told Riokowe where we were.

I afterwards learnt Riokowe's story. Every so often they play the game of the arrows: each man takes the heads off his arrows and in their place ties on leaves of maize-shoots. They often use old arrows or arrows made with the branches of a palm that is commonly found. Each man carries from six to eight arrows. First they prepare the ground, removing the small plants and leaving only the big ones to hide among. The men split up into two groups and begin to throw arrows at each other. They do not play the game inside the *shapuno*, because they might hit small children or women. This game is good for young men to learn to avoid arrows. The two groups must shoot their arrows simultaneously; if the men of one group run away, then hide, the others run after them shooting. It all ends when one half has run away or used up all the arrows. It is a dangerous game; they play it among themselves, because, if they play it with outsiders, it almost always comes to a bad end. My sons' father always used to say: 'Be very careful because the arrow seeks people's eyes. Bend down, turn around, tie the leaves tightly on the arrow, very hard.' My bigger son has a large scar; it seems that the leaves were coming loose and the arrow entered. That time, so long before, the Aramamiseteri were playing that game and the arrow fell above Riokowe's son's groin. The youth lost his senses; the maize leaves had perhaps fallen from the arrow. They carried the boy into the *shapuno*, but he died. During the same night Riokowe burnt the body, collected the bones without a word and said to his mother: 'Mother, go ahead with the women.' Riokowe, his brother Iramame (Jaguar's Eye) and the other brothers did not take vengeance on their companions, but left them and went to the Shamatari. This happened when the Shamatari had been left without a *tushaua*, because my sons' father had killed him. Riokowe was strong and was a great Hekurá. The old father of the dead Shamatari *tushaua*, who had that horrible name, told him to take command; so Riokowe ended up by becoming their *tushaua*.

When Riokowe arrived with the other Shamatari, I heard the shouts of the Pishaanseteri: '*Pei haw*! The Shamatari are arriving, our friends are arriving!' I was in the *roça* and saw those men, all painted brown with beautiful designs, white feathers on their heads, *arara* tails tied to their arms, bunches of feathers of all colours hanging behind them. My son asked me: 'What are they saying, Mother?' I answered: 'The Shamatari are coming; I think they will kill us together with these people.'

Just as I was entering the *shapuno*, returning from the *roça*, other people were also arriving from Mahekototeka (El Platanal). The Pishaanseteri were shouting: 'They are coming from two directions; friends are arriving from two directions.' There were three, an old woman, a man and a young son; the old woman was the mother of Akawe, the man who later became my second husband.

When I saw her, I remembered her; she had come once to our *shapuno*, when my husband was alive and already on that occasion she had said to me: 'There, in the great river, the white men go by; come to us.' I had replied: 'I cannot leave my husband and he will not let me come'; at that time, broadly speaking, he treated me well and I had no wish to leave him. But now he was dead and I could go where I wished. I began to think: 'This old woman lives there, near the big river; what can I do to talk to her, and to escape? If I come there with her, perhaps we shall be safe.'

Late in the evening, the Shamatari rose: two went to speak to Rashawe and said: 'We have come to invite you to a *reaho*.' They had planned to kill them at the third feast! 'We have come to take you; we have many *pupugnas*. I have heard tell that the Namoeteri are attacking and killing you; if you come with me, I can send my men to come here and fight alongside you. From here you will be able to show my men the way to the Namoeteri; we are used to killing!' The man who spoke was Riokowe, my husband's brother-in-law, because he was the brother of the Aramamiseterignuma wife. I was listening to all that he was saying in his formal way of speaking; they talked until it grew late.

When the Shamatari had finished, the man from Mahekototeka got up and said to the Pishaanseteri: 'I have come to invite you; we have *pupugnas*; come.' There were two invitations to *pupugna* feasts; one on one side and one on the other. The man continued: 'We have invited the Patanaweteri, but they have replied that they cannot come, because they are expecting your attack. They are unwilling to leave their *shapuno*, because they do not wish you to say that they are running away for fear of you.' Rashawe then replied: 'Now I will go there to the Shamatari; I will go and hear the sweet songs of the Shamatarignuma; I will go with my men to dance. When our women have learned their beautiful songs, I will come back here, for I must take my vengeance upon the Patanaweteri.' The man said: 'Go, go then to the Shamatari; I will not take it amiss that they have invited you first. I will invite the Kashibueteri who live near to us.' They spoke and spoke together all that night. The son of the man of Mahekototeka at length said: 'You are going to eat *mingau* with the Shamatari, but the Shamatari, who today are friends, will soon be your enemies.' He spoke frankly, because he knew what had been plotted; the Patanaweteri had told those of Mahekototeka all about it.

The next day Riokowe said: 'I want my sister, the dead *tushaua*'s wife.' The woman refused and the man with whom she was staying refused too. Riokowe took her by one arm and dragged her out of the *shapuno*. The man followed her outside and got the woman back with the help of his friends; they said afterwards that for this reason the Shamatari grew even more angry.

As soon as the Shamatari had left, the men began to shout: '*Pei haw*! Let us go to the Shamatari!' Orisiwe (Ori is a poisonous serpent), who was step-brother to Fusiwe on his father's side, came up to my elder son that evening and said to him: 'Prepare your hammock, and let's go to dance in the Shamatari *shapuno*.' I said aloud to my son: 'Answer: "When my father was alive, I never went into other people's territory so far away; now that my father is no longer in this world, I go where my mother goes."' Orisiwe did not answer.

Shortly after Rashawe came to me and asked me: 'Don't you want to come with us to the Shamatari *reaho*?' Next to him stood Orisiwe, a brother of Rashawe and others. I answered: 'I am a woman, so I will not come. Formerly I went where my sons' father went; now I have no one to go with and I am staying here, alone, with my sons.' That lame uncle, Orisiwe's brother, whose name was Amuhune, said: 'I cannot walk; I'm staying with my women, my sons and my mother.' 'Napagnuma can stay with us,' said the old woman.

At that moment I thought: 'I must warn them,' and I said to Rashawe: 'I want to tell you something; I want to tell you, because you saved me when the *tushaua* wanted to kill me; because you saved my sons. I listened when the Namoeteri spoke with the Hasubueteri. They said that they would make an agreement with the Shamatari, who would invite you the first time to a *reaho* of *bejú*; you have already been there. The second time they would invite you and you would still come back alive. The third time the Hasubueteri will take up positions around the Shamatari *shapuno* and, when you are inside, will attack you in order to kill you.' 'So that's it!' exclaimed Rashawe, and he smiled; 'but no one will succeed in holding *me* down and killing me!' 'I don't know,' I said, 'that is what I heard and so I am warning you. You will decide whether to go the third time they invite you.'

A man came out and said: 'The Shamatari are my friends; they do not kill me when I go there, they give me a feast! Riokowe, this *tushaua* who has left today, and his brother Haikiawe are my friends. She is lying and inventing stories, because she is afraid that we will kill her.' 'Yes,' I answered angrily, 'I am lying, I am inventing! When you feel the arrow enter your stomach, then you will think: "It's true what that lying woman said" and you'll remember what I am saying today.' The man sneered and said: 'You are upset.' 'I am upset because, while I warn you, you say that I do it for fear,' I protested. Then Rashawe said: 'I believe it, very often that is what they do. They pretend to be friends, so that people will be calm, then they attack. This is the truth; I believe it. I will go; I will go because I do not want anyone to think: "Our chief was too afraid to go." Get ready and let's go.' That was the last time I saw Rashawe.

Those of El Platanal had not yet left. I was going towards the *igarapé*, when the old woman caught me up and asked me: 'Are you going to fetch water? I am coming too to take a bath with you; I want to talk to you.' Then she went on: 'Why don't you come with us? Over there the whites pass by; over there is a good white man, who has given me clothes; you will be able to talk to him.'[1] I answered: 'If this lame uncle of my children comes, I will come too; invite him!' That man had always been very kind and I did not want to leave him. Then the man from Mahekototeka said to Orisiwe: 'This lame brother of yours can come with his family and with us to the Mahekototeri; the bridge over the great river is strong. So, when the Namoeteri come, they will not find anyone.' The old woman said to me: 'Prepare the bananas for the journey.'

I went to the *roça*; there was no one there. Angrily I began to break the bunches of *pupugnas*, then I tried to break the trees. I managed to break down seven young trees with an old axe which I had. While I was breaking them, the lame man came and snatched the axe away from me. 'It is an evil sign,' he said, 'to break down *pupugna* trees. If you break them, your sons will die; leave them for your sons, so that they may eat the fruit, when they hold a *reaho* for you and consume your ashes in the banana *mingau*.' 'I shall not die here, no! Do you think I shall die here? The land where I shall be buried is very far away from here.' The man went away without another word.

[1] The old woman is referring to the missionary Barker.

CHAPTER 40

Towards the Orinoco

We left the same day for Mahekototeka. We travelled for three days in the forest and at last, on the fourth day, reached the bank of the great river. We found a bridge of tree-trunks and lianas and passed over it; when we were on the other side, the man said: 'We are close. We who belong here will go ahead to warn them.' The man, the old woman and the youth went ahead; I and the children and the lame uncle with his women and his sons followed them more slowly.

We came to the *roça* of the Mahekototeri: there were bananas everywhere. The lame man said: 'Let us paint ourselves!' and we all did so. I painted myself on the legs, chest and face; it was the first time that I had painted myself again after the *tushaua*'s death. So we entered the *shapuno* of the Mahekototeri; it was no longer the one I knew, but had been rebuilt a short distance away. Near the *shapuno*, which was in the plain, flowed the great river; behind it rose a high mountain. In the *shapuno* there were very few men, because the rest had gone hunting.

So I stayed with the Mahekototeri. One day four men arrived from the Kashibueteri (Ant Tribe); three left again soon after and one remained behind. The lame uncle had two wives, one of them younger with a baby girl. What did that Kashibueteri, the brother of the Kashibueteri *tushaua,* do then? He plotted with the woman, and in the night fled with her, taking the small girl as well. The next day the Mahekototeri *tushaua* was filled with rage. He was still that *tushaua* with a slightly twisted mouth whom I knew already; he said: 'This Kashibueteri has taken the woman of one whom I had invited to my *shapuno*: now I will send my men to get her back.' The Mahekototeri immediately followed the tracks of the fugitives and came to their *shapuno*; the Kashibueteri refused to hand over the woman. But the Mahekototeri took the child and went back saying: 'We have taken the girl. Who knows? Perhaps the mother will come back?' But the woman did not come back and to this day she is still there with the Kashibueteri.

One day a man arrived: he was Akawe, son of that old woman with whom we had come. His mother said to him: 'Here is the Namoeteri *tushaua*'s wife whom you used to know; she is here with her sons, whom the Pishaanseteri wanted to kill and whom Rashawe would not allow to be killed. I made her come, thinking of you, who live so far away. If she stays in this *shapuno,* the Pishaanseteri will come and take her back.' Akawe stayed some days with the Mahekototeri; he always came to talk to the lame man. After he had left again, his mother said to me: 'My son has left, because the Punabueteri (Bee Tribe) with whom he lives, are awaiting an attack of the Ihiteri (Tree Tribe). Follow him: he will leave signals on the way, so that you may follow him without going wrong.'

I did not know what to do. Meanwhile the Pishaanseteri, who had been to the second feast of the Shamatari, were arriving at Mahekototeka. The flood water of the great river had carried the bridge away, but some had crossed over by holding onto the lianas. In the *roça* of the Mahekototeri, two Pishaanseteri met some women, who told how the wife of that lame man had fled with the young Kasibueteri. I was afraid.

I was gathering *pataua* fruit in the forest, along with the old woman and other women, when four Pishaanseteri, among whom was Miramawe, brother of Rashawe, came up to us. The old woman said to my elder son: 'Go fishing with them'; the child followed them. I became very worried and asked her: 'But why have you sent him with them? They are Pishaanseteri and they are enemies.' The old woman answered: 'Don't worry, they won't do him any harm.' In the afternoon my son came back; he was sad. He lay down in the hammock weeping: 'Mother,' he said, 'those people wanted to kill me.' 'Why?' I asked. 'While they were fishing, that brother of Rashawe hurt himself; he became very agitated and then said to a friend: "Bring me that child; I want to cut off his head and throw it in the river." I was so frightened.' While he was talking, my son trembled and wept. 'You shouldn't have gone, son! Don't you know that we are among enemies and that you must not go with anyone? Remember that you no longer have a father.' The old woman came up and asked: 'What happened?' I answered: 'You sent my son and they wanted to kill him.' The little boy went on: 'Kosipawe saved me by saying: "The child has done no wrong and you must not kill him," and then he said to me: "Let's run away" and so we ran away.'

I was very worried: I had learnt that the Pishaanseteri had decided to stay a long time with the Mahekototeri. In the evening I went to the *roça*: I in front, the old woman behind, the boy still further behind. On the way we met again some Pishaanseteri and one of them said: 'Here is the son; let us catch him and kill him.' The other answered: 'No, he's too small; if we kill him while he is so small, his uncles will not bear any hatred. Let us leave him to grow bigger and when he and his brother are more grown up then we will kill them.' The child listened to them, ran to me and told me the story. Then I decided and said: 'Son, let us run away at once, otherwise the Pishaanseteri will end up by killing us.' We went back to the *shapuno* immediately; the men had gone hunting and only one was left behind: he had a bad ear. I thought: 'Now is the moment to run away'; I took the younger one in my arms and, without even taking fire, we ran away. The little boy was beginning to walk and he understood. We fled towards the mountain, where I found the path; it was a big path which led to the Kashibueteri. The old woman had told me that on the top was another smaller path. The elder boy was running by my side, when he slipped and fell, and began to cry; I said: 'Don't cry, son; don't you see that we are running away for fear because these people want to kill us?' Then the boy stopped crying. Later we arrived where the path divided; on one side there was a smaller path. I looked carefully and saw two broken leaves on the big path: it obviously meant that I must not go that way. It had been Akawe who left that signal.

I shortened the bark-strip with which I had the younger child strapped round my neck and we began running again. I thought: 'Today no one will persecute us. The Pishaanseteri have not yet entered the *shapuno* and those who live there have gone hunting.' We climbed a new mountain, went down again, and crossed an *igarapé*. When night was falling, we found some old *tapirí* beneath the mountain. I thought: 'These must be the *tapirí* where the Mahekototeri slept, when they went to the Kashibueteri.' In one *tapirí* there was also an old hammock, all mouldy: I washed it and beat it well to dry it. We slept in that hammock without fire and without having had anything to eat.

When day was breaking, I had already got up. That day we ran all the time. The weather was dark and it was raining hard; rotten tree-trunks were falling, but we pressed on. They had told me that we would have to cross a great river. In the evening I saw a bamboo forest and a bright patch on one side of it: it was the river. We reached the bank; the water was high on all sides. Our path ended in the river at an old bridge of trunks, which the water had in great part carried away. Only a few posts could be seen on the other side; I thought: 'Oh my God! If we have to stop here and the Pishaanseteri catch up with us, they will kill us.' It was already late; I made my elder son sit down and put his little brother on his knees: 'Now don't move; we have got to cross the river. I am going to look for lianas.' I left the children sitting down; the water was fast and it bore white foam; the *bodos* (like dolphins) were jumping near the bank. A big liana was hanging from a tree: I pulled it with all my might. It would not break, but at last it snapped off and I fell to the ground. It was not enough; I looked for another, then another. So I took three very long lianas and tied them together; I tied the first to a big tree and rolled that long rope underneath, so that it should not get caught up as I pulled it. I went up to the children and said to the elder one: 'Don't make the baby cry; I don't know whether I shall be able to cross over to the other side, if the current is too strong.' I recited the paternoster and prayed God to help me. I climbed a little way up the bank, tied the liana to one wrist and threw myself into the water, swimming; I swam and swam and swam, gradually pulling the liana after me. The current would have dragged me down; but at last I succeeded in grabbing hold of a tree-trunk on the other side. It was one of the remaining trunks of the bridge. I held it with my hand and rested; I was dead tired. The water was pulling hard on the liana, but I managed to seize a branch of a tree, which was hanging over the water; I came onto dry land. I pulled the whole liana rope, wound it carefully around a trunk and tied it tight. 'I've done it!' I thought. At that moment I heard in the water: *glu, glu, glu* . . . a loud noise. I don't know what animal it was. I thought: 'Now it will certainly eat me.' Lots of *bodos* were to be seen jumping in that river; *bodos* are not dangerous, but that noise in the water had not been made by a *bodo*. I was afraid, but I took other lianas to strengthen the rope which was stretched from one side of the river to the other. Holding on to that rope, I began to return towards the other bank, twisting other lianas which I was pulling after me. When I reached the middle, I felt upon me all those leaves and those rotten branches, which the river was carrying down. The children were crying and calling. I rested for a moment, then continued and at last succeeded in reaching land: 'Now let's go; you hold yourself up with your hand on the liana,' I said to the bigger boy. 'When you feel tired, cling onto my neck.' I took the little one and tied him tight onto that strip of bark which I held around my neck. The child was high up, with one leg in front of my chest and his arms tightly clasping me round the neck. 'Don't be afraid,' I said, and recited the paternoster. I was more afraid of the men who were following us than of the animals and the water.

At that time my bigger boy was quite large, but he did not yet have his second teeth. We began to cross: in the middle the current held my son's legs up high. 'Mother, I am tired, I can't hold myself up any more, I'm letting go.' If he had let himself go, no one would ever have saved him. I stopped and told him: 'Take hold of me with one hand around my neck and with the other to my wrist.' The two children were behind me and I was holding onto the rope. The little one was shouting, because the older one was squeezing him tight; I tried to move, but had to keep still: 'Mother, are you tired?' 'Yes; I am very tired; if you don't let go of my arm, we shall all go to the bottom.' Then the boy seized the liana again. 'Let's go very slowly; when you cannot hold yourself up, take hold of me again as you did before.' My son let go of me and began to move again, while I followed by his side. Then we rested again and he caught hold of me once more: the current was so strong. 'Now careful; we are about to reach that trunk. You climb up straight away, since you're light.' At last we reached the trunk and he climbed up. 'Mother, come on.' I too climbed onto the trunk with the baby; we were now all three safely on dry land. 'I must break these lianas! If the Pishaanseteri arrive, they will come across too.' I broke the liana, which I had tied to the trunk, and threw it into the water; the current bore it away and carried it to the opposite side.

The path continued; near the river we found old *tapirí,* where we slept without fire and with nothing to eat. The next day the boy said to me: 'Mother, I can't go on; I am tired, I am hungry.' But we pressed on and walked all that day. I answered: 'This is what your father wanted to happen; he actually wanted us to run away and to suffer in this forest! We were living peacefully together, but he wanted war; now we are paying for all that he did.'

It must have been eleven o'clock, when I saw from a distance, right down the path, a group of *tapirí*. Slowly we approached them; I thought: 'Here there ought to be the Kashibueteri; they say that if they see strangers, they seize them.' There was nobody, but we could see the fresh tracks from the day before. We continued to walk. It was now beginning to get late; there was a profound silence; I no longer knew where to go. Then I remembered that the old woman had told me: 'Near the *roça,* there is an enormous tree; near there passes the path which leads to the Punabueteri.' I saw an enormous tree, of the kind which they call *wazimaķi* and which produces large fruits like avocados, from which comes a kind of cotton. I went beneath the tree and at last found the path. I saw old footprints: 'My sons,' I said, 'that man passed this way: tomorrow we shall go along this path.' My son wanted to sleep in the *roça,* but I said: 'No, son, because I have seen a jaguar's tracks.' We went to the edge of the *roça.* There was a big tree-trunk; I cleaned the ground around it, surrounded the space with banana leaves and covered it over somewhat with branches; the children lay down on the leaves and I leaned against the trunk.

Night fell and the toads began to sing: *dru, dru, dru.* Around us on all sides there was marshy water. It was now late at night; I was still awake. Suddenly I heard a noise as of men passing by; the noise came nearer, ceased, and then I heard a whistle. I trembled and thought: 'Here are the Pishaanseteri; they have crossed the river and have seen my tracks!' I woke my elder son and said to him in a whisper: 'They are whistling near here; what shall we do?' Another whistle came in answer still nearer, and then I heard a banana tree falling, near to where I had got the *urucú.* 'What do you think? Can it be humans?' 'Mother, it's not humans, it's Poré.' 'Can it be Poré, my son?' 'Yes, Mother, people don't come here at this hour. It's Poré; he has already gone away.' The other child had also woken up and they pressed themselves closely to my side, with their heads resting on my legs.

After a short time I heard a fresh noise in the water; this time I recognized it: it was the jaguar. The toads ceased to sing. The jaguar was walking slowly over the marsh; he was breathing very heavily and going *fum, fum.* I prayed and prayed. The jaguar was looking for toads in the water; then he came near. A slight wind arose and I easily caught the jaguar's scent; the women had caused me to smell it on other occasions, when the jaguar was near. We remained motionless; the jaguar turned and went away.

In the morning I wanted to go and see where I had heard the banana tree being broken down; I approached very slowly. There were no footprints, they had taken no bananas, nor had they broken the tree down; I saw in the *roça* only birds singing and monkeys jumping among the branches of the tallest trees. I went back and told the children: 'Did you hear Poré last night? Perhaps he came before the Pishaanseteri; let us run away.' We took to the path again which I had found: we passed near to some old *tapirí*, and then to a clearing.

About three o'clock we reached an old abandoned *shapuno*. My elder son was running in front, and I came behind with the baby on my back. As I entered the square of that old *shapuno*, a man stood up with his arrow pointing at me: 'Don't shoot me,' I shouted, 'we are fleeing.' Then on all sides men with arrows pointing at us stood up. 'Who are you?' they asked. Then a woman came running towards me: 'It's Napagnuma, it's Napagnuma; don't shoot!' She knew me; her name was Aruma. She had seen me a long time before, when I was with the Namoeteri. The boy had been terror-stricken and had run to me, clinging tightly to me; the woman said: 'Don't frighten the child!'

An old woman came out; it was Akawe's aunt. She said to me: 'You come with me; my nephew was a friend of your sons' father, so you will stay with me. Let's go away at once, because these men are rather dangerous, when they see a woman.' That woman was the wife of the Punabueteri *tushaua*. We then went away, running; we passed through another *roça* laden with ripe bananas and *pupugnas*, and at last we arrived at a big round *shapuno*, with a fine central space and with only two openings; one towards the *igarapé* and the other towards the *roça*; all round was a high palisade. It was the *shapuno* of the Punabueteri; they were expecting the attack of the Ihiteri, the wickedest enemies in those parts.

CHAPTER 41

The Punabueteri

Akawe lived with them, but at that moment he was not there; he had gone to do guard duties on a path against the enemy. It seems that as soon as they saw me, they went to warn Akawe. The sun was already low when he arrived; he was all painted black. I was standing near that woman, who had given me *bacaba* juice. I saw him approach; he was holding arrows in his hand, those with bamboo heads. It seems that they had told him: 'Your aunt has said: "I want her as my companion and she must not go with anyone; he has many women; why does he want her?" ' I knew nothing of it. Akawe was coming to shoot me. I saw the woman get up, while Akawe pointed his arrow at me, and she shouted: 'Why do you want to shoot her? She is doing no harm,' and she seized his bow. He replied: 'Yes, I'll shoot her, because you want her for yourself; she comes to be with me, because my mother has sent her after me.' 'Why do you want yet another woman, if you have others and maltreat them all?' Akawe did not answer, but came close to me, took me by one arm and led me away.

Then that woman's husband, who was the chief of that place, took my elder son, who wanted to come after me, and said to him: 'Your mother will not go far; you stay with me; you will be a companion to my sons.' The boy did not want to stay and wept and wept. So I went to live at Akawe's hearth together with my smaller child. In that *shapuno* he had a Punabueteri wife who was still a girl, living with his mother. I spent the day at his hearth with my small son, but at night I went to sleep at the hearth of Akawe's aunt.

With the Punabueteri lived two Ihiteri women, who had become the wives of two men there. They had seized them and were afraid that the Ihiteri would take vengeance. They said that the Ihiteri are Waika, very wicked, that they kill everybody, even young women, so that they can have no more sons to take vengeance. One day I had gone to the *roça*: I heard a shout in the direction of the *shapuno*.

They had already hit a man in the leg as he was coming out. I ran back desperately, shouting: 'Don't shoot me, I am not a Punabueteri, I am Napagnuma . . .' On all sides there were men painted black; only their eyes were white. They did not shoot me; I ran into the *shapuno*, and ran to hide behind the wooden hedge. I asked: 'Who are those who are attacking?' 'They are Ihiteri,' one of the Ihiteri women replied, and she went on: 'Have you seen near the palisade one man with blond hair? He is a brother of mine.'

The enemy remained at least three hours behind the *shapuno*, shouting; one of them was calling the name of that Punabueteri who had stolen his woman and was saying: 'Kamosiwe (this is a large butterfly), you have taken that young girl who should have been mine, but you won't live long, for I will kill you, I will kill you! You'll not have a son by her! I shall come back, I shall come back until I kill you; there's no one else I wish to kill.' 'No, you will not kill me,' replied the man. 'Yes, I shall kill you, because you are not *waiteri* and I am.' I remember that the enemy were very numerous behind the palisade; the Punabueteri inside the *shapuno* were far fewer. In the evening the Ihiteri shouted and went away; they had wounded only one man. Then the Punabueteri pursued them; they lived a long way off, behind the mountains, behind the Mahekototeri. After four days the men returned; only Akawe did not return. They all said they had killed him. When they heard distant thunder, they said: 'You hear the sad Thunder; they have killed him.' 'No,' I replied, 'he is not dead, he is eating game; he is well.'

After many days Akawe came back and told us that he had come near to the *shapuno* of those Waika; he had hidden in the thickets near an *igarapé*, waiting for someone to arrive. Only many women came to take a bath, but he did not shoot them; he thought then of attacking those in the *shapuno*. There were two palisades; Akawe pulled aside the poles of the first and approached the second. Through the tree-trunks he saw the back of a young man, aimed his arrow between the posts and shot it. The youth shouted loudly and fell; Akawe ran away.

Akawe had many women, one here, one there; to have more he was prepared to kill. Before I arrived, the Igneweteri had invited Akawe to go with them against the Kopariweteri and had promised him a woman. He says they found the Kopariweteri while they were taking a bath and killed many of them; Akawe told how he himself had killed one of them. A second time he went with the Igneweteri to make war on the Watubaweteri: he says that that time he did not kill, but it was the others who killed. The Igneweteri lived on low ground, near the Makiritari; their *shapuno* was near an *igarapé* of water that was as red as blood (*Igne*). Their chief was a strong old man, with an eye that slipped to one side. It seems that Akawe lived with them for some time together with a woman, whom he later left. Her relations had been angry and had sent word to him to say: 'You have deceived that woman, you have only put her in the family way: now we are waiting for you.' Later, however, they became friends again.

We spent much time with the Punabueteri. Akawe's old mother, who lived with the Mahekototeri, came to see us. One day Akawe came into the *shapuno* almost crazy: he was shouting, shouting and biting. Then the men tied him up. An old woman began to make smoke with resin beneath his net, but Akawe said: 'I must go, I must go; those women are calling me; look, they are here.' Then the old woman threw firebrands and said: 'Away; what do you want of my son?' We could not see anything.

The Hekurá began to take *epená*; I was afraid and his mother told me to stay away from Akawe, so that, mad as he was, he should do me no harm. But he could see only those women. 'See how beautiful these women are,' he shouted, and he rolled his eyes, which were all red. They had tied him up very tight and he remained that way day and night. He would not eat anything; the rope wounded him in many places. He shouted: 'Mother, come and set me free; if you do not loose me at once, as soon as you do set me free I will run away. Mother, those women want to get me back.' The old woman then ran behind the *shapuno* and said: 'Why do you want to take my son again? You are Yai; seek as husband one who is Yai as you are; this man is my son.' All around, day and night, the Hekurá took *epená* to terrify Yai, the Amahini and I don't know who else, until they succeeded in making him better. He began to eat again only after he ceased to see those bewitched women! He had become thin and weak.

After some time the Punabueteri went to a feast with the Kashibueteri, where lived that youth who had stolen the wife of the lame man. I did not wish to go, but the Punabueteri *tushaua,* who had my elder son with him, went and took him along. When they came back they told me that the Pishaanseteri had gone to the Kashibueteri to get the woman back: a man had seized her (I do not know whether it was Rashawe), had pinched her, had given her a bite in the ear, removing the bottom half of it, and had then said: 'Now let's leave her here; she no longer has an ear, she has nowhere now to put her ear ornaments.' The old man told me that the Pishaanseteri had said that they would do the same to me: they would remove my ear with a bite.

Then came a brother of Akawe, who lived with his mother among the Mahekototeri, and said: 'The Pishaanseteri have been invited to a *reaho* by the Shamatari; they have said that they will go there, then they will come here to Punabueteka to take back the two children, sons of the *tushaua*.' 'If they want the children, let them take them,' answered Akawe. But the old Punabueteri chieftain said: 'They may come, but from here they are not going to take anyone; first they wanted to kill this child, now they want him.' Another man also said: 'No, we will not let them, otherwise they will think that we have allowed them to take them because we are afraid of them.'

CHAPTER 42

The Witukaiateri

Akawe said one day: 'Let us go to where my father-in-law is, over there in Witukaiateka, with the Witukaiateri.' He had there a wife with a small child. I went with my second son, because the elder one stayed with the old man. When we arrived, we found the *tapirí* empty. We waited; after a few days the father-in-law arrived, with the mother-in-law, Akawe's wife, who had a very small baby, and the others. I was so ashamed; that wife did not want to live with him any more, but wanted to stay with her mother and her small son.

He said to me: 'Go and fetch my son.' I refused; then Akawe asked his brother's wife to fetch him. The woman went, and took the child saying: 'Give him to me, his father wants him!' The mother replied: 'This child must not receive his tendernesses! Let him give them to Karyona, who is her son, not this one.' Karyona was my son and that mother was jealous. The woman began to pull that small boy to one side the mother to the other side, and the child cried. Then Akawe ran up with a *nabrushi*; the mother left the child and fled. When night fell, Akawe began to shout loudly. The father-in-law answered, then he took his bow and arrows. Akawe did the same. The old man came close, threatening Akawe, and saying that he was *waiteri*; Akawe wanted to strike him, but two of the old man's sons came to their father's defence. Akawe said that he would shoot them. Three Igneweteri, who were in the *shapuno*, took Akawe's arrows and said: 'You must not shoot him, he is old. When he is upset, he does not know what he is saying.' 'No; I want to kill the old man; if I don't kill him, I will kill a son.' They took him without arrows into his hammock, but then Akawe turned against me: 'I will kill you, because that woman does not want me to show tenderness to my son, and it's your fault!' I answered: 'I have no blame; I was there with your aunt and you came to take me by force!' All were against him. The next morning he said to me: 'Let us go away,' and he began to walk forward. While I was loosening my hammock to follow him, his old mother-in-law said to me: 'Tell him not to come back any more; you too, don't come back here again. My daughter will find another man; I will give her to the Namoeteri.' I did not answer and came away; Akawe was waiting for me in the *igarapé* and asked me: 'What were they saying? I want to shoot them.' 'They weren't saying anything,' I replied.

I remember that we stopped to sleep in an empty *shapuno*. In the night I heard a strange noise and I said to Akawe: 'Do you hear that noise?' 'Yes,' he replied in a whisper, 'it's the jaguar.' The animal came near, entered the *shapuno,* which was large, and began to eat the bones of wild boar and other animals, which they leave hanging up over their hearths for superstition. It was eating and going *crak, crak, tac* . . . I said to Akawe: 'Shoot it.' 'No, I will shoot it only if it comes near.' He took one of those big sticks with which they fight and put it under his hammock. It was very dark and we could see nothing; I said: 'Raise the flame of the fire, so that you can see and then you can shoot.' 'No, otherwise it will come towards us.' 'Then frighten it; I am afraid.' I was very much afraid; the jaguar was making a great deal of noise, grunting and blowing. Akawe said: 'I will throw pieces of wood which are not alight; if I throw wood which is burning, the jaguar will jump on top of us.' He then threw some big pieces of wood in the direction of the noise which we could hear. When the jaguar heard the wood falling close to it, it roared enough to terrify us. At last it went away. When we could no longer hear it, Akawe asked me: 'Why do you think I did not draw my arrows?' 'Because you were frightened,' I answered. 'No, because I only had four arrows with poisoned heads and I would have wasted them.'

The next morning we came to the Punabueteri. Akawe's aunt asked us: 'Why have you come so unexpectedly?' He answered: 'We have come because this woman has quarrelled with that old Hashowe.' 'It's not true,' I said, 'it was he who quarrelled with his father-in-law. They said they wanted to kill each other; the one showed his arrows to the other; then came the old man's sons. This is why we have come away.' Then the Punabueteri began to laugh, asking: 'What did that old man do in his anger, with that bottom of his stuck up in the air?' and they laughed. In fact the old man was lame on account of an arrow-wound which he had had in the rear. 'You make me laugh,' answered Akawe, 'but I don't wish to.' 'Why did you not give a good blow with your stick on that stuck-up behind and put it in its place?' they continued to ask, sniggering. 'I wanted to shoot him, but I felt too sorry for him.' 'It's not true,' said I; 'it was the others who took away his bow and arrows.' Then that old chief who was looking after my elder son reproved him severely.

At that time I was suffering since many months from a wound in one arm, which continually discharged. If I did not wash it for a day, it smelt like rotten flesh; it swelled up under my arm and it never healed. Akawe's aunt took eight or ten of those enormous hairy spiders. She caught them in their holes: she held them firm with a little stick, then put out her hand and seized hold of them. I have never had the courage to take hold of them, because their bite is very poisonous. She roasted them on the fire and opened them. That white flesh inside is eaten, for it is good. She picked up the rest, put it into leaves and brought it to me saying: 'Take the mud pot, put it on the fire and let it cook.' She pounded the whole with a stone, made a packet out of it and said to me: 'Now go and have a bath, wash your wound, then put ashes on top of it.' Every evening I took a bath, washed myself well and put the dust on me: it burnt, but it really caused the wound to heal. They had given me so many things, but the wound never healed. They had put *epená* on it; but it had done no good. They wanted to put the poison of their arrows on it, but I had refused. Some said that they were tiny, invisible little animals which eat the flesh; others said that the father had eaten harpy flesh, while I was pregnant, and that the harpy came to cause that wound without being seen. The old woman told me that they were tiny little animals, the Hurateri, much smaller than fleas, and that, when that spider remedy is applied, they run away.

Akawe made peace again with his Witukaiateri wife, so we went back to live in that *shapuno*: he had made a separate hearth, where he lived with that wife and with her child. I had my own hearth apart from theirs.

When I was at Witukaiateka, a baby was born with all its fingers joined like a duck's and with one very tiny eye. If they are born deformed, they kill them; they put a tree-trunk on the neck, stamp on it with their feet, until they suffocate them, and then bury them. An Igneweteri woman came running to us and said: 'An ugly baby has been born; let us go and tell the mother not to kill it.' That woman had already lost six children; they died as soon as they began to walk. I went and found the baby abandoned on the ground; the mother was saying: 'I will kill it.' 'She wants to kill it because it is defective,' said the mother-in-law. 'How will he be able to take a *cuia* with his fingers joined together like that?' I looked carefully at him; the Igneweterignuma asked me: 'Shall we try to separate the little fingers and to cut that skin?' I answered: 'Yes, let's try.' We picked up the baby and washed him; we carried him near to the fire. I opened the fingers and the other woman cut right down to the bottom with a cane. Then we looked for small pieces of wood and put them in between all the fingers, so that they would not join together again, tying them up tightly. We did it at once, because we thought that, if some days went by, it would be more difficult to separate the fingers, and his parents would kill him. It was easy work, because that skin had no flesh and no veins: we only had to cut and open it. They said that he was born like that because his mother had eaten many paws of the water tortoise, which has its toes joined together like the duck.

The baby's eye, too, was small and closed. The mother said to us: 'You have given the baby a bath! Whoever gives him a bath must take him and bring him up.' 'I cannot, because I have my own children,' I replied. The mother-in-law was sitting down, looking on; she said: 'Give him to me; I will not kill him, because he is my son's son.' The mother went on: 'I will not give my milk to the baby. Whoever wants to bring him up can give him milk. I don't want a son like a *sabai* (duck); I don't want the other children to laugh at him when he starts to grow up. Then it would be I who had to listen to them laughing.' I said: 'No, he won't stay like this.' At last the father-in-law arrived and said to his wife: 'He who has sons must not kill them; whether they have fingers or not, they must be reared. Take the baby and let's go.' The grandmother then took him and said: 'If anybody wishes to help me let them give a little milk to the child.' The husband's sister gave milk to the baby, because she had another baby born only a few days before. The baby lived. One eye was smaller and round; the other was beautiful. The child was intelligent; the mother often said to me: 'Look, here comes your son, the son whom you would not let me kill.' He then grew bigger, and always brought me the animals which he caught, and fruit; he came to play with my son. I felt very sorry for him on account of his eye; I said: 'If we cut round it, perhaps the eye would see better'; but the eye was set too deep and we did not touch it. When I came away, he was already quite a big boy. Akawe was wicked, and mocked him. The boy called him uncle and Akawe used to answer: 'I don't have a nephew with ugly eyes.'

One day Akawe's Witukaiateri wife ran away with a youth and the two went to a distant group, with the Makiritari: the men there liked the woman very much and took her. The youth protested loudly; after three days the *tushaua* made them give the woman back and told him to go away. He lacked the courage to go to the others, because he knew that they were Akawe's friends, and, after about a month, he ended up by returning to the *shapuno*, together with the woman.

Akawe took a *nabrushi* and said to me: 'Now you will see; you will no longer say that I beat only you.' The woman was near her mother, eating *sauba* (ants)[1]: I heard her shouts. Akawe had struck her on the head and the woman had fallen flat; then came another blow which split open her head in a wound which did not close up for a long time. The woman's mother shouted: 'He must not only strike my daughter; but also the man, who is as guilty as she is.' So then Akawe went up to the man and asked him: 'Well, are you afraid?' The man did not answer; the woman's brother shouted: 'Just as you found the courage to run away with her, so now you must have the courage to fight. You are not a woman who weeps when anyone beats her! Look for your *nabrushi*.' The old mother also came and shouted at that young man: 'What? My daughter has fallen down under the blows and he is not going to get any? If no one hits him, I will hit him myself!'

Meanwhile Akawe had taken a long, heavy pole. The men were saying to the youth: 'Come down from your hammock, take your *nabrushi*, and wait for him with your *nabrushi* in the middle of the square', but the man did not answer, and did not move from his hammock. Akawe, in the middle of the square with his *nabrushi*, called him: 'Come here, I'm waiting for you', then, seeing that he did not move, he ran up to him and hit him on the head while he was still in his hammock. This opened a big cut and the young man's head lost much blood and he grew weak. The men lifted him up and took him reeling across the middle of the square. As soon as the other remained on his feet, Akawe struck him again, near to where he had wounded him: the man fell and Akawe gave him yet another blow. Then the men began to grow agitated, because Akawe had struck again without waiting for the other man's blow. 'Yes,' they said, 'you have struck three consecutive blows without waiting; this is not the way to do it, you are afraid, you are a coward. You only have the courage to give blows and not to receive them!' They shouted at him so much, because this was not the way to behave. That man had been afraid and had not had

[1] Some species of big ants and termites are a much sought-after food.

the courage to answer: when they have courage they get up again and give their blow in return. The men escorted the youth to his hammock: blood kept on dripping from his head. They put a *cuia* under the hammock to collect the blood which was falling: the man almost died.

Then Akawe said: 'Now that woman can stay with him; I don't want her any more; I have already given enough blows to both of them.' He turned to me: 'Among the Kuritateri I have another, very young woman; her mother has promised her to me; as soon as she is a woman, I shall take her.' 'All right, take her,' I replied, 'then she will run away from you just the same as this one.' 'No, that one is good,' he said. 'She is still small, but she doesn't talk to anybody. If anyone calls her, she does not answer, she hates everybody; only when I call her, she comes.' 'Don't you know,' I replied, 'that those women who are afraid of everyone when they are children, when they grow up are no longer afraid of anyone?' 'It's a lie! You'll see, she will be an excellent woman.'

CHAPTER 43

The Slaughter

One day Akawe's mother came from Mahekototeka with a son and other men. They began to recount: 'The Pishaanseteri have gone to the feast of the Shamatari; they have been attacked by the Shamatari and by the Hasubueteri. A few days ago, before we left Mahekototeka, the Pishaanseteri were calling and calling from the other side of the great river and asking them to help them to build a bridge to cross. They said: "Come and take us, come and take us; they have killed our sons." Then the Mahekototeri cut down trunks and lianas; one who knew how to swim passed across pulling the liana from the other side, and then another crossed over and they began to tie the trunks together, until they built the bridge. Now your minds may rest at ease, they have killed almost all the great men, those who thought always of killing; the others are wounded and only the sons are left.' I said: 'I had warned them; they answered that the Shamatari were their friends: this has been Riokowe's greeting.'

One afternoon two Pishaanseteri arrived: I knew them, but the Punabueteri did not know them. '*Pei haw* . . .' shouted those who lived there. The two entered and stood still in the middle of the *shapuno*; soon after, they called them, one on one side and the other on the other. The old chief with whom my son lived came up to me and asked me: 'Who are they?' 'They are Pishaanseteri,' I replied, 'They are the sons of Pakawe,' and I went to hide. The Pishaanseteri wear a smaller tonsure than that of the other Namoeteri; more or less like that of the Shamatari. As it grew late one of them came up to the old *tushaua* and began his chanting speech: 'I have come here; do not think that I want quarrels or death! I have come because my people wish to know whether they may come to these parts, for they are hungry. The Kashibueteri are not friends and refuse to invite us; nor would the Mahekototeri. We have come to learn whether we may come with you.' The old *tushaua* answered: 'I don't know; I want to hear what they say.' Another old man also said: 'I don't know, you live a long way off.' They continued to talk and talk; in the morning the old Punabueteri said: 'We still cannot say what we have decided.' The two men asked for tobacco, were given it and went away. A few days went by and other Pishaanseteri arrived; there came also that old uncle of Rashawe, who wanted to cut off my children's heads. They came to an agreement with him and said: 'You may come and stay with us for some time.'

The Pishaanseteri related how Rashawe had been killed, likewise the brother of Rashawe, Pakawe, and so many more. Almost all the men alive had wounds. So, a few days later, all the Pishaanseteri arrived. What a lot of them were missing! The men had been wiped out, but neither women nor children had been killed. And now Rashawe too was dead: I wept so much when I thought of him. The women said to me: 'Why are you not happy? They have killed all those who were your enemies!' 'They were not my enemies, It was they who considered me an enemy!' The two who had shot my husband had been wounded, but were not dead.[1]

When all those Pishaanseteri who had escaped came to live with the Punabueteri, I was very frightened. I remembered that that night Akawe had changed place: he had gone to sleep near one of his brothers and had left me alone. The old chief, who kept my elder boy with him, brought him to me, saying: 'Keep him near you; with me there are too many Pishaanseteri.' The man who had killed my husband came down from his hammock and took his arrows; he prepared the heads with poison and put them in the canes. His hammock was not far off and I heard when he said to his wife: 'Tomorrow morning, when day breaks, I will shoot these people.' Rashawe was now dead and nobody would defend us. That man lay down in his hammock and went to sleep. Then very quietly I called the children. Behind me, under the roof, all the pieces of wood were well tied together with lianas and further back was the high palisade. I began to bite the lianas which tied the wood; I made an opening and got through the roof of the *shapuno*. I had to pass the palisade; with all my strength I succeeded in raising some posts, opened a hole and got through. I went back in to where the children were; I took a firebrand too and carried the children out through those two holes. I left them sitting down and I said: 'Wait for me, I am going in again, I'll close up the hole which I have made and I'll

[1] The missionary Barker has also published information, which he received from the Indians, on this slaughter of the Pishaanseteri. (*Bol. Indig. Venez.* 7: 151–67, 1959.)

come out through the main entrance.' While I was crawling through the stockade, the younger boy called me: 'Mother, mother.' I ran back. 'For Heaven's sake, keep quiet! There is the man who killed your father, and now he wants to kill us!' The children fell silent; I put the tree-trunks of the stockade back in place; I entered through the wood at the base of the roof and closed the hole that I had made, but I did not tie it again with lianas. I slid through in the darkness of the night across the square and went out of the main entrance without their seeing me. So we remained hidden in the forest. Then my elder son went back to that old chief who defended him and Akawe looked for me. He found me again and said: 'We are going to the Kuritateri.'

Time passed. One evening a strong wind arose and a woman's shout was heard. Akawe and his brother took their arrows and ran out; the voice came from a distant piece of ground. I was pregnant with my third son and an old woman asked me: 'Did Kumareme or Siruruwe shout? If it was Siruruwe, she will devour us tonight, because, when there is a pregnant woman, she becomes fierce. She comes, enters, and sucks people, and only their skin remains.' I was truly frightened; all the women were much afraid. In the night we again heard the shout. It was Kumareme.

There was a feast among the Raharaweteri, who lived far off. A sister, the mother and other relations of Akawe had gone to that feast. Akawe's brother followed that shout and did not come back; we thought the enemy had killed him and we were very much afraid. His little wife wept during those days. When he returned, he told us that he had followed the woman's shout; he shouted again, she replied, and so, running all the time, he had got lost in the forest. When he returned, he continued for some time to see Kumareme still. 'Mother,' he said, 'this woman is standing in front of me, looking at me.' No one saw anything: 'I don't see anything; they are the baskets of *pupugnas*,' replied his mother. 'Frighten her away, Mother, hit her.' Then they began to burn peppers and resin; the Hekurá blew on him and succeeded in sending Kumareme away. Only then did he begin to improve. I believe that it was actually Kumareme who enticed him, because he spent those nights like that, lost in the forest.

CHAPTER 44

Sad Life with Akawe

Meanwhile the Pishaanseteri had separated from the Punabueteri and we returned to live with the latter. There at Punabueteka my third son was born. His father said: 'He is white; he is handsome; the Hekurá have told me that his name is Hoshiweiwe.' Hoshiwei is that beautiful little blue bird of the forest.

But Akawe continued all the time to think of the young Kuritateri girl who was about to become a woman and who had been promised to him. It happened that as soon as she became a maiden, she fled with a young Igneweteri. The two took refuge with the Wakawakateri. Their parents went there and took the girl back, but the man stayed with the Wakawakateri. That time Akawe wanted to kill me; he said: 'That girl, who was so young, has run away and you, who are old, have remained; you ought to have fled!' 'It's no fault of mine,' I answered.

In the night he took *epená* and began to chant. When they take *epená*, they become like drunken men and they tell everything. He chanted: 'Sleep today, and tomorrow morning I will cut off your head. Since the young girl ran away, you have been dead to me. If you wish to live, run away today; tomorrow will be too late.' I pretended to ignore him, but I was listening; I was angry and afraid. Early in the morning Akawe got up, untied the basket where the black *urucú* was and started to paint himself. His mother's sister came up and asked me: 'Why is he painting himself black? No man ever paints himself black without a reason.' 'Because he wants to kill me,' I replied. When I saw that he was approaching me, I took my small son, who was still sleeping in the hammock, put him on my back, and began to run away. He wanted to shoot me, but the men took his arrows from him; he said: 'It doesn't matter, I can also kill her with my bow,' and he tried to strike me with the end of his bow. All were shouting against him.

From that moment I have not been able to bear the sight of him. Fusiwe had never maltreated me thus. I succeeded in escaping from the *shapuno* with my second son and with Akawe's small son. The men meanwhile took up their positions threateningly around Akawe and took away his bow also; I could hear from afar the men and the women, who were shouting against him. I hid in the forest; later I heard him coming, calling and whistling: 'Napagnuma, come back; come back with my son! My son is hungry, come back; I will not harm you,' but I did not answer and I thought: 'Mad is the man who runs away and answers.' At dead of night, when all was now silent, I went back behind the *shapuno*. A dog began to bark, then came up to me, recognized me and wagged its tail. Slowly I approached behind the roof of the old chief, where my elder son was sleeping next to the chief's two children, and I went in under the roof. The wife recognized me at once and made me lie down in the hammock. 'Akawe is looking for you, like a madman.' I started to cry. The old woman continued: 'I will not light the fire, so that, if he comes, he will not see you.'

For some days I used to go and hide in the forest and come back at night; one day the old woman said to me: 'A boat has passed along the big river; when it comes back, run away. I am very sorry for you.' My elder son said: 'As soon as I grow up, I shall go away and take my mother to the white men.'

One morning Akawe came back. I heard him saying: 'You have hidden Napagnuma and my son here; my Hekurá have told me.' Akawe saw me; I was squatting down on one side. He pushed me with his foot in my shoulder and said: 'Go away, you who are occupying my hearth; it is your fault that the young women do not want me any more. If it had not been for you, I should have had three or four young women; they see you and take fright.' I replied: 'Make them come; build your hearth apart and live with them; I don't mind; I have my sons to live with.' Then he gave me a push to throw me to the ground, but he did not succeed; I escaped and he ran after me. It was raining hard: he caught up with me and seized me to throw me to the ground. As I was falling, I caught him with my hands around his neck, here on the throat. He too slipped and fell with me. I turned around and he went underneath. I was squeezing his throat as hard as I could. Akawe began to shout: 'Let me go; pull her off!' But I held on tight to his throat. 'Mother of my son, don't do it, don't do it, you are killing me!' The men came close to look; they said: 'Well done, well done!' In the end a sister-in-law of his came and took my hand off him. He had almost fainted; he was all purple and breathing badly. Slowly he stood up, swaying, and went towards his hammock. 'I don't know whose daughter she is, what kind of people's daughter this woman is!' Around him they were saying: 'Don't you know whose daughter she is? She almost kills you; well done!' Others again were saying: 'Why do you maltreat her? Why do you beat her?'

The Punabueteri wife, who was still very young, and kept with her mother, was looking after him; his sister-in-law went to fetch water to wash him. A little later Akawe took his bow, his arrows and his quiver with the poisoned arrowheads in it. 'Tomorrow I will go to the Mahekototeri, to my mother; I want to see who will catch game, so that you may eat. Since you have the strength to squeeze my throat, go into the forest, seize a wild boar, squeeze his throat until you kill him, and eat his flesh, if you can!' I answered: 'Why must I catch a wild boar by the throat? Will he not attack me and throw me to the ground? Why have you come to do me harm?' 'I will go away,' he replied, 'so that you'll no longer have anything to eat; you will see that nobody will give you anything to eat.' 'I shall not ask for anything, nor shall I sit by them when they eat game, waiting for them to give me something. I have my sons; when they are grown up, they will give me game and I shall not have to expect it from others.' He added: 'You are not human; you have the strength of an animal!' 'Perhaps I am not human, but I am not afraid of the jaguar; you are human, and that is why you were afraid of the jaguar that night.'

From that time on he scarcely ever beat me again; he was always less wicked. Previously, when he used to come back and I had cooked the bananas and brought them to him, he would often throw them away saying: 'I don't like the bananas you prepare; throw them to the dogs.' Other times he would say to me: 'I don't want bananas, I want *uhina*;' I would prepare it and he would say to me: 'I don't want any more of it.'

That day he wanted to take his small son away; I snatched the baby from him; then he went away by himself. After three days he came back: he was happy; he hugged his son and said: 'I have come back, because I love you very much, my son. If it had been for your mother, I would never have come back.' I answered: 'I had heard tell that a certain person would never come back; however he has come back to see where his ashes are hanging up.' They say in fact that, when a man says that he is going away for good, it is as though he were dead, and, if he returns, they ask him whether he has come to see where his ashes have been hung up. I turned the other way and did not look at him; I was cooking *uhina* and I called my son. His girl cousin came up and said to me: 'What are you eating? Give a bit of it to my brother as well;' she called him brother. I answered: 'I cannot give it to him, because otherwise he will grow old, poor boy; with my old hands I have taken this *uhina* and, if he eats it, he too will become old. I am old and everything which I touch grows old, including those who eat whatever I have touched.' Akawe began to laugh and said: 'This kind of people don't know that when a man arrives he is hungry; they won't give him anything to eat.' He took three of those potatoes and went away.

Akawe's aunt then said: 'We cannot understand how you whites think; you remain angry for one day, for two days, for several days.' They, on the other hand, do not remain upset; at one moment they beat their wives and immediately afterwards they are already talking together; the wife does not continue to feel angry. Sometimes I have seen them with a wound still open, with blood flowing, and already they are talking as before. The aunt came up to me and said: 'Don't be upset any longer; he is not upset now; why do you carry on so?' 'Because he has not treated me like a human being; I too am human and if I knew where to go, I would go away.' Meanwhile I was always thinking of going away and did not know where. The old woman asked me: 'Do you really want to go away?' 'Yes, he has treated me too badly; I don't want to stay here any more.'

One day the Witukaiateri, with whom we had gone back to live, killed a tapir, and shared out the meat. Akawe took a little meat and put it in his basket, saying to his other wife: 'Keep it for me; I have no other wife; if I had I would give it to her.' The other woman replied: 'Why don't you give a bit of it to your son's mother?' 'No,' he answered, 'if she wants tapir, let her kill it for herself.' He was remembering the time when I had held him by the throat. He loved his child very much, but he often treated my son Karyona very badly. When he had finished eating, he threw the bone to my son Karyona, who was hungry and was looking at him. I said: 'My son is not a dog to whom bones are to be thrown; he no longer has a father and therefore you treat him like this! When you are dead, will you be glad if they do the same with your son?' He then said to my son: 'Son, go a long way away.'

That day the little boy, Akawe's son, had dysentery badly and the father was worried. After having eaten, while he was going out with his other wife to go to the *roça*, he said to me: 'Don't go anywhere with my son, as he is ill.' I did not answer; I only waited for him to go away, then I untied my hammock, put it in the basket, took my cotton and put it inside. My second son, Karyona, who was by now quite big, took another basket full of cotton and we fled. I knew the Shipariweteri, because I had been with Akawe to get earthenware pots from them. With the Shipariweteri lived a sister of Akawe, who had always been very kind to me: they lived a very long way off, but when one wants to run away, nothing is far off. As we were going out of the *shapuno,* Akawe's mother-in-law understood that I wanted to flee, took Karyona's arm and said: 'Don't go, your step-father will get angry.' The child started to cry, because he wanted to come with me; the father-in-law came up and tried to keep him back. 'Why do you want to keep him?' I said. 'He is no relation of yours, we are different people.' Then the brother-in-law came up and said: 'Let's let them go, he treats them too badly: let's let them go in peace. Haven't you seen that he has not given him any meat and has thrown the bones to him?' That man was good; if he caught an animal, he often called Karyona and gave him a little of the meat and sent it for me; the father-in-law, too, was kind and often gave things for us.

After two days of walking and of hunger, we came to the Shipariweteri. The baby was no longer sucking milk. Perhaps on account of the cold which he had caught in the night, he had grown worse. Then those Hekurá came up to take care of him; Shawarakariwe, chief of that group, came; the husband of Akawe's sister came; one whose names was Hehetawe came and yet another; there were four in all. They began to inhale *epená.* The woman had left the child lying in the hammock. One came and sucked his chest, another came and sucked his throat; they sucked his stomach and his head, because they said that he had the sickness in his head, which was very hot. One finished and the next began: they took *epená* and chanted. I no longer remember those chants of theirs, which were different from those of the Hekurá I knew, because I heard them only once. Shawarakariwe, after he had chanted, said: 'He will get better; we have sucked his chest, we have cleansed him; now he too will begin to suck again; he will not die.' The aunt was weeping and that *tushaua* continued: 'Do not weep, he will not die; when he grows up, he will turn into a white man and when the whites come, he will go away with them. We shall always stay here without clothes; but he will be master of clothes. Do not weep.'

I was so tired that I went to sleep, but later the aunt came, woke me up, gave me the baby, and said: 'While you were asleep, the

Hekurá continued to care for him, until the cold air of the morning began to beat on them.' The men had said: 'Tomorrow we will meet to minister to him again. His father is already thinking of him, and is already coming; he is the son whom he loves most. The son of that other woman, who is bigger, he does not love so much.'

They say that when Akawe returned from the forest and found our hearth empty, without hammocks, without fire, he wept. The mother of that wife sent him banana *mingau*, but he did not want it, and he did not eat that tapir meat which he had left hanging in the basket; he decided to come after us. When he arrived in the *shapuno* of the Shipariweteri and saw his son so ill, he said to me: 'The child is dying; if he dies, you head will fall over there. He is dying because the Hekurá of your white father have come to take him.' 'It is no fault of mine,' I said, 'how can any of the fault be mine? I have no Hekurá; if I had them, I would send them to blow in your eyes to make you blind.' His sister said to him: 'You think only of killing! Well then, kill her and eat her, seeing that you maltreat her so! No one should kill; we must die because of a snake's bite, or of the Hekurá; not by being killed by each other!' The child was in my arms, and he was cold, with his mouth tightly shut.

Towards midnight the baby opened his eyes, looked around, raised his head and saw me lit up by the light of the fire. He wanted to come to me, but the aunt would not let him. At first he would not sleep any more, but then he fell asleep until the morning. He recovered; it had been that old Hekurá who cured him. He would not go away that day because, he said, the enemy Hekurá might return, take the *nohotipe* of the child and kill him once and for all. 'Now,' he said in a chant, 'I will hide *nohotipe* of child in skin of Hekurá of jaguar, so that they never take him back again.' While he was invoking Irariwe, he walked on all fours, and put out his tongue, and showed his teeth, and roared, as though he had been a jaguar.

Time passed: we returned to the Kuritateri, where we lived for a long time. My eldest son, Maramawe, had stayed all the time with the old Punabueteri chief. One day, while I was alone, the Witukaiateri chief arrived with some others; he called Karyona, my second child. They said that he was taking him, so that he could be with the old man's sons. I shouted and wept, but they carried him off. When Akawe returned to the *shapuno*, he said: 'Leave him to them, so that they can bring him up; when he is bigger, we will go there and fetch him back.' The other Kuritateri also said: 'When he is bigger, we will go with Akawe and bring him back.' From time to time the Witukaiateri came to see the Kuritateri, but they did not bring the child: some told me that they were treating him well; others, however, said that they were maltreating him. The son-in-law of that old man was without doubt treating him well; the old man perhaps made him work, loading wood and fetching water.

CHAPTER 45

The First White Men

I was thinking all the time of how to escape. The first time that I had seen the white men had been in Mahekototeka (El Platanal): I had gone with Akawe to spend a little time with his mother. While we were in the *shapuno*, we heard the noise of an engine on the river. They began to say: '*Nape, nape* (the white men, the white men).' I ran to see, because I wanted to speak to them: there were three men, but I did not succeed in speaking to them.

We returned another time later to the Mahekototeri; Akawe said to me: 'Here are the white men.' They lived in a nice little house with a fence round it; they had cultivated maize and fruit-trees. I approached a tall white man and asked where we were; he answered: 'In Venezuela.' I then said to him: 'I used to live with my father; they shot him and seized me; I have been living with them for many years.' I also tried to write my name. I wanted to ask him to help me escape, but at that moment Akawe arrived and asked me: 'What are you saying? Do you want to run away?'; and he made me go away: he was always suspicious.[1]

A long time after that we were again with the Witukaiateri, who had their *shapuno* near to a big *igarapé*. One morning about eight o'clock, I was preparing banana *mingau* and I heard shouting: '*Pei haw, Napeke haw*! (The white men),' and I saw a man with a big hat on his head and a gun; behind him came another man with a gun. Akawe took his arrows and said quietly: 'What do these whites want? Do they really want me to kill them?' And he began to sharpen the head of an arrow. I answered: 'You think of nothing but killing; instead of asking for machetes and knives, you think of killing. What have they done to you?' Akawe went on: 'Yes, I'll kill them.' I then said to him: 'Do you think by chance that to kill a white man is easy? They have a gun and they will kill *you*.' He looked at them fearfully; the *tushaua* then said: 'Leave the arrows,

[1] The white man to whom Helena Valero here refers is the German scientist Otto Zerries of the Frobenius Expedition.

otherwise the white men will be afraid!' They all went to meet them without arrows.

The two men had left their motor boat and had taken a path to come to the *shapuno*; I learnt afterwards that the man with the big hat was a Venezuelan, whose name was Sisto. I wanted to go up and speak to those two, but they were all standing around me and I could not. The men began to offer bunches of bananas; Akawe himself brought two. Sisto would not eat, but he said in Spanish: 'Bring them onto my boat.' I still remembered a few words and translated. So they brought many full baskets onto his boat; he then distributed some machetes, but not to all those who had given the bananas, and he went away with his companion. I heard a man say: 'I have given bananas and he has given me nothing; if he comes back, I will kill him.' All those who had not received anything were very angry; another said: 'He didn't give me anything either; let us kill them if they come back.' Those who had had machetes did not want this, but later they all agreed to kill them.

After perhaps a month the two came back: they arrived at the same point on the *igarapé*, took the path and came towards the *shapuno*; they already knew the way. On that day, I remember, I was lying ill in the hammock, because a river-ray had stung me in the foot: my whole leg was swollen. Sisto entered the *shapuno*, came up to me, asked me what was the matter and told me in Spanish: 'I have a remedy.' Meanwhile the men had congregated on the compound of the *shapuno*; some were painted brown, but not black. Akawe too had painted himself. I heard them saying among themselves: 'Let us kill them!' I saw that they were approaching Sisto and his companion with their bows and arrows and were pointing to one of those ants' nests which are found on the trees and which could easily be seen from the open space within the *shapuno*. They wanted them to shoot, so that they could then kill them. Sisto's companion began to show them how he hunted, because he thought they were joking. He bent down, and pointed his rifle. They went *tum*, *tum*, so that he would shoot. They knew that white men kill with rifles.

When at last Sisto pointed his gun at the *cupim* to shoot, I said in bad Spanish: 'Don't shoot, don't shoot! They want to make you shoot in order to kill you!' The men continued: 'Shori, pan pan,' but Sisto understood. The two whites came close one to the other, with their rifle pointing towards the Witukaiateri. 'Go away,' I said, 'go away, and look behind you, because they will follow you.'

It was already evening and the two men did not go away. I asked: 'Why do you not go away?' 'Because we have seen a big tree near here, fit for making a canoe: it is very difficult to find these trees.' Then I said: 'Do not sleep tonight, otherwise they will kill you; they are angry with you, because the last time they gave you bananas, and you took them and gave many of them nothing in return. If you sleep, they will shoot you. Keep your rifles in your hands all the time, for they are afraid of guns; if they succeed in taking them off you, they will shoot you with arrows.' That night the two did not sleep and kept their rifles in their hands all the time; when the men approached, they showed their cartridges. Early in the morning they went away and distributed many machetes and other gifts.

In the *shapuno* the men afterwards joked with the women and said: 'Go with Sisto; we want to have a white son.' The women grew upset, but they said: 'We are joking, don't get upset.' One man said to a woman: 'Why don't you want to go? A son with curly hair is handsome;' the woman replied angrily: 'Send your own woman.' 'But can't you see that I am joking?' What I have heard tell here is not true, that to have stronger sons, pregnant women go with other men. It may be so in other tribes, but with them it is a lie. The Indians may have said it for a joke as that time, but I have never seen them give their women to their guests.

I was again pregnant and expecting this last son. One day Akawe had killed a crocodile and said to me: 'Go and get water to cook the crocodile;' I took the basket with the *cuias* and went to the river. It was already evening; I left the *shapuno* and set out on my way; behind me came other women. On the path, as I was walking, I trod on something cold. A big snake wrapped itself round my body, with its head down; its tail was squeezing me under my breast. It gave me a bite in the leg, then loosened itself and slithered to the ground. It then raised its head very high and chased me. I ran, but it was faster; it caught up with me and gave me another bite in the leg; its teeth slid down and drew a line without entering the flesh. They have left these two long scars.

I shouted out loudly; the women, who were coming behind me, also shouted: 'Karahirimahe, Karahirimahe (jararaca, jararaca).' 'It is not Karahirima,' I said, 'it's bigger!' I ran to the *shapuno*: dark blood was coming out of the holes made by the teeth. 'It's your fault, for sending me out to get water after dark!' I shouted to Akawe. At that moment I felt no pain, but then it began to hurt more and more; I was shouting. A man came and said: 'Rub tobacco leaves on your leg; in this way you will soothe the pain of the snake-bite somewhat.' A woman squeezed the juice of those leaves and rubbed it on my leg: she was crying for pity, seeing me suffer in that way. The pain went down a little, but then began worse than ever; it was a terrible pain. It grew more and more swollen for four to five days, then burst, and blood and water began to come out; then the pain died down. They used to say that when a snake bites, the leg may stay bent; so they tied it up for me, stretching it out well. To get down from the hammock I had to have someone come and help me. That wound lasted such a long time. Eventually, to put an end to that liquid discharge, I treated it with the hot, roasted dust of the nest of those ants: a great scar is still left.

Karahirima had bitten me a very long time before, when I was a child and lived with the Shamatari. I was going with the other women into the forest to get honey: I was the last in line. It was morning and it seems that the snake was waking up: when I passed, I felt something like a prick caused by a thorn. I shouted and ran ahead; the others tried to kill it, but the creature went inside a hole in a tree: it was small. They said: 'Karahirima.' I became like one stunned: I could neither feel nor understand. Then the pain started, but it was less and I healed in a shorter time. If a big *tocandira* ant or some other poisonous animal bites, they tie tightly above it, so that the pain or the poison shall not rise.

CHAPTER 46

The Unfortunate Son of Riokowe

While I was still suffering from the snake-bite, some Pishaanseteri came to invite Akawe, saying: 'You are *waiteri*, you are famous everywhere; you have killed Waika, you have fought against Shiriana; now you must go there. We will show you the way to the Shamatari and you must avenge our dead. If you kill a Shamatari, we will give you one of our women; you will stay there with us.' I was listening; Akawe said to me: 'I will go, you stay here and do not wait for me.' I answered: 'Go, take a woman there; you say that it is my fault that you have no women; so take a young girl far away over there and stay with her. I am old, you say; you want a young woman; take three, or four, or as many of them as you find and stay with them.' Then I said to those Pishaanseteri who had come to invite him: 'Give him your young women.' They replied: 'Yes, we will give him them, we will give him them; you will weep when you learn that he has two young women.' 'No, I do not weep for a man! I know how to do everything, I know how to prepare food, I know how to cut wood, I know how to live on my own.' Akawe did not speak; he took his hammock, his arrows and the poisoned arrowheads which his brother had sent him from Mahekototeka, because near there are those poisonous lianas. And he left.

Akawe left with the Pishaanseteri and it was he who killed Riokowe, *tushaua* of the Shamatari. He told me later that they travelled a long way, and at last reached a spot near the *igarapé* of the *shapuno*. The Shamatari were making their preparations for a *reaho*. On the lower ground, in the *igarapé*, at a distance, could be seen many men who were bathing; further up, Riokowe was in the water, diving in and rubbing himself; near him was a wife, a sister-in-law and the children who were playing, jumping in the water and singing: '*Shamariwe toko tokoe*.' 'The tapir goes *toko tokoe* [when he falls into the water].' Another was singing: '*Patasiwe toto tokoe.*' (*Pata* means big; the big tapir.) I too have heard the Shamatari and the Karawetari children sing in that way while they are bathing; this is what Akawe repeated to me when he came back.

He crept up, pointed his arrow and hit Riokowe in the chest. The man shouted, tried to get out of the water, then fell backwards with his legs on the land and his head in the water. His wife ran off shouting: Akawe said that he tried to catch her, but did not succeed. A small child, who was near his father, began to run away, but Akawe ran after him and caught him; then he joined the other Pishaanseteri.

He wanted to bring the little boy to Kuritateka, but the Pishaanseteri asked for him and he left him. Then the Pishaanseteri went to the Mahekototeri, bringing that small child with them. One day a woman sent him to fetch water from the river; a Pishaanseteri, son of Pahawe, saw him and said: 'I will kill that Shamatari for vendetta.' The woman said: 'Do not kill him,' but when the child was coming back with his little *cuias*, that wretch hurled his arrow and killed him.[1]

It seems that the Pishaanseteri had already tried to take vengeance on the Shamatari, but had not succeeded; therefore they had invited Akawe; they had promised him a young woman, but after he killed Riokowe, they told him they had only one child, daughter of a man with a big scar. The man had made them tell Akawe: 'My daughter is very young; when it is time, I will give her. Meanwhile continue to kill game for us.' For months Akawe continued to kill game for his parents-in-law, then grew tired of it and came away.

[1] Of this grim episode, too, the missionary James Barker received news. (*Bol. Indig. Venez* 7: 153, 1959.)

CHAPTER 47

The Last Flight

When Akawe came back, I was with the Kuritateri, together with that sister of his who was very kind. My fourth son had been born and was already several months old. I always said that I would run away to the white men. A white man had passed by, whom they called Balachi; when the baby was born, they began to make jokes, saying that he was like that man Balachi and so the name of Balachi stuck to the child.

Akawe asked me: 'So do we want to escape to the white men?' I replied: 'Why ever do you ask me this?' He added: 'I want to escape; too many men want to kill me.' After he had killed that Shamatari chief, he was afraid of a vendetta; he was no longer friendly with the Pishaanseteri. 'The Pishaanseteri have deceived me; if they come here, I will kill them,' he said. I then replied: 'If you bring along all my sons together, I will run away. I cannot leave my sons here, because if we run away, the others will kill them for vengeance.' 'We will all run away,' he answered. He seriously wished to run away and go to the white men; he was afraid.

In the evening he asked the Kuritateri: 'Do you wish to accompany me? I wish to go and fetch back the son of Napagnuma, who has stayed behind with the old Punabueteri; he is now a big boy, he hunts, he must come back with us.' 'It's right,' said the others. I felt happy in my heart. It was night and he shouted: '*Pei haw* let's all go!' I left the two small children with an old woman and we went. When they came near to the *shapuno*, the men painted themselves black: the women did not paint themselves; only the young girls made big black lines on their bodies. The men said: 'You women, hold the bows and arrows; we will enter with *nabrushi* only;' and they prepared short *nabrushi*. 'If you see them getting arrows, then give us our arrows.' I was carrying Akawe's bow and arrows. We ran all the time and when we arrived it was still dark: Akawe entered the *shapuno* first; behind him the other men and then we women. He ran straight to where the boy was in his hammock, took him by the arm and dragged him away. I was waiting in the middle of the square; Akawe said to me: 'Run out with him at once. You women, all of you go out with him; we men are staying here to fight.'

The Punabueteri meanwhile had taken their *nabrushi* and began to give blows. Akawe received a great blow on the head; the wound remained open for a long time. Many men were wounded, but none died. At last that old Punabueteri chief, who was kind, said: 'That's enough; we cannot fight with *nabrushi,* otherwise we shall break our arms. If our enemies come, we shall not even be able to throw our arrows, because our arms will be wounded. Kuritateri! We do not want to quarrel with you!' Then the men went out of the *shapuno,* and joined us, when we were already quite a way off. Akawe said: 'I think that the Punabueteri will pursue us with arrows; it's better that we men wait for them here. You women go on.' In fact, soon afterwards, the Punabueteri arrived all painted black, with bows and arrows, so the men told us later. Akawe then said: 'If you want to die, come close to us; if you wish to live, go back.' He took bow and arrows and stood up, ready. The Punabueteri stopped and the Kuritateri began their journey back home again without being pursued further. When we found ourselves in the *shapuno* again, the men said to me: 'It is your fault that I have this arm almost broken.' 'It is your fault that I have received this blow.' I answered: 'But you are accustomed to fighting.'

After some days some Punabueteri came and, without taking my son back, said: 'We must not fight; the Ihiteri, who are Waika, are saying: "We have already a long time ago wounded one of them with arrows and no arrow has fallen in our *shapuno*." You, Kuritateri, come with us therefore to fight against the Ihiteri.' Akawe said: 'You go; when you come back, I will then go and kill them by myself.'

Almost all the Kuritateri men went to the Punabueteri to attack the enemy together; only the *tushaua* stayed behind with a few men. That same evening Akawe called my son and told him: 'I have come to take you, and so I have received a great blow from a *nabrushi*. Now you go and ask for me the daughter of that old *tushaua*; you must tell the mother to send her daughter to me here as I wish to speak to her.' My son refused to go, but at last he went; the mother answered: 'I will not give my daughter to a man who has so many other women.' The boy came back and said: 'Do not send me again; she said that she would not give her to a man who has so many other wives, but to a man of another tribe.' Akawe was then seized with anger and said: 'Yes; everyone is against me. Let us then escape to the Nape.' 'Let us go,' I answered, 'but I want my other son too.' 'Go and get him then,' he replied, 'I won't come.' I said to Akawe: 'I am going to fetch Karyona from the Witukaiateri.' 'Have you the courage to go?' 'Yes, I know quite well how to get in without being seen.' He was dubious. 'You will see,' I said; 'you get everything ready for running away as soon as I come back.' 'You won't succeed,' he replied; 'a woman cannot do it. There are three mountains of thorns on the path; around the *shapuno* of the Witukaiateri there is a palisade.'

I left at once and ran all night; I passed the *roça,* then entered the forest, found the second *roça* and then came again to the forest; I reached a pretty piece of ground where, they said, the jaguar was always to be found. I crossed an *igarapé*; I was all of a sweat and I took a bath, then went into a *pataua* wood. The way was long, but I ran all the time; at last I reached the spot and heard a dog barking. I stopped, said my prayers and recited it three times; I counted it with my fingers as on the rosary.

In the *shapuno* all was silent; I recited seven more paternosters and seven Ave Marias, and I approached slowly. I met the first barrier of thorns; I took a thick stick and, a little at a time, opened a way through the thorns. Further on I found another barrier of thorns and did the same thing. I came close to the *shapuno*: everywhere was *tucuma* thorns. So I came near to the palisade; I thought: 'Now I will lift only two posts; I am small and I shall get through.' They were high posts, but light; I raised them, moved them away a little, without making a noise, pushed myself through and so entered.

The night was dark, but there were men awake, cooking a monkey. I recall that one of them was asking: 'Is the broth good?' 'It's rather bitter because of the *mamocori* (curare); they have not washed it well.' On the other side they were all asleep; the hearths showed no flames. I tried to see my son, but could not; I passed near to a big dog, which was lying down. The dog raised its head and snarled. I took a leaf that I had in my hand, put it under my tongue and folded the tongue over it, closing the mouth. They say that this is what you do when there is a bad dog. The dog became quiet again. While I was already standing near the boy, on the other side of the *shapuno,* they lit a big fire which made a great deal of light; I crouched down in the dark. An old man warmed himself at the fire and went back to lie down in his hammock.

I came to where my son was. His hammock was hanging above the hammock of one of the old man's sons; the old man was to one side; above him was the hammock of another son and on the other side that of his wife. I blew on my son's face and he woke up. I said to him in a whisper: 'Get up and don't make a noise!' He pointed out to me his small bow and his arrows, which were pushed into the roof, almost above the old man. I took them very slowly, while my son gently came down from his hammock. I untied the hammock and put it on my shoulders. No one awoke and we went out without being seen by anyone; I then came back to all the thorns, and, farther on, with that same stick, I gradually built up again the barricades of thorns. Then I said: 'Now let us run.' The boy was now about ten years old. We ran and ran, ran and ran; we again passed by the same places where I had been before and so we came to the *shapuno*.

It was now daytime. Akawe was waiting, but my eldest son was not there. I had not told him that I wanted to run away and he had gone hunting. We could not wait for him any longer. Akawe's sister, who was always so kind, said to me: 'He has gone hunting with two others.' 'When he comes back, tell him that I have run away towards the great river.' 'Are you really going then?' asked the woman; then she went on: 'Go then, perhaps you'll be better off.' She came close to me and started to cry. I picked up my few things, my *urucú,* my *cuias,* and gave them to her. I took only a small basket which she had made for me.

We set out; we did not pass along the path, but through the wood. I was carrying around my neck the two children whom I had borne to Akawe. My other son, Karyona, was walking; every so often he bumped into the thorns and cried out. We had also taken burning firebrands. The forest was thick: Akawe took from me his bigger son and put him on his shoulders. We passed close to a *roça* full of tobacco. Akawe said: 'I want to get some tobacco leaves.' 'Never mind the leaves,' I replied, 'we are going towards a land where there is plenty of tobacco; anyone who is fleeing does not carry tobacco, and does not take anything to eat.' It began to rain: we reached a big *igarapé*. Karyona said: 'Mother, I came here with the others to fish. There must be a canoe; down there, along the river, live the Igneweteri.' Akawe said: 'Then let's go and look for the canoe.' I waited for them with the other two little ones, but they came back without having found it.

All of a sudden I heard the footsteps of someone running; I turned round: it was my eldest son. 'Mother, the others are coming. I have heard the shouts of the Witukaiateri, who are coming.' As soon as they had realized that I had stolen my second son, they had run to the Kuritateri, had joined the few men there, and were pursuing us. The boy was crying: 'They wanted to kill me. Why did you run away without waiting for me? The old Kuritateri *tushaua* told me: "Run away, run away at once; go to your mother, so that you will die together with your brothers and your stepfather; I do not want to kill you here, because here no one will burn you; let them kill you a long way from here and let your smoke smell from afar!" '

Then my son said: 'I know where the canoe is.' He began to walk forward along the *igarapé*; at last he threw himself into the water. The canoe was hidden at the bottom of the water, covered with branches and tied with lianas; there were also four oars. He held onto the lianas, he went under water, then came out; he pulled, and the canoe appeared. He brought it out of the water. Then we all jumped in. Akawe did not know how to row and remained seated with the babies: he was frightened. I sat down in the stern; I knew how to row, because I used to row as a girl. The two big boys, who had lived near the big river, knew how to row; the two little ones were very frightened. The current helped us to go downstream and, soon afterwards, we reached a big river of white water. It was the Orinoco. We continued to go downstream; at last we came to a place near the Igneweteri. We climbed the bank and found empty *tapirí*; we continued to walk and found a *roça*. Nearby, other *tapirí,* where there were only women and an old man, whom my big son called uncle. He made us space to hang up our hammocks and asked us why we were fleeing; Akawe made up a lie. He did not say that we were fleeing, but told how we had had a quarrel over some women. Then I said quietly to Akawe: 'If you want to stay, then stay; take your two small sons, who are your own. The two big ones, whom I brought with me from the forest, I won't leave with you; I am taking them with me to the white men.'

A woman told us: 'All the rest have gone to a feast; a white man has passed along the river and has pointed out with his fingers when he would come down.' 'How many days?' I asked. The woman showed six fingers. 'So many days have gone by; tomorrow is perhaps the last day.' 'What is his name?' 'Eduardo; he has his wife with him.' Night fell; I went up to a woman whom I knew and said to her: 'I will tell you a secret; don't tell anybody; we are running away to the white men.' 'I will help you,' she answered.

When day broke, the old man said to the boys: 'Near here are some *pataua* palms, where many *arara* go to eat; go and shoot them.' The big boy already had a big bow and went with his brother Karyona and a boy, the old man's son. No sooner had they set out when that old Punabueteri chief arrived, who had brought up my eldest son and loved him so much. They had heard him shout from the other side of the river and the boys there, who had canoes, had gone to fetch him. Akawe was painting himself, because he wanted to inhale *epená*. I saw the old man from a distance and said to the woman who wanted to help me: 'Run along the path; when my eldest son returns, don't let him come, because the old Punabueteri is here.' I knew that my son loved him very much also and I did not want them to meet. The woman ran along the path and met them as they were coming back. They had killed two *araras*; they gave them to her and went back into the bush.

The old man, after having spoken with the man there, came up to us: 'We arrived yesterday,' said Akawe. 'I know,' he answered, 'I have come to tell you not to go back to the Kuritateri any more; they are furious. They have talked so much about you; they have treated you like an animal, every kind of animal, and likewise they have spoken of your dead father. I wanted to defend you and they almost beat me with a *nabrushi*. Those men, where your wife went to steal the boy by night, have run to the Kuritateri to kill all of you with strong poison; they have pursued you not with a *nabrushi,* but with arrows to kill you. I have not come to take the boy back. Where is my Shamatari?' (Sometimes he called my son Namoeteri, sometimes he called him Shamatari.) 'He has gone fishing with the others,' answered Akawe. 'Poor boy, you won't run away from here, will you?' 'No,' answered Akawe, 'I am not going to the white men, for I am afraid of sickness. The others are enemies; I shall stay here.' The old man was weeping, because he had understood and he loved the boy very much. It filled me with pity; I turned my back and I too wept. After a little the old man said: 'I am going; look after that son and the other sons, and stay here; don't run away. Look after my Namoeteri well. One day, perhaps, he will come back with me again.' Then the old man went sadly away. He had brought up that child like a son. Akawe too said: 'It upset me to see that old man's beard. His hair, too, is beginning to turn white.'

As night was falling, we heard from a distance the noise of an engine: 'Eduardo, Eduardo,' they said. He was coming to look for people to tie the cedar trees that he had cut down. The Igneweteri men had returned and three of them went with him to help him make the raft with the cedar-trunks. They left again and I heard the engine going away. The next day they were already back; in front came the raft of trunks and behind came the engine. I took in my arms the two small children, put the hammock in the basket and ran towards the bank. I had no clothes, but I was not ashamed and I thought: 'If I feel ashamed of the white men, I will never go away; when the Kuritateri and the Witukaiateri learn that we are here, they will cross over and come.'

The wife of that white man, whose name was Juan Eduardo, came out of the boat. I spoke to her in bad Spanish: 'Tell me, which way are you going?' 'We are going down to San Fernando.' 'I would like to talk to you.' I spoke badly, but I remembered a little of that Castilian that I used to speak with my father when I was a child. The man asked, 'Who are you?' 'I am the daughter of Carlos Valero,' I answered. Juan Eduardo leapt to the ground: 'Are you the daughter of Carlos Valero?' 'Yes, they seized me when I was a girl. Now I do not know where I am.' 'You don't know where you are? You are in Venezuela, on the Alto Orinoco; San Fernando is farther down.' Then I asked: 'Could you not take me as far as San Fernando?' 'Of course; Carlos Valero is my friend; he has two houses at San Fernando; he is there.'

The man gave me a *cuia* full of manioc flour; I did not feel the desire to eat, but only the desire to leave. Juan Eduardo's wife took one of her dresses and passed it to me; I put it on, took the children and jumped into the big boat. Akawe wanted to jump in; I said: 'Don't come, stay here; I am going alone with my sons. If you wish, take your two. Here you have relations and people who love you; I and these two older children of mine have no relations.' I was angry with Akawe, because he had been wicked too often. 'No, I won't stay; I'm coming with you,' he answered.

We all embarked on the boat and Juan Eduardo gave orders to the Makiritari Indian to set it in motion. When, from that boat driven by a powerful engine, I saw the bank drawing away from us, I felt a great happiness. It felt as though I were already with my mother.

CHAPTER 48

The Wicked World of the White Men

After three days we came to the Protestant missionaries at Tama Tama. We continued the journey and, after a further four days, we reached Juan Eduardo's holding, where he had three houses. A few days later Juan Eduardo went to S. Fernando de Atabapo and told the whole story. At once the missionaries' motor launch came to fetch us. I had very bad stomach-ache and they took me to a hospital; the sisters gave us all clothes. Then they took me to two missionaries and a doctor. They asked me so many questions, but I could not tell them as I am doing now, because I knew so few words: I scarcely remembered any Spanish.[1]

So I came back to Juan Eduardo's house; one day a motor launch arrived. There was my brother Anisio, who worked with the anti-malarial service. They told him: 'Anisio, your sister is here.' He answered: 'Who is my sister?' 'Helena.' 'I don't know her. I'll call again tomorrow.' The next day he came back with other friends; I felt very shy. They sent for me and Eduardo said: 'This is your sister; I found her in the forest. You know what to do; either take her or call your father.' Anisio replied: 'I cannot take her; I have to go to work. I'll send a telegram today.' Then he asked me the name of my father, of my mother and of my brothers. I answered: 'My father's name is Carlos, my mother's is Clemência da Silva; I have two brothers, one named Luis Valero, the younger Anisio, and a sister, Ana Teresa.' He was writing everything down. 'Then it's true,' he said, 'you are my sister. Only a short time ago our father and our mother left, because the authorities here saw that we are not Venezuelans, and so they have sent for some documents to Manaus in Brazil.' My father had lost his documents on one occasion when the boat overturned; Mother did not have them. It seems that

[1] One of these missionaries was father Luigi Cocco.

it is a very important thing to have documents in order to live there. Anisio was not bad; he bought four pieces of material for me and gave some clothes to Akawe.

My parents received the telegram in Santa Rosa on the Rio Negro, before arriving at Cucuí. They say my father asked my mother: 'What shall we do? The Government has only given us a few days to find the documents; if we go back, we shall waste these days.' They went to Cucuí; my father went by air to Manaus and returned a fortnight later, while my mother waited for him at Cucuí. So we met after many days: my brother Luis wrote saying that he did not want us to go to them at Manaus. He was ashamed of me, and asked why I was coming back. I ought to have stayed there in the forest. I wept a great deal with pain and with anger. Akawe spoke to my father and asked me to translate: 'Take this child, bring him up, and when you are very old he will be your companion. I don't want him to suffer hunger and be maltreated, because I love him very much.' He took his elder son by one arm and gave him to my father. (The boy's name is now Carlinhos.) He then went on: 'I think I will go back to my people.' He said to me: 'Your father must look after this son of ours; don't let others take care of him; it is your father who must be responsible for him.'

So I stayed at the missions. A letter arrived in which they said that my mother wept incessantly, because she wanted to see me. I sent word that if my mother wished to see me, she should come to Tapuruquara to the Mission, and that I would not go to my brothers' homes. I did not want to go, but the missionary sister told me: 'Mother is mother, and you must go to see her.' Akawe returned along the Cauaburí to the Kohoroshiwetari and I went down to Manaus. When I saw my brothers, I said so many things: 'I didn't go of my own accord; they seized me; I could not find the way to escape, and so must you treat me this way? And these sons of mine, what blame attaches to them?' I wept and said so many things. They replied that they had written in this way because they were angry with the Indians. 'He came with me and helped me; if it had not been for him, I should still be in the forest; you are more wicked than he is.' (I was referring to Akawe.) When I recall these things today, Luis is sorry; but I remember, because I had been full of joy and now felt such pain. I remained a long time at the mission at Tapuruquara, but later some Marauyá Indians came and wanted to take me away. Akawe went along the Cauaburí, and then came back and wanted his sons back; that is why I went to live at Manaus.

When I arrived at Manaus, I did not know how to live and I started work in a family home. My brother was out of work. The Inspector of the Indians sent for me and said that the children would go to school at their expense; but it was only to get me to tell my story. My father came with me and told me: 'Let's go; if he calls you in order to help you, you tell him the story and I will explain.' But they paid no attention to what I related and I did not wish to go again. They made me so many promises, but they did nothing. If I had not found a post in service, my sons would have died of hunger. Only in the Salesian College of Santa Teresinha they gave me milk, a little rice, and the leftovers of manioc flour. Later a journalist came to see me; he wanted me to tell the story of my life. My brother said: 'My sister must not recount all her sufferings unless she is paid for it while you are writing: it is not fair.' He was telling the truth, and that man did not come back again. The newspapers then began to report so many things, so many brutal stories.

The newspapers said that the government would help, and would give us something to eat, a little house to live in, and for my sons a school where they could study. It seems that they wrote these things three times in the newspapers. One day a lady came to see me and said: 'Let us go to the Parliament House.' I answered: 'I cannot speak'; but they came and took me to the Palace. When we arrived, they said that the President was not there; then they let us in. The President was behind a table; next to him were a man on one side and a man on the other side; it was a long table. The woman who was accompanying me asked if they could help me to find a school for my sons. He replied that he could not help anyone and said: 'We cannot help anyone, or provide schools. You must look for work.' He actually said this to me: 'If you wish to educate your children, look for work, enter their names at the college and make them study; we cannot help anyone.' 'And if I do not find work?' I asked. 'If you don't find work, go back with your children into the forest.' That is what he said to me; I wept with rage. When we came out, I said to that lady: 'I did not want to come; why did you bring me? Why did you bring me to feel such shame in this place?' The woman replied: 'They had told me that he would help; that is what they had written in the newspapers, and that is why I brought you.'

I went to the priests' college, where they answered that they could not accept boys who were still backward. I went to another school where they told me: 'We can do nothing.' At the Mission of

Tapuruquara they would accept them, because my sons know the language of those Indians, but I did not want this, because the Indians of the Cauaburí and of the Marauyá could have carried them off again.

I then went to the Believers in a Protestant Baptist college. There was an American; I talked with him. His wife came, listened, and told me that I could go and work in her house. 'Come tomorrow and we will enter the children's names.' So they entered the eldest, Maramawe, whose name today is José. They bought him uniforms, shoes, notebook, pencil, whatever was necessary for the college. I worked with her, and she gave me something to buy soap, manioc flour, sugar and rice.

How we suffered at that time with these children! Many days we did not eat. My son José, after school, used to go to market to help to carry some parcels. People used to give him a couple of fish; he brought them back, I cooked them, and that is what we all ate. My brother looked for work here and there, but found none; sometimes a lady would send us a plate of food, which we shared among ourselves. At that time the only ones who helped us were the Baptists. I worked with the lady and she gave me a few clothes. She gave me a hammock and something for my mother; she also gave me six plates, a dozen glasses and a few knives and forks. I also earned something from her, but it was not enough to feed José and the other two little ones. The second son, Karyona, whose name is today Manoel, had stayed behind with my sister in Venezuela. No one else has helped me: neither the government nor the Inspector of the Indians. The newspapers had written so many things and people believed them; they used to ask me: 'What? Don't you receive food from the government?' I didn't even answer; everything had been invented by the newspapers.

I went to speak on behalf of Carlinhos with a Redemptorist Father, and I succeeded in getting him put in a kindergarten; so he has begun to study. A nun from there has helped me and has bought various things for the child, as the Baptists had done. Manoel, poor boy, has only just now begun to study. A soldier had started to teach him something. He has come after spending two years in Brazil with my sister. I then went to the Collegio Domingo Savio and I succeeded in speaking with the Salesian Father Schneider. The following Sunday, the missionary came to see me here in my house; he knew where I lived and he informed himself fully as to whether the children were studying and whether the government was helping. I answered that no one had helped and that only Carlinhos was studying a little, because I had tried to make sacrifices by going back to the Protestants too. I said: 'The priests here do not speak with the people; the priests here, if anyone says good morning to them, do not even answer, they are so proud; but with the rich the priests here behave very nicely; with the poor people the priests here don't behave at all.' He asked me a lot about the language of the Indians. He was interested in their language; he asked me if I would help. I replied: 'I work at such-and-such a place; you may speak to my mistress.' I went to him four times. He was generous and gave me four *contos*.

After a short time I received a call from the Father Director of the Collegio Domingo Savio and I went there with my sons. There was a letter from Father Schneider at the mission at Taraquá. He read the letter and asked me to which mission we wished to go. I answered: 'I do not wish to go to Tapuruquara, because too many of those from the Cauaburí and the Marauyá arrive there. I want to go to Taraquá, because there I began to study, there I took my first communion. I would also like my sons to begin to study and take their first communion in the same mission.' He said: 'Very well,' and gave me a note for the sister in charge of the Santa Teresinha college, Sister Luizinha. She read it and said: 'All right, I will send you with one of these planes of the Brazilian Air Force which go to the missions.' So we departed: therefore Manoel is today studying at Taraquá. It was Father Schneider who found this opportunity for him, otherwise he would not be studying yet. Manoel used to say to me: 'Mamma, if we go to Manaus and I find work in the daytime, I will study at night.' Carlinhos and John are younger. I do not know whether I shall succeed in getting them educated in the future.

I thought that everything would be different among the white men.

PHOTOGRAPHIC DOCUMENTATION

(The following photographic documentation, which refers to aspects of Yanoáma life, has been compiled by Missionary Luigi Cocco and the author, among some of the groups with whom Helena Valero lived.)

Dwellings
(Photos 3, 4, 24, 25, 26, 32, 36, 43, 45, 47, 52, 53)

(*a*) The *shapuno* is a large collective dwelling which may be more than 100 yards in diameter. It consists of a large central open area, surrounded by one single sloping roof, underneath which the separate families live around their respective hearths. In the periods of war between groups, the *shapuno* can be protected on the outside by palisades and reinforced on the inside with barriers of tree-trunks.
(*b*) The *tapirí* is a little hut, always with one sloping roof, which the Yanoáma build in order to take shelter during their journeys.

Designs on the body and adornments
(Photos 16, 17, 18, 19, 20, 22, 23, 37)

Men and women often paint their bodies elegantly with various designs. Thin lines and the colours red and brown indicate joy; broad lines and the colour black indicate mourning and death. As adornment, they push smoothed sticks, leaves, feathers, etc. through the holes in their noses, the lobes of their ears and the corners of their mouths.

Tobacco
(Photos 12, 19, 25, 31, 39)

The Yanoáma do not smoke, but men and women put between their lower lip and their teeth enormous wads prepared with tobacco leaves.

Food and cooking
(Photos 14, 15, 28, 29, 30, 31, 43, 44)

The men hunt big wild animals and are the owners of the conical earthenware pots in which they boil the meat with all the hair on it; the men also prepare the big receptacles of the bark of trees for holding banana pap. The women however thread cotton, make baskets, carry wood and cook—on embers or inside leaves—fruit, roots and small animals (birds, fish, reptiles, amphibians and arthropods).

Curare or Mamocori
(Photos 7, 8, 9, 10, 11)

Curare, the poison used in hunting and in war, is prepared by the Yanoáma by a method which has until now remained completely unknown and which consists of the roasting and percolation of barks and roots of trees belonging above all to species of the genus *Strychnos*. Here is the first documentation of this new method of preparing curare, studied by the author in collaboration with D. Bovet and G. B. Marini Bettolo.

Drugs (*epená*)
(Photos 33, 34, 35)

The men inhale vegetable hallucinatory powders (*epená*), prepared from plants of the genus *Piptadenia*, *Virola*, etc., which are blown into the nostrils by means of a cane. Thus they have visions which are especially luminous and believe they are entering into contact with the Hekurá, the eternal spirits of nature. The use of these drugs is forbidden to women and to the uninitiated. The hallucinatory alkaloids of the *epená* of seeds, studied by the author in collaboration with G. B. Marini Bettolo and colleagues, belong to the group of bufotenine and dimethyltriptammine.

Shamanism and shamanic therapies
(Photos 36, 37, 38, 39, 40)

Under the effect of *epená*, the shamans sing, dance, assume ecstatic positions to carry out imaginary flights towards the Sun, the Moon, Night, etc. They cure the sick by extracting the sickness from the suffering body, finding and bringing back into the body the lost soul, driving away enemy Hekurá, etc.

Reaho or great feast
(Photos 1, 2, 41, 42, 43, 44, 45, 55)

The Yanoáma groups meet frequently at the time when the *pupugnas* or other fruit are ripening, almost always to celebrate their dead with great feasts or *reaho*, which may even last many days.
During their moves they walk along the paths, in Indian file. Women with small children carried across their shoulders in bark strips regularly go in the middle of the file carrying the loads, while

the majority of the warriors, with bows and arrows, go in front and behind the group. The chief generally travels together with the women. On the occasion of the *reaho*, the representatives of the various groups hold amongst themselves characteristic, rhythmic ceremonial discussions; the young men carry out dances, sing nocturnal responsorial chants, fight duels, sometimes violent and dramatic, to resolve questions of honour or misunderstandings, or to cement old friendships.

Endocannibalism
(Photos 54, 55, 56)

The dead are regularly burnt on the *shapuno* compound. The bones, pounded and reduced to dust, are then mixed with banana pap and eaten by the dead man's relatives, to give peace to the troubled spirit of the departed. If death strikes a Yanoáma far away from the *shapuno*, his comrades hang the body up on high in the forest, wait for the flesh to fall off the bones, then burn them and eat them in the *shapuno*. Weeping and funereal chants accompany the solemn ceremony of endocannibalism, which usually concludes the great collective feasts or *reaho*.

1. Warriors dancing during the *reaho* of the Kohoroshiwetari

2. Dance of the palm branches during the *reaho*

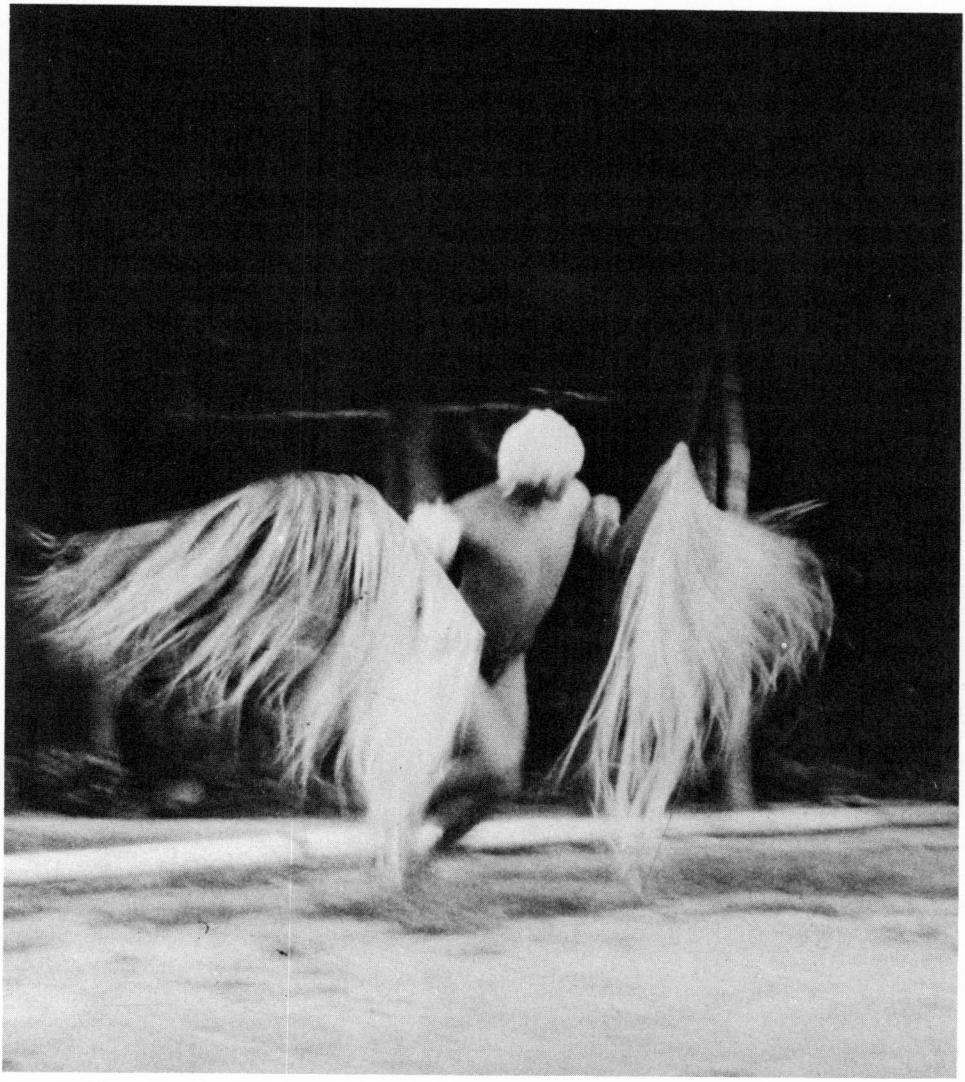

4. A *shapuno* of the Mahekototeri (upper Rio Orinoco)

3. The great *shapuno* of the Kohoroshiwetari (Rio Maturacá)

5. A group of Yanoáma warriors in the forest

6. Pishaanseteri family (Rio Maraca)

7. Opening the package of mamocori bark

Preparing curare in the *shapuno* of the Kohoroshiwetari:

8. Roasting the bark and roots

Preparing curare 9. Powdering the roasted material 10. Adding hot water to the powder 11. Applying curare to the arrow points

12. Ignewetari warrior

13. Kashihewe, chief of the Mahekototeri

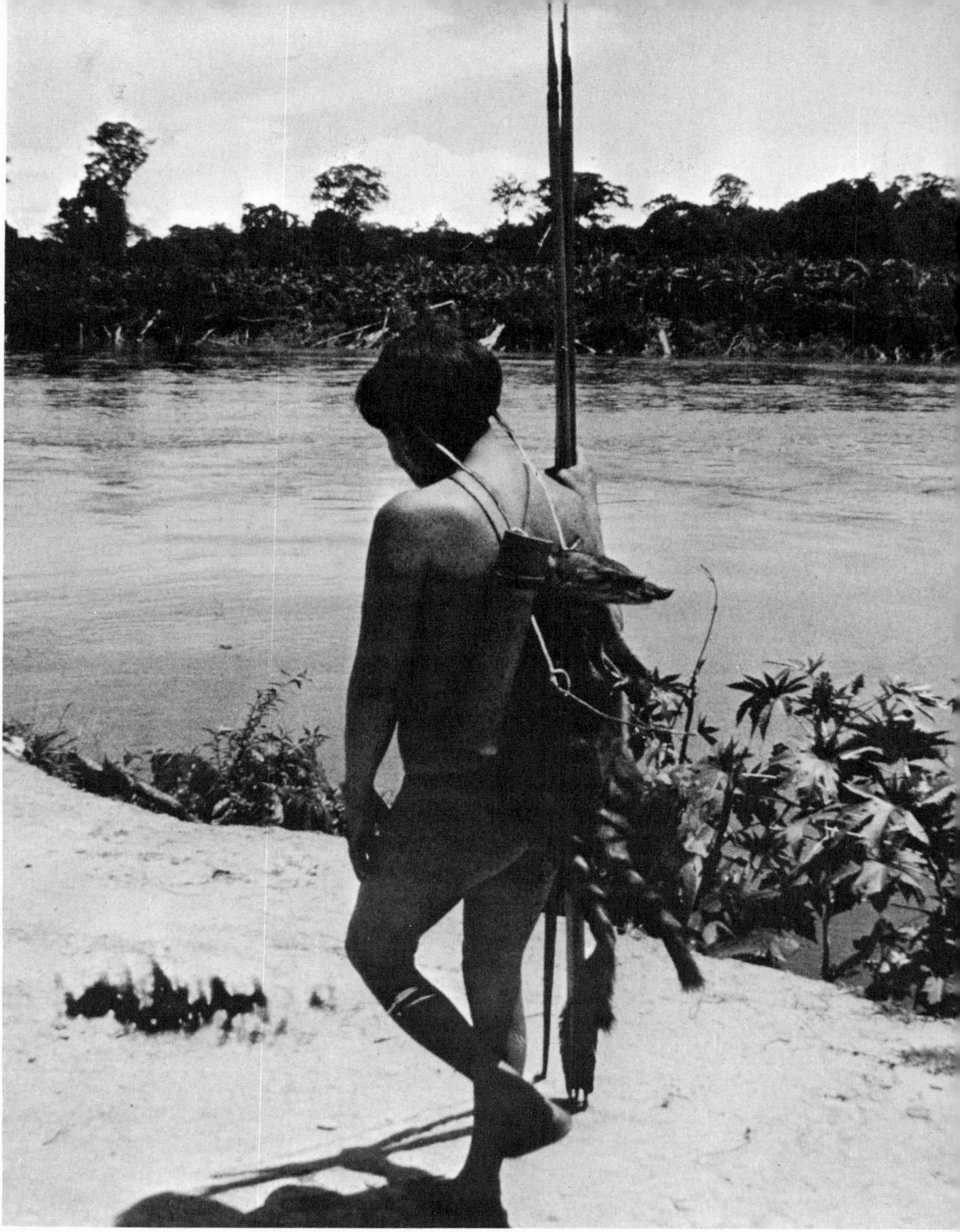

15. Returning with game

14. Returning from the hunt with an ocelot

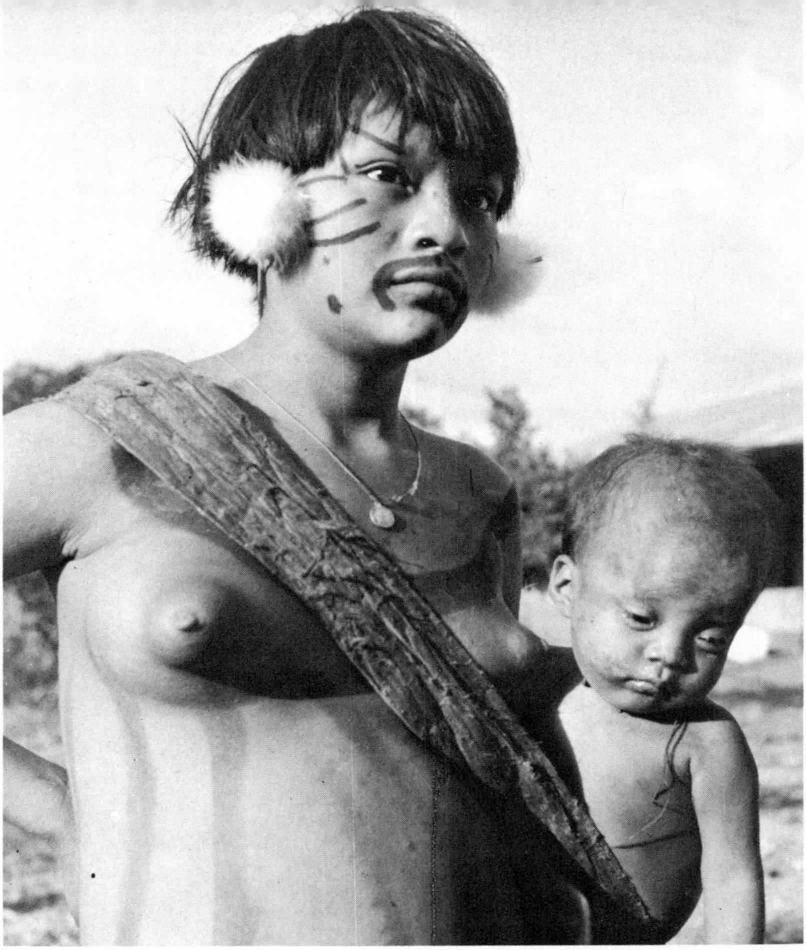

16. Ignewetari mother (Rio Ocana)

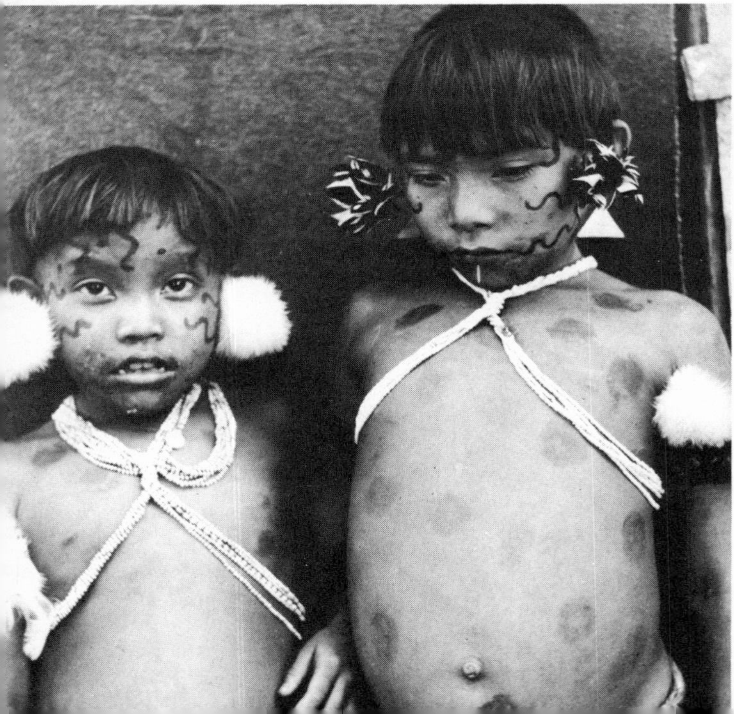

17. Young Ignewetari girls decorated for a feast

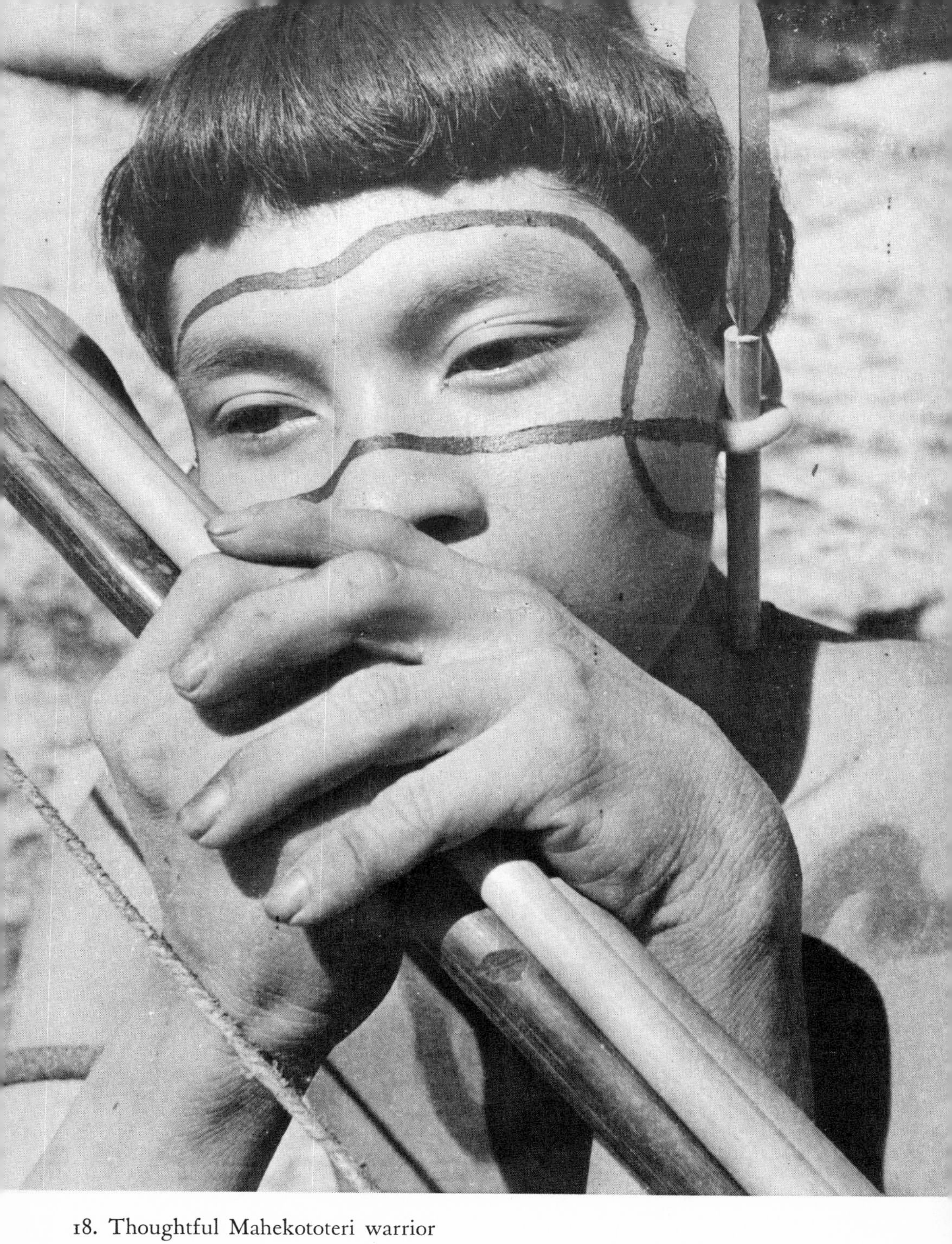

18. Thoughtful Mahekototeri warrior

19. Yanoáma men of the Upper Orinoco hold large lumps of tobacco between lips and teeth

20. Group of Yanoáma warriors

21. Akawe, one of Helena Valero's husbands

22–23. Yanoáma women, showing face ornaments

24. A fortified *shapuno* (upper Rio Orinoco)

25. A group of hunters inside a fortified *shapuno*

26. Young Witukaiateri mother

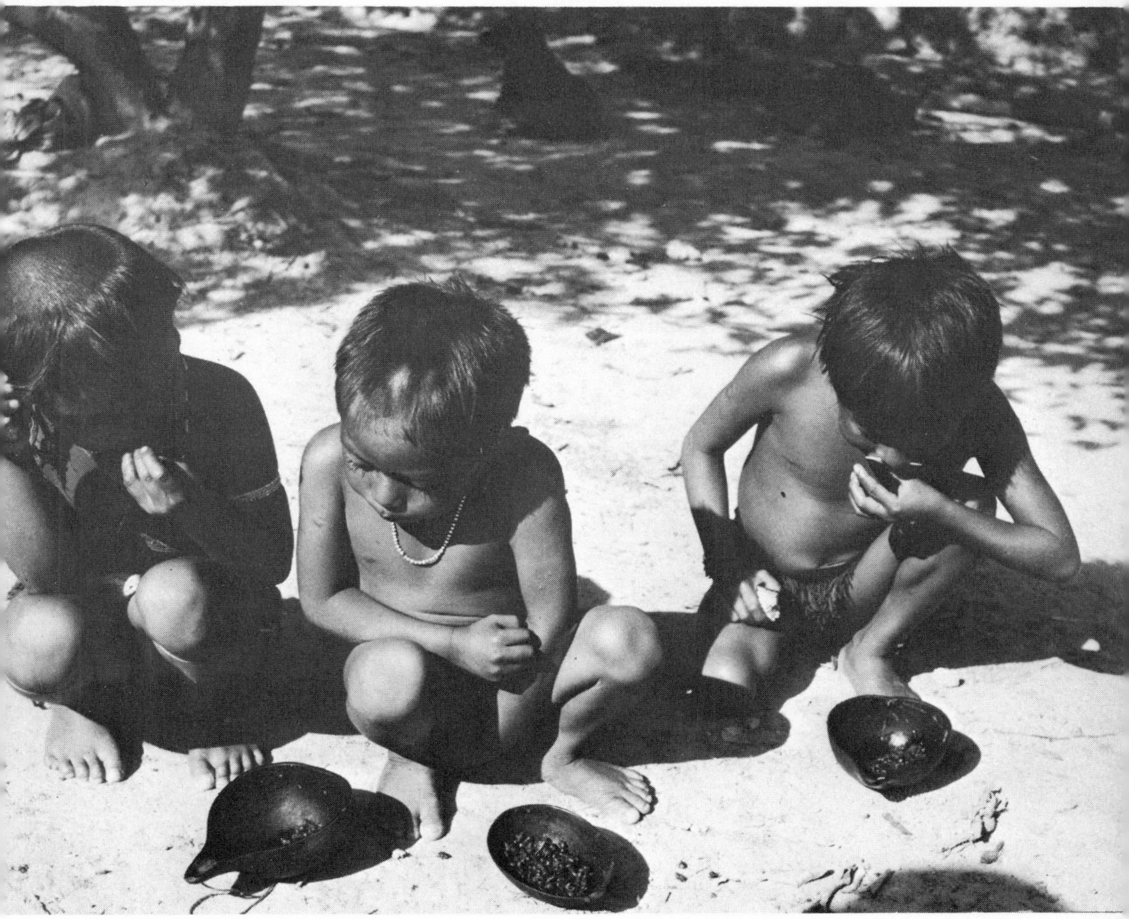

27. Children eating live ants

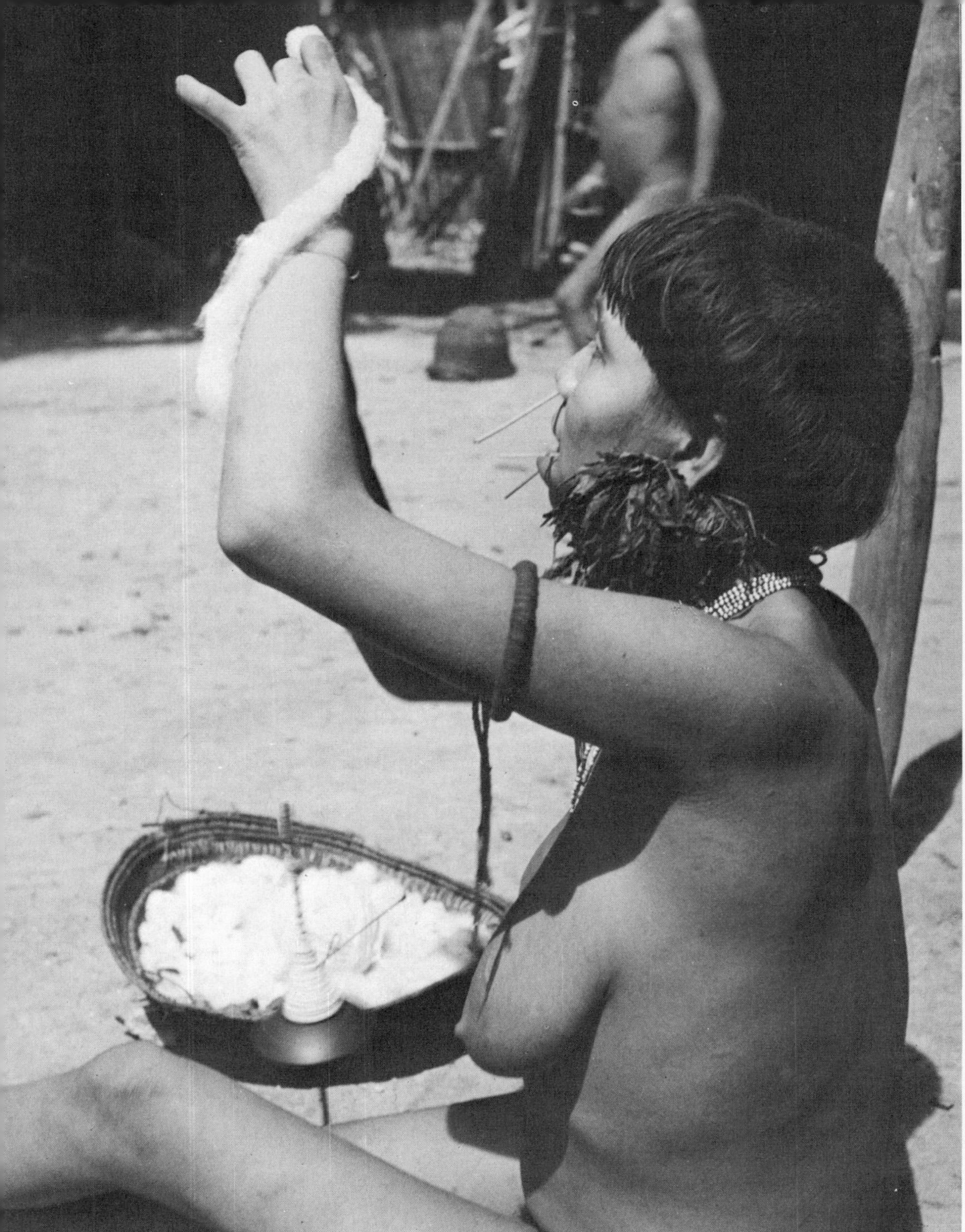

28. The humming-bird has taught the Yanoáma how to cultivate and thread cotton

29. Returning from the *roça* with *pupugnas*

30. Making fire

31. Pot for boiling game

32. Mahekototeri around the *epená,* a hallucinatory powder

34. Inhaling *epená*

35. The results of taking *epená*

33. Man filling the pipe with *epená*

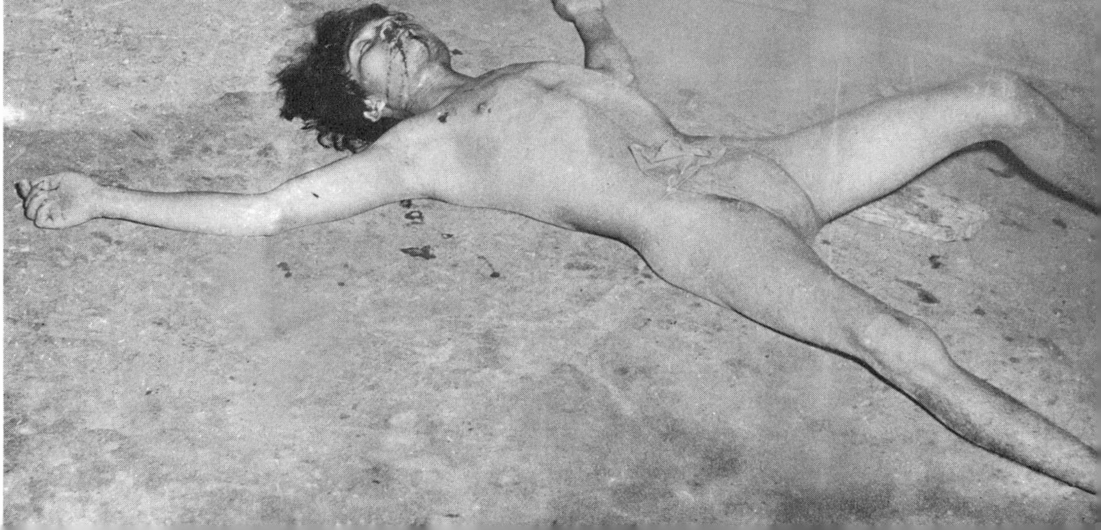

36. Dance of a shaman in the Kohoroshiwetari *shapuno*

37. Mahekototeri shaman invoking the Hekurá

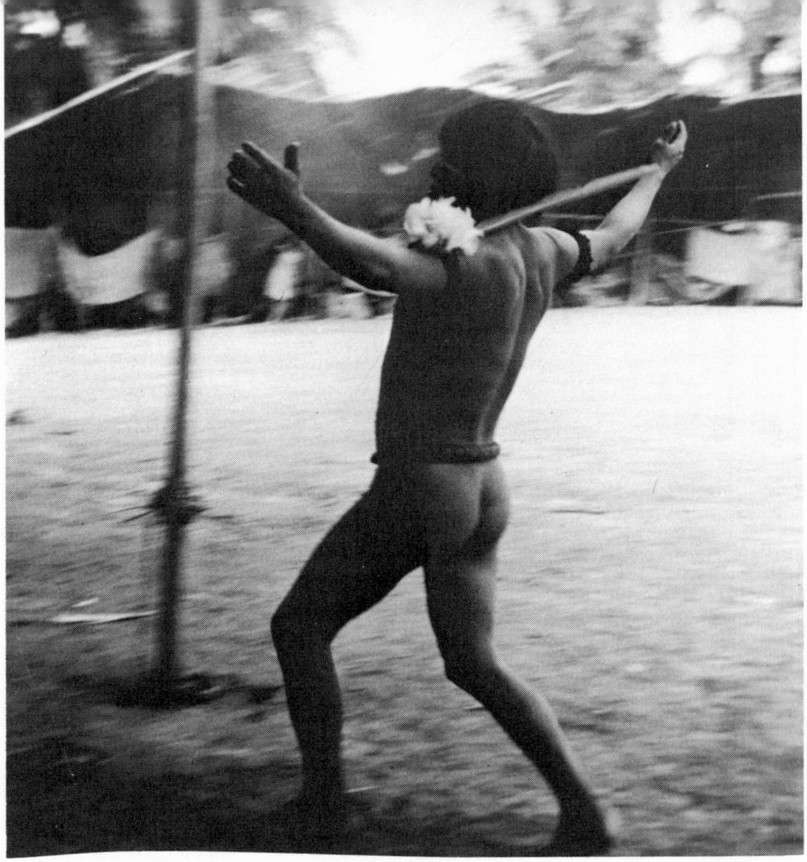

38. Shaman in ecstatic posture

39. Witukaiateri shaman drawing sickness out of a patient

40. Struggle of a Mahekototeri shaman against death

41. The Pishaanseteri on a journey

42. Arrival of the guests at the *reaho* of the Mahekototeri

43. Banana pap in the bark canoe

44. The canoe, close-up

45. Dances during the *reaho* of the Witukaiateri

46. Ceremonial rhythmic speeches

47–48. Duels with blows of the hand in order to become friends again

49. Participants in a dance of exaltation

50. Women help a fallen Witukaiateri

51. Dramatic moment

52. Women paint their cheeks black in mourning with ashes and tears

53. Resenting the photographer

54. Body of a dead Igneweteri suspended high in the forest

55. Ceremony of endocannibalism during the *reaho* of the Witukaiateri: the relatives drink the ashes of the dead in banana pap

56. Shamatari warriors

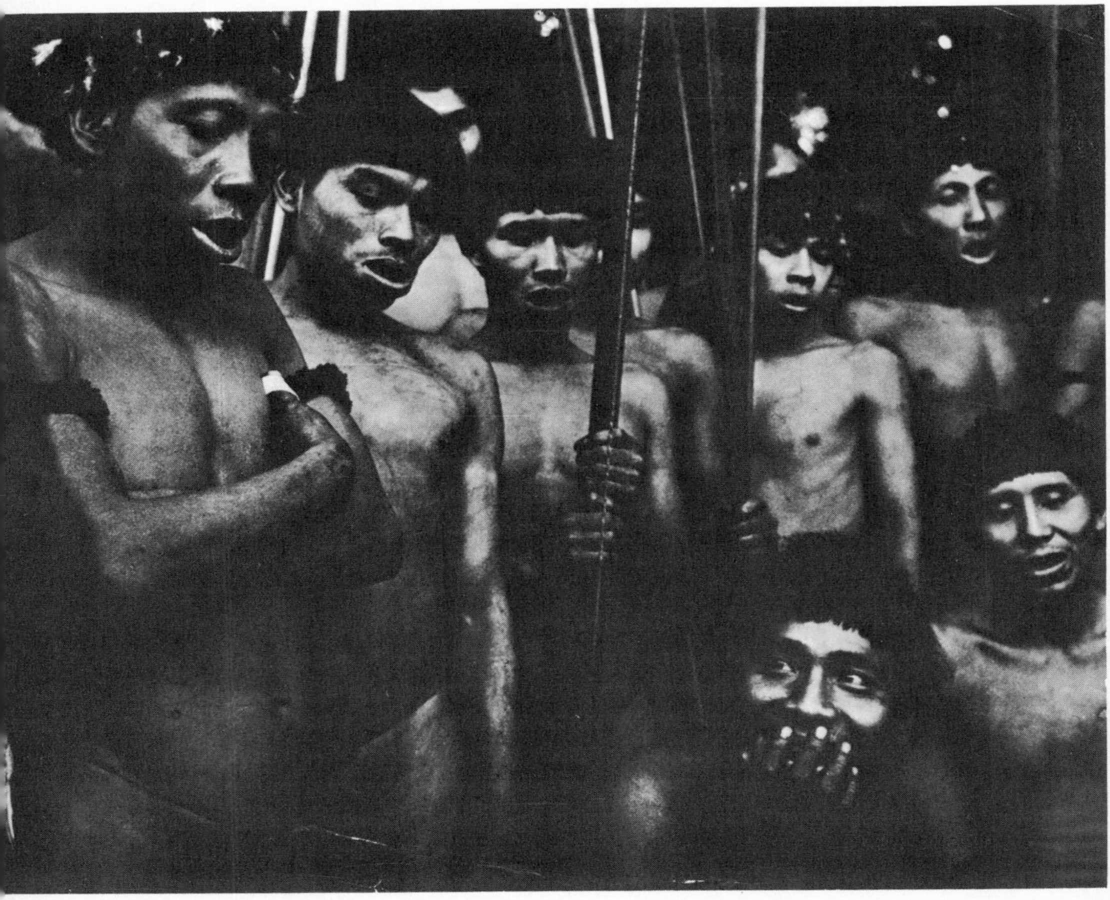

57. Helena Valero with three of her children, Akawe, and her father

GLOSSARY

Amahini:	spirits of the woods
arara:	a kind of parrot
aroari:	a magic poison
assaí:	a palm-tree (*Euterpe*)
bacaba:	a palm-tree (*Oenocarpus*)
balata:	a tree from which is extracted a liquid similar to india-rubber for preparing chewing-gum
bejú:	manioc cake
burití:	a palm-tree (*Mauritia*)
cajú:	a fruit (*Anacardiaceae*)
cará:	edible roots (*Dioscoreaceae*)
cotia:	the agouti, a South American rodent, like a large guinea pig (*Dasyprocta*)
cuia:	a vessel for holding liquids; often consisting of a gourd or other dried shell of a hard fruit
cupim:	a termites' nest
curare:	a poison used on arrows
curuba:	a skin disease
embauba:	a tree (*Cecropia*)
epená:	a powder or snuff, which has hallucinatory effects when inhaled
Gnaru:	a mythical being, Thunder
gnuma:	a woman
guariba:	a monkey
Hekurá:	the word has two meanings, (1) a supernatural spirit, (2) a shaman or witch-doctor
igarapé:	a stream in the forest
inajá:	a palm-tree of the genus *Maximiliana*
ingá:	a forest fruit
Jabutí:	a forest tortoise (*Testudo tabulata*)
japim:	a bird (*Cacicus*)
jararaca:	a snake (*Bothrops*)
Jurupuri:	worms which attack the uhina plant
Kumareme:	a female spirit of the woods
mamocori:	a liana which the Indians use to make curare
mingau:	banana pap
mumbu-hena:	a kind of leaf

mumu:	an edible fruit
mutum:	a bird (*Cracidae*)
nabrushí:	enormous stick or club for fighting
nohotipe:	spirit, shade
okhoto:	a snake
pagé:	shaman or witch-doctor in 'lingua geral'
pashuba:	a palm-tree (*Iriartea exorrhiza*)
patauá:	a palm-tree (*Oenocarpus*)
piassaba:	a palm-tree (*Leopoldinia* or *Attalea*)
piripirioca:	a magic plant
pishaansi:	a large leaf used as a receptacle
Poré:	the spirit of death
pupugna:	a palm-tree (*Bactris*)
rahakashiwa:	the magic point of an arrow
reaho:	a feast, usually to celebrate the dead
roça:	a cultivated piece of land over burned forest
sauba, sauva:	a kind of ant (*Atta*)
Shapori:	witch-doctor, shaman
shapuno:	a Yanoáma village
Siruruwe:	a female spirit of the woods
tamanduá:	a large anteater
tapirí:	a native hut built in the forest
terçado:	a large knife in Portuguese
tipití:	fibre tube for squeezing manioc
tocandira:	a poisonous ant
tushaua:	a headman, chief
uhina:	plant (*Colocasia*), producing a kind of potato
unucai:	men who have killed an enemy
urucú:	a vegetable colouring matter extracted from *Bixa*
wahati:	orphan, cold
Waikugna:	the anaconda (*Eunectes murinus*)
waiteri:	brave, courageous
Washò:	a bat
wishá:	a monkey
wishasina:	monkey's tail worn as an ornament

BIBLIOGRAPHICAL NOTE

The following are the principal writings, from the time of the conquest to date, which refer to the country and the customs of the Yanoáma:

1. ANDUZE, PABLO J. (1958), *Shailili-ko. Descubrimiento de las fuentes del Orinoco.* pp. 412. Talleres Gráf. Caracas.
2. BARKER, JAMES P. (1953), 'Memoria sôbre la cultura de los Guaika', *Boletín Indigensita Venezolano, 1*: 433–99.
3. *Id.* (1959), 'Las Incursiones entre los Guaika', *ibid.*, 7: 151–67.
4. BECHER, H. (1957), 'Die Yanonámi: ein Beitrag zur Frage der Völkergruppierung zwischen Rio Branco, Uraricuréra, Serra Parima und Rio Negro'. Vienna *Völkerkundliche Mitteilungen*, v. 5, 13–20.
5. *Id.* (1960), Die Surára und Pakidái: Zwei Yanonámi-Stämme. pp. 138. *Ed. Hamburg Museum f. Völkerkunde u. Vorgesch.*
6. BIOCCA, E. (1966), *Viaggi tra gli Indi Alto Rio Negro—Alto Orinoco*, 4 vol., Consiglio Nazionale delle Ricerche, Rome.
7. GHEERBRANT, A. (1953), *L'expédition Orénoque—Amazone*, 1948–1950. pp. 391. Paris, Gallimard.
8. GRELIER, J. (1954), *Aux sources de l'Orénoque.* pp. 283. Paris, La Table Ronde. (English translation published 1957.)
9. HUMBOLDT, A. von, and BONPLAND, A. (1852), *Personal narrative of travels to the Equinoctial regions of the New Continent during the years 1799–1804.* 3 vol., London, Bohn.
10. KOCH-GRÜNBERG, TH. (1917–1923), *Vom Roroima zum Orinoco.* 5 vol., Stuttgart, Strecker & Schröder.
11. PIZARRO, G. in MEDINA, T. (1934), *The Discovery of the Amazon according to the account of Friar Gaspar de Carvajal and other documents.* American Geographical Society. Special Publication No. 17 New York.
12. RALEIGH, SIR WALTER (1596), *The Discovery of the large, rich, and beautiful Empire of Guiana, with a relation of the great and golden city of Manoa, performed in the year 1596 by Sir Walter Raleigh.* Reprinted from the edition of 1596 by Sir R. H. Schomburgk; Hakluyt Society, London, 1848.
13. RICE, H. A. (1921), 'The Rio Negro, the Cassiquiare Canal and the Upper Orinoco (September 1916–April 1920)', *Geographical Journal, 58*: 321–344.
14. RODRIGUES, JOÃO BARBOSA (1885), *Rio Jauapery. Pacificação dos Chrichanás.* pp. 275. Rio de Janeiro.

15. SCHOMBURGK, SIR ROBERT H. (1841), *Reisen in Guiana und am Orinoko während der Jahre 1835–1839*. pp. 510. Leipzig.

16. SEITZ, G. (1960), *Hinter dem grünen Vorhang*. pp. 311. Wiesbaden, F. A. Brockhaus.

17. SONAGLIA, MARIA (1959), *Il Dramma di Napaiuma*. Scuola tipografica privata. Instituto Figlie di Maria Ausiliatrice, Torino.

18. STRADELLI, E. (1964), *'La leggenda del Jurupary' e outras lendas amazonicas*. Caderno no. 4, Instituto Cultural Italo-brasileiro, S. Paulo.

19. VINCI, A. (1956), *Samatari (Orinoco-Amazzoni)*. pp. 390. Bari, Leonardo da Vinci Editrice.

20. VOLTAIRE, F. M. de (1952), *Romans. Candide ou L'Optimisme*. pp. 162. Paris, E. Gibert jeune.

21. ZERRIES, OTTO (1964), *Waika*. pp. 312. München, Klaus Renner Verlag.